ACCOUNT RENDERED

ACCOUNT RENDERED
Extraordinary Rendition and Britain's Role
Andrew Tyrie MP, Roger Gough and Stuart McCracken
Biteback

Biteback Publishing

First published in Great Britain in 2011 by
Biteback Publishing Ltd
Westminster Tower
3 Albert Embankment
London
SE1 7SP

ISBN 978-1-84954-109-1
10 9 8 7 6 5 4 3 2 1

A CIP catalogue record for this book is available from the British Library.

Set in Adobe Garamond
Printed and bound in Great Britain by TJ International

CONTENTS

List of Illustrations

Acknowledgements

THE ALL-PARTY PARLIAMENTARY Group (APPG) on Extraordinary Rendition was founded in December 2005, following the emergence of allegations that the United States had been operating a programme of 'ghost flights' and 'black sites'. In the five years since then the Group has played a role in establishing Britain's involvement in the programme as well as raising public awareness about rendition.

Two important tasks remain: to get to the truth and to ensure that the government does what is necessary to give the public more confidence that the UK will not be involved in extraordinary rendition in the future. This compendium, which is a compilation of facts and documents on rendition, is intended to assist in the first of these. It is the product of several years of work and preparation, based on information discovered by the APPG through Parliamentary Questions, Freedom of Information Act requests and other sources, and by others working in this field.

Many individuals and organisations have provided advice, assistance and inspiration. MPs and Peers in this country, along with Senators and Congressmen in the United States gave encouragement and moral support, particularly in the early days when this issue was far from fashionable. The informal advice of former and some serving civil servants was greatly valued in pursuing this subject. Investigative journalists and NGOs uncovered much of what is known about rendition and highlighted issues that became part of the APPG's campaign. Ian Cobain, Stephen Grey, Clara Gutteridge, James Hanning, Robin Hodgson, Norman Lamb, Ann Marsh, Brent Mickum, Chris Mullin, Richard Norton-Taylor, Mark Pallis, Clive Stafford Smith, Robert Verkaik and Stuart Wheeler fall into one, or more often more, of these categories.

Much of the Group's work would not be possible without the generous pro bono support of Freshfields Bruckhaus Deringer and Hogan Lovells, and counsel they have instructed. This includes sections of this compendium. In particular, Deba Das, Patrick Doris, Amanda Hennedy, Maziar Jamnejad, Paul Lomas and Clarissa O'Callaghan at Freshfields; Jonathan Abram, Harry Caldecott, Eric Chang, Emma Colquhoun, Derek Craig, Joe Cyr, Paul Dacam, Michael Davison, Adam Feeney, Daniel Gritten, Johanne Houbouyan, Carolyn Kruk, Eric Lashner, Kathryn Long, Audrey Moog, Jamie Potter, Cordelia Rayner, Michael Roffe and David Spinley at, or formerly at, Hogan Lovells; and Joanne Clement, Richard Drabble QC, Toby Fisher, Michael Fordham QC and Tom Hickman, have been a huge help at various times over the last three years.

Professor Margaret Satterthwaite of New York University School of Law kindly gave the authors sight of an important article on rendition and international law in advance of its publication.

Sam Carter, Iain Dale, Mick Smith and James Stephens at Biteback Publishing, along with John Schwartz at Soapbox Communications, have given strong backing to this book and brought it to a speedy and efficient conclusion.

Foundation Open Society Institute (Zug), the Oak Foundation, the Persula Foundation, Mark Moody-Stuart and Stuart Wheeler have been generous in their financial support. Finally, particular thanks are due to Zoe Oliver-Watts, the former Coordinator of the APPG, for all her help with this compendium and her wider work for the Group.

The above list of acknowledgements is long – but it will inevitably have excluded many others. One of the most refreshing aspects of the APPG's work has been the full-hearted support and encouragement we have received from people in other countries and across all party boundaries.

1. Introduction: Reckoning with Rendition

Andrew Tyrie MP

*[The rendition programme] has produced valuable
intelligence, but the question is at what cost?*

- Senator John D Rockefeller IV, then Chairman of the
Senate Intelligence Committee, October 2007[1]

*Killing, capturing terrorists keeps them at bay and protects our
people, but defeating the world view responsible for producing
those terrorists diminishes the threat itself. Winning the war
of ideas actually defines the long-term victory that we seek*

- General Michael Hayden, then CIA Director, 7 September 2007[2]

IN ITS STRUGGLE against international terrorism, and especially in the years
after the attacks of 11 September 2001, the United States developed rendition – the international transfer of an individual without customary due
processes such as extradition or deportation – as an instrument of policy.
Rendition became associated with the willingness of the administration
of President George W. Bush to sanction the use of coercive interrogation
techniques. These techniques approached and, in many cases, crossed the
threshold of torture, in violation of international standards to which successive American administrations had committed themselves. To a degree
yet to be fully established, Britain – among a number of the US's Western
allies – was implicated in that American policy.

The incoming coalition government has recently established an inquiry
to examine the UK's role in rendition and maltreatment of detainees.[3] I

argued vigorously for such an inquiry with senior Conservative colleagues before the election, having also pressed Prime Ministers Blair and Brown to get to the truth. The Prime Minister's decision to set aside a number of objections that were doubtless put to him and to hold a judge-led inquiry is a huge step forward. It is the only way in which the public can have confidence that the truth will come out, and in which the damage done to Britain's moral reputation abroad and probably to the morale of our security services can be addressed.

It is regrettable that in the United States the Obama administration has missed the opportunity to do something similar. Such an inquiry need not have led to prosecutions, which would have produced the most divisive trials in modern American history. Nonetheless some form of commission was probably needed in order to secure the truth. This would have worked against conspiracy theories and the wilder claims about rendition activity. It would also have provided a basis for more widespread acceptance of new policies. Defenders of previous policies, such as former Vice President Cheney, would have been able to present their argument that rendition, detention and aggressive interrogation had indeed prevented attacks and saved lives. Some, but certainly not all, claims for the policy have recently been undermined.[4]

Whatever the alleged benefits of the policy, its enormous cost is already clear – not simply in terms of the human impact of the abuses, but also in terms of the huge damage done to the moral authority of America, and, by implication, of the West in general. On the basis of what I have seen in the public domain my view remains that, even setting aside ethical considerations, this policy has made the West less safe. The case on grounds of expediency seems weak. Only with the information that an inquiry can secure can a firm judgement be made about this question.

The damage done to the moral authority of the US and the West is supported by considerable evidence. For example, the Pew Research Center Global Attitudes Project showed steep falls in positive images of America between the turn of the millennium and 2007–08 (before partially rebounding in the Obama presidency). 51 per cent of British respondents had a favourable view of America in 2007, compared with 83 per cent in 1999/2000. Perhaps more significantly, in Indonesia, the world's largest Muslim country, there was a decline in the same period from 75 per cent to 29 per cent. In Turkey, favourability ratings were in single digits (9 per cent) in 2007, and the figures were almost as dismal in much of the Arab Middle East. This could not all be put down to rendition, secret detention and coercive interrogation – the Bush administration was capable of giving offence in a variety of ways – but they undoubtedly made a significant contribution.[5]

By creating a powerful image of injustice, rendition gave Islamist radicals a recruiting and propaganda tool. For many British observers, the obvious comparison was with the mishandled attempt in the early 1970s to break the IRA by harsh interrogation methods (some of them exactly the same as the 'enhanced' techniques used in the War on Terror); the result was 'hundreds of young men in working class nationalist communities joining the IRA and creating one of the most efficient insurgency forces in the world'.[6] The British government renounced the use of such methods in 1972.

The fear and revulsion generated by the Bush era policies have prejudiced cooperation with the West, whether at a governmental or an individual level, across the Muslim world. Sir Richard Dearlove, the former head of the SIS (Secret Intelligence Service, otherwise known as MI6) was quoted as saying in 2006 that 'the rendition issue has hindered the ability of Western intelligence agencies to recruit moderate Muslims because they no longer think countries like the UK are on the right side of the argument'.[7] The same goes for efforts by the security services to gain recruits and reliable sources of information within Muslim communities in Britain.

Finally, the policy was a severe setback for the steady efforts over recent decades to enhance shared international standards in humanitarian and human rights laws and agreements, and in the rule of law generally. These standards have enshrined the values that the West seeks to export; that the assault on them was led by a country which had previously played such a strong role in the worldwide spread of free institutions and limited government was all the more damaging. What has dismayed democrats has delighted dictators; both Zimbabwe's Robert Mugabe and Iran's Mahmoud Ahmadinejad have used the War on Terror as a debating tactic to deflect attention from their own, much more severe human rights violations.[8]

One other feature of the Bush era is worthy of reflection: not just a lack of transparent public debate as to what was being done at the time but a misleading economy of the truth. The President and other senior figures insisted that America did not torture and respected its international obligations, often using carefully crafted definitions and legal formulations; meanwhile, the administration's lawyers gave justifications for harsher interrogation techniques in private memoranda that did not survive the scrutiny even of their colleagues but which nonetheless provided the basis for policy. This approach has left an enduring legacy of distrust.

The Bush approach is at the opposite end of the spectrum from Alan Dershowitz's argument for 'torture warrants'. Dershowitz's argument, first advanced in early 2002, applied to the 'ticking bomb' scenario; a catastrophic attack is imminent, and the only way to prevent it is to coerce knowledge out of a captured terrorist. In these circumstances, Dershowitz argued, 'The real question is not whether torture would be used – it would – but whether it would be used outside of the law or within the law.' If such actions could take place only through the issue of a torture warrant by a judge, then there would at least be accountability. In a later publication, Dershowitz cited the emerging policies of the Bush administration as an example of the covert use of maltreatment that he wished to avoid.[9]

Other arguments have been put for methods of combining coercive methods with some form of accountability. The Brookings Institution's Benjamin Wittes has argued for a system whereby 'the tiniest, most committed, subset of America's enemies' can be subjected to interrogations that go beyond established rules (though still stopping short of torture) on the explicit order of the President. It is argued that such approaches represent the only way in which a democracy might properly choose to apply coercive methods.

My own view is that the 'ticking bomb' crisis is something of an artificial exercise; the lawyer Clive Stafford Smith challenged a number of eminent commentators to come up with a real example of such a case and found that no one could. If, however, one did exist, it would be better to rely on the principles set out by Jessica Montell of the Israeli human rights groups B'Tselem: 'I imagine that [as an interrogator] I would do what I would have to do in order to prevent that catastrophe from happening. The state's obligation is then to put me on trial, for breaking the law … and then the Court decides whether or not it's reasonable that I broke the law in order to avert this catastrophe.'[10]

The Gibson Inquiry will give the British government an opportunity – which it must take – to address the issues raised by rendition. Britain should not wait for an American lead. The UK can act both to set our own house in order and to seek to shape the international debate. Although the Obama administration has made significant policy changes, it has left open the possibility of some forms of rendition. Nor is there any guarantee that earlier practices will not return. This could come with a change of administration, or even without it; a successful attack on the United States would leave the administration open to massive pressure to revert to policies that, critics would argue, kept America safe in the years after 9/11.

The necessary precondition for British leadership is that Sir Peter Gibson's inquiry does its job effectively. It has a number of essential tasks. First it must get to the full truth. It has long been clear that the slow drip-drip of revelations has been hugely damaging to trust in government and in particular in the security services. Following the two Court of Appeal rulings in the Binyam Mohamed case in February 2010, this loss of trust reached serious proportions. The inquiry needs to establish, once and for all, the limits of Britain's involvement in rendition, secret detention and interrogation methods that amounted to cruel, inhuman and degrading treatment or worse. This must include transfer of detainees 'in theatre', that is, Iraq and Afghanistan. The biggest beneficiaries of this clarity would probably be the intelligence services themselves, as well as the military.

Secondly, the inquiry will need also to establish the shortcomings in the provision of information and assurances to Parliament, notably to the Intelligence and Security Committee (ISC). It is clear that – whatever the reason – the UK's parliamentary tool for bolstering trust in the security services failed in its primary task of obtaining the truth on the public's behalf. The Court of Appeal's 26 February 2010 judgment raised the possibility of suppression of evidence by members of the security services; at the very least, shoddy record-keeping has been a constant theme as each new revelation has emerged.

Thirdly, reliance on assurances from the Americans needs also to be examined, not least because it is likely that the UK will in some circumstances need to rely on such assurances again. The Foreign Affairs Select Committee argued that the government should ask the Obama administration to provide a thorough search of its records in relation to the use of Diego Garcia in connection with rendition, and this request should be made to assist the inquiry, in relation not only to Diego Garcia but to rendition 'circuit flights' (that is, flights travelling to or from carrying out a rendition but without a detainee on board).

The issue of assurances also arises with respect to the handover of individuals held by British military forces overseas to the Americans, and the human rights law obligations that should govern such transfers. A legal opinion I commissioned in 2008 raised a number of concerns about such transfers, some (but not all) of which will have been eased by changes to interrogation policy under the Obama administration. The opinion also noted that: 'If United States authorities breached assurances in the past, this will make it very difficult for the British government to satisfy its stringent obligations under the HRA [Human Rights Act] in the future by accepting assurances from United States authorities as to the treatment of detainees handed-over to their custody by British military authorities.'[11] Subsequent to this opinion being issued, the rendition of two military detainees who had been transferred to US custody has come to light, raising precisely these concerns. A thorough examination of past assurances is needed if future assurances are to carry credibility. This will be a matter not only for Sir Peter Gibson's inquiry, but for the separate investigations into military detention operations in Iraq and Afghanistan being carried out by the Ministry of Defence.[12]

Fourthly, as I argued in a consultation paper issued in late 2009, we probably need specific changes to legislation to strengthen the disincentives for Britain to take part in extraordinary rendition.[13] The Gibson Inquiry should examine this issue closely. In theory, there are already some legal provisions against extraordinary rendition. In addition to Britain's obligations under international law, discussed in the next section of this report, the criminal law, common and statutory, creates a number of offences that relate to actions inherent to rendition. These include kidnapping, false imprisonment and various offences against the person (such as actual or grievous bodily harm). Aviation law (Articles 148 and 149 of the Air Navigation Order 2005) criminalises actions that have in some cases been associated with rendition flights, such as falsification of flight documents. International aviation law also has relevance; under the Chicago Convention, Britain has the power – and the duty – to require an aeroplane suspected of carrying out an extraordinary rendition while passing through British airspace to land.[14] However, given the scale of air traffic through British airspace, the current approach would have to be based on highly specific intelligence, and there are serious questions as to the practicality of applying this power.

In spite of all this, there is no specific offence that criminalises the extraordinary rendition process. In addition, the perpetrators of these main offences are likely to be foreign intelligence agents, who may well be difficult to bring to trial. Evidence for this comes from the case of Khaled el-Masri, discussed later in this report, in relation to which the German courts issued arrest warrants for thirteen US citizens, most or all of them CIA officers. In response, the US government made very clear that it would not respond to extradition requests; we also now know from the WikiLeaks revelations that American diplomats apparently warned the Germans that 'issuance of international arrest warrants would have a negative impact on our bilateral relationship'. The German Ministry of Justice did not issue any extradition request. In the case of Abu Omar, also discussed later, the Italian government showed no interest in pursuing extradition.[15]

Existing law, notably Britain's obligations under the Torture Convention and the offence of torture under the Criminal Justice Act 1988, may be able to deal with active involvement in the maltreatment of prisoners. However, the alleged British role in extraordinary rendition appears usually to have been a more accessory one, such as technical support, refuelling and clearances for rendition flights. The threshold for demonstrating this sort of liability is high. The existing law does not create enough pressure on those controlling transport facilities to ensure that they do not facilitate extraordinary rendition.

To remedy this, the APPG on Extraordinary Rendition has made proposals to improve the law. The proposals, published in November 2009, set out firstly that there should be a specific offence of using transport facilities for the transfer of persons without their consent and without lawful excuse. Secondly, they propose creating an offence of facilitating extraordinary rendition, rather than relying on the uncertainties of accessory liability. Thirdly, they would create a 'failure to prevent' offence, so that those in the management or control of key infrastructure take reasonable steps to ensure that their facilities are not used for extraordinary rendition; to limit the risk to these individuals, there would be a 'safe harbour' of appropriate procedures that they could demonstrate that they had undertaken. Fourthly, the prohibitions would extend to 'circuit flights' rather than embracing only planes with detainees on board.

The occasion should also be taken – although this raises wider issues than that of rendition alone – to make changes to the ISC. On this, the

Gibson Inquiry should be forthright in making recommendations for reform in order to restore its credibility. Since 1994, when the committee was established by John Major, it has provided Parliamentary oversight of the security services. It was specifically designed to give the public confidence. It failed. Firstly, it appeared to be slow off the blocks on rendition. Secondly, it did not get to the truth. And thirdly, there has been an apparent reluctance to recognise that this left a problem. It is possible that the ISC's justification for its failure to get to the truth – sloppy record keeping on the part of the security services – is a full explanation. However, these failings have not done much to bolster public confidence.

Under its new Chairman, Sir Malcolm Rifkind, the committee should examine and report on what went wrong and recommend ways to improve its standing. Those recommendations should be submitted to the Gibson Inquiry. As for the means by which credibility can be restored, this can partly be achieved through a re-examination of its investigatory powers, but wider changes are probably also needed. While I am not yet convinced by the suggestion attributed to the former head of the SyS (the Security Service, otherwise known as MI5), Lady Manningham-Buller, that the ISC can become a full Select Committee of Parliament, I am clear that its perceived independence should be strengthened. We should adopt the Wright Committee's recommendation that the chairman, instead of being appointed by the Prime Minister, should be elected by secret ballot of the House of Commons, albeit subject to prime ministerial veto.

Finally, having put its own house in order, Britain can better play a full role in the international debate about rendition. One such issue is the use of assurances that an individual transferred to a third country will not be ill-treated. There was much criticism of the use of this device by both the Clinton and Bush administrations, and a number of cases demonstrated that, where countries with poor human rights records were involved, the assurances were not to be relied upon. Nonetheless, the Obama administration has committed itself to making use of assurances, albeit with more robust monitoring mechanisms than those applied in the past. The UN-attached bodies concerned with human rights issues have taken subtly different views on such matters. Both the Human Rights Committee and the Committee Against Torture have insisted on the application of very strict safeguards, but the latter has also argued that assurances can in no case be relied upon in the case of countries that systematically violate the

Torture Convention. However, the former Special Rapporteur on Torture, Manfred Nowak, has taken a more stringent line in opposition to all use of assurances.[16]

Britain has every reason to address the issue. At home, in June 2010 the then independent reviewer of terrorism legislation, Lord Carlile, raised the question of reliance on assurances following the failure to deport two men accused of planning attacks in Manchester. He indicated that they could be an acceptable policy option if applied on a case by case basis and supported by strong subsequent contact with the individuals who had been removed. Internationally, human rights bodies are still developing standards to be applied by countries whose facilities – such as airports – are used in transfers that rely on assurances so that they do not incur liability for breaches of human rights law.[17]

The APPG's legal proposals, if adopted, would put Britain in the forefront of measures to end extraordinary rendition. At the same time, it will be necessary to address what might be described as the 'hard cases'. These were the dilemmas often rhetorically posed by John Bellinger in his time as Legal Adviser to the State Department. What is the West to do when reliable intelligence suggests that an individual in a failed state, with which no extradition treaty exists, and which does not possess an effective domestic legal structure, means it harm? What if the state is unwilling rather than unable to discharge its obligations to hand over suspected terrorists instead of shielding them? The seizure of an individual under such circumstances without the normal process of extradition, but with the purpose of bringing them to a properly constituted trial, would be a return to what has been called 'rendition to justice', rather than the rendition away from justice that became such a feature of US policy during the Bush years. Even renditions that 'permit governments who are either unwilling or unable to transfer fugitives publicly via extradition to do so through quiet means', although difficult if not impossible to justify legally, were accepted practice in some cases in the 1990s.[18]

The establishment of a firm legal basis for rendition to justice is not straightforward. As the Appeals Chamber of the International Criminal Tribunal for the Former Yugoslavia (ICTY) put it when assessing a defendant's challenge to his detention on the basis that he had been rendered to the court, there is a balance to be struck 'between the fundamental rights of the accused and the essential interests of the international community in the prosecution of persons charged with serious violations of international humanitarian law'.[19] Much the same could be argued with respect to terrorism, an act that violates a large number of international norms.[20] Human rights groups are also divided on such issues. Some see rendition to justice as an inadequate and dangerous procedure, while others have accepted that renditions may sometimes be necessary and even 'celebrated' to prevent offenders acting with impunity, especially in relation to offences such as terrorism and genocide.[21]

There is a need to 'ensure that procedural protections for individuals do not create perverse incentives – such as the incentive to kill a suspected terrorist instead of detaining and transferring him'. The operation of these perverse incentives has arguably been present during the Obama presidency; bringing suspects into American custody is viewed as sufficiently difficult that the administration has relied instead on encouraging proxy arrests by local security forces (some of them with questionable human rights records) and the aggressive use of attacks by drone aircraft. More than 700 people have been killed in drone attacks in Pakistan's tribal areas since President Obama took office, compared with fewer than 200 under his predecessor.[22]

Although the solution is unclear, there can be no doubt that a structure of core principles for a legitimate rendition policy, carefully regulated by law, subjected to review by the courts, and used as a last resort in certain extremely limited circumstances, would have merit. The APPG's legal proposals would criminalise support to transfers of individuals 'without lawful excuse'. The latter proviso, borrowed from the law of kidnap and false imprisonment, could provide a basis for the courts to assess, and under some circumstances accept, rendition to justice.

It is now apparent that the most far-reaching application of extraordinary rendition and other features of the War on Terror was in the period between 9/11 and the Abu Ghraib scandal in mid-2004. This was the period in which the Bush administration was espousing its ill-conceived effort at an almost revolutionary recasting of the international order, an effort foreshadowed in part in the then Prime Minister Tony Blair's Chicago speech in 1999. The Obama administration has reversed the rhetoric and many of the policies of its predecessor. David Cameron's 2006 foreign policy and national security speech, among others, signalled a similar return to more orthodox foreign policy thinking in the UK. The 2001–04 period is also, not coincidentally, the time during which there is the strongest evidence of the authorities in Britain and other western countries being, to adopt the phrase cited in legal arguments in the Binyam Mohamed case, 'mixed up in wrongdoing'.

The reversal of policy on extraordinary rendition, and cleaning up the mess, is a necessary part of the process of reappraisal. Rendition became a symbol of much that was wrong with American foreign policy in the years after 9/11. To a degree yet to be fully established, Britain was drawn into that policy, a sign that the UK too had to some extent lost its moorings. It is time for Britain to reckon with and move on from the past, and having done so, to make a self-confident contribution to the construction of better foreign and security policies in the field. In my view doing so is not only required on ethical grounds, it will make Britain safer. This is why the work of the Gibson Inquiry will be so crucial.

2. Rendition, Extraordinary Rendition and International Law

... the torturer has become like the pirate and slave trader before him, hostis humani generis, *an enemy of all mankind*

- United States Court of Appeals for the Second Circuit, Verdict in *Filártiga v. Peña-Irala*, 30 June 1980[1]

... it was often liberal democratic societies – States that previously lauded the importance of the rule of law and human rights protections – that are now at the forefront of undermining those protections

- The Eminent Jurists' Panel, 2009[2]

A DECADE AGO, the term 'rendition' was known only to specialists. Now it is a common part of political and wider public debate, a central part of the controversies over the counter-terrorism policies of the United States. It has even provided the title of a Hollywood movie. Yet rendition is not a term defined by law; nor is its common variant, extraordinary rendition. They describe the procedure by which a detainee is transferred from one state to another, outside normal legal processes, in some cases to a destination where he or she faces a real risk of torture. They have often been used as if they are interchangeable, but they are not; and even within the scope of these terms there are more narrowly defined categories.

Taking *rendition* first, it can be described simply as 'the involuntary transfer of an individual across borders without recourse to extradition or deportation proceedings'.[3] A leaked memo from the British Foreign Office to the Prime Minister's Office in 2005 offered a similar definition: 'the transfer of a person from one jurisdiction to another, outside the normal legal processes such as extradition, deportation, removal or exclusion'. It added that 'this does not necessarily carry any connotation of involvement in torture'.[4]

Extraordinary rendition, however, usually does carry such a connotation. There have occasionally been other definitions. The Venice Commission, an advisory body to the Council of Europe of experts in constitutional law, defined it in 2006 as merely applying 'when there is little or no doubt that the obtaining of custody over a person is not in accordance with the existing legal procedures applying in the State where the person was situated at the time'.[5] However, the more common use of the term describes a situation in which a detainee, rather than being rendered for the purpose of being brought to trial, is transferred away from justice: to indefinite detention, secret detention, or to a place where he or she is at real risk of facing torture or cruel, inhuman or degrading treatment.

However, as later chapters of this book show, even extraordinary rendition has taken on a variety of different forms in the last two decades, as policy has shifted within and between different US administrations. A comprehensive effort at definition was made by the ISC in its 2007 *Report on Rendition*, which elaborated on these variants:

> **'Rendition':** Encompasses any extra-judicial transfer of persons from one jurisdiction or State to another.
>
> **'Rendition to Justice':** The extra-judicial transfer of persons from one jurisdiction or State to another, for the purposes of standing trial within an established and recognised legal and judicial system.
>
> **'Military Rendition':** The extra-judicial transfer of persons (detained in, or related to, a theatre of military operations) from one State to another, for the purposes of military detention in a military facility.
>
> **'Rendition to Detention':** The extra-judicial transfer of persons from one jurisdiction or State to another, for the purposes of detention and interrogation outside the normal legal system.
>
> **'Extraordinary Rendition':** The extra-judicial transfer of persons from one jurisdiction or State to another, for the purposes of detention and interrogation outside the normal legal system, where there is a real risk of torture or cruel, inhuman or degrading treatment (CIDT).[6]

These elaborations were criticised by some non-governmental organisations, concerned that the definitions used were not generally accepted, and that the distinctions made between different types of rendition seemed to legitimise some of its forms. Clive Stafford Smith, Director of the human rights group Reprieve, told the House of Commons Foreign Affairs Select Committee that: 'I wish someone could tell me what the difference is. As a lawyer, the legal term is kidnapping. Rendition is one of these euphemisms that we have seen far too many of in this whole process. .. It is not actually a useful term at all. I think that we should just get back to the rule of law—if you want to move someone involuntarily from one country to another, you use legal procedures.'[7]

However, quite apart from the arguments over 'rendition to justice', a categorisation of the kind set out by the ISC is helpful, since it helps track changes in approach. We have therefore adopted the ISC's nomenclature in this report, with the exception that we sometimes also use the term 'rendition to third countries' for situations in which detainees were transferred to the custody of another country (for example, transporting a detainee from Croatia to Egypt) rather than to that of a US agency such as the CIA. In practice, like 'rendition to detention', this can often be considered a subset of extraordinary rendition. However, it is important to make the distinction; rendition to third countries was the main strand of American policy in the 1990s, whereas rendition to detention, notably under the auspices of the CIA, became more important after 9/11.

Much of this was in clear conflict with emerging and established international law. For some forms of rendition, there are ambiguities. The Venice Commission noted that:

> Whether a particular 'rendition' is lawful will depend upon the laws of the States concerned and on the applicable rules of international law, in particular human rights law. Thus, even if a particular 'rendition' is in accordance with the national law of one of the States involved (which may not forbid or even regulate extraterritorial activities of state organs), it may still be unlawful under the national law of the other State(s). Moreover, a 'rendition' may be contrary to customary international law and treaty or customary obligations undertaken by the participating State(s) under human rights law and/or international humanitarian law.[8]

Rendition to justice is therefore a somewhat ambiguous area, and one in which national practice varies. American courts have tended to take the pragmatic approach of *male captus, bene detentus*; put simply, if the court feels that there is a legitimate case to answer, then it is not too concerned as to how the defendant got there. This is the so-called Ker-Frisbie doctrine.[9]

It has been modified a little by more recent judgments; in *United States v. Toscanino* (1974), the court ruled if that a rendition were carried out with great brutality – conduct which 'shocks the conscience' – jurisdiction could be denied, and there were similar conclusions from *United States v. Gengler* (also 1974).[10] Broadly speaking, however, Ker-Frisbie still stands. English courts used to take a similar view, but of late have taken a stricter line against rendition, even to justice, notably in *Ex Parte Bennett* (1994) and *R. v Nicholas Mullen* (1999). The latter is particularly significant since it involved terrorism charges.[11]

In international law, there have been a number of high-profile examples of renditions to justice. These include Adolf Eichmann, rendered from Argentina to stand trial in Israel in 1960; Ilich Ramírez Sánchez, the terrorist known as Carlos the Jackal, rendered from the Sudan to France in 1994; the Kurdish leader Abdullah Öcalan, rendered from Kenya to Turkey in 1999; and a number of cases relating to the former Yugoslavia and the ICTY. Each generated legal or political challenges.

In both the Carlos and Öcalan cases, there was clear cooperation between the authorities involved that offset concerns regarding infringement of national sovereignty. Carlos' attempt to claim wrongful arrest was rejected by the European Commission of Human Rights. In this, the cooperation between the French and Sudanese authorities was an important factor in the Commission's thinking; however, so was the fact that Sudan was not bound by the European Convention. Interestingly, such cooperation was seen as particularly relevant with respect to terrorism. 'It does not appear to the Commission that any cooperation which occurred in this case between the Sudanese and French authorities involved any factor which could raise problems from the point of view of Article 5 of the Convention, particularly in the field of the fight against terrorism, which frequently necessitates cooperation between States.' In the case of Öcalan, the Court was similarly influenced by the cooperation between the Turkish and Kenyan authorities in the absence of an extradition treaty. In both cases, the Court also relied on the existence of lawful domestic warrants in the countries to which the detainees were transferred.

In Eichmann's case, however, there was no such consent by the host country and the Argentinean government protested to the UN. The Security Council passed Resolution 138, which judiciously indicated disquiet over the violation involved in the abduction while making clear that it was desirable that Eichmann be brought to justice. Israel was asked to make reparation to Argentina, though the latter was content to accept an apology for the violation of its sovereignty; given the charge sheet against Eichmann, there was no interest in taking matters further.[12]

The pragmatic international resolution of the dispute over Eichmann was a clear indication that, in the case of very grave crimes, the severity of the charges against the detainee is a factor weighing against concerns over state sovereignty or violations of procedure. As noted in the Introduction, the ICTY has taken a similar view with respect to crimes against humanity committed during the Yugoslav wars of the 1990s (though unlike purely national courts it is also buttressed by the Security Council resolution which established it and which required Member States to cooperate with it). In the *Nikolic* case, the Appeal Chamber upheld the *male captus, bene detentus* approach while also noting that 'certain human rights violations are of such a serious nature that they require that the exercise of jurisdiction be declined' (though it did not believe that such violations had taken place during Nikolic's rendition).[13] This is a position very similar to that which US courts have reached with the modified Ker-Frisbie doctrine.

Thus there have been a number of occasions on which rendition to justice has achieved a degree of acceptance by domestic and international courts, even though a growing emphasis on arguments about individual rights (notably, the rights that a detainee might expect the host state to uphold with regard to full lawful procedures) rather than focusing solely on national sovereignty concerns may raise a further hurdle.[14]

However, none of these ambiguities can apply to extraordinary rendition. The British government's official position in 2008 was that 'if we were requested to assist another state in a rendition operation, and our assistance would be lawful, we would decide whether or not to assist taking into account all the circumstances'; in other words, this left open the possibility of some lawful types of rendition. However, for extraordinary rendition, 'we unreservedly condemn any rendition to torture'. This would clearly be in conflict with Britain's international obligations.[15]

The centrepiece of these obligations – for the United States as for Britain – is the Convention Against Torture and Other Cruel, Inhuman and Degrading Treatment or Punishment (the Convention Against Torture, or CAT), adopted by the United Nations General Assembly in December 1984. The Convention (Article 1) offers a broad definition of torture:

... any act by which severe pain or suffering, whether physical or mental, is intentionally inflicted on a person for such purposes as obtaining from him or a third person information or a confession, punishing him for an act he or a third person has committed or is suspected of having committed, or intimidating or coercing him or a third person, or for any reason based on discrimination of any kind, when such pain or suffering is inflicted by or at the instigation of or with the consent or acquiescence of a public official or other person acting in an official capacity. It does not include pain or suffering arising only from, inherent in or incidental to lawful sanctions.

Signatories are required to take action to prevent torture taking place within their jurisdiction (Article 2). And: 'No exceptional circumstances whatsoever, whether a state of war or a threat of war, internal political instability or any other public emergency, may be invoked as a justification of torture.' Article 3 has particular relevance to rendition: 'No State Party shall expel, return ('refouler') or extradite a person to another State where there are substantial grounds for believing that he would be in danger of being subjected to torture.' Article 4 requires states to ensure that acts of torture are criminalised in their domestic law, which in the UK has been effected through the Criminal Justice Act 1988. The Article also requires the criminalisation of complicity in torture; this is particularly relevant to Britain, given that the allegations made against the British authorities have been those of complicity rather than of direct perpetration of torture. Later articles of the CAT establish effective universal jurisdiction over torture and require states both to act against perpetrators (wherever the act of torture is alleged to have taken place) and to cooperate with others in doing so. The treatment of Cruel, Inhuman and Degrading Treatment (CIDT) within the CAT is less sweeping than that of torture; it is not, for example, included within the *non-refoulement* provisions of Article 3. Nonetheless, a signatory state is required to prevent CIDT 'in any territory under its jurisdiction' (Article 16) and the Committee Against Torture has interpreted the prohibition on CIDT widely, so as to extend to Article 3.[16]

The prohibition on torture is so fundamental that it has taken on the status of *jus cogens*, a 'peremptory norm'. This is categorised as 'a norm accepted and recognized by the international community of States as a whole as a norm from which no derogation is permitted and which can be modified only by a subsequent norm of general international law having the same character'.[17] While there is no single source of authority as to which norms have the status of *jus cogens*, it is generally accepted that the ban on torture is one of them.

This is reinforced by the International Covenant on Civil and Political Rights (ICCPR), which was approved by the UN General Assembly in December 1966 and which came into force a decade later. The ICCPR states simply (Article 7) that: 'No one shall be subjected to torture or to cruel, inhuman or degrading treatment or punishment.' While some derogations from the ICCPR are permitted under conditions of national emergency, Article 7 is explicitly excluded from this.[18] The United Nations Convention Relating to the Status of Refugees also has *non-refoulement* provisions, albeit in more restrictive terms than the CAT.[19] For member states of the Council of Europe, Article 3 of the European Convention on Human Rights (ECHR) has very similar wording to that of the ICCPR: 'No one shall be subjected to torture or to inhuman or degrading treatment or punishment.' The European Court has interpreted this as incorporating a concept of *non-refoulement*.[20] Under the Human Rights Act 1998, the ECHR is incorporated into British law.

Thus, there have for some time been clear commitments – by the British and other European governments, as well as (with the exception of the ECHR and its jurisprudence) the United States government – that would appear to preclude extraordinary rendition.

However, when the CAT was ratified by the United States Senate in 1994, it was with a variety of 'reservations' and 'declarations'. Among the former was that the US felt itself bound to prevent CIDT only insofar as it was consistent with the Fifth, Eighth and/or Fourteenth Amendments of the US constitution; that it offered a somewhat tighter definition of torture as an act 'specifically intended to inflict severe physical or mental pain or suffering', with a particular emphasis on actions that caused 'prolonged mental harm'. Most significantly, the US interpreted the *non-refoulement* article as follows:

> (2) That the United States understands the phrase, 'where there are substan-
> tial grounds for believing that he would be in danger of being subjected to
> torture,' as used in article 3 of the Convention, to mean 'if it is more likely
> than not that he would be tortured.'[21]

Although, as General Michael Hayden, CIA Director between 2006 and 2009, put it much later, the United States was 'not looking to do this

49/51', this provision set the bar significantly differently from that applied by European countries.[22]

In time, some of these differences of interpretation, coupled with other policy choices and further exercises in legal definition, would be used to help give a legal basis for extraordinary rendition. The following chapters set out how this happened.

3. Rendition before 9/11

*George W. Bush was still struggling to coax oil out of the ground when
the United States 'rendered to justice' its first suspect from abroad*

Daniel Benjamin, National Security
Council Staff member 1994–9[1]

*Each time a decision to do a rendition was made, we reminded the
lawyers and policy makers that Egypt was Egypt, and that Jimmy
Stewart never starred in a movie called 'Mr. Smith Goes to Cairo'.
They usually listened, nodded, and then inserted a legal nicety*

Michael Scheuer, head of the CIA rendition programme 1995–9[2]

RENDITION, IN ITS various forms, has been used by successive American
administrations since the mid-1980s. Its use has been almost exclu-
sively linked to the struggle against terrorism.

By 1984–5, the increasing incidence of terrorism was a major concern
for senior members of the Reagan administration. Secretary of State
George Shultz, an outspoken advocate of an activist approach, argued that
'it is increasingly doubtful that a purely passive strategy can even begin to
cope with the problem. ... When – and how – should we take preemptive
action against known terrorist groups?' The hijacking of flight TWA847
in June 1985, and that of the Italian cruise ship, the *Achille Lauro* the
following October raised the stakes further. In the latter case, the administration attempted an unorthodox seizure of the terrorists, intercepting
their getaway aeroplane and forcing it to land at the Sigonella NATO base
in Sicily. The Americans intended to transfer the terrorists to another plane
to fly them to stand trial in the United States: an early form of rendition
to justice. However, the Italian authorities insisted on taking the terrorists
into custody; to American exasperation, two detainees who had not been

on the boat, including the 'ringmaster' Abu Abbas, were released, though the remaining four were tried and imprisoned.[3]

The CIA's Director, William Casey, under pressure from Reagan to develop a more aggressive and effective counter-terrorism strategy, commissioned the head of the European Division, Duane R. Clarridge, to bring forward proposals in early 1986. Clarridge argued that the Agency had to overcome its 'defensive mentality' which meant that 'terrorists had operated knowing there was little chance of retribution or of their being brought to justice'. In particular, there should be 'action teams', operating worldwide and authorised to kill terrorists or seize them and bring them to justice. The report led to the formation of the CIA's Counterterrorist Center (CTC), with Clarridge as Director, on 1 February 1986. At the same time, President Reagan signed National Security Decision Directive NSDD-207, 'The National Programme for Combating Terrorism', alongside a highly classified Presidential Finding (the authorisation required from the President for covert operations) endorsing a variety of measures, including the establishment of 'action teams'.[4] The ability to act in more offensive fashion was assisted by two acts of Congress – the Comprehensive Crime Control Act of 1984, and the Omnibus Diplomatic Security and Anti-Terrorism Act of 1986 – which established extraterritorial jurisdiction of federal law in matters relating to terrorism.

The caution induced by the Iran-Contra scandal meant that many of Clarridge's ambitious plans failed to materialise. Nonetheless, 1987 saw the first rendition or, to use the term preferred at the time, 'extraction'. On 18 September, Fawaz Yunis, a Lebanese militant who had played a secondary role in the TWA847 seizure, and who had been indicted in the US for his role in another 1985 hijacking, was lured onto a boat in international waters off Cyprus and seized by FBI agents (the CIA could legally 'render assistance', but not carry out the arrest). Yunis was flown to the United States, where he was tried and sentenced to thirty years' imprisonment. This was clearly a rendition to justice, and in a style that indicated a relatively circumspect approach by the Reagan administration: 'Yunis had to be apprehended by the FBI in international waters or airspace, remain in constant custody of the feds, and remain clear of the turf of any sovereign nation – for the entire duration of his four-thousand-mile journey to the United States.'[5]

In 1988, the Justice Department issued a memo authorising rendition as a tactic for use by the CIA and FBI, and in 1989 the then Director of the CIA, William Webster, described its possible use and justification in relation to plans to seize the perpetrators of the Lockerbie bombing and bring them to the US for trial:

> ...the Justice Department, he said, has created a new term, 'rendition,' to describe the act of capturing and bringing back to the United States a criminal suspect. Webster confirmed that the United States believes it has the legal basis for kidnapping a terrorist in another country even without the knowledge and permission of its government. The term was contained in a Justice Department legal opinion issued last June and is particularly aimed at allowing the CIA or Federal Bureau of Investigation to seize a terrorist in countries like Lebanon, where there is no longer any rule of law.[6]

Clearly, the aim was still to render suspects *to* justice. This was also evident during the presidency of Reagan's successor, George H.W. Bush. The 1990 capture of the Mexican Dr Humberto Álvarez Machain is a rare case of a rendition not related to terrorism; Álvarez was accused of involvement in the murder of an American Drug Enforcement Agency officer. He was acquitted by a District Court in 1992; however, his case provided an important legal benchmark, since his efforts to challenge the legality of his rendition failed in the Supreme Court. In *United States v. Álvarez-Machain,*[7] the Court sustained the Ker-Frisbie doctrine that a US court could have jurisdiction over an individual, regardless of how that person was brought to them. They applied the same doctrine when the ousted Panamanian leader, Manuel Noriega, sought to challenge his transfer to Florida on narcotics charges after he was arrested by US forces invading his country.

The first Bush administration also saw some development of policy through National Security Directive NSD-77, which was written in 1992 and remains classified. According to Richard Clarke, who as chairman of the National Security Council's Counterterrorism Security Group (CSG), would continue his role as the main coordinator of policy regarding terrorism during the succeeding Clinton Presidency, it 'laid down a procedure under which we could do snatches'.[8]

It was under President Bill Clinton that rendition became an important policy tool, and began to change its form. Terrorism made itself felt early in the administration's term. On 25 January 1993, a few days after Clinton's inauguration, the Pakistani Mir Aimal Kasi killed two CIA employees outside the Agency's headquarters in Langley, Virginia, and wounded three others. On 26 February, a car bomb was detonated under the World Trade Center in New York, killing six people and injuring over a thousand.

Clinton's approach to rendition was soon tested by Clarke:

> The first time I proposed a snatch, in 1993, the White House Counsel, Lloyd Cutler, demanded a meeting with the president to explain how it violated international law. Clinton had seemed to be siding with Cutler until Al Gore belatedly joined the meeting, having just flown overnight from South Africa. Clinton recapped the arguments on both sides for Gore: Lloyd says this. Dick says that. Gore laughed and said, 'That's a no-brainer. Of course it's a violation of international law, that's why it's a covert action. The guy is a terrorist. Go grab his ass.'

The 'snatch' was approved, though it proved unsuccessful. This set the pattern for the President's term of office. 'The fact is,' Clarke recalled, 'President Clinton approved every snatch that he was asked to review.'[9]

Thus, 'by the mid-1990s these snatches were becoming routine CSG activity'. Initially, these appear to have been renditions to justice in the United States. Ramzi Yousef, organiser of the World Trade Center attack, was captured by Pakistani intelligence officers in Islamabad in February 1995 and handed over to the Americans without a formal extradition process. As with the 1997 rendition of the Langley assassin Mir Aimal Kasi, 'both were apprehended in Pakistan, whose leaders decided that the nation would rather not have those two - folk heroes to some - sitting in jail, awaiting extradition. Pakistan's leaders feared that cooperating with the United States would be dangerously unpopular, so they wanted the suspects out of the country quickly.'[10]

However, there were significant policy changes in 1995. The Oklahoma City bombing in April, though carried out by domestic rather than international terrorists, raised the salience of the issue; so did the sarin gas attacks carried out on the Tokyo subway in March. On 21 June, President Clinton signed Presidential Decision Directive PDD-39. This emphasised the need to seek cooperation from other states in handing over terrorists wanted by the US authorities, and where this was not forthcoming, 'return of suspects by force may be effected without the cooperation of the host government, consistent with the procedures outlined in NSD-77, which shall remain in effect'. This still sounds like rendition to justice; however, according to the staff work carried out for the 9/11 Commission, 'the United States could seek the local country's assistance in a rendition, secretly putting the fugitive in a plane back to America or some third country for trial'. By some accounts, this was authorised by sections of the Directive that remain classified. In any case, the CIA now began to render suspects to third countries, and to do so under circumstances that match the definition of extraordinary rendition.[11]

According to its colourful author Michael Scheuer, 'The CIA's rendition programme began in late summer, 1995 ... The Rendition Program was initiated because President Clinton, and Messrs. Lake [Anthony Lake, National Security Adviser 1993–97], Berger [Sandy Berger, National Security Adviser 1997–2001], and Clarke requested the CIA begin to attack and dismantle AQ [al Qaeda]. These men made it clear that they did not want to bring those captured to the US.'[12] Much of the evidence surrounding terrorist groups, such as that gathered by intercepted messages, was difficult to use in a normal open court; some of the sources, notably governments in the Islamic world, could be expected to be uneasy at the scale of their cooperation with the US being brought to public view. While there was political commitment to acting against terrorist groups and their leaders – among whom, at that time, Osama bin Laden was only one name, and chiefly seen as a financier rather than an organiser of terrorism – there was no will to undertake fundamental changes, such as a new legal regime aimed specifically at terrorists. Rendition to third countries was thus adopted as a policy that could damage terrorist networks while staying within the political constraints of the pre-9/11 world.[13]

The programme was not designed to gather intelligence. At best, this was a helpful by-product: 'hard copy or electronic documents in [the terrorists'] possession when they were arrested ... could provide options for follow-on operations'. In sharp contrast to the post-9/11 rendition programme, 'interrogation was never a goal under President Clinton'. Among the reasons for this was that 'torture might be used and the information might be simply what an individual thought we wanted to hear'.[14]

The bulk of third country renditions in the years after 1995 were to Egypt, long a close US ally and one confronting a strong domestic Islamist movement. As Scheuer pointed out, 'What was clever was that some of the senior people in Al Qaeda were Egyptian. It served American purposes to get these people arrested, and Egyptian purposes to get these people back, where they could be interrogated.' The CIA's international network was made available to the Egyptian authorities in an effort to stamp out their domestic terrorist opposition. The first case was that of Talaat Fouad Qassem, whose terrorist record, according to the Egyptian authorities, included a role in the assassination of President Sadat in 1981. Qassem had fled to Croatia. American agents assisted the local police in arranging his arrest in September 1995; he was then interrogated by the Americans on a ship in the Adriatic before being handed over to the Egyptians. He is believed to have been executed.[15]

There were two large-scale renditions to Egypt in the second half of 1998. The first was in Albania; the CIA assisted the intelligence services to monitor a cell of Egyptian militants suspected of planning to bomb the US Embassy in Tirana. The Egyptian authorities were prevailed upon to issue an arrest warrant for one of them. Four of the suspects were arrested by the Albanians and interrogated by the Americans before being transferred to Egypt; a fifth was shot by the Albanian police, a sixth was arrested in Bulgaria, while two others escaped capture. By the time that the 'Albanian returnees' stood trial in Cairo, they were joined by three others who, arrested while attempting to take part in the Nagorno-Karabakh conflict, had been transferred from Azerbaijan.[16]

Two of the 'Albanian returnees' were hanged for offences for which they had been tried in absentia; there were strong allegations that the others were tortured. Such cases highlight the more general question of the human rights record of governments – above all, that of Egypt – to which suspects were handed over. In the words of the former CIA officer Robert Baer: 'If you want a serious interrogation, you send a prisoner to Jordan. If you want them to be tortured, you send them to Syria. If you want someone to disappear – never to see them again – you send them to Egypt.'[17]

This sat uneasily with the United States' obligations under the CAT. The 'more likely than not' reservation entered by the Senate to the CAT's *non-refoulement* article gave some latitude, but in addition the administration sought to cover itself by seeking assurances from the Egyptians and others regarding the treatment of prisoners. Daniel Benjamin, who served on the Clinton era National Security Council, has argued that 'subjects could be sent only to countries where they were not likely to be tortured – countries that gave assurances to that effect and whose compliance was monitored by the State Department and the intelligence community. ... At a minimum, countries with indisputably lousy human rights records (say, Syria) were off-limits.'[18]

This is hard to reconcile with the State Department's consistent reports of torture and brutality by the Egyptian authorities, and especially by the political police, the Mukhabarat.[19] The assurances have been widely viewed as having little value. Edward Walker Jr, US ambassador to Egypt at the time of the Clinton administration's rendition programme, told the journalist Stephen Grey: 'I can't say to you with any candour that there was anything more than the verbal assurance, or even a written assurance. There was very little effort to follow up on that.'[20] In his congressional testimony, Scheuer was (characteristically) more trenchant:

> Mr. MARKEY. ... Now, how do you feel about this idea of accepting diplomatic assurances from countries like Syria that they won't torture someone who we send to them?
> Mr. SCHEUER. It isn't, sir, as Mr. Roosevelt's Vice President said at one time, worth a bucket of warm spit, sir.
> Mr. MARKEY. So you don't feel comfortable accepting a diplomatic assurance then?
> Mr. SCHEUER. If you accepted an assurance from any of the Arab tyrannies who are our allies that they weren't going to torture someone, I have got a bridge for you to buy, sir.[21]

Throughout the later 1990s, and into the new millennium, both terrorist activity and the measures against it escalated. In early 1996, the CIA set up a bin Laden unit, headed by Scheuer; initially, this was focused on bin Laden's role as a financier but within a year it had become clear that he was a leader and organiser of terrorism rather than simply a financier, and the unit consequently broadened its scope. The CTC established a Renditions Unit in 1997. Bin Laden himself was the target of a scheme to use Pashtun tribesmen with whom the CIA had long-standing contacts to capture him and get him out of Afghanistan. He would have been brought to the US to face charges under a sealed indictment issued by a grand jury in the southern district of New York. 'Had it worked, it would have been ... [a] rendition – and Americans would have cheered.' The capture plan was close to being authorised in May 1998, but was eventually pulled when its chances of success appeared too slight to justify the civilian casualties involved. Later variants on the plan ran into similar obstacles.[22]

On 23 February 1998, bin Laden and his Egyptian associate, Ayman al-Zawahiri, announced the formation of an 'International Islamic Front for Jihad Against Jews and Crusaders'. The group's manifesto, signed by a variety of militant groups, urged Muslims to kill Americans and their allies across the world. In May, Clinton signed a further directive, PDD-62, which reinforced the counter-terrorist strategy of PDD-39. The first of its ten programmes of activity was 'Apprehension, Extradition, Rendition and Prosecution'.[23] August saw the twin attacks on American embassies in Nairobi and Dar es Salaam, killing more than 200 people, 12 of them Americans; in response President Clinton launched cruise missile strikes on what were believed to be al Qaeda sites in Sudan and Afghanistan. In 1999, the CTC developed 'The Plan', an attempt at a comprehensive strategy against bin Laden and his associates, including 'renditions and disruptions'. The period around the millennium, as well as the Ramadan season of 2000, saw high levels of alert; a number of planned terrorist attacks were prevented, though al Qaeda succeeded in bombing the USS *Cole* in October 2000.

Rendition was used extensively during this period. The exact number of those rendered to the authorities – whether in the United States or elsewhere – in the pre-9/11 period is not known, but appears to have been in the higher double digits. Testifying before the 9/11 Commission, then CIA Director George Tenet remarked, '... we used all the tools at our disposal. There were – you know, I've testified that there were over 80 renditions.' Previously, he had given the figure as 70; in a speech prior to 9/11, he had indicated that 'we have helped to render more than two dozen terrorists to justice' over an eighteen month period between July 1998 and early 2000. Also testifying to the 9/11 Commission, former National Security Adviser Sandy Berger stated that 'the CIA, together with foreign intelligence services, tracked down and captured more than 50 terrorists abroad'.[24] Scheuer, meanwhile, estimated that 'the operations that I was in charge of concerned approximately 40 people at that time [i.e. before September 2001]'[25]; however, since he left his post in 1999, he may not have had the full picture.

Efforts to identify individuals have produced only about half this number; for example, Stephen Grey's *Ghost Plane* records twenty-four individuals (starting with Yunis in 1987) rendered before 9/11. Another investigation found twenty-nine cases of rendition during this period, fourteen of which could be considered 'extraordinary'. Of these, twelve were to Egypt, with the Albanian and Azerbaijanian cases accounting for eight.[26] The difference is probably accounted for in the flurry of activity around various terrorist alerts, including (under the George W Bush administration) the months leading up to 9/11. In his written testimony to the 9/11 Commission, Tenet described how, during 'the Millennium threat period', actions were taken successfully against 21 individuals that 'included arrests, renditions, detentions and surveillance. … During this same period, unrelated to Millennium threats, we conducted multiple operations in East Asia, leading to the arrest or detention of 45 members of the Hizballah [sic] network.' Similar operations were carried out during Ramadan 2000, while among the initiatives taken in summer 2001, 'we assisted another foreign partner in the rendition of a senior bin Laden associate'.[27]

The increasing use of rendition took place amid an ambiguous phase in American counterterrorism policy. In some respects, American policy – like its European counterparts – approached terrorism as a law enforcement issue. Yet the strand of policy that had gradually developed since the foundation of the CTC in 1986 had represented a more preemptive, national security driven approach. In the later 1990s, Clinton signed various Memorandums of Notification (MONs) – which authorise significant actions under a Presidential Finding – authorising operations against bin Laden and his associates, some of which could only be justified under the law of armed conflict.[28] Yet the MONs were sometimes contradictory and policy remained ambivalent. The President's inner group of advisers debated 'whether to consider this a law enforcement matter demanding a judicial response or a military matter in which the use of armed force was justified,' Madeleine Albright recalled. 'We decided it was both.'[29] The attacks of 11 September 2001 produced a decisive lurch in policy – and in the forms and uses of rendition.

4. The Bush Administration Goes to War

*... at about 9:45 [on 9/11] the President told the Vice President:
'Sounds like we have a minor war going on here, I heard about
the Pentagon. We're at war ... somebody's going to pay'*

- From the 9/11 Commission Report[1]

*... the war against terrorism is a new kind of war. ... The nature
of the new war places a high premium on other factors, such as the
ability to quickly obtain information from captured terrorists and
their sponsors in order to avoid further atrocities against American
civilians, and the need to try terrorists for war crimes such as wantonly
killing civilians. In my opinion, this new paradigm renders obsolete
Geneva's strict limitations on questioning of enemy prisoners and
renders quaint some of its provisions requiring that captured enemy
be afforded such things as commissary privileges, scrip (i.e. advances
of monthly pay), athletic uniforms, and scientific instruments.*

- Alberto R. Gonzales, White House Legal
Counsel to President George W. Bush[2]

THE DEADLY ATTACKS of 11 September 2001 produced a step change in the US administration's efforts to fight terrorism. In the days, weeks and months after 9/11, senior figures in the Bush administration were haunted by fear of another attack, perhaps involving biological weapons. 'They thought they were going to get hit again. They convinced themselves that they were facing a ticking time bomb.' The intelligence agencies in particular were under enormous pressure to compensate for their failure to prevent 9/11.[3]

If fear was an important driver of what followed, so was ideology. Two of the key figures in the administration – Vice President Dick Cheney and Defense Secretary Donald Rumsfeld – had been witnesses to the wreckage of presidential authority in the Vietnam and Watergate era by what they viewed as a presumptuous Congress and an intrusive press, contributing to America's military defeat. As Cheney put it: 'Watergate and a lot of the things around Watergate and Vietnam served, I think, to erode the authority I think the president needs to be effective, especially in the national security area.'[4] This new crisis would be met by a tough-minded assertion of executive power.

As a result, rendition would change significantly in the details of its operation, while also shifting from a somewhat ad hoc operation to an element in a comprehensive strategy, the 'Global War on Terror' that would be the signature policy of George W. Bush's presidency.

In the immediate aftermath of 9/11, on 17 September 2001, President Bush issued a wide-ranging MON that gave the CIA 'exceptional authorities to detain al Qaeda operatives worldwide'; this was a blanket authority, with decisions on individual cases delegated to the CIA Director. The British intelligence agencies were given some indication of these new powers, but were sceptical about them 'because there had been a great deal of "tough talk" following 9/11'. However, some elements of the new powers were brought into the public domain when, on 13 November, Bush issued a Presidential Military Order authorising detention of suspects with no certainty of trial, and raising the prospect that trials that did ensue could be carried out by military commissions.[5]

In contrast to the Clinton era, there were almost no renditions to US justice after 9/11. However, extraordinary renditions to third countries continued apace. One case that attracted considerable subsequent attention was that of Mohammed al-Zery and Ahmed Agiza, who were rendered from Sweden, where they were seeking asylum, to their native Egypt in December 2001. Both were alleged to be involved in the Egyptian Islamist opposition, though in both cases the scale and nature of their involvement was disputed. The Egyptian government had issued warrants for their arrest. On 30 October, SÄPO, the Swedish security service, recommended that their applications be refused for security reasons; Sweden's Migration Board, aware of the security service's view but concerned that the men might be at risk of maltreatment if returned to Egypt, referred the matter to the government for decision.

By some accounts, the Swedish government was by this stage coming under severe American pressure to deport the two men. It asked for and received assurances from the Egyptian authorities that the two men would be treated 'with full respect to their personal and human rights ... according to what the Egyptian constitution and law stipulates'. The cabinet approved immediate deportation of the two men during a morning session on 18 December. Al-Zery and Agiza were arrested during the afternoon and taken to Bromma airport near Stockholm, where they were handed over to a group of hooded CIA officers, accompanied by two Egyptian officials and two representatives from the American Embassy. Although still on Swedish soil, the Americans took charge of the operation. Agiza and al-Zery were flown to Cairo that night on an American plane.[6]

The American role in this transfer – apart from the alleged pressure on the Swedish government – was for the CIA to act as 'a travel agency'. The aeroplane used was an executive jet, a Gulfstream V, later alleged by investigative journalists to be one of the flagships of a twenty-six strong fleet operated by a set of linked companies that carried out work for the CIA.[7]

The procedure at Bromma airport matches what was by many other accounts a standard modus operandi in renditions. 'The hooded agents slit the author's [al-Zery's] clothes with a pair of scissors and examined each piece of cloth before placing it in a plastic bag. Another agent checked his hair, mouth and lips, while a third agent took photographs ... When his clothes were cut off his body, he was handcuffed and chained to his feet. He was then drugged per rectum with some form of tranquilliser and placed in diapers. He was then dressed in overalls and escorted to the plane blindfolded, hooded and barefooted.'[8] The two men were chained to the floor and remained blindfolded and hooded during the flight to Cairo.

Despite the assurances about their treatment given to the Swedish government, there are strong allegations that on their return to Egypt the two men suffered torture, including electric shock treatment. Al-Zery was released after two years, though he was required to remain in his village; Agiza was jailed for twenty-five years (later reduced to fifteen) by a military tribunal, to which Swedish officials were denied access.[9]

The scale of renditions to third countries appears to have been comparable to but a little less than that during the Clinton years. CIA Director General Michael Hayden stated that they were 'mid-range, two figures since September 11, 2001. A pace somewhat behind the number of renditions conducted in the 1990s'. Independent investigators identified fifty-three third country renditions between 9/11 and early 2008.[10] However, this form of rendition was now only part of the picture.

Meanwhile, military rendition and rendition to detention grew apace. The first of these developed as a result of the successful invasion of Afghanistan, and the need to decide how to handle captured al Qaeda and Taliban prisoners. In January–February 2002, John Yoo of the Justice Department's Office of Legal Counsel (OLC) and the White House counsel, Alberto R. Gonzales, argued that neither the Geneva Convention on Prisoners of War, nor Common Article 3 of the Geneva conventions – which set a minimum requirement of humane treatment of non-combatants, including prisoners, in a conflict – should be applied to detainees in Afghanistan. Alongside legal justifications, Gonzales argued that 'the war against terrorism is a new kind of war … The nature of the new war places a high premium on other factors, such as the ability to quickly obtain information from captured terrorists and their sponsors in order to avoid further atrocities against American civilians.'[11] Captured al Qaeda and Taliban fighters were to be treated neither as prisoners of war nor as civilians against whom criminal charges might be brought, but rather as 'unlawful combatants' who had the protection of neither status and who could in principle be held indefinitely.

Secretary of State Colin Powell and the State Department were strongly opposed to this approach; the Department's Legal Adviser, William Howard Taft IV, described the Yoo-Gonzales arguments as 'seriously flawed' in matters both of fact and law.[12] However, Bush sided with the OLC. In the Memorandum that he issued to establish the new approach on 7 February, the President insisted that the United States remained 'a strong supporter of Geneva and its principles'. He added that, 'As a matter of policy, the United States armed forces shall continue to treat detainees humanely and, to the extent appropriate and consistent with military necessity, in a manner consistent with the principles of Geneva.'[13] However, Geneva's automatic protections, and in particular those of Common Article 3 had been discarded.

What was most striking about this decision was the way in which it was taken. The concept of the unlawful combatant still existed in American theory (though less in practice) about the laws of war; in 1987, President Reagan had refused to submit Protocol 1 of the Third Geneva Convention for Senate ratification because it blurred the distinction between regular and irregular fighters. The International Committee of the Red Cross (ICRC) has insisted that 'contrary to some assertions, the ICRC has never stated that all persons who have taken part in hostilities in an international armed conflict are entitled to POW status'. However, a 'competent tribunal' was required to rule on the merits of each individual case; by categorising detainees without a hearing, the Bush administration was visibly disregarding the Conventions.[14]

While excluding the prisoners from Geneva Convention protection, the administration sought also to keep them outside the American legal system. The US naval base at Guantánamo Bay, Cuba – leased from the Cuban government in 1903, and theoretically under Cuban rather than US sovereignty – matched these requirements. The two previous administrations had seen its advantages as a place of detention for unwanted aliens who, because of its status, would have 'no judicially cognizable rights in US courts'.[15] The first prisoners of the war in Afghanistan were transferred there in January 2002; in total, more than 800 people would enter it in the years that followed. This was 'military rendition': an extra-judicial transfer of people captured in a theatre of military operations to military captivity elsewhere. Guantánamo would become part of an international network of sites linked by other forms of rendition.

Many of those held in Guantánamo had been handed over to the Americans by the Pakistani authorities or the Afghan Northern Alliance in exchange for bounties; it seems very likely that many were innocent, or were at most foot soldiers. A senior CIA analyst who questioned a random sample of prisoners in the summer of 2002 concluded that a third of them had no connection to terrorism at all. Similarly, as early as May, Major General Michael Dunlavey, the commanding officer in charge of interrogations at Guantánamo, 'had concluded that half the detainees had no intelligence value at all'. However, his civilian superiors in the Department of Defense had no interest in freeing any detainees at this point.[16]

According to Lawrence Wilkerson, a career soldier, former Chief of Staff to Colin Powell and a strong critic of many features of the Bush administration's policies, the large-scale detentions, not only at Guantánamo but also at sites such as Bagram air base in Afghanistan, reflected the thinking of key Pentagon officials. 'And so you sweep all these people up in this "mosaic theory", and you question them, and then you plug all of this into an analytical computer … and suddenly the patterns begin to appear, and you begin to know more about al Qaeda, or al Qaeda-like people, than you otherwise would know. And you don't care where you got the information, or the fact that 29 of the 30 people you swept up didn't give you a thing that was worthwhile, because one did. And maybe even that one was innocent.' Wilkerson has subsequently alleged in a signed declaration in support of a case brought by a former Guantánamo detainee that President Bush, Vice President Cheney and Secretary Rumsfeld knew that many of those held at Guantánamo were innocent but did not believe that it was politically acceptable to release them.[17]

If many of those transferred to Guantánamo during the earlier stages of the War on Terror had little if any connection to the higher reaches of al Qaeda, the same could not be said of the group known as the 'High-Value Detainees' (HVDs), who were believed to be senior al Qaeda figures and so in possession of vital information. In the words of a senior figure within the CTC: 'If a guy is captured on the battlefield and sent to [Guantánamo], that's got nothing to do with it. But I think there is a tendency in the media, in Europe and in America, to blend together what the FBI is doing, what the military is doing and what the CIA is doing – to attribute it all to the same programme. And frankly, you can't do that. The HVD programme is a very structured, very rigorous programme.'[18] This was the group on which the CIA focused its efforts: 'we didn't want the insurgents; we wanted the leadership'.[19] The Agency did not trust HVDs to others, whether foreign intelligence services or the US military.

The HVD programme generated a new form of extraordinary rendition, making use of secret prisons – the so-called 'black sites' – operated by the CIA in various parts of the world. From early 2002 onwards, a number of those identified by the US administration as important al Qaeda figures were arrested and disappeared from outside view into this network. The first such figure was Abu Zubaydah, a Saudi believed to be an important organiser for bin Laden, who was captured after a gunfight in Faisalabad, Pakistan, on 28 March 2002. Perhaps the biggest success was the arrest of Khalid Sheikh Mohammed, a Kuwait-born Pakistani who was the self-proclaimed organiser of the 9/11 attacks and involved in many other acts of terrorism, in Rawalpindi, Pakistan, on 1 March 2003. Nor were the arrests limited to Middle Eastern linked operatives; on 11 August 2003, Riduan Isamuddin, an Indonesian also known as Hambali and considered 'the bin Laden of South East Asia' for his reported role as head of operations for the militant group Jemaah Islamiyah, was arrested in Ayutthaya, Thailand.

While most of the black sites appear to have been far from the theatre of conflict, some interrogation sites were not. The section of Bagram air base in Afghanistan known as 'the hangar', along with two prisons reportedly close to Kabul, known as 'the dark prison' (so called because of the complete lack of light in the cells) and 'the salt pit', served both as transition points and places of interrogation for CIA prisoners. In Iraq, Abu Ghraib held prisoners detained by the military, but also 'ghost detainees', brought in by the CIA or by US Special Forces, some of whom were moved around the prison to prevent the ICRC having access to them.[20] However, unlike the Afghan prisons, Abu Ghraib does not appear to have been used for prisoners rendered from outside the country.

While most interrogation at Guantánamo was carried out by the military, there are reports of a separate interrogation facility on the base, run by either the CIA or Special Forces. This was reportedly abandoned in 2004 when Supreme Court rulings regarding the detainees held by the military were seen as threatening greater judicial intervention. An alternative explanation for these allegations may be provided by recent reports suggesting that four HVDs were held at Guantánamo for six months in 2003–04 before being returned to the black sites, again because of looming litigation before the Supreme Court.[21] Guantánamo's major and visible link to the HVD programme came later, when prisoners were transferred there after the reported closure of the black sites in September 2006.

The distinction between rendition to third countries and rendition to detention in the network of secret CIA prisons is not entirely rigid. For example, the British resident Binyam Mohamed – whose case will be examined in more detail in a later chapter – was allegedly put though both systems. Arrested in Pakistan in April 2002, he was by his own account rendered to Morocco three months later. In January 2004, he was transferred to the 'dark prison', then to Bagram in May and finally to Guantánamo in September. In addition, a majority of those who had been held within the CIA programme appear to have been returned to their home countries when their intelligence value was exhausted.[22]

It is possible to be quite precise about the numbers put through the secret prisons programme. According to a memo written by Steven G. Bradbury, Principal Deputy Assistant Attorney General, in May 2005, 'To date the CIA has taken custody of 94 detainees … [redacted] and has employed enhanced techniques to varying degrees in the interrogations of 28 of these detainees.' Bradbury's memo was not published until 2009, but similar information was in the public domain from Michael Hayden in 2007: 'Fewer than 100 hardened terrorists have gone through the program since it began in 2002, and, of those, fewer than a third have required any special methods of questioning.'[23]

The 'enhanced techniques' and 'special methods of questioning' were to be one of the most troubling features of the secret prisons programme. Their starting point was the capture of Abu Zubaydah in March 2002, six months after 9/11. Senior CIA officials believed that he was withhold-

Maher Arar and Khaled el-Masri: Caught in the dragnet

Some of those subject to rendition faced long charge sheets; in some other cases, the evidence was very mixed. But there were also a number of cases of individuals caught in the rendition net through error.

Maher Arar, a telecommunications engineer with joint Syrian and Canadian citizenship, was arrested during a stopover at New York's John F. Kennedy airport on his way back to Canada from a family holiday on 26 September 2002. Detained for thirteen days, he was then deported to Syria via Jordan. He was held in Syria for a year, beaten with cables and kept in a six foot by three windowless cell. He was released in October 2003 as a result of a campaign that his wife ran on his behalf in Canada, and the realisation by his Syrian jailers that he had no vital information to give them. No charges were brought against him.

A Commission of Inquiry established by the Canadian government concluded that there was no evidence to link Arar to terrorism. He had drawn the attention of the Canadian authorities because of indirect links to members of the Canadian-Syrian community suspected of terrorist activity; these made him a 'person of interest' (but not a suspect) to the Canadian security services. This information, passed on to the US authorities without provisos, triggered his arrest and deportation. The Canadian government gave Arar an apology and a C$10.5m compensation settlement.

Khaled el-Masri, a German citizen of Lebanese origins, was arrested at the Serbian-Macedonian border while on a brief holiday on 31 December 2003. His arrest was apparently triggered by suspicions – which proved unjustified – about the validity of his passport (it was a new style of German passport with which the border guards were apparently unfamiliar). He was held incommunicado and interrogated in a hotel in Skopje for three weeks before being flown to Afghanistan, where he was held in the 'salt pit' and subject to cold temperatures, poor food and threatening interrogations. He was eventually released on 28 May 2004 and returned to Germany via a 'reverse rendition' to Albania.

It is possible that el-Masri's attendance at a radical mosque in his home town of Ulm contributed to his arrest, though he was not a central figure in the mosque and there were no grounds to associate him with terrorism. The most common explanation given for his detention is mistaken identity: an unrelated Khalid al-Masri (the transliteration used in the 9/11 Commission's report) was believed to be a key link between the al Qaeda leadership and the 'Hamburg cell' that carried out the 9/11 attacks. By several accounts, a number of CIA officers realised from quite early in el-Masri's detention that he was innocent, but efforts to release him were blocked by more senior figures in the Agency. He was eventually released on the instruction of CIA Director George Tenet, who reportedly said, 'Are you telling me that we've got an innocent guy stuck in prison in Afghanistan? Oh shit! Just tell me – please – we haven't used "enhanced" interrogation techniques on him, have we?'[62]

ing information that might help prevent another attack. A 'more robust approach' was therefore needed. 'This accelerated CIA's development of an interrogation program.'[24]

Under pressure to show results, the Agency had begun examining 'enhanced' interrogation techniques in November 2001. Two independent contractors were taken on to produce a paper on al Qaeda operatives' resistance to interrogation, and ways in which this resistance might be broken. Their expertise lay in the SERE (Survival, Evasion, Resistance, Escape) programme, overseen by the Department of Defense's Joint Personnel Recovery Agency (JPRA) and designed to assist US service personnel withstand torture and other coercive interrogation methods if captured by an enemy. This approach was then 'reverse engineered' to generate 'enhanced interrogation techniques' (EITs) that could be applied to al Qaeda suspects.[25] The aim was to break resistance; or, in the jargon-heavy terminology of a later report by the CIA's Inspector General, 'An interrogator transitions the detainee from a non-cooperative to a cooperative phase in order that a debriefer can elicit actionable intelligence through non-aggressive techniques during debriefing sessions.'[26]

The analysts' paper recommended the use of eleven (later reduced to ten) such techniques; these included the 'facial or insult slap', 'cramped confinement' in a dark box, sleep deprivation, the use of insects and, most notoriously, simulated drowning or 'waterboarding'. The CIA's Office of Technical Services (OTS) secured opinions from psychologists and reports from SERE training that justified use of the EITs on the grounds that they did not have long-lasting psychological effects (although it appeared that the use of waterboarding in training was limited 'because of its dramatic effect on the students who were subjects').[27]

Excluding detainees from the Geneva Conventions gave interrogators some protection against the application of the 1996 War Crimes Act. However, domestic and international law still put severe limits on the methods that they could employ – at a time when interest in 'enhanced interrogation techniques' was growing. In particular, the United States had obligations under the CAT; furthermore, in accordance with the convention, legislation enacted in 1994 (18 USC §§2340 – 2340A: the 'torture statute'), the year of the CAT's ratification, made clear that under the federal criminal code use of torture was a punishable offence.

The CIA asked for advice from the OLC, which issued a series of documents on 1 August 2002, later to become notorious as the 'torture memos'. The first was addressed to Gonzales and went under the signature of the Assistant Attorney General, Jay S. Bybee; however, the authorship is widely attributed to Deputy Assistant Attorney General John Yoo.[28] This focused on what interrogation techniques would be forbidden by the torture statute, which prohibited actions 'specifically intended to inflict severe mental pain or suffering'. Citing health benefits legislation, the memo offered an extremely restrictive definition of 'severe':

> Physical pain amounting to torture must be equivalent in intensity to the pain accompanying serious physical injury, such as organ failure, impairment of bodily function, or even death. For purely mental pain or suffering to amount to torture under Section 2340, it must result in significant psychological harm of significant duration, e.g., lasting for months or even years.

The memo offered further scope to interrogators by arguing that 'in the circumstances of the current war against al Qaeda and its allies, prosecution under Section 2340A may be barred because enforcement of the statute would represent an unconstitutional infringement of the President's authority to conduct war'. A further justification might be provided by 'necessity or self-defense'.

The second document, which took the form of a letter from Yoo to Gonzales, addressed the issue of whether or not the interrogation methods violated US commitments under the CAT or could provide the basis for a prosecution at the International Criminal Court. Yoo concluded that, as with the domestic statute, international obligations did not preclude the interrogation techniques. He based his argument on interpretations issued by the first Bush administration at the time that the US acceded to the CAT, and on the February decision not to apply the Geneva conventions to Taliban and al Qaeda fighters.[29]

The third memo, addressed to John Rizzo, Acting General Counsel to the CIA and once more signed by Bybee but written by Yoo, addressed the specific issue of the Agency's desire to move to an 'increased pressure phase' in its interrogation of Abu Zubaydah. Following through the arguments of the first memo, it examined each of the 'enhanced' techniques in detail and concluded 'that the interrogation procedures that you propose would not violate Section 2340A'.[30]

This exercise in definition served to argue that, in applying 'enhanced' techniques, officers were not violating either the CAT or domestic laws. However, it did not address the question of how adoption of the techniques was consistent with the United States' obligations under Article 16 of the CAT to prevent CIDT (as interpreted by the Senate to reflect the Fifth, Eighth and Fourteenth Amendments to the Constitution), merely noting that while the latter were acts 'that are not to be committed' they were 'without the stigma of criminal penalties'.[31]

The issue was taken up to some extent in a further document (undated, but apparently completed in June 2003), 'Legal Principles Applicable to CIA Detention and Interrogation of Captured Al-Qa'ida Personnel'. It argued that 'the [Torture] Convention permits the use of [cruel, inhuman, or degrading treatment] in exigent circumstances, such as a national emergency or war', presumably on the basis that the CAT's provision that this justification cannot be used applies only to torture. It also argued that the Fifth and Fourteenth Amendments did not apply extraterritorially, while the Eighth applied only to those on whom criminal sanctions had been imposed. In addition to restating the position that the EITs were permissible under torture statutes, the paper also emphasised that al Qaeda operatives were not prisoners of war and so not entitled to the protections of the laws of war.[32] It made clear that the arguments justifying the use of EITs on Abu Zubaydah could be applied more generally.

The application of these techniques to fourteen key HVDs – including Khalid Sheikh Mohammed and Abu Zubaydah – was documented by the ICRC after it had access to the men for the first time soon after their arrival in Guantánamo in September 2006. They recorded widespread use of the EITs: beatings, prolonged standing in 'stress positions', sleep deprivation, confinement in boxes, exposure to cold and other methods. Waterboarding was used on three of the detainees, Khalid Sheikh Mohammed, Abu Zubaydah, and Abd al-Rahim al-Nashiri.[33]

Most of these techniques had been approved in the OLC memos; some, however, (such as forced shaving and dousing with cold water) were not in the original CIA proposals but instead belong to lists of techniques approved separately for military interrogators. In addition, there were occasions on which interrogators went beyond what had been authorised. In some cases, waterboarding was carried out in a way that went beyond the OLC guidelines, in terms both of the methods used and its frequency. The CIA Inspector General's report recorded that Khalid Sheikh Mohammed 'received 183 applications of the waterboard in March 2003', while Abu Zubaydah was waterboarded at least 83 times during August 2002.[34] On some other occasions, interrogators introduced techniques of their own, such as mock executions, threats to prisoners' families and threatening a detainee with a power drill.[35]

The treatment of these fourteen prisoners represents only part of the overall picture. Others who passed through jails such as the 'dark prison' described experiencing threats, sleep deprivation, the playing of very loud music and being held in cold and confined cells.[36] A prisoner held by the CIA in the 'salt pit' was reported to have died of hypothermia as a result being left chained, wet and naked from the waist down in a freezing cell overnight and was buried in secret. The death was first reported, but not officially confirmed in 2005. More recent reports have given the detainee's name (Gul Rahman) and the date of his death (20 November 2002). A footnote in a recently released document gives considerable substance to the story. It has also been reported that Rahman's death triggered an investigation by the CIA's Inspector General, but that the Justice Department did not press charges at the time.[37]

The CIA was not the only agency to apply aggressive interrogation techniques, and the black sites were not the only places at which they were used. Developments in CIA interrogation techniques were paralleled by those in the military, whose practices had previously been set by the Army Field Manual, itself heavily informed by the Geneva conventions. As in the CIA, military policymakers began to examine and adopt the techniques taught by the JPRA. In December 2001, at around the same time that the CIA was in contact with SERE experts, the Defense Department's Office of the General Counsel contacted JPRA about methods of detainee 'exploitation'.[38] For the military as for the CIA, it was the apparent recalcitrance of a prisoner believed likely to hold important intelligence – Mohammed al-Qahtani, the alleged 'twentieth hijacker' for the 9/11 attacks – that accelerated the drive for more aggressive interrogation methods. Rendered from Pakistan to Guantánamo in February 2002, al-Qahtani was believed by his interrogators to be holding back important information. He was held in strict isolation from August and as the Guantánamo authorities investigated the use of harsher interrogation techniques, they were advised by the JPRA and had some input from the CIA. The training provided to Guantánamo staff at Fort Bragg, North Carolina, in September 2002 was described by a JPRA officer as 'similar in nature to what we did for OGA [Other Government Agency, i.e. the CIA] on the last iteration'.[39]

The final link between the development of the CIA's HVD programme and interrogations at Guantánamo was the role played by legal advice. When in October 2002, Major General Dunlavey sent a formal request to his superiors to use more aggressive techniques outside those sanctioned by the Army Field Manual, he accompanied it with a hastily drawn up legal justification by a relatively junior legal adviser, the Guantánamo Staff Judge Advocate, Lieutenant Colonel Diane Beaver. However, there are strong indications that senior figures in the Pentagon were aware of the justifications that the Bybee/Yoo memos had already provided for the CIA to use similar techniques; General Counsel Haynes later stated that it was 'very, very likely' that he had read the OLC opinion by this stage.[40]

The interrogation techniques requested escalated from Category I (yelling at the detainee and various forms of deception) to the more severe Category II, which included stress positions lasting up to four hours; isolation for up to thirty days; hooding; twenty-hour interrogations; deprivation of light and auditory stimuli; stripping the detainee of his clothes; forced shaving; and 'using detainees' individual phobias (such as fear of dogs) to induce stress'. Most serious were the four techniques included in Category III, which required more senior approval and 'are required for a very small percentage of the most uncooperative detainees (less than 3%)'. These were death threats to the individual or his family; exposure to cold temperatures or water; waterboarding; and 'mild, non-injurious physical contact, such as grabbing, poking in the chest with the finger, and light pushing'. Following the advice of his Counsel Jim Haynes, Defense Secretary Rumsfeld approved the use of all techniques in the first two categories and one (physical contact) in Category III. The other techniques were not approved 'at this time. Our Armed Forces are trained to a standard of interrogation that reflects a tradition of restraint.' This approval came on 2 December 2002; however, by that time al-Qahtani had already been subject to the techniques for more than a week, indicating that approval was seen as something of a formality.[41]

However, following protests by the Navy's Advocate General, Alberto Mora, authorisation was rescinded on 15 January 2003. During the review that followed, the OLC advice resurfaced once more in the form of a memorandum (dated 14 March) from John Yoo that restated its essential arguments. This was taken as the legal template for the review, which recommended thirty-five techniques for use. On 16 April, Secretary Rumsfeld issued a further memorandum authorising the use of twenty-four of the techniques, five of which were outside the Army Field Manual, including isolation, environmental manipulation (such as adjustments to temperature) and 'sleep adjustment'. Although the memorandum emphasised certain safeguards, it also provided for case by case approval by the Defense Secretary of 'additional interrogation techniques for a particular detainee'.[42] In the summer, the Defense Secretary approved the application of more aggressive techniques (loud noise and sleep deprivation) to another detainee, the Mauritanian Mohamedou Ould Slahi; in practice, threats, prolonged standing and a darkened cell appear also to have been used. The Guantánamo authorities asked for permission for special interrogation plans for two other detainees, although it is unclear whether or not this was granted.[43]

Although Rumsfeld's was a relatively limited approval, there are reports of a number of cases of abuse that involved techniques that were not on the approved list. Furthermore, 'in addition to the use of strobe lights and loud music, techniques such as forced shaving, sensory deprivation and even implied threats of death were either used or planned for use' in interrogations at the camp in 2003 (in some cases, this appears to have been based on a broad or mistaken interpretation of the guidelines, such as seeing the use of noise and strobe lights as 'environmental manipulation'). Official investigations provide some support for these accounts, while considering that some of the techniques applied were acceptable; for example, the use of loud music was considered part of an 'incentive and futility' technique allowable under the Army Field Manual, with playing of 'cultural music' the incentive, while the 'futility technique included the playing of Metallica, Britney Spears, and Rap music'. Prolonged 'short shackling' of prisoners to the floor – recognised as an improper technique – was considered by the Schmidt-Furlow army investigation to have taken place on 'at least a two occasions', though there are other indications that it may have been more frequent. There was also quite frequent use of 'sleep adjustment', notably the 'frequent flyer programme', under which the sleep of detainees deemed uncooperative was disrupted by transferring them to a different cell every few hours.[44]

The combination of pressure to get results and guidance from the top that was contradictory but leaning towards permissiveness contributed to the development of similar techniques in Afghanistan and Iraq. In part, this was through 'a store of common lore and practice within the interrogator community circulating through Guantánamo, Afghanistan and elsewhere'[45] However, some of the links were more direct. In Afghanistan in 2002, the only official guidance was the Army Field Manual, but 'more aggressive interrogation of detainees appears to have been ongoing'; the deaths in Military Intelligence custody of two detainees at Bagram in December 2002, and reports of frequent abuses at the facility at that time reinforce this conclusion.[46] Standard Operating Procedures (SOPs) issued by both special and conventional forces in Afghanistan in January 2003 appear to have been influenced by JPRA methods and incorporated a range of aggressive techniques. When it came to Iraq, a Special Forces task force took a copy of the SOPs for Afghanistan, 'changed the letterhead, and adopted the SOP verbatim'. Conventional forces initially took a similar approach, although this was later reversed in light of the recognition that in Iraq, as opposed to Afghanistan, the Geneva Conventions were applied (though, to complicate matters further, the military leadership in Iraq ruled that some detainees could be considered unlawful combatants on the model applied in Afghanistan).[47]

Detainee abuse culminated in the eruption of the Abu Ghraib scandal in April 2004. In its report, the Independent Panel set up to review detention operations, chaired by the former Republican Defense Secretary James R. Schlesinger, noted that the incidents captured in the notorious photographs taken at the prison 'were not part of authorized interrogations nor were they even directed at intelligence targets'. However, it added that other abuses did take place in interrogation sessions and that there was 'both institutional and personal responsibility at higher levels'. A vast array of factors lay behind the abuses, including understaffing, the pressures of trying to respond to a growing insurgency and failures at many levels of command. In addition, however, 'the changes in DoD interrogation policies between December 2, 2002 and April 16, 2003 were an element contributing to uncertainties in the field as to which techniques were authorized. Although specifically limited by the Secretary of Defense to Guantánamo, and requiring his personal approval (given in only two cases), the augmented techniques for Guantánamo migrated to Afghanistan and Iraq where they were neither limited nor safeguarded.' These ambiguities were reinforced by frequent changes in approach at an operational level. The CIA's activities were also a factor: 'Some of the abusers believed other governmental agencies were conducting interrogations using harsher techniques than allowed by the Army Field Manual 34-52, a perception leading to the belief that such methods were condoned.'[48]

Just as Abu Ghraib was dominating the world's television screens, the CIA Inspector General, John Helgerson, submitted his (then) secret review of the Agency's interrogation methods. He noted that 'the Agency's detention and interrogation of terrorists has provided intelligence that has enabled the identification and apprehension of other terrorists and warned of terrorist plots planned for the United States and around the world'. He qualified this by adding that 'the effectiveness of particular interrogation techniques in eliciting information that might not otherwise have been obtained cannot be so easily measured, however'.[49] He also noted that some agents were uneasy about the ethical and legal implications of methods that contradicted many of the stated aims and values of US policy and which might one day result in prosecutions. The new methods marked a sharp departure in CIA policy and posed 'potentially serious long-term political and legal challenges … particularly [the] use of EITs and the inability of the US Government to decide what it will ultimately do with terrorists detained by the Agency'.[50]

This warning proved timely, since mid-2004 saw a major shift in sentiment against the administration. The Abu Ghraib scandal had a dramatic effect on opinion both at home and abroad; an important element in it was the death in custody of Manadel al-Jamadi in November 2003, in which CIA interrogators were implicated. The 'torture memos' were made public in June, and were shortly afterwards scrapped by the OLC head Jack Goldsmith, who had already concluded that their legal reasoning was outlandish. However, in May 2005, a series of memos by the acting head of the OLC, Steven Bradbury, found new grounds to justify the EITs, both singly and in common. Bradbury's papers argued that the techniques did not generate suffering of sufficient intensity and duration to meet the definition of torture; nor did they violate Article 16 of the CAT, since they were applied outside US jurisdiction and in any case should not be considered executive actions that would 'shock the conscience' and so be forbidden by the Fifth Amendment.[51]

Also in June 2004, the Supreme Court handed down two verdicts clearly inimical to the administration's wide-ranging interpretation of the War on Terror. In *Rasul v. Bush* (28 June 2004), the Court voted 6-3 to assert its right to hear habeas corpus petitions from Guantánamo detainees, asserting that the prison was not beyond the reach of US law. This provided 'a vivid illustration of the Court's willingness to alter doctrine to ensure accountability in the war against terrorism'.[52] On the same day, in *Hamdi v. Rumsfeld*, the Court voted 8-1 that a 'citizen-detainee' (Hamdi was a Saudi who had been born in Louisiana and so held American citizenship) had a right to counsel, to know the accusations against him and 'a fair opportunity to rebut the Government's factual assertions before a neutral decision-maker'.

The administration sought to reverse the effects of these judgments, especially the potentially wide-ranging *Rasul*. It set up Combatant Status Review Tribunals (CSRTs) to examine the status – though not the guilt or innocence – of detainees, along with Annual Review Boards (ARBs) to determine whether or not a detainee remained too dangerous to the United States to be released or transferred to a third country. In addition, the 2005 Detainee Treatment Act allowed the verdicts of these bodies to be reviewed by the Circuit Court of Appeals in Washington DC; apart from this, it stated that 'no court, justice or judge' would be able to consider habeas corpus applications from Guantánamo detainees. The Act also incorporated the McCain amendment, intended to prevent ill-treatment of those in US custody; however, the administration interpreted the legislation in such a way as to largely negate these provisions.

Nonetheless, the War on Terror continued to lose ground during President Bush's second term, with rendition increasingly centre stage. The practice had been noted by some journalists from the turn of 2001–02, and increasing evidence had come to light through the work of NGOs and investigative journalists, making use of flight data (much of it available on the internet), information from plane spotters and information from within the air traffic control sector.[53] However, it was the journalist Dana Priest's exposé of the CIA's secret prisons network in *The Washington Post* in late 2005 that gave it large-scale notoriety. The immediate storm around the issue generated defensive comments from Secretary of State Condoleezza Rice as she embarked on a European tour. 'Rendition is a vital tool in combating transnational terrorism. Its use is not unique to the United States, or to the current administration.' The Secretary of State's remarks blurred the distinction between rendition to justice and other forms of rendition, and took a carefully legalistic approach to the question of maltreatment of suspects ('torture is a term that is defined by law … The United States government does not authorise or condone torture of detainees').[54]

Some of the most troubling individual cases gained increasing publicity. A Swedish television investigation of the al-Zery/Agiza case was broadcast in May 2004; the affair was subsequently investigated by the Parliamentary Ombudsman and by two United Nations committees, both of which were highly critical of Sweden's reliance on assurances from the Egyptians. In 2007, the government revoked the deportations of both men, and awarded them compensation the following year. In the Maher Arar case, the Canadian government launched a Commission of Inquiry in January 2004; its report in September 2006 exonerated Arar of links to terrorism and was followed by a formal apology and compensation settlement by the government. Khaled el-Masri's case became front page news in the *New York Times* in January 2005, and later (like a number of others) the subject of a lawsuit.

Perhaps most embarrassing was the case of the '*Imam rapito*', Abu Omar. An Egyptian preacher suspected of terrorist links, Abu Omar had been abducted from the street in Milan on 17 February 2003. He had been flown to Egypt, where he later reported that he was tortured. For over a year, nothing was known of his whereabouts; however, when a phone call that he made to his wife after his release in April 2004 was intercepted by the Italian security services, it triggered a magistrates' investigation into his disappearance. This led rapidly to the CIA station in Italy, and in the summer of 2005 magistrates indicted twenty-five CIA officers and an Air Force colonel, following up with indictments of Italian military intelligence officers the following year. The officers' trial began in Milan in June 2007; prison sentences for most of the officers were handed down in November 2009 (three, including the former head of the CIA's Rome station, were cleared on grounds of diplomatic immunity). The sentences were purely symbolic, since the Italian government refused to issue extradition requests for the Americans, but the investigation and trial generated several years of news stories of how the CIA had kidnapped a man from the streets of a NATO ally.[55]

A further important milestone was the Supreme Court's judgment in *Hamdan v. Rumsfeld* in June 2006. This threw a spoke in the wheel of the Detainee Treatment Act, arguing that it did not bar habeas corpus hearings from Guantánamo detainees launched before the Act came into force. It insisted that the executive have full authorisation from Congress before it could hold trials by military commissions. Most significantly, it held that Common Article 3 of the Geneva Conventions, with its broad guidelines for the humane treatment of prisoners, applied to those held in the War on Terror. On the administration's urging, Congress passed the Military Commissions Act, giving the commissions legislative backing and once more blocking off Guantánamo detainees' access to the courts. It also offered a narrow definition of the 'grave breaches' of Common Article 3 that could result in prosecution.

However, the *Hamdan* ruling increased the already growing unease within the CIA about the secret prisons programme. In a speech on 6 September, the President gave the first public acknowledgement of its existence. He insisted that 'the United States does not torture. It's against our laws, and against our values. I have not authorised it, and I will not authorise it.' However, he explained that in the secret prisons, the CIA had employed 'an alternative set of procedures. These procedures were designed to be safe, to comply with our laws, our Constitution and our treaty obligations.' As a result, the United States and its allies had been able to thwart a number of planned attacks, including 'a plot to hijack passenger planes and fly them into Heathrow or the Canary Wharf in London'. He announced that fourteen of very 'highest value' detainees had been transferred to Guantánamo for trial by military commissions. The secret prisons were now empty, but as and when other terrorists were captured 'having a CIA programme for questioning terrorists will continue to be crucial to getting lifesaving information'.[56]

Thus the President left the door open to a continuation of the programme, and in June 2007 issued Executive Order 13440, which provided a framework for CIA interrogations that would be compliant with Common Article 3. The detailed guidelines emanating from the Executive Order were not published; however, administration sources indicated that waterboarding (which had not been used since 2003) was no longer permissible, but other methods (such as sleep deprivation) might be.[57] Two further HVDs were transferred from CIA custody to Guantánamo in 2007–08, suggesting that some forms of black sites were still operating. However, given the growing legal pressures that it faced, the administration seems to have relied more in its last two years on supplying information to allies, notably in the Middle East, and leaving arrests and interrogations to them.[58]

This more indirect approach may also be reflected in the 'Horn of Africa renditions' in early 2007. These were a consequence of the long-running civil war in Somalia, which in June 2006 had seen the Islamic Courts Union (ICU) take control of Mogadishu. The ICU incorporated radical Islamist elements and reportedly sheltered a number of individuals linked to al Qaeda and the 1998 embassy bombings in Kenya and Tanzania. Ethiopia, which was alarmed at the ICU's alleged links to its neighbour and rival Eritrea and to insurgencies within its own borders, intervened and drove the ICU from Mogadishu in December. This operation, in support of the Transitional Federal Government of Somalia, reportedly had US backing. As many individuals fled towards the Kenyan border, the Kenyan authorities arrested at least 150 of them; during January and February 2007, at least eighty-five were allegedly rendered back to Somalia, where they were either questioned by Ethiopian officers or transferred to Ethiopia itself for interrogation over possible links to Islamist groups. Ethiopian forces made other arrests within Somalia itself. Former detainees have made allegations of mistreatment.

Reportedly some of the questioning was carried out by American intelligence officers, operating out of a villa in Addis Ababa to which detainees were brought. There are also accounts of British intelligence officers carrying out questioning, since four British nationals were among those detained. In response to a Parliamentary Question by Andrew Tyrie, the then Foreign Office Minister Bill Rammell MP confirmed that British officials spoke to a number of people in Ethiopian detention during that period, but that the government was not aware that their detention was unlawful. In further correspondence with the APPG, while re-iterating its position on counter-terrorism cooperation with foreign governments, the government failed to address these specific allegations in more detail.[59] Most of those held were released after a few months; however, a Kenyan citizen, Mohammed Abdulmalik, who was arrested while trying to return to Kenya from Somalia, was transferred to Guantánamo in March 2007. The unusual and large-scale operation in the Horn of Africa is not included in the figures usually given for renditions during the Bush administration.[60]

The ping-pong between the administration and the Supreme Court continued when the Court ruled once more against the administration in *Boumediene v. Bush* in June 2008. Just as *Hamdan* had dealt a blow to the Detainee Treatment Act, the *Boumediene* ruling struck down the Military

Commissions Act's provisions that barred detainees from bringing habeas corpus writs to US courts. The procedures of the Detainee Treatment Act, the Court ruled, were not adequate substitutes for habeas corpus writs.

In any case, even though some HVDs had been transferred there, overall numbers at Guantánamo were falling sharply as a result of the operation of ARBs and agreements to transfer prisoners – most notably a large-scale agreement for Saudi prisoners to return home and undergo a 'reintegration programme'. At the time of Bush's speech in September 2006, there were 455 detainees in Guantánamo. This was down sharply from its peak, and would almost halve by the time that Bush handed over to Obama in January 2009. As the new President noted some months later, 'two-thirds of the detainees were released before I took office'.[61]

Thus, by the end of the Bush administration, policy had retreated somewhat from its most aggressive phase in 2001–04; nonetheless, the President was fighting a rearguard action to defend as much as possible of the rendition and detention programme. The victory of Barack Obama in November 2008 brought to power a severe critic of the War on Terror, and offered the prospect of major policy change.

What were the benefits?

It is hard to give a precise verdict on rendition and the wider War on Terror of which it was a part. In part, this is because of the impossibility of running counterfactuals, but also because many key issues remain disputed. For example, Abu Zubaydah – whose arrest accelerated the use of 'enhanced' techniques – was seen by many in the administration as a senior al Qaeda figure and a key source of information. Yet others have argued that he was a delusional personality whose significance was vastly overrated. 'They [the CIA] thought he was a big shot, but he was just a hotel clerk.'[63]

Senior Bush administration officials continue to insist that their programme yielded vital intelligence; in March 2010, Bush's adviser Karl Rove insisted that he was 'proud that we kept the world safer than it was, by the use of these techniques',[64] while the former President similarly insisted on their validity in his memoirs. In the years after 9/11, there was no successful attack on the US and many senior al Qaeda leaders were arrested or killed, although new structures have emerged to replace them and attacks have continued around the world. Intelligence was central to this counter-attack, and according to the CIA Inspector General 'the reporting of detainees' was assessed as 'one of the most important sources for finished intelligence'.

In July 2008, under questioning from the House Judiciary Committee, former US Attorney General John Ashcroft referred to indications that George Tenet had given him about what had been obtained through the use of enhanced interrogation techniques: 'the value of the information received from the use of enhanced interrogation techniques, I don't know whether he was saying waterboarding or not, but assume that he was for a moment, the value of that information exceeded the value of information that was received from virtually all other sources.'[65] CIA Director Hayden also espoused the intelligence benefits of the Agency's secret detention and interrogation programme: 'These fewer than a hundred detainees that we've had have created just under nine thousand intelligence reports. They comprise some of the most critical information we've ever gained on al-Qaeda... this did work. It provided us with very reliable, massive amounts of information.'[66]

The Inspector General's report listed a number of plots of which the Agency became aware through interrogations, though 'this review did not uncover any evidence that these plots were imminent'. These included plots later referred to by President Bush when he finally disclosed the HVD programme in September 2006, including planned attacks on the US consulate in Karachi and on Heathrow.[67] From the British end, the head of the Security Service, Eliza Manningham-Buller, told the ISC that 'when [Khalid Sheikh Mohammed] was in detention in 2003, place unknown, he provided [the pseudonyms of] six individuals... who were involved in AQ activities in or against the UK. The Americans gave us this information... These included high-profile terrorists – an illustration of the huge amount of significant information that came from one man in detention in an unknown place.' Similarly, the head of SIS told the committee that 'with the arrest of Khaled [sic] Sheikh Mohammed in 2003 ... information came through, for example, on terrorist planning against Heathrow'.[68]

What none of this can answer is whether the same results could have been achieved by different means. Some of those who took part in the interrogations were convinced that they could not. Against this, FBI interrogators were strongly of the view that their 'rapport-based approach' could yield at least as much intelligence; in the case of Abu Zubaydah, they claimed that he was cooperating well with them and then ceased to do so – at least temporarily – when the CIA took over and applied more aggressive methods.[69] (Of course, institutional rivalry may well have influenced the respective CIA and FBI views of the issue). The CIA Inspector General hedged his bets: 'Measuring the effectiveness of EITs, however, is a more subjective process and not without some concern.'[70]

Some of the negative consequences of coercive interrogation have already been noted: the loss of Western powers' moral authority, and a consequent reduction in the willingness to cooperate on the part of potential intelligence sources. There is the further problem that, in the words of a senior FBI figure, 'if "aggressive" techniques are used long enough, detainees will start saying things they think the interrogator wants to hear just to get them to stop'. Notoriously, this was the case with Ibn al-Shaykh al-Libi, whose false confessions about links between al Qaeda and Saddam Hussein's Iraq helped to buttress the case for war.

However, there are other accounts of detainees triggering a series of false alerts as they confessed to 'half-hatched or entirely imaginary plots'.[71]

A final consequence of the use of these techniques has been an inability to bring cases to trial. In the closing days of the Bush administration, Susan J. Crawford, convening authority of the military commissions, insisted that in the case of al-Qahtani, 'His treatment met the legal definition of torture. And that's why I did not refer the case [for prosecution] ... [T]here still has to be a line that we should not cross. And unfortunately what this has done, I think, has tainted everything going forward.'[72]

5. The Obama aftermath

We reject as false the choice between our safety and our ideals

- President Barack Obama, inaugural address, 20 January 2009

We campaign in poetry, but when we're elected
we're forced to govern in prose

- Mario Cuomo, former Governor of New York[1]

PRESIDENT OBAMA'S INAUGURAL address suggested a sharp change in direction from his predecessor's policies, and decisions taken in his first few days in office appeared to confirm this. Military trials at Guantánamo were suspended immediately and the prison was to be closed within twelve months. The secret prisons were also to be closed. The OLC opinions endorsing more aggressive interrogations were revoked. There was to be an end to 'enhanced interrogation techniques'; pending a further review, US government bodies interrogating prisoners (including the CIA) were to apply the rules of the Army Field Manual.

Under executive orders issued by President Obama on 22 January 2009, three task forces were set up to develop the detail of the new policy directions:

- *Guantánamo*. A group led by the Attorney General was to review the status of detainees at the prison and determine the best course of action regarding them, given the intended closure of the prison:

- *Special interagency task force on detainee disposition*. This group, led jointly by the Attorney General and the Secretary of Defense, was to examine the options for 'the apprehension, detention, trial, transfer, release, or other disposition of individuals captured or apprehended in connection with armed conflicts and counterterrorism operations':

- *The special task force on interrogations and transfer policies.* This group was to be chaired by the Attorney General, with the Secretary of Defense and Director of National Intelligence as deputies. It was to determine whether the Army Field Manual was an appropriate guide for non-military interrogators, or whether 'any different additional or different guidance for other departments or agencies' was needed. The task force was also 'to study and evaluate the practices of transferring to other nations' to ensure that such practices were consistent with US law and did not, through 'the transfer of individuals to other nations to face torture', circumvent the country's international obligations. In other words, it was to rein in extraordinary rendition.[2]

In April, despite fierce opposition from a number of previous CIA directors (and the reported misgivings of the new appointee, Leon Panetta), the President authorised the publication of the 'torture memos' – the original Bybee/Yoo memo, as well as subsequent refinements. In August, the CIA Inspector General's report of 2004 was published; while significantly redacted, the published version made clear some unpalatable details (such as the 183 waterboardings of Khalid Sheikh Mohammed). It also demonstrated the unease within parts of the CIA at the legal and ethical implications of what had been done; the uncertainty over whether such methods were needed to gain valuable intelligence; and evidence that in some cases even the wide remit given to interrogators by the Bush administration's legal team had been exceeded. As Attorney General Eric Holder made clear, the latter disclosure opened up the prospect of prosecutions.

To Obama's Republican critics, this was an irresponsible gamble with national security, throwing away policies that had ensured that there had been no repetition of 9/11, and plunging the CIA into its worst crisis of morale since the Church Committee investigations of the mid-1970s. Former President Bush kept his counsel until the publication of his memoirs in late 2010, but his deputy, Dick Cheney, was outspoken in his denunciation of the new policies as 'recklessness cloaked in righteousness'.[3]

However, as the new administration settled in and had to make more detailed policy choices, it also ran into increasing criticism from liberal commentators and lawyers. In their eyes, many of the administration's changes were at best symbolic. While the black sites were to be closed, there had been little sign of their use during the last two years of the Bush administration. Similarly, the high value detainees were no longer subject to enhanced interrogation techniques by the time of Bush's handover to Obama. The proposed closure of Guantánamo raised as many questions as it answered. In the eyes of one critic: 'The regrettable fact is that the policies implemented by Mr Obama are materially indistinguishable from those of George Bush at the end of his second term.'[4] On this – perhaps over-harsh – view, the biggest changes took place during the Bush administration, not following its departure; and just as practices such as rendition had not started with George W. Bush, neither had they ended with him. The forces of continuity, favouring an approach to counterterrorism that went well beyond law enforcement, were simply too strong to be cast aside.

By the spring, there were increasing signs that the new administration accepted more of its predecessor's paradigm than its more idealistic supporters had hoped, and that in some areas at least its course was one of policy modification rather than radical change. The disclosure of the 'torture memos' notwithstanding, there was no interest in a comprehensive examination of the past, which was seen as a divisive waste of energy. Parts of the Democratic Party base were eager to call former administration officials, above all perhaps the authors of the memos, to account. The Obama administration did not oblige them, the very partial example of interrogators who had violated the policy of the time notwithstanding. Senator Leahy, chairman of the Judiciary Committee, called for a blue ribbon 'truth commission', to examine what had happened rather than to launch prosecutions; this too fell on stony ground.

In the courts, the administration invoked the same very wide interpretation of the state secrets privilege used by the Bush administration to block Binyam Mohamed's and four other Guantanamo detainees' court claim against Jeppesen Dataplan Inc (*Mohamed v. Jeppesen Dataplan, Inc.*) alleging that its logistical services had been used by the CIA for its rendition flights. It also opposed efforts to have intelligence information relevant to rendition cases disclosed as a result of legal action abroad, and made clear its displeasure when the British Court of Appeal forced the disclosure of sensitive information in the case of the British resident and former Guantánamo detainee, Binyam Mohamed.

Obama gave another clear and early sign of an incremental approach towards the military commissions established under Bush. As a candidate, Obama had sounded as though he were opposed to them in principle; however, he had been careful to frame his opposition with reference to the

2006 Military Commissions Act. By May 2009, the President had made it clear that he wanted military commissions to continue, albeit in modified form, with better safeguards for the accused and an end to the admission of evidence secured by coercive methods. His hope was that these reforms 'will begin to restore the commissions as a legitimate forum for prosecution, while bringing them in line with the rule of law'.[5]

This was in advance of the formal report by the 'detainee disposition' task force, which was due in July. On 20 July, the Detention Policy Task Force issued an interim report, which indicated a wide range of issues on which decisions were deferred for another six months. However, it gave some detailed judgements on the reform of military commissions, expanding on the thinking set out by the President in May, as well as a process for assessing whether individual cases should be tried by the commissions or by federal courts. Congress passed legislation setting up the new commissions in October 2009.

Guantánamo, which held 242 prisoners when Obama was inaugurated, offered the most symbolically powerful change. However, the administration was soon struggling to reach the President's January 2010 deadline for closure, and by the autumn of 2009 it was clear that it would be missed. Obama had to grapple with the same problems that had dogged the Bush administration as it had reduced detainee numbers. The first was to find suitable places to which released prisoners could be sent. Congress was hostile to their coming to the United States. In some cases (such as the Chinese Uighurs) the detainees had clear and understandable grounds to fear persecution in their home countries. Some American allies, such as Saudi Arabia, were unwilling to accept the remaining, potentially most difficult returnees. In other cases – notably Yemen, about which the administration had severe reservations even before the Christmas Day 2009 Detroit bomb plot came to light – there was a lack of trust in the authorities to maintain surveillance of those who might yet be drawn into or return to Islamist radicalism. The Detroit and Times Square plots have only hardened attitudes, with the administration holding on to a significant number of relatively low-level Yemeni detainees 'who would already have been repatriated had they been from a more stable country'.[6] The October 2010 parcel bomb plot reinforced this position.

Secondly, there was the question of which detainees might be brought to trial, and in what kind of court. Both the new-style military commis-

sions and the federal courts offered possible routes. Only in the autumn
of 2009, however, were the new commissions given legislative backing
and in due course a number of cases were slated to be brought before
them. Three detainees whose cases were outstanding, Ibrahim al-Qosi,
Omar Khadr and Noor Uthman Muhammed, were sentenced by military
commissions in August 2010, October 2010 and February 2011 respectively, though all three cases involved plea bargains. In March 2011 the
Obama administration announced plans for new charges to be brought
before military commissions after a two-year moratorium. In the civilian
courts, the first trial of a former Guantánamo detainee (and one of the
fourteen HVDs transferred there in September 2006), the Tanzanian
Ahmed Khalfan Ghailani, opened in New York in October 2010. The
prosecution suffered a setback when a witness was disqualified because
he was identified through statements by Ghailani allegedly made under
duress. In November Ghailani was found guilty on only one of the 285
charges brought against him; enough to ensure him a life sentence, but
nonetheless widely seen as a setback for the administration's approach.
A year earlier, with obvious symbolism, Attorney General Holder had
announced that Khalid Sheikh Mohammed and four others implicated
in the 9/11 attacks would stand trial in a civilian court in New York. The
proposal, however, provoked fierce opposition and the administration
after months of delay continued to keep a variety of options open, including use of a military commission, although it seemed increasingly likely
that Mohammed and the others would remain in indefinite detention.[7]
By early 2011, the administration was fighting Congressional moves to
restrict any prosecution of Guantánamo detainees in Federal courts.

The last problem was the knottiest one. By the time that the Guantánamo
Task Force reported in January 2010, the number of detainees was down
to 198. Of these, some eighty-two were proposed for release, assuming
that suitable destinations could be found for them; in some cases this has
been achieved (as of February 2011 the total number of detainees had
reportedly fallen to 172). The security worries about Yemen kept thirty
of its nationals in 'conditional' detention. Thirty-six detainees were lined
up for trials, whether military or civilian. The question was what to do
with the remainder. In this area too, the administration had indicated as
early as the spring significant continuity with its predecessor. In its eyes,
some forty-eight remained too dangerous for release, yet with evidence

that was insufficient – or too tainted by how it had been gained, or considered likely to compromise intelligence operations – for any sort of trial. This was a return to the legal limbo that had characterised larger numbers of detainees during the Bush era.[8] Under an executive order issued in March 2011, the President established a process of periodic review for those who would continue to be held without trial.

Some of the more moderate critics of the Bush administration's War on Terror – such as Benjamin Wittes of the Brookings Institution – had argued that, since situations of this kind were bound to arise, Congress should create a legal framework for detention without trial that offered at least some safeguards. Speaking in May 2009, Obama seemed to accept this view. He insisted that, 'I am not going to release individuals who endanger the American people'; what was needed was 'a legitimate legal framework' for their 'prolonged detention'. He promised to 'work with Congress to develop an appropriate legal regime so that our efforts are consistent with our values and our Constitution'.[9]

By the autumn, however, he had abandoned the attempt, falling back instead on the powers given to his predecessor following the 9/11 attacks. In December, the administration announced that it was buying from the state government a largely unused maximum security prison – in Thomson, in the President's home state of Illinois – and planned to transfer the remaining prisoners there. To liberal critics, Thomson was 'Gitmo North'; Amnesty International's US policy director, Tom Parker, argued that 'the only thing that President Obama is changing with this announcement is the zip code of Guantánamo'.[10] And even this plan ran into difficulties in its turn, with the House and Senate Armed Forces Committees voting to block appropriations to upgrade Thomson to take the prisoners. It is now widely accepted that Guantánamo will be open at the end of President Obama's current term in 2013.[11]

Thus, even if Guantánamo were to close, the form of detention for which it became notorious will continue. This conclusion is reinforced by the continuing operation of the prison at Bagram Air Base (Bagram Theater Internment Facility, formerly known as the Bagram Collection Point). There have been reforms to the prison; a $60m upgrade has improved conditions, and some of the secrecy surrounding it has been eased. In January 2010 the names of 645 prisoners held there were released. A new review system was announced in autumn 2009, assigning military officials to detainees to gather evidence that could challenge their detention; some fifty prisoners have been released under this regime. However, the process is still a relatively modest step, and was designed to buttress the administration's opposition to habeas corpus suits by detainees. In April 2009, a District Court had ruled in favour of three non-Afghan detainees' habeas corpus application, citing the precedent of *Boumediene v. Bush* and concluding that the system of review instituted by the Bush administration in 2007 'falls well short of what the Supreme Court found inadequate at Guantánamo'.

In contesting this verdict (which it won in the appeals court in May 2010), the administration maintained its predecessor's desire to hold suspects beyond the reach of American courts. Intriguingly, unnamed senior officials implied a link to rendition when they told the *New York Times* that 'the importance of Bagram as a holding site for terrorism suspects captured outside Afghanistan and Iraq has risen under the Obama administration, which barred the Central Intelligence Agency from using its secret prisons for long-term detention and ordered the military prison at Guantánamo closed within a year'. Some thirty of the detainees are non-Afghan; it is not clear how current plans for the prison to be handed over to the Afghan authorities will affect their detention.[12] There are also continuing allegations of a separate facility, a 'black prison' (not to be confused with the dark prison in Kabul) in which harsher 'restricted' methods, drawn from Appendix M of the Army Field Manual and including cramped cells, noise and sleep deprivation are applied, albeit on a time limited basis and in less extreme form than had been the case in previous years. The facility is reportedly operated by a unit within the Defense Intelligence Agency (DIA).[13]

Like its counterpart on detainee policy, the Special Task Force on Interrogations and Transfer Policies was expected to report in July 2009, but was granted an extension (of two months). In fact, it reported on 24 August. The Task Force concluded that the Army Field Manual was undoubtedly sufficient for military interrogators, 'and that no additional or different guidance was necessary for other agencies'. However, it established the High Value Detainee Interrogation Group (HIG) an elite and specialist group to interrogate the most dangerous terrorist suspects. The HIG was also mandated to undertake scientific research as to the effectiveness of different methods of interrogation. These proposals, swiftly adopted by

Obama, marked a fundamental shift from the Bush era; a further sign of change was that the HIG was to be housed at the FBI, but overseen by the National Security Council. The CIA was to be only one of the organisations influencing its operation.

Rendition – specifically, rendition to third countries – was addressed by the task force along with other forms of 'transfer', ranging from extradition to military rendition. The terms of reference in the executive order of 22 January made clear that rendition in some form was likely to continue, and this was confirmed by the new CIA Director, Leon Panetta, in remarks to the Senate Intelligence Committee on 5 February. Panetta stated the new administration's opposition to 'that kind of extraordinary rendition - when we send someone for the purpose of torture or actions by another country that violate our human values'. However, 'I think renditions where we return individuals to another country where they prosecute them under their laws, I think that is an appropriate use of rendition.'[14]

To achieve this balance, the task force sought to address the thorny issue of assurances from other countries about the treatment of those who were transferred. It recommended measures to strengthen confidence in these assurances, chiefly through greater involvement of the State Department in their evaluation and an annual review of transfers that had relied on them. Assurances should incorporate a 'monitoring mechanism', enabling regular and private access to the person transferred. The task force also made recommendations, which remain classified, to ensure the proper treatment of individuals 'should the Intelligence Community participate in or otherwise support a transfer'.[15]

There has been only one case of rendition reported from the Obama era so far, and that a somewhat idiosyncratic one: that of Raymond Azar, a Lebanese construction manager working on projects for the US military in Afghanistan, who was rendered from that country to the US on charges of corruption in April 2009. This was a rendition to justice, and not related to terrorism, though Azar has alleged mistreatment and threats to his family by those who transferred him.[16] However, the task force's policy prescription is an ambiguous one, and the continuing reliance on assurances was criticised by human rights groups. This was scarcely surprising; even if the new policy sought to strengthen oversight, the history of reliance on assurances was not a happy one. And, while there are no longer black sites to which detainees can be rendered, there is still scope for them to be sent to 'prolonged detention'.

Civil libertarians made a downbeat assessment of Obama in office: the American Civil Liberties Union entitled its report on his first year, *America Unrestored*, and picked out extraordinary rendition as a conspicuous area of policy disappointment.[17] At the same time, some of those associated with the previous administration could find a certain amount to praise in Obama's pragmatism. Though the term 'War on Terror' was no longer used, some elements of the thinking behind it continued; as the President emphasised in his May 2009 speech on civil liberties and national security, 'Let me be clear. We are indeed at war with al Qaeda and its affiliates. We do need to update our institutions to deal with this threat.'[18] In that war, rendition – even if modified significantly in its operation – remains a weapon that can be used.

6. The Conduct of the Allies

*Noting that some of the European shock about renditions/
flights is disingenuous, he recalled Captain Louis Renault's
line from Casablanca: 'I am shocked, shocked to find that
gambling is going on in here!' Reporters captured the parallel.*

- Internal State Department email on a press briefing by
Legal Adviser John Bellinger, 5 December 2005[1]

*Any operation in Europe was done with the cognizance, support
and approval of the European security services involved*

- Michael Scheuer, 17 April 2007[2]

IN NOVEMBER 2005, European Governments, responding to grow-ing press revelations, took up the rendition issue with the Bush administration. The response was telling. Secretary of State Condoleezza Rice explained – perhaps somewhat pointedly – that 'the United States has respected – and will continue to respect – the sovereignty of other countries'. Her predecessor, Colin Powell, was more explicit. 'Well, most of our European friends cannot be shocked that this kind of thing takes place... The fact [is] that we have, over the years, had procedures in place that would deal with people who are responsible for terrorist activities, or suspected of terrorist activities, and so the thing that is called rendition is not something that is new or unknown to my European friends.'[3]

Investigations of rendition quickly demonstrated that the United States could only carry out this policy with quite widespread cooperation from its allies, in Europe and elsewhere. Firstly, a number of those rendered were residents or citizens of allied states, raising the question of the role of the domestic authorities in their removal. Secondly, there was the matter of hosting the black sites. Thirdly, there was the question of logistics: the ability for rendition flights to cross countries' airspace, and to land for refuelling, with or without a prisoner on board. The unifying element in all this was cooperation by the allies' military forces and intelligence services.

This was not limited to Europe. Detainees were taken into custody in a variety of countries, from Pakistan to Thailand. In the case of Maher Arar, the Commission of Inquiry was critical of the role of the Royal Canadian Mounted Police (RCMP) in providing information to the US authorities about Arar that was misleading and not accompanied by the appropriate caveats. While the Canadian authorities appear not to have played any role in Arar's detention and transfer, the Commission judged that, in carrying out these actions, 'it is very likely that ... Americans authorities relied on information about Mr Arar provided by the RCMP'. The Commission also found that, subsequent to Arar's transfer, the Canadian Security Intelligence Service (CSIS) did not properly assess whether information that it received from the Syrian authorities was likely to be the product of torture.[4]

However, the most wide-ranging investigation has concerned the role of European countries. The Council of Europe's investigation, led by the Swiss Liberal politician and former prosecutor Dick Marty, built on the work of investigative journalists and others and added important new information through its access to the European air traffic agency Eurocontrol, government sources in a variety of countries and, increasingly, participants in the rendition programme from both sides of the Atlantic. These were later supplemented by 'data strings', raw communications data concerning flight movements from the worldwide Aeronautical Fixed Telecommunication Network (AFTN), some of which demonstrated that on occasion false flight information had been provided to Eurocontrol.[5] In the first of two reports, Marty remarked that, 'The impression which some Governments tried to create at the beginning of this debate – that Europe was a victim of secret CIA plots – does not seem to correspond to reality.' He produced a charge sheet against a number of European countries:

> 288. In this sense, it must be stated that to date, the following member States could be held responsible, to varying degrees, which are not always settled definitively, for violations of the rights of specific persons identified below (respecting the chronological order as far as possible):
> - Sweden, in the cases of Ahmed Agiza and Mohamed Alzery;

- Bosnia-Herzegovina, in the cases of Lakhdar Boumediene, Mohamed Nechle, Hadj Boudella, Belkacem Bensayah, Mustafa Ait Idir and Saber Lahmar (the 'Algerian six');
- The United Kingdom in the cases of Bisher Al-Rawi, Jamil El-Banna and Binyam Mohamed;
- Italy, in the cases of Abu Omar and Maher Arar;
- 'The former Yugoslav Republic of Macedonia', in the case of Khaled El-Masri;
- Germany, in the cases of Abu Omar, of the 'Algerian six', and Khaled El-Masri;
- Turkey, in the case of the 'Algerian six'

To this list he added those who could be held to account for 'collusion':

- Poland and Romania, concerning the running of secret detention centres;
- Germany, Turkey, Spain and Cyprus for being 'staging points' for flights involving the unlawful transfer of detainees;
- Ireland, the United Kingdom, Portugal, Greece and Italy for being 'stop-overs' for flights involving the unlawful transfer of detainees.[6]

Sweden's role in the rendition of Agiza and al-Zery has already been described. However, in a number of other cases there were indications of European involvement, in one form or another, in the rendition pro-gramme. In the case of Khaled el-Masri, there was strong evidence of the involvement of the Macedonian security services, and their cooperation with the CIA in spite of official denials.[7] The German government has maintained the position that it knew nothing about el-Masri's disappear-ance until his return to the country at the end of May 2004. However, el-Masri believed that some of the questioning that he experienced could only have come from Germany, and claimed that in the later stages of his captivity he was visited by an agent who identified himself as 'Sam' and whom he believed to be German. Nonetheless, a later Bundestag commit-tee report was supportive of the government's position.[8]

In a separate case, there are allegations that another detainee, Moham-med Haydar Zammar, was interrogated by German officers while being held in Syria.[9]

In the case of Abu Omar, the Italian government initially demonstrated its indignation, with Prime Minister Berlusconi summoning the Ameri-can ambassador to demand that the United States show 'full respect' for Italian sovereignty. However, even though Abu Omar's kidnapping was investigated by one arm of the Italian state, there were strong suspicions that it was carried out with at least the complicity of others. This was duly confirmed; in 2006, senior figures in SISMI (Italian military intelligence), including its head, Nicolò Pollari, were indicted for their role in the abduction. Some accounts suggested that the initiative had come from the Italian rather than the American side; one CIA officer involved in the rendition told Stephen Grey that the Italians 'requested us to *disappear him*'. A committee of the European Parliament went further, arguing that it was 'very likely, in view of the involvement of its secret services, that the Italian government of the day was aware of the extraordinary rendition of Abu Omar from within its territory'.[10] In any case, the Italian government sat on extradition requests for the CIA agents and invoked state secrecy to hold back documents from the case.

Perhaps the most significant contribution made by a number of allied countries was the hosting of the black sites used by the CIA for interrogation of the High Value Detainees. When the *Washington Post* reporter Dana Priest broke the 'secret prisons' story in December 2005, she referred to 'sites in eight countries, including Thailand, Afghanistan and several democracies in Eastern Europe, as well as a small center at the Guantánamo Bay prison in Cuba'.[11] At the request of the Bush administration, the *Post* did not name the European countries involved. Many countries allegedly involved, both within and beyond Europe, have denied that the prisons were ever on their territory and there are some discrepancies of detail; nonetheless, a combination of investigative journalism, accounts by former detainees and analysis of flight records come up with many of the same names.

- *Stare Kiejkuty intelligence training base, Poland.* This site, near Szymany airport in the north-east of the country, was named in the Council of Europe investigation. At least eight of those thought to be the most important HVDs, including Khalid Sheikh Mohammed and Abu Zubaydah, were reportedly held there between the end of 2002 and 2005. The Council of Europe report identified eight flights of CIA-linked aircraft that landed at Szymany during this period, while demonstrating that in many cases false flight plans had been filed in an effort to conceal the nature of the flights; it also drew on CIA sources who reported that detainees had been held at Stare Kiejkuty. [12]

This allegation was long denied by the Polish authorities, although the matter has been the subject of a prosecutors' investigation since March 2008. However, further investigations have added details that strengthen the allegations. A United Nations report, published at the beginning of 2010, showed further evidence from analysis of aeronautical data that rendition flights landed at Szymany. It also indicated that sections of the CIA's Inspector General's report, released in 2009, remain redacted because they would disclose the rendition of another HVD, Abd al-Rahim al-Nashiri to Poland. In February 2010, the Warsaw-based Helsinki Foundation for Human Rights and the Open Society Justice Initiative published the results of a freedom of information request to the Polish Air Navigation Services Agency. This provided raw data about six flights of CIA-associated aircraft which had landed at Szymany between February and September 2003; five from Kabul, one from Rabat. The data also revealed how false flight plans had been filed. However, the release did not address questions about other landings in 2002 and 2003 that had been raised in the freedom of information request. In September 2010 al-Nashiri filed a petition with prosecutors in Warsaw concerning his alleged treatment in Poland, which led to the public prosecutor's office launching an investigation.[13]

The timing of several of the flights can be linked to movements of particular detainees. On 5 December 2002, aircraft N63MU (a Gulfstream) flew from Bangkok to Szymany via Dubai; this matches the reported transfers of Abu Zubaydah, who was allegedly held for some months in Thailand, and al-Nashiri. The flight of N379P, a Gulfstream reported to have been frequently used in renditions, from Kabul to Szymany on 7 March 2003 came days after the arrest of Khalid Sheikh Mohammed. By Mohammed's own account, he was held for five days after his arrest – in Pakistan and Afghanistan – before being flown to an unnamed detention site. While being held there, he was on one occasion given a bottle of water from which the label had not been removed, and which 'had [an] email address ending in ".pl"'. On 22 September 2003, aircraft N313P – a Boeing 737, a much larger aeroplane – came to Szymany and left, reportedly with five unnamed passengers. The airport facilities manager, Mariola Przewlocka, who spoke about the flights in late 2010, remembered this occasion. 'It was extremely dangerous, because the airstrip at Szymany isn't suitable for such big aircraft. But we had to do it.' This aircraft carried out a four-day circuit in which its stops included Bucharest, Tashkent and

Rabat before flying on to Guantánamo Bay. The timing and nature of the flight are consistent with the reports of a number of HVDs being flown to Guantánamo in the autumn of 2003, only to be returned to black sites six months later.[14]

Various accounts describe the secrecy in which the flights arrived at Szymany: an advance call from the headquarters of the Border Guards; the runway cleared and Polish staff removed to the air terminal; the securing of the airport perimeter; American officials waiting in vans near the runway; the arrival of the aircraft, which taxied to a far corner of the airfield where officials from the vans boarded it. Mariola Przewlocka recalled that on one occasion 'the director of the airport at the time called me in, and said that this plane – it was a Gulfstream – had to be allowed to land, or, as he put it, heads would roll. He looked very frightened.'[15]

- *Mihail Kogalniceanu airport and base, Romania*. According to the Council of Europe report, this site, near Constanța on the Black Sea, was added in late 2003 as the number of HVDs grew and operated until 2005. The detainees, while far from being foot soldiers, were of lesser significance than those held in Poland. They included individuals 'extracted from the theatre of conflict' in Iraq and Afghanistan, and often linked to the insurgencies in those countries. However, other accounts suggest that the prison was in Bucharest, while the Romanian authorities have continued to deny that there was any facility on their soil.[16]

- *Other European sites.* In the second half of 2009, there were allegations that a facility for around eight detainees had operated at a former riding school in Antaviliai, Lithuania in 2004–05. Rolandas Paksas, President of Lithuania in 2003–04, subsequently claimed that he was approached by the head of the country's State Security Department in the summer of 2003, who asked for permission for 'our foreign partners to bring people in secret to Lithuania and hold them there'. Paksas alleged that he refused this request. During 2004, a group of Americans built a large warehouse on the site of the former riding stables. A parliamentary inquiry concluded that a secret prison was built in 2004, although it could not confirm whether or not any prisoners had been held there. At its conclusion in December 2009, the parliamentary inquiry recommended that the Prosecutor General's Office should investigate the actions of three former senior State Security Department officials. The investigation began in January 2010, but was closed in January 2011, with prosecutors apparently citing the operation of a statute of limitations. There have also been allegations that two US bases in the Balkans – Camp Bondsteel in Kosovo, and Eagle Base in Tuzla, Bosnia – were used.[17]

- *Royal Thai Air Force Base, Udon Thani, north-eastern Thailand.* There are widespread reports of detention facilities being used in Thailand, particularly in 2002–03, early in the War on Terror. Abu Zubaydah is believed both to have received treatment for wounds suffered during his arrest and to have been interrogated there. Ramzi Binalshibh, a Yemeni accused of a leading role in the 9/11 attacks and arrested in Pakistan in September 2002, is also believed to have been held in Thailand. The site has often been identified as the Udon Thani air base, which had long-standing CIA links (it had served as the Asian headquarters of the CIA-linked airline, Air America, during the Vietnam War), though other accounts speak of a facility outside Bangkok known as 'the Cat's Eye'. The Thai authorities have denied the existence of any such site; however, UN investigators continue to 'take it as credible that a CIA black site existed in Thailand'.[18]

Finally, a number of European airports appear to have played a significant logistical role in rendition. Among the 'staging points' (airports from which operations were launched) that the Marty report identified were Palma de Mallorca in Spain, airports in Cyprus and in Turkey, and two airports in Germany. Ramstein, a NATO base, was used as a transit point for the flight taking Abu Omar to Egypt. Frankfurt, which was also identified as a key staging point, was reportedly the CIA's 'main logistics base in Europe'. Marty's 'stopover points' (for refuelling, often on the way back from a rendition) included Glasgow Prestwick, Shannon in the Republic of Ireland, Rome Ciampino, Athens and Santa Maria in the Azores.[19]

When EU Foreign Ministers raised their concerns about rendition with the Bush administration, Britain held the rotating presidency of the Council of Ministers. Thus it fell to the British Foreign Secretary, Jack Straw, to write on behalf of his colleagues. But, like many of its European partners, Britain had questions to answer over its role in rendition. It is to those questions that we now turn.

7. 'More than a bystander': The British role

Unless we all start to believe in conspiracy theories and that the officials are lying, that I am lying, that behind this there is some kind of secret state which is in league with some dark forces in the United States, and also let me say, we believe that Secretary Rice is lying, there simply is no truth in the claims that the United Kingdom has been involved in rendition full stop...

- Rt Hon Jack Straw MP, then Foreign
Secretary, 13 December 2005[1]

I am very sorry indeed to have to report to the House the need to correct those and other statements on the subject

- Rt Hon David Miliband MP, then Foreign
Secretary, 21 February 2008[2]

THERE IS NO question that Britain has been involved in rendition. However, the nature and scale of this involvement remains unclear; there has been an unhappy history of intermittent revelations and official statements that have had to be corrected.

The starting point for investigations into British involvement in rendition was the growing revelations about the CIA network of secret prisons in late 2005. It was at this time that Andrew Tyrie created the All-Party Parliamentary Group (APPG) on Extraordinary Rendition. The first government statement came in a Written Answer to Sir Menzies Campbell on 12 December 2005 by the then Foreign Secretary Jack Straw. He confirmed that two rendition flights had gone through British airspace in 1998, during the Clinton administration; these had been approved by

Straw in his previous role as Home Secretary. Both were renditions to justice. Mohammed Rashid was rendered from Egypt to the US in June 1998, charged with bombing a Pan Am aircraft in August 1982. The flight carrying him stopped at Prestwick. In August the flight carrying Mohamed Rashed Daoud Al-Owhali, rendered from Kenya to the US and charged in connection with the Nairobi Embassy bombing, stopped at Stansted. Both men were subsequently tried and are now serving prison terms in the US.[3]

The Foreign Secretary identified at least one further occasion on which the US had asked permission to conduct a rendition through the UK, and which appeared to have been refused. Information at this stage was incomplete: 'The search for records continues.' He also stated:

> Careful research by officials has been unable to identify any occasion since 11 September 2001, or earlier in the Bush administration, when we received a request for permission by the United States (US) for a rendition through UK territory or airspace, nor are we otherwise aware of such a case.[4]

In a Written Statement on 10 January 2006, the Foreign Secretary stated that the search of all relevant records back to May 1997 had now been completed, and that it had established one further case, also in 1998, where the government refused a request to refuel a flight carrying two detainees to the US.[5] Following the publication of a leaked government memo[6] about rendition, from the Foreign Office to Number 10, the Foreign Secretary made a second Written Statement on 20 January 2006. This confirmed that there had been four occasions, all in 1998, where the US had requested permission to render one or more detainees through UK airspace. On two occasions, this request had been granted, and on the other two, refused.

Information provided to the ISC later added some detail about the requests that were refused. One was for a flight carrying two unnamed Hezbollah members to the US to refuel at Akrotiri Air Base in Cyprus. However, the second involved a third country; the US requested that an aeroplane carrying Muhammed Ibid al-Ibid, an alleged member of the militant group GIA, from Ecuador to Egypt should be able to refuel at Prestwick. 'There is no record of whether this request was agreed or refused … the recollection of some of those present at the time is that the request was refused.' (The leaked memo to Number 10 stated as fact that a request was turned down 'because the individual concerned was to be transported to Egypt'). [7]

In his second Written Statement, the Foreign Secretary referred to the heightened media interest following the leak of the Foreign Office memo and strongly denied suggestions that 'the Government may be aware that there have been cases of "extraordinary rendition" through UK territory or airspace about which it has not informed Parliament'. He insisted that 'we have found no evidence of detainees being rendered through the UK or Overseas Territories since 1997 where there were substantial grounds to believe there was a real risk of torture'. Emphasising the close relationship with the US, he added, 'We are also clear that the US would not render a detainee through UK territory or airspace (including Overseas Territories) without our permission. As noted above, the US has sought such permission in the past.' [8]

In a subsequent letter to the then Shadow Foreign Secretary, William Hague, Straw set out that there had been a further occasion, in 2004, when the US Administration had made enquiries about conducting a rendition 'via one of the Overseas Territories'. It was indicated to the US that any such request would be refused. The Intelligence and Security Committee later confirmed that this rendition was to take place through Diego Garcia. [9]

It was this Indian Ocean island, site of one of the world's largest US naval bases, that was to be the subject of the next significant revelation about British links to the rendition programme. From 2002 onwards, there had been press reports of prisoners being held on the island, or on ships anchored in its waters. Barry McCaffrey, a retired four-star general and West Point professor, spoke twice publicly about use of the island for detention, although he later retracted the claims. [10] The reports met with frequent denials from the British government. A Written Answer by Jack Straw on 21 June 2004 is representative of the position taken: 'The United States authorities have repeatedly assured us that no detainees have at any time passed in transit through Diego Garcia or its territorial waters or have disembarked there and that the allegations to that effect are totally without foundation. The Government are satisfied that their assurances are correct.' [11]

However, 2007 saw fresh allegations. In January, Stephen Grey's investigations of flight logs revealed that a Gulfstream V linked to rendition flights had landed on the island. The second Marty report for the Council of Europe, released in June, noted that 'we have received concurring confirmations that United States agencies have used the island territory of **Diego Garcia**, which is the international legal responsibility of the United Kingdom, in the "processing" of high-value detainees. It is true that the UK Government has readily accepted "assurances" from US authorities to the contrary, without ever independently or transparently inquiring into the allegations itself, or accounting to the public in a sufficiently thorough manner.'[12]

Nonetheless, on 11 October the then Foreign Office Minister for the Overseas Territories Meg Munn gave the standard response in a Written Answer: 'The US authorities have repeatedly given us assurances that no detainees, prisoners of war or any other persons in this category are being held on Diego Garcia, or have at any time passed in transit through Diego Garcia or its territorial waters or airspace. This was most recently confirmed during the 2007 US/UK Political Military Talks held in Washington on 11 and 13 September.'[13] In November, the then Foreign Office Minister for Counter-Terrorism Dr Kim Howells refused further requests to investigate these allegations, stating in a letter to Andrew Tyrie that 'as recently as September, we have had robust assurances from the US that at no time have there been any detainees either on Diego Garcia, or transiting through the UK's territorial seas or airspace surrounding Diego Garcia. I have confidence in these assurances.'[14]

By this stage, however, media and other interest in the issue was intensifying. Following urging from both Reprieve and the APPG, the Foreign Affairs Committee decided in October 2007 to investigate Diego Garcia's role.[15] Within a few months, the government had to change its stance. On 21 February 2008, the Foreign Secretary, David Miliband, gave an Oral Statement in the Commons. He recalled previous statements on the subject, noting that the previous March the then Prime Minister, Tony Blair, 'gave an assurance to the Intelligence and Security Committee that he was satisfied that the US had at no time since 9/11 rendered an individual through the UK or through our overseas territories'. However:

> I am very sorry indeed to have to report to the House the need to correct those and other statements on the subject, on the basis of new information passed to officials on 15 February 2008 by the US Government.

Contrary to earlier explicit assurances that Diego Garcia had not been used for rendition flights, recent US investigations have now revealed two occasions, both in 2002, when that had in fact occurred. An error in the earlier US records search meant that those cases did not come to light. In both cases, a US plane with a single detainee on board refuelled at the US facility in Diego Garcia.

The Foreign Secretary stressed that both American assurances and British government statements had been made in good faith, that no other renditions had been carried out through Diego Garcia or any other British Overseas Territory, and that 'the US Government have assured us that no US detainees have ever been held on Diego Garcia'.[16] It emerged subsequently that the US administration had given the British government assurances that no rendition flights had landed on Diego Garcia no less than seven times between June 2003 (nine months after the second incident) and US-UK talks about the island in September 2007.[17]

In his statement, the Foreign Secretary did not disclose the identity of the two individuals who had been transferred through Diego Garcia. However, he did reveal that 'neither of the men was a British national or a British resident. One is currently in Guantánamo Bay. The other has been released.' Almost a year later, on 11 February 2009, a Parliamentary Question on behalf of the APPG revealed further information:

Mr. Tyrie: To ask the Secretary of State for Foreign and Commonwealth Affairs whether one of the detainees rendered through Diego Garcia is still being held in the Guantanamo Bay detention centre.

    Bill Rammell: Both of the individuals rendered through Diego Garcia in 2002 have been returned to their countries of nationality.[18]

The human rights group Reprieve, working from the information that one of the individuals involved had been released from Guantánamo between February 2008 and February 2009, and taking account of factors such as the plausibility of Diego Garcia as a stop-off point in their transfer, identified the detainee as Mohammed Saad Iqbal Madni. He had been arrested in Indonesia in January 2002 on suspicion of a link to the 'shoe bomber', Richard Reid, and rendered to Egypt, where he alleges that he was brutally tortured; he was later transferred to Bagram and finally to Guantánamo. He was eventually released without charge.[19] In July 2009, Reprieve launched legal action against the government over Madni's case.

Following a High Court hearing in March 2010, Reprieve and Madni's legal team argued that the government had made a last-minute reversal of its position. Having argued that it had no documents relevant to the case, government lawyers declared on the eve of the hearing that 'the defendant [the Foreign Secretary] has possession of documents which have a bearing (to use a neutral phrase) on whether any British or American authorities were mixed up in wrongdoing against the claimant'. The case is currently stayed.[20]

While the Foreign Secretary in his February 2008 statement insisted that Diego Garcia had been used only as a refuelling point, claims have continued to be made that the island played a bigger role in rendition. As the Foreign Affairs Select Committee put it in summer 2009, continued allegations that the two reported renditions 'do not represent the limit of the territory's use for this purpose' are 'a matter for concern'. That concern is deepened by, once again, lack of records; flight data for the period around the time when the two renditions took place have been destroyed.[21]

In March 2008, Manfred Nowak, then UN Special Rapporteur on Torture, 'said he had received credible evidence from well-placed sources familiar with the situation on the island that detainees were held on Diego Garcia between 2002 and 2003', though 'there were only a few of them and they were not held [there] for a long time'. Some months later, *Time* quoted a 'former senior American official' that 'a CIA counterterrorism official twice said that a high-value prisoner or prisoners were being held and interrogated on the island'. The source also believed that prisoners may have been held on ships in Diego Garcia's territorial waters. Like Nowak, the *Time* story placed these events 'in 2002 and possibly 2003'.[22]

However, other accounts suggest that Diego Garcia may have been used more recently. In late 2009, UN experts investigating secret detentions contacted a number of governments, including the British government, concerning the disappearance of Mustafa Setmariam Nasar, a Spanish citizen of Syrian origin. Nasar, an author of extensive writings on jihad and wanted in connection with both 9/11 and the March 2004 Madrid bombings, was reported to have been arrested in Pakistan in October 2005. There has been no official news of his whereabouts since and his name disappeared from the US government's 'Rewards for Justice' website. Unconfirmed reports suggest that he was held on Diego Garcia in November 2005 before being transferred to detention in Syria. In its response to the UN experts, the British government relied as before on assurances from the US administration that there had been no such detention of Nasar on Diego Garcia.[23]

Up until the February 2008 statement, the government had relied solely on such assurances with regard to rendition flights either landing in British territory or making use of British airspace. This stance was widely criticised; in the spring of 2006, the parliamentary Joint Committee on Human Rights argued that it was utterly inadequate to satisfy 'the obligation under domestic and international human rights law to investigate credible allegations of renditions of suspects through the UK to face torture abroad'. It urged that 'the Government should now take active steps to ascertain more details about the flights which it is now known used UK airports, including, in relation to each flight, who was on them, and their precise itinerary and the purpose of their journey. If evidence of extraordinary renditions come to light from such investigations, the Government should report such evidence promptly to Parliament.' The committee further argued that the government should take more aggressive steps to challenge flights that might be returning from renditions.[24]

In his statement on Diego Garcia, the Foreign Secretary made some movement towards the government's critics, explaining that 'I have asked my officials to compile a list of all the flights where we have been alerted to concerns regarding rendition through the UK or our overseas territories. Once it is ready we will be sending the list to the US and seeking their specific assurance that none of those flights was used for rendition purposes.'[25] In May, a list of 391 flights – drawing on concerns raised by parliamentarians, NGOs and others – was submitted to the Americans. The Foreign Secretary reported back to Parliament on 3 July.

> The US Government received the list of flights from the UK Government. The US Government confirmed that, with the exception of two cases related to Diego Garcia in 2002, there have been no other instances in which US intelligence flights landed in the United Kingdom, our overseas territories, or the Crown dependencies, with a detainee on board since 11 September 2001.[26]

The renewed assurances from the US government thus referred only to rendition flights *landing* in the UK. The possibility remained that rendition flights with detainees onboard transited UK territory, airspace, or territorial waters (although, as the Foreign Secretary pointed out, the various lists of flights submitted to him did not include any overflights). The Foreign Secretary also refused to ask about flights on the way to or from carrying out a rendition. This ignored the issue raised by the Foreign Affairs Select Committee in its Human Rights Annual Report 2007, which was also published in July 2008:

> 47. We conclude that the Government has a moral and legal obligation to ensure that flights that enter UK airspace or land at UK airports are not part of the 'rendition circuit', even if they do not have a detainee on board during the time they are in UK territory. We recommend that the Government should immediately raise questions about such flights with the US authorities in order to ascertain the full scale of the rendition problem, and inform the Committee of the replies it receives in its response to this Report.[27]

Research into flight logs by the journalist Stephen Grey and others showed that the three countries most used for landings by CIA flights were Germany, the United Kingdom and the Republic of Ireland. As Grey pointed out, the bulk of these hundreds of flights had nothing to do with rendition. The Council of Europe's Dick Marty remarked that, 'We should not lose our sense of proportion. It would be exaggerated to talk of thousands of flights, let alone hundreds of renditions concerning Europe.' He agreed with Michael Scheuer's assessment that '98% of those flights are about logistics!'

Nonetheless, some flights – and some airports – appeared to be linked to the rendition circuit. As noted in the previous chapter, Glasgow's Prestwick airport was among those listed by Marty as 'Category A', a stopover point for refuelling, usually on the way home after a rendition. A CIA pilot told Grey, 'It's an 'ask no questions' type of place, and you don't need to give them any advance warning you're coming.'[28]

The ISC, drawing on Grey's research, identified four cases in which aircraft returning from rendition operations are alleged to have landed in Britain (in all four cases at Prestwick):

- 24 October 2001 – N379P refuelled at Prestwick airport, returning from the rendition of Jamil Qasim Saeed Mohammed from Pakistan to Jordan on 23 October

- 20 December 2001 – N379P refuelled at Prestwick airport, returning from the transfer of Ahmed Agiza and Mohammed al-Zery from Sweden to Egypt on 18 December
- 15 January 2002 – N379P refuelled at Prestwick airport, returning from the rendition of Mohammed Saad Iqbal Madni from Indonesia to Egypt on 11 January
- 24 July 2003 – N379P refuelled at Prestwick airport, returning from the rendition of Saifulla Paracha from Thailand to Afghanistan on 22 July[29]

Given the American response reported by the Foreign Secretary in July 2008, it is impossible at present to determine the truth of these allegations. The picture with respect to the use of British airspace is even less clear. As with Diego Garcia, important questions remain unanswered.

The government had to revise its position on another issue. On 25 February 2008 former SAS soldier Ben Griffin alleged that UK forces in Iraq had been capturing people who were handed over to US forces, and subsequently rendered or mistreated. 'Throughout my time in Iraq I was in no doubt that individuals detained by UKSF [United Kingdom Special Forces] and handed over to our American colleagues would be tortured.'[30] He suggested that a policy of detaining people without arresting them had been adopted in an attempt to avoid the UK's legal obligations to those it captured. These claims appear to have been lent further credibility by evidence provided to the Australian Senate, which indicated that Australian forces had a similar policy with the effect that any detainees they captured were officially detained by US personnel in the group. This was regardless of the nationality of the bulk of the capturing force.[31]

The APPG had already been investigating detention practices in Iraq and Afghanistan, and made detailed submissions to the Defence and Foreign Affairs Select Committees on the issue. In December 2007 the British government was unable to confirm whether or not anyone captured by UK forces had subsequently been held at Guantánamo Bay detention centre, stating only that 'we have an understanding with the relevant government that the transferred individual cannot be removed from the country without our agreement. We have at no time given our consent for any individual to be transferred to the detention facility at Guantánamo Bay.'[32] Following further questions and correspondence from the APPG, the then Defence Secretary Des Browne qualified the picture still more in a letter on 31 January 2008: 'Whenever we have passed an individual from UK jurisdiction into the jurisdiction of the Iraqi, Afghan or US authorities, we have had in place an understanding that they would not transfer that individual to a third country without first seeking our consent *or at least informing us of their intention*' (emphasis added).[33]

The Ministry of Defence was highly resistant in its responses to Freedom of Information Act requests by the APPG concerning the understandings agreed with the US and other governments, and the details of those detained by British forces. Eventually, however, in an evidence session with the Defence and Foreign Affairs Committees in October 2008 the government was able to confirm that no one captured by British forces had ever been held at Guantánamo Bay. Under questioning during the same hearing, the government committed to a further examination of its records.[34]

Following this review, the then Defence Secretary, John Hutton, told the House of Commons on 26 February 2009 that two individuals captured by UK forces in Iraq in February 2004 had been handed over to the Americans and then rendered to Afghanistan. It subsequently emerged that the two individuals, allegedly members of the al Qaeda-linked organisation Lashkar-e-Taiba, had been transferred to Bagram. The Secretary of State was deeply apologetic that once again 'inaccurate information on this particular issue has been given to the House', but insisted that the transfer had been because of a lack of linguists with the right skills to interrogate them effectively in Iraq, that the detainees had been treated humanely and that the Red Cross had access to them. The Defence Secretary insisted that Ben Griffin's allegations had been examined and refuted by a senior general, and that the review had been comprehensive, although a number of MPs were clearly still uneasy. Reviewing the matter some months later, the Foreign Affairs Committee found the explanation of the reason for the transfer unconvincing and remained concerned about allegations that the case was not an isolated one.[35]

The Defence Secretary made clear that the British had not been aware when transferring detainees to the Americans that they would be rendered, but that 'officials were aware of the transfer in early 2004'. He added that 'the transfer ... should have been questioned at the time', implying that officials had been aware of it before the fact. This was confirmed by Hutton's successor, Bob Ainsworth, who explained that the records 'suggest that British officials became aware of an intention to transfer in March 2004, although this was some days after the initial capture had occurred. British officials had learned by mid-June 2004 that the individuals had been transferred to Afghanistan.' The minister remained 'satisfied that these assurances [that the detainees were being treated humanely] are reliable'.[36]

The picture that ministers presented of these events was of a British government deeply reliant on assurances from the US administration, and not always aware of what was happening, even on British territory. The ISC, reporting on rendition in mid-2007, painted a similar picture of the government and intelligence services being sometimes behind the pace of events and with limited leverage over the Americans. The committee found that the security services had been 'slow to detect the emerging pattern of "Renditions to Detention" that occurred in 2002'. Only as the picture became clearer in the course of 2003 did they take a more cautious approach, increasingly seeking ministerial approval and assurances on humane treatment 'in operations that involved any risk of rendition and/or US custody'. Record keeping had been poor. In one case, 'it is regrettable that assurances regarding proper treatment of detainees were not sought'. Above all, it was clear that 'the US will take whatever action it deems necessary, within US law, to protect its national security from those it considers to pose a serious threat. Although the US may take note of UK protests and concerns, this does not appear materially to affect its strategy on rendition.'[37]

However, evidence from a series of high-profile individual cases raises questions as to whether the British position was one of more active complicity than this rather hapless picture implies.

The first case concerns the arrest of Bisher al-Rawi and Jamil el-Banna on a visit to the Gambia in November 2002, and their subsequent rendition to Afghanistan and thence to Guantánamo. Both men were British residents but not citizens. Al-Rawi, an Iraqi national who arrived in Britain in 1984, had exceptional leave to remain, while el-Banna, a Jordanian Palestinian, had refugee status. The Security Service assessed both men to be extremists. 'Mr al-Rawi and Mr el-Banna were known to the Service prior to their detention in The Gambia. Whilst in the United Kingdom, both were in contact with a number of individuals considered by the Service to be Islamist extremists, including Abu Qatada, the radical cleric...'[38]

However, the Security Service had been in contact with both men. A member of the Security Service and a Special Branch officer visited el-Banna on 31 October 2002, attempting to win his cooperation: 'if he chose to help us by providing details of all his activities and contacts, we would assist him to create a new life for himself and his family'. El-Banna was 'welcoming and apparently friendly' but showed no interest in the offer.[39] Al-Rawi, by his own account, served as an intermediary between the security services and Abu Qatada, particularly in the months after 9/11. He met Security Service officers who introduced themselves as Alex, Matt and Martin, and later – when he became anxious that his work for them might somehow incriminate him – he met a Security Service lawyer who introduced himself as Simon and promised help if he was ever arrested.[40]

On 1 November – the day after the visit to el-Banna – al-Rawi, el-Banna and a third man, Abdullah el-Janoudi (a British citizen) travelled to Gatwick airport to fly out to The Gambia. The stated purpose of the trip was to join al-Rawi's brother Wahab (who, unlike Bisher, had taken British citizenship) who was planning to develop a peanut oil business. They were arrested at Gatwick when suspicious items were found in al-Rawi's luggage. That day, the Security Service sent a telegram to the US authorities informing them of the arrests. The telegram described al-Rawi as 'an Iraqi Islamic extremist who is a member of Abu QATADA's close circle of associates', while el-Banna was 'formerly assessed to be Abu QATADA's financier'. It described the item that led to their arrest as 'some form of home-made electronic device. Preliminary enquiries including X-ray suggest that it may be a timing device or could possibly be used as part of a car-based IED [Improvised Explosive Device].'[41] The ISC in its later assessment of the case described such a telegram as 'routine, and a fundamental part of the work of the Security Service'.[42]

The three men were held and questioned between 1 and 4 November, before being released. According to their lawyer, the device was a home-made battery charger, apparently for use in connection with the peanut project and 'this was confirmed by the Anti-terrorist squad at 5.22 pm on 4 November who informed their solicitors that they had found it to be "an innocent device" and that they were therefore being released'. In releasing the men, the police did not make use of the full detention powers at their disposal.[43] On the day of the release, the Security Service (SyS – otherwise known as MI5) sent a second telegram to the Americans, suggesting that 'the following form of words can be passed to Gambian liaison'. It mentioned that the three men, whose links with Abu Qatada were referred to again, were due to fly to The Gambia. 'We would be grateful for feedback on the reaction of the Gambians to this intelligence. In particular, we would be interested to learn if they are able to cover these individuals whilst they are in Gambia.' Like the previous telegram, this carried the standard caveat that it was 'for research and analysis purposes only and may not be used as the basis for overt, covert or executive action'.[44]

On 8 November, el-Banna, al-Rawi and el-Janoudi flew out to the Gambia. A further telegram to the US, which followed on from a telephone conversation, gave the details of their flight and the names under which they were travelling.[45] Shortly after their arrival at Banjul airport, the three – along with Wahab al-Rawi and a Gambian citizen, both of whom had come to meet them – were arrested by the Gambian authorities concerning suspicious items in their luggage. They were soon transferred to American custody. The Foreign Office asked for access to the two British nationals, but – in contravention of the Vienna Convention on Consular Relations – this was denied. In late November, the British authorities were told of plans to render the four men to Afghanistan, and protested at the proposal. Ultimately the two British citizens were allowed to return to the UK (on 4-5 December), but el-Banna and Bisher al-Rawi were allegedly rendered to the dark prison on 8 December, to Bagram on 22 December and to Guantánamo in February 2003. They recalled experiencing severe maltreatment in all three places.[46]

In Guantánamo, al-Rawi was reportedly visited by a Security Service officer in the autumn of 2003, who remarked apologetically, 'Sorry about all this.' He was later seen by the three agents who had met him in London, and the possibility of his working for the SyS again if he was released was discussed. At his CSRT in October 2004, al-Rawi asked for the three agents to be called as witnesses. After making inquiries, the Tribunal President reportedly told him: 'We have contacted the British Government and at this time, they are not willing to provide the tribunal with that information … The British Government didn't say they didn't have a relationship with you, they just would not confirm or deny it. That means I only have your word.' His witness request was denied. The official record, while heavily redacted, confirms that al-Rawi asked for 'Alex', 'Matthew' and 'Martin' to be called as witnesses, and that the Tribunal President attempted to arrange this; however, for reasons that remain undisclosed, 'the witnesses could not be identified'.[47]

In 2004 and 2005, the British government had made formal requests for the return of its nationals from Guantánamo; the last of these were released in January 2005. However, this did not cover al-Rawi and el-Banna, since they were residents but not citizens. Lawyers acting on their behalf applied for Judicial Review to require the Foreign Secretary to intercede on their behalf. The case was heard in the Administrative Court in February 2006, and then in the Divisional Court on 22–23 March. The judgment handed down in May went in favour of the government. However, just before the hearing on 22 March, the Treasury Solicitor informed al-Rawi's lawyers that, on the basis of a 'fact specific claim' by al-Rawi – widely taken to be his allegation of having worked for the Security Service – the Foreign Secretary would approach the Americans to ask for his release. The British government would nonetheless maintain its general stance that it would not intercede on behalf of non-citizens. At the end of that year, Margaret Beckett (who had succeeded Jack Straw as Foreign Secretary) told the Intelligence and Security Committee that *the previous Foreign Secretary made an exception, in the case of Mr al-Rawi, somewhat late in the day, because he was informed, rather late in the day, of information [redacted]*.[48] In the event, al-Rawi was released in April 2007. In August the British government changed its stance and asked for the release of British residents; in December three of them, including el-Banna, were returned to the UK.

Was the British government, or the British security services, responsible for the rendition of al-Rawi and el-Banna? There is secondary evidence to suggest so. El-Banna stated that his American interrogators told him: 'Why are you so angry at America? It is your government, Britain, the MI5, who called the CIA and told them that you and Bisher were in the Gambia and to come and get you. Britain gave everything to us. Britain sold you out to the CIA.' According to Wahab al-Rawi, when he asked for the British High Commissioner to be informed of his arrest, one of the Gambian officials laughed and said, 'It was the British who told us to arrest you.' El-Janoudi recalled a CIA officer named Lee telling him that the British had 'sold you out'.[49]

However, the documentary evidence is ambiguous, and the intelligence agencies insisted to the ISC that the wording of the caveats on the telegrams – that they were not to be used for action – was not merely a formality but a central part of the intelligence-sharing that the Americans had honoured for many years. The authorities also presented evidence to the ISC to indicate that they had been taken aback at the prospect of the men's rendition. The Committee accepted this account, while noting that unilateral American action 'shows a lack of regard, on the part of the US, for UK concerns ... [with] serious implications for the working of the relationship between the US and the UK intelligence and security agencies'.[50]

At the very least, two significant questions remain. The first is that the two telegrams sent in early November 2002 contained information about el-Banna and al-Rawi (their alleged affiliations and the 'suspicious device' found at Gatwick) that would have raised major suspicions about them; indeed, it may be that this is what the comments attributed to CIA officers referred to. However, it seems that at no point were the police conclusions about the 'device' relayed. Secondly, while the exact nature of Bisher al-Rawi's relationship with the Security Service is unclear, facts significant enough to change the Foreign Secretary's mind about making representations on his behalf remained undisclosed over a long period. As the ISC put it, 'we consider that the Security Service should have informed Ministers about the case at the time, and [we] are concerned that it took [redacted] years, and a court case, to bring it to their attention'.[51]

If the al-Rawi and el-Banna case remains somewhat ambivalent, that of Binyam Mohamed has produced much sharper disclosures of what at least parts of the security services knew was happening. Strikingly, these events took place early in the 'War on Terror', raising questions as to whether the British authorities could or should have been quite as much in the dark about American methods and intentions as the ISC's report suggested.

Binyam Mohamed, an Ethiopian national born in 1978, lived in Britain between 1994 and 2001. Although his asylum claim was refused, in 2000 he was given leave to remain for four years. However, by this time he had made a strong commitment to Islam, and left in 2001, first for Pakistan, then for Afghanistan. His account was that he wanted to get away from an environment in which he had been caught up in drug-taking and to see a pure version of Islam. However, he was later to be accused of having received military and explosives training from al Qaeda, and to have plotted a variety of terrorist attacks with the former Chicago street gang member and convert to Islam José Padilla, including reviewing the possibility of constructing an improvised radioactive ('dirty') bomb. Arrested at

Karachi airport on 10 April 2002 while trying to fly to the UK on a forged passport, he was held incommunicado in Pakistan for several months. By his own account he was flown to Morocco in July 2002, and tortured brutally there before being sent to Afghanistan; first to the dark prison in January 2004, then to Bagram in May, before being taken to Guantánamo in September.[52]

The British role in Binyam Mohamed's treatment emerged gradually, starting with his accounts of what had happened to his lawyer, Clive Stafford Smith, in 2005.[53] However, the catalyst for further revelations came when he was charged in May 2008 with offences that could have carried the death penalty and faced the imminent possibility of trial before a military commission. Legal action was launched in Britain to release documents that, his lawyers contended, demonstrated that confessions he had made to these offences reflected the coercive treatment to which he had been subjected. In its August 2008 judgment, the Court concluded that, in its handling of the affair, 'the relationship of the United Kingdom Government to the United States authorities in connection with BM was far beyond that of a bystander or witness to the alleged wrongdoing'. On the contrary, the British authorities had 'facilitated' these actions.[54]

In October 2008, the charges against Binyam Mohamed were dropped, and he was released from Guantánamo in February 2009. Legal challenges now focused on the government's wish to withhold from public disclosure a summary of US intelligence material that gave more details about his interrogation. The government argued that the release of this information would damage intelligence sharing between the US and the UK. In February 2010, to the evident disquiet of the US administration, the Court of Appeal ruled that the summary should be released.

The events at issue took place in the weeks and months after Mohamed's arrest in April 2002. While he was held incommunicado and interrogated in Pakistan, some information was passed to the British security services. From this – which included the 'dirty bomb' allegations – it was clear 'that B[inyam] M[ohamed] was a person whose activities would be of importance to the SyS in protecting the vital interests of the national security of the United Kingdom'. The British supplied questions to be asked and expressed an interest in interviewing Mohamed themselves. This was with full knowledge that Mohamed was being held incommunicado, circumstances that the ISC later (without specific reference to this case) characterised as 'of itself mistreatment'.[55]

This was agreed, and the interview – carried out by a Security Service officer identified in the court case as 'Witness B' – took place on 17 May.[56]

However, before the interview took place, both the SyS and the Secret Intelligence Service (SIS – otherwise known as MI6) received reports about Mohamed's treatment in Pakistan. It was the summary of these reports that was 'redacted at the request of the Foreign Secretary' but eventually released in February 2010. The redacted paragraphs read:

> iv. It was reported that a new series of interviews was conducted by the United States authorities prior to 17 May 2001 as part of a new strategy designed by an expert interviewer.
>
> v. It was reported that at some stage during that further interview process by the United States authorities, BM had been intentionally subjected to continuous sleep deprivation. The effects of the sleep deprivation were carefully observed.
>
> vi. It was reported that combined with the sleep deprivation, threats and inducements were made to him. His fears of being removed from United States custody and 'disappearing' were played upon.
>
> vii. It was reported that the stress brought about by these deliberate tactics was increased by him being shackled during his interviews.
>
> viii. It was clear not only from the reports of the content of the interviews but also from the report that he was being kept under self-harm observation, that the interviews were having a marked effect upon him and causing him significant mental stress and suffering.
>
> ix. We regret to have to conclude that the reports provided to the SyS made clear to anyone reading them that BM was being subjected to the treatment that we have described and the effect upon him of that intentional treatment.
>
> x. The treatment reported, if had been administered on behalf of the United Kingdom, would clearly have been in breach of the undertakings given by the United Kingdom in 1972. Although it is not necessary for us to categorise the treatment reported, it could readily be contended to be at the very least cruel, inhuman and degrading treatment of BM by the United States authorities.[57]

ABOVE Architects of the Global War on Terror: President George W. Bush, Vice President Dick Cheney (right) and Defense Secretary Donald Rumsfeld (left). © PA Photos Ltd.

BELOW Gulfstream N379P, claimed to have been frequently used in rendition flights.

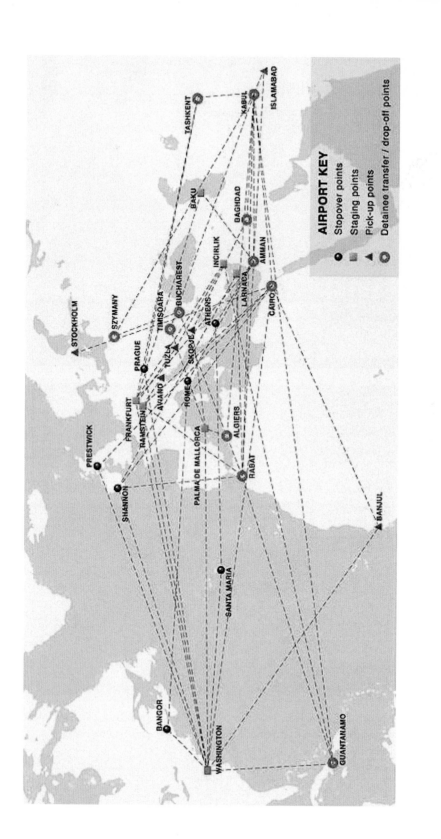

AIRPORT KEY

Stopover points
Staging points
Pick-up points
Detainee transfer / drop-off points

OPPOSITE The Council of Europe's diagram of the CIA's global network of renditions and 'black sites'. Reproduced by kind permission of Once Were Farmers and The Council of Europe.

ABOVE LEFT Stare Kiejkuty, Poland, widely alleged to have been the site of a CIA secret prison in which 'High Value Detainees' underwent 'enhanced' interrogations. © PA Photos Ltd.

ABOVE RIGHT Guantánamo Bay, Cuba, to which many rendered detainees were eventually transferred. © PA Photos Ltd.

BELOW Diego Garcia: allegations that this British Overseas Territory in the Indian Ocean was used for renditions were repeatedly denied by the Government. By kind permission of Dr. J. David Roberts.

ABOVE LEFT 21 February 2008: Foreign Secretary David Miliband, flanked by Jack Straw (left) and Meg Munn (right) confirms that two detainees were rendered through Diego Garcia in 2002. © PA Photos Ltd.

ABOVE RIGHT RAF Northolt, 23 February 2009: a Gulfstream jet brings Binyam Mohamed back to the UK. © PA Photos Ltd.

BELOW Former SAS soldier Ben Griffin alleges that individuals detained by British forces in Iraq were handed over to the US and subsequently mistreated. © Getty Images.

The Court found it 'inconceivable' that the reports had not been studied by 'Witness B', either before or after his interview with Mohamed; it also determined subsequently that the reports were read by other desk officers.[58] In other words, an unspecified number of officers within the SyS were aware of the treatment of Mohamed in Pakistan, treatment which was against the UK's legal obligations and the Service's stated values. Subsequently, when the ISC asked whether the reports had also been seen by officers within SIS, it was initially told that they had not. However, 'We asked SIS to check its records again and were subsequently told that at least four members of staff saw the information, including the team leader covering [redacted], and their section head.'[59]

During his meeting with Mohamed, whom he believed to be withholding information, 'Witness B' warned him that 'if he wanted my help [in persuading the Americans to be more lenient with him], he would need to be completely forthcoming'. This, he argued in court exchanges, was a statement of fact rather than a threat. Mohamed's own account of the meeting included a curious and oblique threat:

> They gave me a cup of tea with a lot of sugar in it. I initially only took one. 'No, you need a lot more. Where you are going you need a lot of sugar.' I didn't know exactly what he meant by this, but I figured he meant some poor country in Arabia. One of them did tell me I was going to get tortured by the Arabs.[60]

By his own account, Mohamed was rendered from Pakistan to Morocco on 22 July 2002. There he was treated with the utmost brutality with a variety of tortures, including repeated cuts with a scalpel to his chest and penis. Much of the questioning related to his time in Britain: 'They also showed me photographs and files that they said came from Britain, from MI5. They called it the British file. It was then that I realised that the British were sending questions to the Moroccans.'[61]

Judge Kessler of the Sixth District Court of the District of Columbia, ruling on a habeas corpus case in which Binyam Mohamed's testimony played a central role, stated that 'the [US] government does not challenge or deny the accuracy of Binyam Mohamed's story of brutal treatment'. In addition, the flight logs show that there was a flight of the Gulfstream V jet linked to renditions from Pakistan to Morocco at the time that he claimed to have been rendered. (There is similar supporting evidence for his transfer to Afghanistan in January 2004).

There is also corroboration that questions were being put from the British side. In the months following 'Witness B's' interview with Mohamed, the SyS tried – with increasing frustration, since Mohamed was 'one of their highest priorities' – to get access to him again. The Americans indicated that he was likely to be transferred to Afghanistan, but this did not happen. 'By 19 August 2002, the SyS were aware that BM was being held in a covert location where he was being debriefed. Direct access was not possible but the SyS were able to send questions to the US authorities to be put to him.' In the autumn, the Americans continued to refuse access; however, the SyS, anxious that Mohamed might have information about an attack in the UK that they believed to be a serious possibility, was allowed to pass on more questions. Reports of interviews were passed back on several occasions between September 2002 and March 2004.[62]

In contrast to the situation when Mohamed was held in Afghanistan, the British intelligence services apparently had no direct evidence of where he was and how he was being treated. However, the government has admitted that it was 'apparent that he was in the custody of a third country and not yet in United States custody'. It was also clear that he was still being held incommunicado; nonetheless, 'the SyS continued to facilitate interviews by the United States authorities after September 2002'.[63] It also emerged from documents supplied to the High Court that Witness B visited Morocco three times during the time that Mohamed was held there; once in November 2002, and twice in February 2003. The Court declared itself 'unable to determine the significance (if any) of Witness B's visits to Morocco' and added that 'we have been informed that the SyS maintains that it did not know that BM was in Morocco in the period in question'.[64] Others have, however, argued that there was a link between Witness B's visits and an alleged undercover agent – referred to as Informant A – who reportedly already knew Mohamed from London and sought to 'turn' him while he was held in Morocco.[65]

Given what was already known in at least some parts of the Service about Mohamed's treatment while in Pakistan, it is at the very least striking that few if any questions seem to have been asked about his treatment. The then head of the Service, Lady Manningham-Buller, stated in March 2010 that 'the Americans were very keen that people like us did not discover

what they were doing.' A senior Pentagon official was quoted as responding that 'the Brits were always very happy to receive information we gave
them emanating from Mohamed'.[66]

The reverberations of the Court findings in the Binyam Mohamed
affair continued throughout 2009 and into 2010. The case highlighted
the issue of the guidance to intelligence and service officers on detention
and interviewing of detainees overseas. In its report on treatment of such
detainees (2005), the ISC had referred to the case of an SIS officer who had
raised concerns over the treatment of a detainee in January 2002. While
the committee found that the officer had been told that such treatment
of a detainee was unacceptable, it concluded that the instructions given
to him – 'if circumstances allow, you should consider drawing this to the
attention of a suitably senior US official locally' – did not go far enough,
and that there was a tendency to treat such cases as isolated incidents.
The ISC also found that intelligence officers deployed to Afghanistan,
Guantánamo and Iraq were insufficiently trained in the Geneva conventions and other requirements for detainee treatment. While new guidelines
were issued by the intelligence agencies in September 2004, the ISC was
'concerned at how long it took to issue this formal guidance. The need for
this should have been recognised much earlier.' The ISC returned to this
theme in its 2007 Report on Rendition, noting that by 2004 the agencies
realised that their guidance on dealing with foreign intelligence services
was 'insufficiently detailed' and that there were revisions in 2005–06.[67]

On 18 March 2009, the then Prime Minister Gordon Brown issued a
Written Statement on detainee policy.[68] Among its provisions was that the
ISC should update its two reports on detainees and rendition, and that
it should review the outstanding guidance to officers. These would then
be published and reviewed annually for compliance by the Intelligence
Services Commissioner, Sir Peter Gibson. However, it was not until mid-
November that the government was able to consolidate existing guidance
and hand it to the committee for review. The committee submitted its
report to the Prime Minister on 5 March 2010, making clear its exasperation at the delays and with the strong expectation that the report would
be published promptly. That the report was not made available for the
parliamentary debate on the ISC's annual report on 18 March was another
source of frustration.[69]

Following the General Election and the formation of the coalition government, the new Prime Minister David Cameron announced the publication of new guidance on 6 July, along with the establishment of the Gibson Inquiry.[70] However, the guidance that had been in place in the years immediately after 9/11, which the previous administration had declined to reveal, remained an issue between the legal teams representing the government and those representing the former detainees. On 21 June the High Court ordered the disclosure of the documents referred to in the ISC reports. The material was released, but the guidance issued to the SIS officer (and copied to others serving in Afghanistan) in January 2002 was subject to significant redaction, so that it added little to what had already been disclosed by the ISC. The guidance issued in 2004–06 was less heavily redacted, but the question of how satisfactory and comprehensive the pre-2004 guidance was remains unanswered.[71] In the view of at least some observers, what is known of the guidance falls short of the UK's obligations, notably under the CAT.[72]

On 26 March 2009 the Attorney General announced that she had referred the Binyam Mohamed affair to the police for possible criminal investigation; in July the police confirmed that the investigation was under way. This focused on the officer known as 'Witness B'; however, in November 2010, the Director of Public Prosecutions, Keir Starmer, announced that there was insufficient evidence to bring a criminal case against the officer 'arising from the interview of Binyam Mohamed in Pakistan on 17 May 2002'. However, a 'wider investigation into other potential criminal conduct arising from allegations made by Mr Mohamed' continued.[73] This was not the only such case. In February 2010, the Metropolitan Police were reported to be investigating allegations that a British official was present when Shaker Aamer, the last British resident held in Guantánamo was allegedly beaten by US interrogators in Bagram, and that other interrogators from SyS were aware of his maltreatment. The government had initially been unwilling to make documents relating to the allegations available to Aamer's lawyers, but released them after a High Court ruling in Aamer's favour in December 2009.[74] In addition, there are wider allegations of complicity by the British security services in the mistreatment or torture of a number of individuals held in other countries, notably Pakistan. These cases do not contain any element of rendition and so are beyond the scope of this book, although the apparent shift in

Western policy in recent years towards reliance on allied governments to detain suspects adds to the salience of the allegations.[75]

The release of the redacted seven paragraphs on the instructions of the Court of Appeal on 10 February 2010 was not the end of the Binyam Mohamed affair. There was a further controversy when it emerged that, following an intervention by the government's legal representative, the judges – led by the Master of the Rolls, Lord Neuberger – had heavily amended a section (Paragraph 168) of the verdict that included hard-hitting comments on the security services. Other parties to the case objected strongly. In announcing the verdict on 10 February, Lord Neuberger conceded that 'it was over-hasty of me' to withdraw the original paragraph, and set out a timetable for reviewing the paragraph and receiving any comments on it.

On 26 February a revised version of the original paragraph was published. It included the comment that 'some Security Services officials appear to have a dubious record relating to actual involvement, and frankness about any such involvement, with the mistreatment of Mr Mohamed when he was held at the behest of US officials. I have in mind in particular witness B, but the evidence in this case suggests that it is likely that there were others.' A later section addressed the role of the security services in advising the Foreign Secretary – whose good faith was not questioned – on preparation of the Public Interest Immunity certificates that justified the original redaction of the seven paragraphs about Binyam Mohamed's treatment.

> Regrettably, but inevitably, this must raise the question whether any statement in the certificates on an issue concerning the mistreatment of Mr Mohamed can be relied on, especially when the issue is whether contemporaneous communications to the Security Services about such mistreatment should be revealed publicly. Not only is there some reason for distrusting such a statement, given that it is based on Security Services' advice and information, because of previous, albeit general, assurances in 2005, but also the Security Services have an interest in the suppression of such information.

This represented a slight toning down of the original version, which had referred (more colourfully) to 'an obvious reason for distrusting any UK Government assurance, based on SyS advice and information, because of previous "form"...' and included the Foreign Office as another organisation with an interest in suppressing such information.[76] Nonetheless, the wording – and especially the reference to 'suppression' – compounded the already severe damage to public confidence, even though government ministers gave strong support to the head of the Security Service, Jonathan Evans, as he defended its record and values.

The ISC, hitherto the watchdog of the security services, also found the conclusions of its earlier reports undermined by the court judgments. In particular, the conclusion of its 2007 Report on Rendition had been that the security services' main failing had been to be relatively slow in grasping what the new US approach was, and that this was relatively understandable given the information available. This conclusion was no longer tenable; as the High Court ruling of 4 February 2009 put it, 'It is now clear that the 42 documents disclosed as a result of these proceedings were not made available to the ISC. The evidence was that earlier searches made had not discovered them. The ISC Report could not have been made in such terms if the 42 documents had been made available to it.'

The Court ruling also suggested that the committee was in a position to ask 'searching and difficult questions of witnesses from the SyS and SIS on the very important issues identified … it is in a position to conduct a most thorough and wide ranging enquiry.' The ruling indicated that there might be other, similar cases to be examined and that the committee could hold both the security services and ministers to account. However, by this stage the committee's critics were asking whether it was properly constituted to do so. Lady Manningham-Buller remarked that 'I would not be surprised if the committee becomes a select committee at some stage'. The committee's then chairman, Kim Howells, spoke of 'essential changes' needed to safeguard its independence. However, the committee's favoured solution – that it should be hosted in a department less closely linked to the intelligence services than the Cabinet Office – elicited little enthusiasm from the government.[77]

Further revelations emerged as a result of a civil suit brought by al-Rawi, el-Banna, Mohamed and three other Guantánamo detainees (Richard Belmar, Omar Deghayes and Martin Mubanga) against the security services, the Attorney General and the Foreign and Home Offices for alleged complicity in their detention and maltreatment. The case was dropped in November 2010 when the government reached an out of court settlement with the former detainees; this agreement removed a major obstacle to the Gibson Inquiry beginning its work. However, in the preliminary stages of the case in July 2010, some documents were released. There was dispute between the two sides' legal representatives over the release of government documents and the degree of redaction necessitated by security concerns. Some of the documents released were heavily redacted. Others, while suggestive, are cryptic; for example, a handwritten note headed 'Warriors 14/1' includes the words 'interview conditions cold beaten up' and refers later to 'ill-treatment' and 'collusive deportation [deleted] extradition'.[78] However, the disclosures from the case shed some additional light on the British authorities' approach.

In the weeks after the Afghan campaign concluded, the government had to decide its view on the fate of British citizens detained by coalition forces. As early as 10 January 2002, an internal Foreign Office memorandum was suggesting that 'transfer of UK nationals held by US forces in Afghanistan to the US base in Guantánamo is the best way to meet our counter-terrorism objective by ensuring that they are securely held'.[79] A telegram sent to leading British embassies a week later (and signed 'STRAW') advised that there was 'no objection to American plans to transfer UK detainees from Afghanistan to Guantánamo Bay'. It went on:

> The UK approach on the repatriation and prosecution of UK nationals is still being considered. Nevertheless, we accept that the transfer of UK nationals held by US forces in Afghanistan to the US base in Guantánamo is the best way to meet our counter-terrorism objective by ensuring that they are securely held. However, a specialist team is currently in Afghanistan seeking to interview any detainees with a UK connection to obtain information on their terrorist activities and connections. We therefore hope that all those detainees they wish to interview will remain in Afghanistan and will not be among the first groups to be transferred to Guantánamo. A week's delay should suffice. UK nationals should be transferred as soon as possible thereafter.[80]

At the same time, however, Guantánamo was causing concern among senior ministers. A Foreign Office memorandum to the Prime Minister Tony Blair, dated a day after Straw's telegram, warned that 'this [Guantánamo] will continue to be a difficult issue to handle, both in procedural and legal terms with the US and in handling Parliament and the media here'. A handwritten comment, almost certainly by the Prime Minister, reads: 'The key is to find out how they are being treated. Though I was initially sceptical about claims of torture we must make it clear to the US that any such action wd be totally unacceptable & v. quickly establish that it isn't happening.'[81]

However, Jack Straw's telegram proved a more durable guide to policy than Tony Blair's anxieties, although thinking within government was divided. A briefing written a few months later noted that in mid-March 'British Embassy officials told Americans informally that it was possible that we would revert with formal (and public) requests for legal access. FCO had wanted to do this (and wanted to be seen to be doing it) but had been overruled by No. 10.'[82]

An account of an interdepartmental meeting to discuss the issue on 25 February gives more detail as to government thinking. While 'the Americans currently take the view that "the ball [is] in the UK court" and wish to know how we would handle any detainees', there was little enthusiasm at the prospect. 'The meeting agreed that UK should not be in any hurry to take back the detainees though FCO was quiet on the point.' It was recognised that British citizens going before US military tribunals might create 'problems of public presentation'; however, 'these are likely to be preferable to those associated with the detainees being released in the UK'.[83]

Later on the government appears to have changed its stance. According to Lawrence Wilkerson, 'Secretary Powell received frequent phone calls from British Foreign Minister Jack Straw, who had consulted with Secretary Powell frequently about repatriating the British Guantánamo detainees. Mr Straw would call and remind Secretary Powell that the UK is our closest ally, was fully capable of detaining terrorists, equally capable of trying them in its courts, and that he should push the repatriations ahead.'[84] In 2002, however, the government appears to have had very little confidence that it could bring effective cases against the detainees and feared the American reaction if they were to be freed.

A number of these elements are present in the rendition of Martin Mubanga from Zambia to Guantánamo. Mubanga, a dual British-Zambian national who had grown up in Britain, had a troubled youth and spent six months in Feltham Young Offenders' Institution, during which time he became interested in Islam. He attended Abu Qatada's mosque, spent time in Bosnia, and later (in 2000–01) travelled to Pakistan and Afghanistan. He was arrested by the Zambian authorities in March 2002. He claimed that he had travelled there from Pakistan because his British passport had been lost, and to visit relatives. However, the British and American intelligence agencies believed that his account 'lacked credibility' and that instead his 'escape [from Afghanistan] may have been arranged by an Islamist network and that he could well have been given a terrorist remit to pursue'. The latter allegation appears to have concerned targeting Jewish organisations in New York.[85]

On 19 March, the British indicated 'that we were keen to obtain access to MUBANGA and could deploy at short notice'. At around this time, a telegram was sent, which 'raises the possibility that MUBANGA might be sent to GTMO', stating that, 'Whether they do so is a matter solely for the US. However, we would hope that they would have legitimate reasons, and see real advantage in taking this action.' While redaction of key sentences leaves many details unclear, it appears that at this point the British authorities favoured Mubanga's removal to Guantánamo.[86]

A few days later, SyS officers conducted two lengthy interviews with Mubanga (on 23 and 24 March). They concluded that his account was 'in many cases unbelievable' and that he appeared to be 'emotionally unstable and committed to violence'. The officers cited the opinion of other observers (whose identity remains redacted) that 'if released, Martin MUBANGA was likely to continue to try to further the cause in which he believes. As such, he would be a danger to national (and international) security.' Under the heading 'Future Action', the officers concluded – after a sentence which remains redacted – that 'if this were to take place, MM is likely to be sent to Guantánamo Bay'.[87]

A few days later, the head of SyS, Eliza Manningham-Buller, wrote to the Permanent Secretary at the Home Office, John Gieve, summarising the interview with Mubanga and assessing that he 'would pose a serious threat if he were to be released'. Legal proceedings were seen as a poor option. 'We fear, and the Anti-Terrorist branch of the Metropolitan Police (SO13) have since confirmed, that there is insufficient evidence at present to charge MUBANGA if he were to be returned to the UK. ... We are therefore faced with the prospect, as anticipated in earlier discussions, of the return of a British citizen to the UK about whom we have serious concerns, whom it may be difficult to prosecute and whose release could trigger hostile US reaction.'[88]

There was, however, a significant prospect that this could happen. As the Deputy Head of Mission in Lusaka wrote afterwards, 'any UK national, no matter what they are alleged to have done, has a right to Consular assistance'. In Mubanga's case, 'if we requested consular access ... thereby de facto acknowledging him as a UK national, he would have been handed over to us'. On 26 March, at a meeting with SO13, the FCO's Consular Department indicated that it wished to 'avoid inconsistencies' in the treatment of detainees. It had asked for access to other detainees, 'and therefore planned to send a message to Consul in Lusaka to ask them to seek consular access for MUBANGA on normal channels'.[89]

However, this direction, if sent, was not acted on. By the Deputy Head of Mission's account, 'instructions from London were unequivocal. We should not accept responsibility for, or take custody of him. This was subsequently reinforced by the message from No 10 that under no circumstances should Mubanga be allowed to return to the UK.' The view from the Lusaka mission was that they had been put in an 'impossible position' by 'the constraints under which [we] were placed by edicts from London', which had acted in a 'schizophrenic way'. An official in the Consular Division in London reflected that, by not seeking consular access to Mubanga, 'we broke our policy despite us knowing that there was a significant question mark over the Zambian aspect of his nationality ... we are going to be open to charges of a concealed extradition.'[90]

Redactions in the documents make what happened next very unclear. A telegram of 26 March (apparently from SyS) indicates that they had sought 'legal and political advice' as to what to do about Mubanga. Direct British involvement in a rendition was ruled out: 'The option of MUBANGA's transfer to US custody through UK officials will not be accepted by HMG under any circumstances.' However, Mubanga was rendered to Guantánamo a few weeks later (on 20 April); the British government insisted afterwards that this was done by the Zambians, with no British involvement.[91] What is clear from the record, however, is the degree to which the British authorities wished to avoid responsibility for Mubanga. His dual nationality and the fact that he was held in Zambia created some ambiguity; the government later argued to the ISC that by policy convention responsibility fell on the Zambians to make representations on his behalf. However, this was not how officials viewed things at the time, not least because the Zambians 'do not recognise dual nationality'. The decision not to offer consular assistance appears to have been a conscious choice rather than, as the government later implied, the consequence of a previously established policy.[92]

Evidence that has emerged in the case of Omar Deghayes raises questions similar to those in the Binyam Mohamed case concerning awareness on the part of intelligence officers of possible maltreatment. Deghayes is a Libyan national but long-term refugee in Britain; his family were opponents of the Gaddafi regime and his father had reportedly been killed in prison in 1980. After studying law in England, Deghayes spent some time in Afghanistan. He was arrested in Pakistan in early 2002 and rendered from there, first to Bagram and then in the autumn to Guantánamo. He has alleged that he was subject both to physical maltreatment and to a threatening interrogation by agents of the Libyan government.[93]

The British and American intelligence agencies believed that Deghayes was actively involved with the radical Libyan Islamic Fighting Group (LIFG) and that he had undertaken jihad in Bosnia. They were suspicious of his reasons for travelling to Afghanistan; in the case later made against him at his ARB hearings in Guantánamo, it was alleged that his travel to Afghanistan had been facilitated by a senior al Qaeda figure, and that he had undergone military training there. A further claim – that his presence in a jihadist video demonstrated his involvement in the Chechen conflict – was long believed by his captors but later demonstrated to be unsubstantiated: the man in the video was a well-known Chechen warlord.[94]

Deghayes was interviewed by an SyS officer known as Andrew in Islamabad on 22 May 2002. He was 'fit and mentally competent', and – both by the officer's account and his own – confrontational, insisting that he had been wrongly detained and that he would launch a lawsuit when he returned to the UK. He made an unsuccessful attempt to pass himself off as his brother (who had taken British citizenship) and denied the allegations of taking part in jihad in Bosnia and of active involvement in the LIFG. The SyS officer 'closed the interview by telling DEGHAYES he needed to think very carefully about the gravity of the situation he was in. He was a Libyan citizen who had been arrested in Pakistan as an illegal entrant.' The officer's assessment was that Deghayes 'is obviously lying about the depth and extent of his involvement. He fits the pattern of a mujahid recruited in the UK.'[95]

By the time of Deghayes' next interview by SyS – on 24 June – he had been transferred to Bagram. His conditions were very different from those of the previous interview. 'DEGHAYES was brought to the interview room manacled and hooded. When the hood was removed, DEGHAYES looked pale and shaky.' The officers – 'Paul' and 'Martin' – did ask him whether he felt well enough to continue and offered to stop the interview if he did not. However, they also warned him that 'he was being held in custody solely by the Americans, and as we understood it he could face a long period of incarceration. We may be able to help him but the only circumstances in which we would even consider this is if he were to be completely honest and tell us everything that we wanted to know.' However, although the officers felt that they had made some progress – 'particularly his admission of being a Bosnian vet' – they were dissatisfied by his answers concerning the LIFG and Afghanistan. They also disbelieved him when 'he swore to Allah that he had never been to Chechnya'.[96]

The available sections of two other interviews with Deghayes at Bagram – on 3 and 11 July – are very fragmentary. However, in the first Deghayes complained of ill-treatment, 'with head-braces and lock-down positions being the order of the day. He was treated better by the Pakistanis; what kind of world was it where the Americans were more barbaric than the Pakistanis? We listened but did not comment.' In the second interview, which lasted for only fifteen minutes, the SyS officer 'told DEGHAYES that I didn't have much time and was about to leave Bagram. ... Would he come clean?' When Deghayes insisted that he had told the truth, 'I asked [redacted] a senior officer in the facility, to come into the room. I told [redacted] in DEGHAYES's hearing that DEGHAYES was not cooperat-ing.'[97]

Limited as these extracts from the interviews are, they raise questions as to the stance taken by SyS officers towards incommunicado detention, reports of maltreatment and the use of threats of continuing US detention or, by implication, transfer to the custody of Libya, a state with a poor human rights record and from which the Deghayes family had already taken refuge in Britain.

The evidence that has emerged from the court cases leaves vital ques-tions unanswered. The same can be said for almost all aspects of the British role in rendition. What was the attitude of the British authorities towards the rendition of a number of its nationals to detention, especially in 2002? What approach did the security services – or at least a number of offic-ers – take towards the possible maltreatment of detainees? At what level of decision-making was this authorised, and what if any was the degree of ministerial knowledge and involvement? Under what guidance were the officers operating? What is the truth about the use of Diego Garcia? What use has been made of British airports in rendition, including circuit flights? Was the one case so far identified of rendition after capture by British military forces and handover to the Americans truly an isolated incident, or a more widespread practice? On what occasions have US assurances been relied on and found wanting? What lies behind the failure by the security services to provide adequate information, notably to the ISC; was it simply a matter of shoddy record-keeping, or more deliberate suppression?

These among other questions must, finally, be resolved. That is why the work of the Gibson Inquiry is so welcome and so essential.

Notes

Chapter 1: Introduction

1. Scott Shane, 'On Torture, 2 Messages and a High Political Cost', *The New York Times*, 30 October 2007, see: http://www.nytimes.com/2007/10/30/washington/30torture.html?_r=1&ref=us&oref=slogin

2. Council on Foreign Relations, 'Transcript: A Conversation with Michael Hayden', 7 September 2007, see: http://www.cfr.org/publication/14162/conversation_with_michael_hayden_rush_transcript_federal_news_service.html

3. Letter from the Prime Minister, Rt Hon David Cameron MP, to Sir Peter Gibson, 6 July 2010, see: http://download.cabinetoffice.gov.uk/intelligence/pm-letter-gibson.pdf

4. For example, the claim by the CIA officer John Kiriakou that he had witnessed the waterboarding of a suspect, Abu Zubaydah, and that one application of the waterboard had induced him to give up significant information was eagerly seized on by the Bush administration's supporters. However, it emerged subsequently that Abu Zubaydah had been waterboarded 83 times in one month, and Kiriakou admitted that he had never been present at a waterboarding but had relied on second-hand reports within the Agency. Alex Sundby, 'CIA Agent Takes Back Waterboarding Claims', CBS News World Watch, 27 January 2010, see: http://www.cbsnews.com/8301-503543_162-6146610-503543.html

5. Pew Research Center, 'Confidence in Obama Lifts US Image Around the World', Pew Global Attitudes Project, 23 July 2009, see: http://pewglobal.org/reports/display.php?ReportID=264

6. Eminent Jurists Panel, *Assessing Damage, Urging Action: Report of the Eminent Jurists Panel on Terrorism, Counter-terrorism and Human Rights* (International Commission of Jurists, Geneva, 2009), p. 30, see: http://ejp.icj.org/IMG/EJP-Report.pdf

7. Julianne Smith, Center for Strategic and International Studies, testimony at 'Extraordinary Rendition in US Counterterrorism Policy: The Impact on Transatlantic Relations', Joint Hearing of subcommittees of the US House of Representatives Committee on Foreign Affairs, 17 April 2007, p. 10, see: http://foreignaffairs.house.gov/110/34712.pdf

8. CNN report, 'Iran's leader slams "arrogant" powers in U.N. address', CNN.com, 25 September 2007, see: http://edition.cnn.com/2007/US/09/25/un.iran/index.html; Claudia Parsons, 'Mugabe slams Bush "hypocrisy" on human rights', Reuters, 26 September 2007, see: http://www.reuters.com/article/idUSN2627903020070926

9. Alan Dershowitz, 'Want to torture? Get a warrant', *San Francisco Chronicle*, 22 January 2002, see: http://articles.sfgate.com/2002-01-22/opinion/17527284_1_physical-pressure-torture-terrorist; and, 'The Torture Warrant: A Response to Professor Strauss', *New York Law School Law Review*, Volume 48 (2003), see: http://www.nyls.edu/user_files/1/3/4/30/53/55/56/v48n1-2p275-294.pdf

10. Benjamin Wittes, *Law and the Long War: The Future of Justice in the Age of Terror* (Penguin, New York, 2008), pp. 184, 209-14; Clive Stafford Smith, *Bad Men: Guantánamo Bay and the Secret Prisons* (Weidenfeld and Nicolson, London, 2007), pp. 47-8

11. All Party Parliamentary Group (APPG) on Extraordinary Rendition, 'Legal Opinion on Detainee Handovers by UK Forces', by Michael Fordham QC and Tom Hickman (Blackstone Chambers) on instruction from Michael Davison and Emma Colquhoun (Lovells LLP), July 2008, pp. 16-7, see: http://www.extraordinaryrendition.org/index.php/component/docman/cat_view/30-all-other-documents?start=10

12. Letter from the Prime Minister to Sir Peter Gibson, 6 July 2010, pp. 1-2

13. APPG, *Extraordinary Rendition: Closing the Gap* (November 2009), see: http://www.extraordi-naryrendition.org/index.php/component/docman/cat_view/30-all-other-documents?start=5.

14. APPG, *Extraordinary Rendition: Closing the Gap*, pp. 77-8

15. Amnesty International, *State of Denial: Europe's role in rendition and secret detention,* (Amnesty International Publications, London, 2008), Case Sheets: Khaled el-Masri and Abu Omar, see: http://www.amnesty.org/en/library/asset/EUR01/003/2008/en/2ceda343-41da-11dd-81f0-01ab12260738/eur010032008eng.pdf; Telegram from American Embassy in Berlin to State Department, 6 February 2007, 'Al-Masri case – Chancellery aware of USG concerns', see: http://www.nytimes.com/interactive/2010/11/28/world/20101128-cables-viewer.html#report/cables-07BERLIN242

16. Margaret L. Satterthwaite, 'The Legal Regime Governing Transfer of Persons in the Fight Against Terrorism', *NYU School of Law, Public Law Research Paper No. 10-27* (May 2010), pp. 30-1, see: http://papers.ssrn.com/sol3/papers.cfm?abstract_id=1157583&reason=0

17. Duncan Gardham, 'Britain should be tougher on foreign terrorist suspects, watchdog says', *Daily Telegraph*, 23 June 2010, see: http://www.telegraph.co.uk/news/uknews/terrorism-in-the-uk/7849405/Britain-should-be-tougher-on-foreign-terrorist-suspects-watchdog-says.html; Satterthwaite, 'Legal Regime', p. 31

18. J.E. Baker, *In the Common Defense: National Security Law for Perilous Times* (2007), cited in Satterthwaite, 'Legal Regime', p. 9 n. 46

19. ICTY ruling in the case of Dragan Nikolic, cited in Satterthwaite, 'Legal regime', p. 13

20. Gregory S. McNeal and Brian Field, 'Snatch and Grab Ops: Justifying Extraterritorial Abduction', *University of Iowa: Journal of Transnational Law and Contemporary Problems* 16.9 (2007), pp. 500-1, see: http://works.bepress.com/gregorymcneal/7/ For a lengthy list of the international conventions relating to terrorism, see Satterthwaite, 'Legal regime', p.1 n.1

21. Tom Malinowski of Human Rights Watch, quoted in Greg Miller, 'Obama preserves renditions as counter-terrorism tool', *Los Angeles Times*, 1 February 2009, see: http://articles.latimes.com/2009/feb/01/nation/na-rendition1; Redress, *The United Kingdom, Torture and Anti-Terrorism; Where the Problems Lie* (The Redress Trust, London, 2008), pp. 8-9, see: http://www.redress.org/downloads/publications/Where%20the%20ProblemsLie%2010%20Dec%2008A4.pdf; Dick Marty (rapporteur), *Alleged secret detentions and unlawful inter-state transfers of detainees involving Council of Europe member states: report* (Council of Europe, Strasbourg, 2006), p. 14, see: http://assembly.coe.int/Documents/WorkingDocs/Doc06/EDOC10957.pdf; Satterthwaite, 'Legal Regime', p. 2

22. Satterthwaite, 'Legal Regime', pp. 35-6; 'Is Obama tough enough?', *The Economist*, 27 February 2010; BBC News South Asia, 'Mapping US drone and Islamic militant attacks in Pakistan', 22 July 2010, see: http://www.bbc.co.uk/news/world-south-asia-10648909

Chapter 2: Rendition, Extraordinary Rendition and International Law

1. *Filártiga v. Peña-Irala*, 630 F.2d 876 (30 June 1980)

2. Eminent Jurists Panel, *Assessing Damage, Urging Action*, p. 12

3. Satterthwaite, 'Legal Regime', p. 2

4. Foreign Office Memorandum to 10 Downing Street, 7 December 2005, see: http://www.extraordi-naryrendition.org/index.php/document-library-mainmenu-27/all-other-documents?start=25

5. European Commission for Democracy through Law (Venice Commission), *Opinion on the international legal obligations of Council of Europe member states in respect of secret detention facilities and inter-*

state transport of prisoners, Opinion No. 363/2005, adopted at the 66th Plenary Session (Venice, 17–18 March 2006), paragraph 31, see: http://www.venice.coe.int/docs/2006/CDL-AD(2006)009-e.asp

6. Intelligence and Security Committee (ISC), *Report on Rendition* (July 2007), p. 6, see: http://isc.independent.gov.uk/committee-reports/special-reports

7. Clive Stafford Smith OBE, Evidence Session 10 June 2009, in Foreign Affairs Select Committee, *Human Rights Annual Report 2008*, (July 2009), Ev 3, see: http://www.publications.parliament.uk/pa/cm200809/cmselect/cmfaff/557/557.pdf; Redress, 'Smoke and Mirrors Remain', 30 July 2007, see: http://www.redress.org/documents/ExtrRenditionResponsetoISCReport30July07.pdf

8. Venice Commission, *Opinion*, paragraph 30

9. The nineteenth century precedent of *Ker v. Illinois* (119 US 436 (1886)) involved the abduction of Ker, who was wanted on larceny charges, by a federal agent. He was brought back from Peru to stand trial in Illinois, and the fact that he had not been brought through the normal extradition channels was not deemed an impediment to a trial. The case of *Frisbie v. Collins* (342 US 519 (1952)) involved a suspect who had been abducted by the Michigan authorities while he was in Chicago

10. McNeal and Field, 'Snatch and Grab Ops', pp. 502-5

11. McNeal and Field, 'Snatch and Grab Ops', pp. 514-7; ISC (2007), *Report on Rendition*, p. 7

12. Alberto Costi, 'Problems with Current International and National Practices Concerning Extraterritorial Abductions', *Yearbook of the New Zealand Association for Comparative Law*, Volume 8 (2002), pp. 61-3, see: http://www.victoria.ac.nz/law/NZACL%20web%20page/PDFS/Vol_8_2002/Costi.pdf; McNeal and Field, 'Snatch and Grab Ops', pp. 510-11

13. Satterthwaite, 'Legal regime', p. 13

14. Costi, 'Problems', p. 67ff

15. Foreign and Commonwealth Office, *Annual Report on Human Rights 2008*, pp. 16-17; see: http://www.fco.gov.uk/resources/en/pdf/pdf15/human-rights-2008

16. Convention against Torture and Other Cruel, Inhuman or Degrading Treatment or Punishment, New York, 10 December 1984, No. 24841 United Nations, *Treaty Series*, vol. 1465, p. 85. See: http://www2.ohchr.org/english/law/pdf/cat.pdf; The Committee Against Torture has stated that the prohibitions on torture and CIDT are 'indivisible, interdependent and interrelated ... The Committee considers that articles 3 to 15 are likewise obligatory as applied to both torture and ill-treatment', UN Committee Against Torture, General Comment No.2: Implementation of Article 2 by States Parties, 24 January 2008, CAT/C/GC/2. See: http://www.unhcr.org/refworld/docid/47ac78ce2.html

17. Article 53, Vienna Convention on the Law of Treaties, Vienna, 23 May 1969, No. 18232, United Nations, *Treaty Series*, vol. 1155, p. 331, see: http://untreaty.un.org/ilc/texts/instruments/english/conventions/1_1_1969.pdf

18. International Covenant on Civil and Political Rights, New York, 16 December 1966, No. 14668 United Nations, *Treaty Series*, vol. 999, p. 171 and vol. 1057, p. 407. See: http://www2.ohchr.org/english/law/ccpr.htm

19. APPG, *Extraordinary Rendition: Closing the Gap*, pp. 70–1

20. Convention for the Protection of Human Rights and Fundamental Freedoms, as amended by Protocols No. 11 and No. 14, Council of Europe, Rome, 4.XI.1950. See: http://conventions.coe.int/treaty/en/Treaties/Html/005.html; APPG, *Extraordinary Rendition: Closing the Gap*, pp. 71–2

21. U.S. reservations, declarations, and understandings, Convention Against Torture and Other Cruel, Inhuman or Degrading Treatment or Punishment, Cong. Rec. S17486-01, see: http://www.bayefsky.com/html/usa_t2_cat.php

22. 'Transcript: Charlie Rose interviews Michael Hayden', *The New York Times*, 23 October 2007,

p. 6, see: http://www.nytimes.com/2007/10/23/world/americas/23iht-23hayden.3.8014027.html?pagewanted=6&_r=2

Chapter 3: Rendition before 9/11

1. Daniel Benjamin, '5 Myths About Rendition (and That New Movie)', *The Washington Post*, 20 October 2007, see: http://www.washingtonpost.com/wp-dyn/content/article/2007/10/19/AR2007101900835.html

2. Michael Scheuer, 'A Fine Rendition', *The New York Times*, 11 March 2005, see: http://www.nytimes.com/2005/03/11/opinion/11scheuer.html

3. George P. Shultz, *Turmoil and Triumph: My Years as Secretary of State* (Scribner, New York, 1993), pp. 645–9 and 669–77; quotation on p. 646

4. Steve Coll, *Ghost Wars: The Secret History of the CIA, Afghanistan and bin Laden, from the Soviet invasion to September 10, 2001* (Penguin, New York, 2004), pp. 139–40; Duane R Clarridge, with Digby Diehl, *A Spy for All Seasons: My Life in the CIA* (New York, Scribner, 1997), pp. 320–9

5. Clarridge, *A Spy for All Seasons*, p. 351

6. David B. Ottaway and Don Oberdorfer, 'Administration Alters Assassination Ban', *The Washington Post*, 4 November 1989

7. *United States v. Álvarez-Machain*, 504 US 655 (1992)

8. Richard A. Clarke, declassified testimony to Joint Inquiry by Senate and House Intelligence Committees, 11 June 2002, p. 6; see: http://intelligence.senate.gov/clark.pdf

9. Richard A. Clarke, *Against All Enemies: Inside America's War on Terror* (New York, Free Press, 2004), pp. 144–5

10. Benjamin, '5 Myths About Rendition'

11. Presidential Decision Directive PDD-39, see: www.fas.org/irp/offdocs/pdd39.htm; The National Commission on Terrorist Attacks Upon the United States (The 9/11 Commission), 'Staff Statement No. 5: Diplomacy', p. 2, see: http://govinfo.library.unt.edu/911/staff_statements/staff_statement_5.pdf. Stephen Grey, *Ghost Plane: The True Story of the CIA Rendition and Torture Program* (St Martin's Griffin, New York, 2007), p. 136 indicates that this was a classified 'additional component' to the Directive, parts of which remain redacted

12. Michael Scheuer, testimony at 'Extraordinary Rendition in US Counterterrorism Policy: The Impact on Transatlantic Relations', 17 April 2007, p. 12

13. Grey, *Ghost Plane*, pp. 129–39

14. Scheuer testimony, p. 12

15. Jane Mayer, *The Dark Side: The Inside Story of How the War on Terror turned into a War on American Ideals* (Anchor Books, New York, 2009) (revised edition), p. 113–4; for a breakdown of renditions that demonstrates Egypt's predominant role, see Grey, *Ghost Plane*, pp. 277–9

16. Grey, *Ghost Plane*, pp. 143–4, 278–9; Mayer, *The Dark Side*, p. 114

17. Robert Baer, quoted in American Civil Liberties Union (ACLU), 'National Security Fact Sheet: Extraordinary Rendition', see: http://www.aclu.org/safefree/extraordinaryrendition/22203res20051206.html

18. Benjamin, '5 Myths About Rendition'

19. For an example from the period in question, see US Department of State, *Egypt Country Report on Human Rights Practices for 1998*, see: http://www.state.gov/www/global/human_rights/1998_hrp_report/egypt.html

20. Grey, *Ghost Plane*, p. 223

21. Scheuer testimony, p. 36

22. Benjamin, '5 myths about rendition'; The National Commission on Terrorist Attacks Upon the United States, *The 9/11 Commission Report* (W.W. Norton, New York, 2004), pp. 108–15, 126–34, see: http://www.9-11commission.gov/report/911Report.pdf,; Coll, *Ghost Wars*, pp. 371–96. Benjamin refers to the Bin Laden plan as 'an extraordinary rendition', which on our definition it would not have been

23. 9/11 Commission, 'Staff Statement No. 5: Diplomacy', p. 7. The full text of PDD-62 is still classified

24. Transcripts of the second day of the Eighth Public Hearing of the National Commission on Terrorist Attacks Upon the United States, 24 March 2004; see: http://govinfo.library.unt.edu/911/archive/hearing8/9-11Commission_Hearing_2004-03-24.pdf Tenet's estimate of 80 renditions is on p. 30; a reference to his estimate of 70 renditions is on p. 3; Berger's estimate is on p. 69. Tenet's earlier comments are in 'Statement by Director of Intelligence George J. Tenet Before the Senate Select Committee on Intelligence on The Worldwide Threat in 2000: Global Realities of our National Security', 21 March 2000, see: https://www.cia.gov/news-information/speeches-testimony/2000/dci_speech_032100.html

25. Thomas Kleine-Brockhoff, 'The Origins of the Rendition Program: Does the CIA Have the Right to Break *Any* Law? An Interview with Michael Scheuer', *Counterpunch*, 7/8 January 2006, translated from the original German language article published in *Die Zeit*, see: http://www.counterpunch.org/kleine01072006.html

26. Grey, *Ghost Plane*, pp. 277–9; Peter Berger and Katherine Tiedemann, 'Disappearing Act: Rendition by the Numbers', *Mother Jones*, 3 March 2008, http://www.motherjones.com/politics/2008/03/disappearing-act-rendition-numbers

27. George J. Tenet, *Written Statement for the Record of the Director of Central Intelligence Before the National Commission on Terrorist Attacks Upon the United States, March 24, 2004*, pp. 22–3, see: http://www.9-11commission.gov/hearings/hearing8/tenet_statement.pdf

28. Wittes, *Law and the Long War*, pp 19–21

29. Coll, *Ghost Wars*, p. 427; the ambiguities of policy are described fully on pp. 423–30. See also *The 9/11 Commission Report*, pp. 131–3

Chapter 4: The Bush Administration Goes to War

1. *The 9/11 Commission Report*, p. 39

2. Alberto R. Gonzales, 'Memorandum for the President: Decision re application of the Geneva Convention on Prisoners of War to the conflict with al Qaeda and the Taliban', 25 January 2002, see: http://www.torturingdemocracy.org/documents/20020125.pdf

3. Mayer, *The Dark Side*, pp. 1–6; quotation (from Roger Cressey of the National Security Council) on p. 4

4. Mark Danner, 'On Dick Cheney'. *The Guardian*, 19 January 2009, see: http://www.markdanner.com/articles/show/on_dick_cheney

5. Mayer, *The Dark Side*, pp. 38–43: ISC (2007), *Report on Rendition*, pp. 19–20

6. Grey, *Ghost Plane*, p. 25–30, 33; United Nations Human Rights Committee, Views on *Alzery v. Sweden*, Communication No. 1416/2005, pp. 4–7, see: http://www.bayefsky.com/pdf/sweden_t5_iccpr_1416_2005.pdf; Craig Whitlock, 'A Secret Deportation of Terror Suspects', *The Washington Post*, 25 July 2004, see: http://www.washingtonpost.com/wp-dyn/articles/A11976-2004Jul24.html

7. Grey, *Ghost Plane*, pp. 105–28

8. United Nations Human Rights Committee, *Alzery v. Sweden*, p. 7

9. Grey, *Ghost Plane*, pp. 25–30, 33; United Nations Human Rights Committee, *Alzery v. Sweden*, No. 1416/2005, pp. 4–7

10. 'Transcript: Charlie Rose interviews Michael Hayden', p. 5; Berger and Tiedemann, 'Disappearing Act'

11. Gonzales, 'Memorandum for the President', p. 2

12. Unclassified memorandum from William H. Taft to John C. Yoo, 'Your Draft Memorandum of January 9', 11 January 2002, see: http://www.torturingdemocracy.org/documents/20020111.pdf

13. Memorandum from President George W. Bush to Vice President Cheney and others, 'Humane Treatment of al Qaeda and Taliban detainees', 7 February 2002, see: http://www.torturingdemocracy.org/documents/20020207-2.pdf

14. Wittes, *Law and the Long War*, pp. 38–41; Grey, *Ghost Plane*, p. 361, n. 8

15. Wittes, *Law and the Long War*, pp. 30–2. The George H.W. Bush and Clinton administrations had detained Haitian refugees in Guantánamo.

16. Stafford Smith, *Bad Men*, pp. 162–4, 169–70; Philippe Sands, *Torture Team: Deception, cruelty and the compromise of law* (Penguin, London, 2008), p. 52; Mayer, *The Dark Side*, pp. 183–4

17. Lawrence Wilkerson, interviewed by Stephen Grey, PBS 'Frontline/World: Extraordinary Rendition', see: http://www.pbs.org/frontlineworld/stories/rendition701/interviews/wilkerson.html; Declaration by Colonel Lawrence B. Wilkerson (Ret.) in the case of Adel Hassan Hamed v. George W. Bush, Donald Rumsfeld, Jay Hood and Brice Gyurisko, US District Court for the District of Columbia, CV 05-1009 JDB, 24 March 2010, see: http://www.truth-out.org/files/Wilkerson.pdf

18. Dick Marty (rapporteur), *Secret detentions and illegal transfers of detainees involving Council of Europe member states: second report*, Committee on Legal Affairs and Human Rights, Council of Europe, Strasbourg, 2007), p. 13, see: http://assembly.coe.int/Documents/WorkingDocs/Doc07/edoc11302.pdf

19. Marty (2007), *Secret detentions*, p. 14

20. Martin Scheinin, Manfred Nowak, the Working Group on Arbitrary Detention and the Working Group on Enforced and Involuntary Disappearances, *Joint Study on Global Practices in relation to secret detention in the context of countering terrorism* (United Nations Human Rights Council, 2010), pp. 79–81, see: http://www2.ohchr.org/english/bodies/hrcouncil/docs/13session/A-HRC-13-42.pdf; Independent Panel To Review DoD Detention Operations, *Final Report*, (Department of Defense, Washington, August 2004), p. 87, see: http://www.defense.gov/news/Aug2004/d20040824finalreport.pdf

21. Scheinin, Nowak et al, *Joint Study on Global Practices*, p. 65; Matt Apuzzo and Adam Goldman, 'AP Exclusive: CIA Whisked Detainees from Gitmo', Associated Press, 6 August 2010, see: http://www.washingtonpost.com/wp-dyn/content/article/2010/08/06/AR2010080600487.html

22. International Committee of the Red Cross (ICRC), *ICRC Report on The Treatment of Fourteen "High Value Detainees" in CIA Custody* (ICRC, 2007), p. 25, see: http://www.nybooks.com/media/doc/2010/04/22/icrc-report.pdf; President George W Bush, 'President's Speech on the Global war on Terror', 6 September 2006, see: http://www.america.gov/st/texttrans-english/2006/September/20060906155503eaifas0.8319666.html

23. Office of Legal Counsel, 'Memorandum for John A. Rizzo, Senior Deputy General Counsel, Central Intelligence Agency', 30 May 2005, p. 5, see: http://www.aclu.org/accountability/olc.html; General Michael Hayden, 'Director's Statement on the CIA Terrorist Interrogation Program', 5

October 2007, see: https://www.cia.gov/news-information/press-releases-statements/press-release-archive-2007/terrorist-interrogation-program.html; CIA response statement in Mayer, *The Dark Side*, pp. 389-90

24. Office of Inspector General, Central Intelligence Agency (OIG/CIA), *Special Review: Counterterrorism Detention and Interrogation Activities (September 2001–October 2003)*, pp. 2–3, 12, see: http://www.gwu.edu/~nsarchiv/torturingdemocracy/documents/20040507.pdf

25. OIG/CIA, *Special Review*, p. 13; Mayer, *The Dark Side*, pp. 156–64. The starting point of the SERE programme had been the maltreatment of American POWs by the North Koreans during the Korean War

26. OIG/CIA, *Special Review*, p. 6. n. 6

27. OIG/CIA, *Special Review*, p. 14 n. 14

28. Office of Legal Counsel (OLC), 'Memorandum for Alberto R. Gonzales, Counsel to the President Re: Standards of Conduct for Interrogation under 18 U.S.C && 2340-2340A', 1 August 2002, see: http://www.torturingdemocracy.org/documents/20020801-1.pdf For Yoo's role, see, for example, Mayer, *The Dark Side*, p. 151

29. Letter from John C. Yoo to Alberto R. Gonzales, 1 August 2002, see: http://www.torturingdemocracy.org/documents/20020801-3.pdf

30. OLC, 'Memorandum for John Rizzo, Acting General Counsel of the Central Intelligence Agency: Interrogation of al Qaeda Operative', 1 August 2002, see: http://www.aclu.org/accountability/olc.html

31. OLC, 'Memorandum Re: Standards of Conduct', p. 15; OIG/CIA, *Special Review*, p. 101

32. OIG/CIA, *Special Review*, p. 22

33. ICRC, *ICRC Report on The Treatment of Fourteen "High Value Detainees"*, pp. 8–9; General Michael Hayden, Testimony to Senate Select Committee on Intelligence, Hearing on 'Current and projected threats to the national security of the United States', 5 February 2008, pp. 71–2, see: http://intelligence.senate.gov/pdfs/110824.pdf; OIG/CIA, *Special Review*, pp. 90–1

34. OIG/CIA, *Special Review*, p. 91

35. OIG/CIA, *Special Review*, pp. 44–5, 69–78, 104

36. Scheinin, Nowak et al, *Joint Study on Global Practices*, p. 70

37. The original story was Dana Priest 'CIA Avoids Scrutiny of Detainee Treatment', *Washington Post*, 3 March 2005, see: http://www.washingtonpost.com/wp-dyn/articles/A2576-2005Mar2.html; also Mayer, *The Dark Side*, p. 225. More recent details are in Adam Goldman and Kathy Gannon, 'AP Investigation: Cautionary Tale from CIA Prison', *Associated Press*, 28 March 2010, see: http://abcnews.go.com/Politics/wirestory?id=10222080&page=1 A memorandum prepared by Jay Bybee's lawyers in response to the initial findings of the Office of Professional Responsibility refers (p. 29, n. 28) to 'the declination memorandum prepared by the CIA's Counterterrorism Section regarding the death of Gul Rahman … If [redacted] as manager of the Saltpit site, did not intend for Rahman to suffer severe pain from low temperatures in his cell, he would lack specific intent under the anti-torture statute.' Counsel for Jay S. Bybee, *Classified Response to the US Department of Justice Office of Professional Responsibility Classified Report Dated July 29, 2009*, see: http://judiciary.house.gov/hearings/pdf/BybeeResponse090729.pdf

38. Committee on Armed Forces, United States Senate, *Inquiry into the Treatment of Detainees in US Custody* (2008), pp. 3–4, see: http://armed-services.senate.gov/Publications/Detainee%20Report%20Final_April%2022%202009.pdf

39. Senate Armed Forces Committee, *Inquiry into the Treatment of Detainees*, p. 44

40. Senate Armed Forces Committee, *Inquiry into the Treatment of Detainees*, p. 95; Sands, *Torture Team*, pp. 91–2, 113–4, 123–4

41. Major General Michael Dunlavey, 'Memorandum for Commander, United States Southern Command', 11 October 2002, see: http://www.torturingdemocracy.org/documents/20021011.pdf; William J. Haynes, 'Action Memo for Secretary of Defense', 27 November 2002, see: http://www.torturingdemocracy.org/documents/20021127-1.pdf; Sands, *Torture Team*, pp. 128–31, 137–8

42. Senate Armed Forces Committee, *Inquiry into the Treatment of Detainees*, p. 119–22; OLC, 'Memorandum for William J. Haynes II, General Counsel of the Department of Defense, Re: Military Interrogation of Alien Unlawful Combatants Held Outside the United States,' 14 March 2003, see: http://www.torturingdemocracy.org/documents/20030314.pdf; Secretary of Defense, 'Memorandum for the Commander, US Southern Command,' 16 April 2003, see: http://www.torturingdemocracy.org/documents/20030416.pdf

43. Senate Armed Forces Committee, *Inquiry into the Treatment of Detainees*, pp. 134–48, pp. 143–6 heavily redacted

44. Senate Armed Forces Committee, *Inquiry into the Treatment of Detainees*, pp. 134–5; Lieutenant General Randall Schmidt and Brigadier General John Furlow, *Investigation into FBI Allegations of Detainee Abuse at Guantánamo Bay, Cuba Detention Facility* (Department of Defense, 2005), pp. 9, 10–11, 12, see: http://www.defense.gov/news/Jul2005/d20050714report.pdf; Office of the Inspector General, US Department of Justice (OIG/DoJ), *A Review of the FBI's Involvement in and Observations of Detainee Interrogations in Guantánamo Bay, Afghanistan and Iraq* (2008), pp. 171–3, 179–84, see: http://www.justice.gov/oig/special/s0805/final.pdf

45. Independent Panel, *Final Report*, p. 37

46. Independent Panel, *Final Report*, p. 8; Senate Armed Forces Committee, *Inquiry into the Treatment of Detainees* pp. 151–2; Tim Golden, 'In US Report, Brutal Details of 2 Afghan Inmates' Deaths', *The New York Times*, 20 May 2005, see: http://www.nytimes.com/2005/05/20/international/asia/20abuse.html?_r=1&ex=1274241600&en=4579c146cb14cfd6&ei=5088

47. Senate Armed Forces Committee, *Inquiry into the Treatment of Detainees*, pp. 151, 154–5, p. 158 (quotation), pp. 200–01, 204–6; Independent Panel, *Final Report*, pp. 36–8, 82

48. Independent Panel, *Final Report*, pp. 5, 14, 29-30

49. OIG/CIA, *Special Review*, p. 100

50. OIG/CIA, *Special Review*, p. 8

51. Mayer, *The Dark Side*, pp. 266-9, 281-2, 287-94, 308-10; OLC, 'Memorandum for John A Rizzo, Senior Deputy General Counsel, Central Intelligence Agency' (two memoranda of this title dated 10 May 2005, one dated 30 May 2005), see: http://www.aclu.org/accountability/olc.html In a memorandum written in the closing days of the Bush administration, Bradbury reiterated that a number of OLC opinions issued in 2001-03, including the first Bybee memo of 1 August 2002 and John Yoo's memorandum on military interrogation of 14 March 2003 'do not reflect the current views of this office.' In particular, Bradbury was keen to distance the OLC from the earlier opinions' advocacy of extremely strong Presidential decision-making at the expense of Congress. OLC, 'Memorandum for the Files. Re: Status of Certain OLC Opinions Issued in the Aftermath of the Terrorist Attacks of September 11, 2001', 15 January 2009, see: http://www.gwu.edu/~nsarchiv/torturingdemocracy/documents/20090115.pdf

52. Wittes, *Law and the Long War*, p. 65. The reference to altering doctrine is to a 1950 case (*Johnson v. Eisentrager*) in which the Court ruled against a habeas corpus petition by German prisoners of war who had been convicted of war crimes by a military commission.

53. For an account of this investigative work by one of its foremost practitioners, see Grey, *Ghost*

Plane, pp. 109-25

54. 'Remarks by Secretary of State Condoleezza Rice on her departure for Europe', 5 December 2005, see: http://2001-2009.state.gov/secretary/rm/2005/57602.htm

55. Grey, *Ghost Plane*, pp. 190-213, 267-9; Marty (2006), *Alleged secret detentions*, p. 37; 'CIA agents guilty of Italy kidnap', BBC News Europe, 4 November 2009, see: http://news.bbc.co.uk/1/hi/world/europe/8343123.stm

56. 'President's Speech on the Global war on Terror', 6 September 2006

57. Executive Order 13440 of 20 July, 2007, see: http://www.fas.org/irp/offdocs/eo/eo-13440.htm; 'Bush alters rules for interrogations', Associated Press, 20 July 2007, see: http://www.msnbc.msn.com/id/19873918/; 'Prepared Statement of Steven G. Bradbury, Principal Deputy Assistant Attorney General', 14 February 2008, see: http://judiciary.house.gov/hearings/pdf/Bradbury080214.pdf

58. Scheinin, Nowak et al, *Joint Study on Global Practices,* pp. 68-9, Eric Schmitt and Mark Mazzetti, 'US Relies More on Aid of Allies in Terror Cases', *New York Times*, 23 May 2009, see: http://www.nytimes.com/2009/05/24/world/24intel.html

59. Bill Rammell MP, Hansard, HC Written Answers, 26 November 2008, vol. 483, column 1772W, see: http://www.publications.parliament.uk/pa/cm200708/cmhansrd/cm081126/text/81126w0063.htm; Letter from Rt Hon David Miliband MP to Andrew Tyrie MP, 16 March 2009, see: http://www.extraordinaryrendition.org/index.php/document-library-mainmenu-27/appg-letters/cat_view/35-appg-letters/39-foreign-office?start=10

60. Scheinin, Nowak et al, *Joint Study on Global Practices,* pp. 94-5; Human Rights Watch, *'Why Am I Still Here?' The 2007 Horn of Africa Renditions and the Fate of Those Still Missing* (Human Rights Watch, New York, 2008); see: http://www.hrw.org/en/reports/2008/09/30/why-am-i-still-here-0

61. 'Remarks by the President on National Security', National Archives, Washington DC, 21 May 2009, see: http://www.whitehouse.gov/the_press_office/Remarks-by-the-President-On-National-Security-5-21-09; Wittes, *Law and the Long War*, p. 79; Josh White and Robin Wright, 'After Guantánamo, "Reintegration" for Saudis', *Washington Post*, 10 December 2007, see: http://www.washingtonpost.com/wp-dyn/content/article/2007/12/09/AR2007120901411.html?sid=ST2007121000474

62. Arar Commission (Commission of Inquiry into the Actions of Canadian Officials in Relation to Maher Arar), *Report of the Events Relating to Maher Arar: Analysis and Recommendations* (Public Works and Government Services Canada, Ottawa, 2006), see: http://www.sirc-csars.gc.ca/pdfs/cm_arar_rec-eng.pdf; Mayer, *The Dark Side*, pp. 129-34, 282-7; Grey, *Ghost Plane*, pp. 62-78, 82-102, 264-6; Marty (2006), *Alleged secret detentions*, pp. 25-32, 40-1; *The 9/11 Commission Report*, p. 165

63. Mayer, *The Dark Side*, p. 178. The argument that Abu Zubaydah's significance was exaggerated was first set out in Ron Suskind, *The One Percent Doctrine* (Simon & Schuster, New York, 2006)

64. 'Rove "proud" of US waterboarding terror suspects', BBC News, 12 March 2010; see: http://news.bbc.co.uk/1/hi/8563547.stm

65. John Ashcroft, testimony at 'From the Department of Justice to Guantánamo Bay: Administration lawyers and Administration interrogation rules (Part V)', Hearing before the US House of Representatives Committee on the Judiciary, 17 July 2008, p. 33, see: http://judiciary.house.gov/hearings/printers/110th/43527.PDF

66. 'Transcript: Charlie Rose interviews Michael Hayden'

67. OIG/CIA, *Special Review*, pp. 87-8

68. ISC (2007), *Report on Rendition*, pp. 12, 24

69. OIG/DoJ, *A Review of the FBI's Involvement*, p. 68; Mayer, *The Dark Side*, pp. 155-7

70. OIG/CIA, *Special Review*, p. 85

71. Mayer, *The Dark Side*, pp. 134-8, 178-9. See also Khalid Sheikh Mohammed's comment to the Red Cross that 'I gave a lot of false information in order to satisfy what I believed the interrogators wished to hear in order to make the ill-treatment stop.' ICRC, *ICRC Report on The Treatment of Fourteen "High Value Detainees"*, p. 37

72. Bob Woodward, 'Detainee tortured, says US official', *Washington Post*, 14 January 2009, see: http://www.washingtonpost.com/wp-dyn/content/article/2009/01/13/AR2009011303372.html

Chapter 5: The Obama Aftermath

1. Governor Mario Cuomo, speech at Yale University, 15 February 1985

2. Executive Order 13491, 'Ensuring Lawful Interrogations', 22 January 2009, see: http://www.whitehouse.gov/the_press_office/Ensuring_Lawful_Interrogation
    Executive Order 13492, 'Closing Guantánamo Detention Facilities', 22 January 2009, see: http://www.whitehouse.gov/the_press_office/Closure_Of_Guantanamo_Detention_Facilities
    Executive Order 13493, 'Review of Detention Policy Options', 22 January 2009, see: http://edocket.access.gpo.gov/2009/pdf/E9-1895.pdf

3. 'Remarks by Richard B. Cheney', American Enterprise Institute, 21 May 2009, see: http://www.aei.org/speech/100050

4. Joseph Margulies, letter to *The Economist*, 15 August 2009

5. 'Statement of President Barack Obama on Military Commissions', 15 May 2009, see: http://www.whitehouse.gov/the_press_office/Statement-of-President-Barack-Obama-on-Military-Commissions

6. Charlie Savage, 'Closing Guantánamo Fades as a Priority', *The New York Times*, 25 June 2010, see: http://www.nytimes.com/2010/06/26/us/politics/26gitmo.html?_r=1

7. Anne E. Kornblut and Peter Finn, 'Obama advisers set to recommend military tribunals for alleged 9/11 plotters', *Washington Post*, 5 March 2010, see: http://www.washingtonpost.com/wp-dyn/content/article/2010/03/04/AR2010030405209.html; Associated Press, 'US Stalls On Sept. 11 Trial for 5 At Gitmo', 1 August 2010, see: http://abcnews.go.com/International/wireStory?id=11298211; Anne E. Kornblut and Peter Finn, 'White House undeterred after Ghailani terror case verdict', *Washington Post*, 18 November 2010, see: http://www.washingtonpost.com/wp-dyn/content/article/2010/11/17/AR2010111705663.html?sid=ST2010111706077; The White House, Office of the Press Secretary, 'Fact Sheet: New Actions on Guatánamo and Detainee Policy', 7 March 2011, see: http://www.whitehouse.gov/sites/default/files/Fact_Sheet_--_Guantanamo_and_Detainee_Policy.pdf; Carol Rosenberg, 'Sudanese war criminal turns government witness', *Miami Herald*, 18 February 2011, see: http://www.miamiherald.com/2011/02/18/2074391/sudanese-war-criminal-at-guantanamo.html; Laura Trevelyan, 'Ahmed Ghailani sentence: The future of Guantánmo', BBC News US & Canada, 25 January 2011, see: http://www.bbc.co.uk/news/world-us-canada-12282218

8. Guantánamo Review Task Force, *Final Report* (2010), p. ii, see: http://www.justice.gov/ag/guantanamo-review-final-report.pdf; 'Suspected Taliban commander held at Guantanamo Bay dies after exercising', *The Daily Mail*, 4 February 2011, see http://www.dailymail.co.uk/news/article-1353459/Taliban-commander-Awal-Malim-Gul-dies-exercising-Guantanamo-Bay.html; Executive Order 13567, 'Periodic Review of Individuals Detained at Guantánamo Bay Naval Station Pursuant to the Authorization for Use of Military Force', 7 March 2011, see: http://www.whitehouse.gov/the-press-office/2011/03/07/executive-order-periodic-review-individuals-detained-guant-namo-bay-nava

9. 'Remarks by the President on National Security'

10. Olivia Hampton, 'It's Gitmo Up North', *The Guardian* Comment is Free, 27 December 2009, see: http://www.guardian.co.uk/commentisfree/cifamerica/2009/dec/27/guantanamo-bay-obama-detainees

11. Savage, 'Closing Guantánamo Fades as a Priority'

12. Eric Schmitt, 'US to Expand Detainee Review in Afghan Prison', *New York Times*, 12 September 2009, see: http://www.nytimes.com/2009/09/13/world/asia/13detain.html?_r=2&hpw; Andy Worthington, 'Is Bagram Obama's New Secret Prison?', *Huffington Post* 15 September 2009, see: http://www.huffingtonpost.com/andy-worthington/is-bagram-obamas-new-secr_b_287215.html

13. Hilary Andersson, 'Bagram Airbase', BBC Radio 4, 16 May 2010; Marc Ambinder, 'Inside the Secret Interrogation Facility at Bagram', *The Atlantic*, 14 May 2010, see: http://www.theatlantic.com/politics/archive/2010/05/inside-the-secret-interrogation-facility-at-bagram/56678/

14. CBS News, 'Panetta: No "Extraordinary Rendition"', 5 February 2009, see: http://www.cbsnews.com/stories/2009/02/05/politics/main4777980.shtml?source=related_story

15. Department of Justice News Release, 'Special Task Force on Interrogations and Transfer Policies Issues Its Recommendations to the President', 24 August 2009, see: http://www.justice.gov/opa/pr/2009/August/09-ag-835.html

16. Scott Horton, 'Target of Obama-Era Rendition Alleges Torture', *Huffington Post*, 11 August 2009, see: http://www.huffingtonpost.com/2009/08/11/target-of-obama-era-rendi_n_256499.html

17. American Civil Liberties Union, *America Unrestored: An assessment of the Obama administration's fulfilment of ACLU recommended 'Actions for Restoring America'* (ACLU, Washington, 2010), see: http://www.aclu.org/files/pages/americaunrestored_11_20100119.pdf

18. 'Remarks by the President on national security'

Chapter 6: The Conduct of the Allies

1. Email sent on 5 December 2005, see: http://www.state.gov/documents/organization/125134.pdf

2. Scheuer testimony, p. 21

3. 'Remarks by Secretary of State Condoleezza Rice on her departure for Europe'; Colin Powell, interview with Sir David Frost, BBC World, 18 December 2005

4. Arar Commission, *Report of the Events*, pp. 13-5

5. Marty (2007), *Secret detentions*, pp. 36-7 and n. 158, p. 67

6. Marty (2006), *Alleged secret detentions*, p. 60.

7. Marty (2006), *Alleged secret detentions*, pp. 27-31

8. Amnesty International, *State of Denial*, Case sheet on Khaled el-Masri; Marty (2006), *Alleged secret detentions*, pp. 30-1

9. Scheinin, Nowak et al, *Joint Study on Global Practices*, p. 98

10. Grey, *Ghost Plane*, pp. 212, 269; Scheinin, Nowak et al, *Joint Study on Global Practices*, p. 100

11. Dana Priest, 'CIA Holds Terror Suspects in Secret Prisons', *Washington Post*, 2 December 2005, see: http://www.washingtonpost.com/wp-dyn/content/article/2005/11/01/AR2005110101644.html

12. Marty (2007), *Secret detentions*, pp. 25, 36-8

13. Marty (2007), *Secret detentions*, p. 25; Scheinin, Nowak et al, *Joint Study on Global Practices*, pp. 58-62; Open Society Justice Initiative (2010), 'Fresh Evidence Shows Polish Government, CIA Cooperation on Renditions', Press release, with flight records and interpretation, 22 February 2010, see: http://www.soros.org/initiatives/justice/focus/foi/news/poland-rendition-20100222; Nicholas Kulish and Scott Shane, 'Flight Data Show Rendition Planes Landed in Poland', *New York Times*, 22 February 2010, see: http://www.nytimes.com/2010/02/23/world/europe/23poland.html; Rafal Kiepuszewski, 'Polish prosecutors to investigate CIA black site torture allegations', *Deutsche Welle*, 7 October 2010, see: http://www.dw-world.de/dw/article/0,,6091363,00.html

14. Scheinin, Nowak et al, *Joint Study on Global Practices*, pp. 59-61; ICRC, *ICRC Report on The Treatment of Fourteen "High Value Detainees"*, pp. 33-5; Daniel Sandford, 'Europe's Secret Prisons', BBC News Channel, 9 October 2010

15. Marty (2007), *Secret detentions*, pp. 39-40; Sandford, 'Europe's Secret Prisons'

16. Marty (2007), *Secret detentions*, pp. 25-6: Scheinin, Nowak et al, *Joint Study on Global Practices*, pp. 57, 61-2

17. Scheinin, Nowak et al, *Joint Study on Global Practices*, pp. 62-6; Sandford, 'Europe's Secret Prisons'; Amnesty International, 'Lithuania Must Reopen CIA Secret Prison Investigation', 18 January 2011, see: http://www.amnesty.org/en/news-and-updates/lithuania-must-reopen-cia-secret-prison-investigation-2011-01-18

18. Scheinin, Nowak et al, *Joint Study on Global Practices*, pp. 54-6; Marty (2007), *Secret detentions*, p. 16 and n. 27

19. Marty (2006), *Alleged secret detentions*, pp. 16, 37; Grey, *Ghost Plane*, p. 100

Chapter 7: 'More Than a Bystander': The British Role

1. Rt Hon Jack Straw MP, House of Commons Foreign Affairs Select Committee, Uncorrected Oral Evidence, 13 December 2005, see: http://www.publications.parliament.uk/pa/cm200506/cmselect/cmfaff/uc768-i/uc76802.htm.

2. Rt Hon David Miliband MP, Oral Statement, 'Terrorist Suspects (Renditions)', Hansard, HC Deb, 21 February 2008, vol. 472, col. 547, see: http://www.publications.parliament.uk/pa/cm200708/cmhansrd/cm080221/debtext/80221-0007.htm#08022198000007

3. Letter from Dr Kim Howells MP to Andrew Tyrie MP, 19 October 2006, see 'Letter from Kim Howells 19.10.06' at http://www.extraordinaryrendition.org/index.php/appg-letters-on-extraordinary-rendition/foreign-office?start=40; ISC (2007), *Report on Rendition*, p. 16

4. Rt Hon Jack Straw MP, Hansard, HC Written Answers, 12 December 2005, vol. 440, col. 1652W, see: http://www.publications.parliament.uk/pa/cm200506/cmhansrd/vo051212/text/51212w19.htm.

5. Rt Hon Jack Straw MP, Hansard, HC Written Statements, 'Rendition: Additional Information', 10 January 2006, vol. 441, col. 5WS, see: http://www.publications.parliament.uk/pa/cm200506/cmhansrd/vo060110/wmstext/60110m01.htm#60110m01.html_sbhd3.

6. Foreign Office Memorandum to 10 Downing Street, 7 December 2005

7. ISC (2007), *Report on Rendition*, p. 16; Foreign Office Memorandum to 10 Downing Street, 7 December 2005

8. Rt Hon Jack Straw MP, Hansard, HC Written Statements, 'Rendition Allegations (Inquiries)', 20 January 2006, vol. 441, col. 38WS, see: http://www.publications.parliament.uk/pa/cm200506/cmhansrd/vo060120/wmstext/60120m01.htm#60120m01.html_sbhd2

9. Rt Hon Jack Straw MP, Letter to Rt Hon William Hague MP, 6 February 2006; ISC (2007), *Report on Rendition*, p. 61

10. Human Rights Watch, 'Letter to Prime Minister Tony Blair', 30 December 2002, see: http://www.hrw.org/en/news/2002/12/30/letter-prime-minister-tony-blair; Ian Cobain, 'Is there a CIA prison on Diego Garcia?', *The Guardian* News Blog, 19 October 2007, see: http://www.guardian.co.uk/news/blog/2007/oct/19/isthereaciaprisonondiego1; Jamie Doward, 'British island 'used by US for rendition'', *The Observer*, 2 March 2008, see: http://www.guardian.co.uk/world/2008/mar/02/ciarendition.unitednations; email from General McCaffrey to Stuart McCracken, 16 January 2008

11. Rt Hon Jack Straw MP, Hansard, HC Written Answers, 21 June 2004, vol. 422, col. 1221W:

http://www.publications.parliament.uk/pa/cm200304/cmhansrd/vo040621/text/40621w13.htm#40621w13.html_wqn9

12. Richard Norton-Taylor, 'Records show Diego Garcia link to alleged torture flights', *The Guardian*, 4 January 2007, see: http://www.guardian.co.uk/uk/2007/jan/04/usa.world; Marty (2007), *Secret detentions*, p. 16

13. Meg Munn MP, Hansard, HC Written Answers, 11 October 2007, vol. 464, col. 703W: http://www.publications.parliament.uk/pa/cm200607/cmhansrd/cm071011/text/71011w0006.htm#07101133000060

14. Letter from Dr Kim Howells MP to Andrew Tyrie MP, November 2007, see 'Correspondence on David Miliband's Conference speech' at. http://www.extraordinaryrendition.org/index.php/appg-letters-on-extraordinary-rendition/foreign-office?start=35

15. Ian Cobain and Richard Norton-Taylor, 'Claims of secret CIA jail for terror suspects on British island to be investigated', *The Guardian*, 19 October 2007, see: http://www.guardian.co.uk/world/2007/oct/19/alqaida.usa

16. Rt Hon David Miliband MP, Oral Statement, 'Terrorist Suspects (Renditions)', 21 February 2008

17. The documents were released to the APPG in September 2008, see 'Diego Garcia assurances – FCO – 02.09.08' at: http://www.extraordinaryrendition.org/index.php/appg-letters-on-extraordinary-rendition/foreign-office?start=20

18. Bill Rammell MP, Hansard, HC Written Answers, 11 February 2009, vol. 487, col. 2002W, see: http://www.publications.parliament.uk/pa/cm200809/cmhansrd/cm090211/text/90211w0007.htm#09021189000154

19. Reprieve, 'Reprieve Announces Legal Action Against British Government', 28 July 2009, see: http://www.reprieve.org.uk/mohammedsaadiqbalmadniactionagainstbritishgov; APPG, 'Madni Action Press Release', 28 July 2009, see: http://www.extraordinaryrendition.org/index.php/extraordinary-rendition-press-releases/cat_view/27-press-releases/55-2009

20. *R (Madni) v Secretary of State for Foreign and Commonwealth Affairs*, Claim No. CO/9212/2009, see: http://www.reprieve.org.uk/static/downloads/2010_03_04_Madni_secret_evidence_argument.pdf; Peter Walker, 'Man claiming torture believes British agent was present, court hears', *The Guardian*, 5 March 2010, see: http://www.guardian.co.uk/world/2010/mar/04/terror-detainee-english-intelligence-court; Clive Stafford Smith, 'Another mess on Miliband's doorstep', *The Guardian* Comment is Free, 5 March 2010, see: http://www.guardian.co.uk/commentisfree/libertycentral/2010/mar/04/saad-madni-rendition-torture

21. Foreign Affairs Select Committee, *Human Rights Annual Report 2008*, Seventh Report 2008-09, (21 July 2009), pp. 25-8, see: http://www.publications.parliament.uk/pa/cm200809/cmselect/cmfaff/557/557.pdf

22. Jamie Doward, 'British island 'used by US for rendition'', *The Observer*, 2 March 2008, see: http://www.guardian.co.uk/world/2008/mar/02/ciarendition.unitednations; Adam Zagorin, 'Source: US Used UK Isle for Interrogations', *Time*, 31 July 2008, see: http://www.time.com/time/world/article/0,8599,1828469,00.html

23. Scheinin, Nowak et al, *Joint Study on Global Practices*, pp. 66-8; BBC 2, *Newsnight*, 31 July 2008, see: http://news.bbc.co.uk/1/hi/programmes/newsnight/7536477.stm

24. Joint Committee on Human Rights, *Report on the UN Convention against Torture*, Nineteenth Report 2005-06, 26 May 2006, paragraphs 168, 170, see: http://www.publications.parliament.uk/pa/jt200506/jtselect/jtrights/185/18511.htm

25. Rt Hon David Miliband MP, Oral Statement, 'Terrorist Suspects (Renditions)', 21 February 2008

26. Rt Hon David Miliband MP, Oral Statement, 'Terrorist Suspects (Renditions)', 21 February 2008

27. Foreign Affairs Select Committee, *Human Rights Annual Report 2007*, Ninth Report 2007-08, (20 July 2008), p. 23, see: http://www.publications.parliament.uk/pa/cm200708/cmselect/cmfaff/533/53306.htm#a8

28. Marty (2006), *Alleged secret detentions*, pp. 16-18; Grey, *Ghost Plane*, pp. 230-1

29. ISC (2007), *Report on Rendition*, pp. 57-8

30. Stop the War Coalition, 'Former SAS soldier blows apart Miliband denial of UK torture involvement', 25 February 2008, see: http://www.stopwar.org.uk/index.php?option=com_content&task=view&id=533

31. Commonwealth of Australia, Official Committee *Hansard*, Senate Foreign Affairs, Defence and Trade Legislation Committee, 31 May 2004, pp. 163-4, see: http://www.aph.gov.au/hansard/senate/commttee/S7646.pdf

32. Rt Hon Des Browne MP, Hansard, HC Written Answers, 5 December 2007, vol. 468, col. 1224W, see: http://www.publications.parliament.uk/pa/cm200708/cmhansrd/cm071205/text/71205w0004.htm#07120552000518

33. Letter from Rt Hon Des Browne MP to Andrew Tyrie MP, 31 January 2008, see 'Correspondence with Des Browne re Guantánamo' at: http://www.extraordinaryrendition.org/index.php/appg-letters-on-extraordinary-rendition/ministry-of-defence?start=15

34. Oral Evidence before the Defence and Foreign Affairs Select Committees, 28 October 2008, Questions 21 to 29, see; http://www.publications.parliament.uk/pa/cm200708/cmselect/cmdfence/1145/8102803.htm,

35. Rt Hon John Hutton MP, Oral Statement, 'Records of Detention (Review Conclusions),' Hansard, HC Deb, 26 February 2009, vol. 488, col. 394, see: http://www.publications.parliament.uk/pa/cm200809/cmhansrd/cm090226/debtext/90226-0008.htm; Rt Hon Bob Ainsworth MP, Hansard, HC Written Answers, 6 July 2009, vol. 495, col. 549W, see: http://www.publications.parliament.uk/pa/cm200809/cmhansrd/cm090706/text/90706w0010.htm#09070625001976; Foreign Affairs Select Committee, *Human Rights Annual Report 2008*, p. 53. With respect to MPs' unease, the Liberal Democrat Nick Harvey warned that, 'The statement raises almost as many questions as it answers' while the Conservative spokesman Crispin Blunt argued that it 'avoids the principal public issue, which is the charge about complicity by UK forces operating in Iraq outside the Multi-National Division (South-East)'.

36. Rt Hon John Hutton MP, Oral Statement, 'Records of Detention (Review Conclusions)', 26 February 2009; Rt Hon Bob Ainsworth MP, Written Answer, 6 July 2010

37. ISC (2007), *Report on Rendition*, pp. 64-7

38. Open statement of Security Service Witness 'A', dated 14 March 2006, in *R (Al Rawi and others) v Secretary of State for Foreign and Commonwealth Affairs and Another* [2006] EWHC 972 (Admin), see: http://www.bailii.org/cgi-bin/markup.cgi?doc=/ew/cases/EWCA/Civ/2006/1279.html, cited in ISC (2007), *Report into Rendition*, p. 36

39. 'Note for file: meeting with Abu ANAS', 31 October 2009, see 'Documents released to APPG by Foreign Office' at: http://www.extraordinaryrendition.org/index.php/information-sessions/bisher-al-rawi-a-jamil-el-banna

40. David Rose, 'I helped MI5. My reward: brutality and prison', *The Observer*, 29 July 2007, see: http://www.guardian.co.uk/world/2007/jul/29/usa.guantanamo; George B. Mickum, 'MI5, Camp Delta and the Story that Shames Britain', *The Guardian*, 16 March 2005, see: http://www.independent.co.uk/news/world/americas/mi5-camp-delta-and-the-story-that-shames-britain-470074.html

41. 'Out-telegram: Detention of Islamists at Gatwick Airport', 1 November 2002, see 'Documents released to APPG by Foreign Office' at: http://www.extraordinaryrendition.org/index.php/information-sessions/bisher-al-rawi-a-jamil-el-banna

42. ISC (2007), *Report on Rendition*, pp. 37-8

43. Gareth Peirce, memo for APPG Information Session 'Bisher al-Rawi, Jamil el-Banna and Rendition', 27 March 2006, see 'Information Session: BRIEFING PACK' at: http://www.extraordinaryrendition.org/index.php/information-sessions/bisher-al-rawi-a-jamil-el-banna?start=5

44. 'Out-telegram: Travellers to Gambia', 4 November 2002, see 'Documents released to APPG by Foreign Office' at: http://www.extraordinaryrendition.org/index.php/information-sessions/bisher-al-rawi-a-jamil-el-banna

45. 'Out-telegram: Individuals Travelling to Gambia', 4 November 2002

46. ISC (2007), *Report on Rendition*, pp. 41-3

47. George B. Mickum, 'MI5, Camp Delta …'; Bisher al-Rawi (Internment Serial Number 906), CSRT Records Publicly Filed with the US District Court for the District of Columbia, p. 4116, The Office of the Secretary of Defense and Joint Staff Reading Room, *Combatant Status Review Tribunal (CSRT) and Administrative Review Board (ARB) Documents*, see: http://www.dod.mil/pubs/foi/detainees/csrt_arb/

48. ISC (2007), *Report on Rendition*, p. 45

49. APPG, 'Briefing note prepared by George Mickum', March 2006, see: http://www.extraordinaryrendition.org/index.php/information-sessions/bisher-al-rawi-a-jamil-el-banna?start=5; Judgment in *R (al-Rawi and Others) v. Secretary of State for Foreign and Commonwealth Affairs and Another*, paragraph 7

50. ISC (2007), *Report on Rendition*, p. 43

51. ISC (2007), *Report on Rendition*, p. 46

52. *R (B Mohamed) v Secretary of State for Foreign and Commonwealth Affairs*, Open Judgment (21 August 2008) as revised on 31 July 2009, [2008] EWHC 2048 (Admin), [2009] 1 WLR 2579, paragraphs 7, 8, 10, 47(i), see: http://www.bailii.org/ew/cases/EWHC/Admin/2008/2048.pdf; Grey, *Ghost Plane*, pp. 45-53; OIG/CIA, *Special Review*, p. 87

53. Stafford Smith, *Bad Men*, pp. 49-80

54. *R (B Mohamed) v Secretary of State for Foreign and Commonwealth Affairs*, Open Judgment, paragraph 88(5)

55. ISC (2007), *Report on Rendition*, p. 68

56. *R (B Mohamed) v Secretary of State for Foreign and Commonwealth Affairs*, Open Judgment, paragraphs 12-17

57. *R (B Mohamed) v Secretary of State for Foreign and Commonwealth Affairs*, Court of Appeal Judgment 10 February 2010, [2010] EWCA Civ 65, Appendix, see: http://www.bailii.org/ew/cases/EWCA/Civ/2010/65.html

58. *R (B Mohamed) v Secretary of State for Foreign and Commonwealth Affairs*, Open Judgment, paragraph 87(iv) – (vii)

59. ISC, *Annual Report 2008-09* (March 2010), p. 45

60. *R (B Mohamed) v Secretary of State for Foreign and Commonwealth Affairs*, Open Judgment, paragraphs 20-1, 26(v)

61. Grey, *Ghost Plane*, pp. 57-9

62. *R (B Mohamed) v Secretary of State for Foreign and Commonwealth Affairs*, Open Judgment,

paragraphs 29-30

63. *R (B Mohamed) v Secretary of State for Foreign and Commonwealth Affairs,* Open Judgment, paragraphs 32 and 88(iv)

64. *R (B Mohamed) v Secretary of State for Foreign and Commonwealth Affairs,* Open Judgment, paragraphs 88 and 35 (a)

65. Vanessa Allen, 'MI5 'used Muslim 007' to turn British torture victim in Moroccan prison', *Mail on Sunday*, 18 May 2009, see: http://www.dailymail.co.uk/news/article-1183183/MI5-used-Muslim-007-turn-British-torture-victim-Moroccan-prison.html; Andy Worthington, 'What the British Government Knew About The Torture Of Binyam Mohamed', 5 August 2009, see: http://www.andyworthington.co.uk/2009/08/05/what-the-british-government-knew-about-the-torture-of-binyam-mohamed/

66. Kim Sengupta, ''24', a diplomatic row and a spy chief's lecture on torture', *The Independent*, 11 March 2010, see: http://www.independent.co.uk/news/world/americas/24-a-diplomatic-row-and-a-spy-chiefs-lecture-on-torture-1919444.html

67. ISC, *The Handling of Detainees by UK Intelligence Personnel in Afghanistan, Guantánamo Bay and Iraq* (March 2005), pp. 13-4, 30-2, see: http://isc.independent.gov.uk/committee-reports/special-reports; ISC (2007), *Report on Rendition*, p. 26 and n. 65

68. Rt Hon Gordon Brown MP, Hansard, HC Written Statements, 'Detainees', 18 March 2009, vol. 489, col. 55WS, see: http://www.publications.parliament.uk/pa/cm200809/cmhansrd/cm090318/wmstext/90318m0001.htm#09031892000039

69. ISC press release on its 2008-09 Annual Report, 11 March 2010, see: http://isc.independent.gov.uk/news-archive/11march2010; and on its 2009-10 Annual Report, 18 March 2010, see: http://isc.independent.gov.uk/news-archive/18march2010; Letter from the Chairman of the ISC, Rt Hon Dr Kim Howells MP, to Human Rights Watch, 19 February 2010, see: http://www.extraordinaryrendition.org/index.php/appg-letters-on-extraordinary-rendition/uk-committees

70. Rt Hon David Cameron MP, Oral Statement, 'Treatment of Detainees', Hansard, HC Deb, 6 July 2010, col. 175, see: http://www.publications.parliament.uk/pa/cm201011/cmhansrd/cm100706/debtext/100706-0001.htm#10070631000625; Cabinet Office, *Consolidated Guidance to Intelligence Officers and Service Personnel on the Detention and Interviewing of Detainees Overseas, and on the Passing and Receipt of Intelligence Relating to Detainee*s (July 2010), see: http://download.cabinetoffice.gov.uk/intelligence/consolidated-guidance-iosp.pdf

71. *Al Rawi and others v Security Service and others,* Claim Nos. HQ08X01180/HQ08X01413/HQ08X01416/HQ08X03220/HQ08X01686, Exhibit SM22, see: http://www.reprieve.org.uk/2010_07_14_al_rawi_court_revelations

72. Philippe Sands QC, quoted in Ian Cobain, 'The truth about torture', *The Guardian*, 8 July 2009, see: http://www.guardian.co.uk/politics/2009/jul/08/mi5-mi6-acccused-of-torture

73. The Attorney General (Baroness Scotland of Asthal), Hansard, HL Written Statements, 'Binyam Mohamed', 26 March 2009, vol. 709, col. WS51, see: http://www.publications.parliament.uk/pa/ld200809/ldhansrd/text/90326-wms0001.htm#09032631000003; James Sturcke, 'Police launch investigation into Binyam Mohamed torture allegations', *The Guardian*, 10 July 2009, see: http://www.guardian.co.uk/world/2009/jul/10/binyam-mohamed-torture-investigation-police; Ian Cobain, 'Police investigate MI5 officer who interrogated Binyam Mohamed', *The Guardian*, 11 February 2010, see: http://www.guardian.co.uk/uk/2010/feb/11/mi5-binyam-mohamed; Crown Prosecution Service press release, 'CPS Decision on Witness B', 17 November 2010, see: http://www.cps.gov.uk/news/press_releases/141_10/

74. *Shaker Aamer v. Secretary of State for Foreign and Commonwealth Affairs* [2009] EWHC 3316

(Admin); Richard Norton-Taylor and Vikram Dodd, 'Police investigate claim MI5 was complicit in Shaker Aamer's torture', *The Guardian*, 19 February 2010, see: http://www.guardian.co.uk/uk/2010/feb/19/police-claims-shaker-aamer-torture-mi5-complicit; Ian Cobain and Richard Norton-Taylor, 'Police to interview last Briton in Guantánamo over 'torture'', The Guardian, 20 November 2010, see: http://www.guardian.co.uk/world/2010/nov/20/shaker-aamer-interview-guantanamo

75. Cobain, 'The truth about torture'; Scheinin, Nowak et al, *Joint Study on Global Practices*, pp. 97-8; Rt Hon David Davis MP, 'Government Policy (Torture Overseas)', Hansard, HC Deb, 7 July 2009, vol. 495, cols. 940-3, see: http://www.publications.parliament.uk/pa/cm200809/cmhansrd/cm090707/debtext/90707-0020.htm#09070793000426

76. *R (B Mohamed) v Secretary of State for Foreign and Commonwealth Affairs*, Court of Appeal Judgment 26 February 2010, [2010] EWCA Civ 158, paragraphs 18 and 29, see: http://www.bailii.org/ew/cases/EWCA/Civ/2010/158.html

77. *R (B Mohamed) v Secretary of State for Foreign and Commonwealth Affairs*, Approved Judgment 4, High Court, 4 February 2009, [2009] EWHC 152 (Admin), paragraphs 88 and 90; http://www.judiciary.gov.uk/docs/judgments_guidance/mohamed-judgment4-04022009.pdf; Richard Norton-Taylor and Ian Cobain, 'MPs step up demands for inquiry into MI5 torture claims', *The Guardian*, 15 March 2010, see: http://www.guardian.co.uk/uk/2010/mar/15/inquiry-calls-mi5-torture-row; *ISC Annual Report 2009-10* contains (p. 4) complaints about encroachment on its independence; for the report and government response to it, 18 March 2010, see: http://isc.independent.gov.uk/committee-reports/annual-reports

78. *Al Rawi and others v Security Service and others*, Exhibit SM21

79. FCO Memorandum, 'Afghanistan: UK detainees', 10 January 2002, *Al Rawi and others v Security Service and others*, Exhibit LC13

80. FCO Telegram, 'Afghanistan: Detainees', 17 January 2002, *Al Rawi and others v Security Service and others*, Exhibit SM21

81. FCO Memorandum, 'UK Nationals Held in Afghanistan and Guantánamo', 18 January 2002, see: http://news.bbc.co.uk/1/shared/bsp/hi/pdfs/blair29092010.pdf

82. Note by Stuart Horlock, 'John Gieve's Meeting with Sir Anthony Jay, 12 April 2002, *Al Rawi and others v Security Service and others*, Exhibit SM21

83. Note by Stuart Horlock, 'UK Nationals Held in Guantánamo Bay', 26 February 2002, *Al Rawi and others v Security Service and others*, Exhibit SM21

84. Declaration by Colonel Lawrence B. Wilkerson (ret.), p. 3

85. Letter from Eliza Manningham-Buller to John Gieve, 27 March 2002; 'Loose Minute: Martin Mubanga: Interviews', 2 April 2002, *Al Rawi and others v Security Service and others*, Exhibit LC14. Mubanga's account is in David Rose, 'How I entered the hellish world of Guantánamo Bay', *The Observer*, 6 February 2005, see: http://www.guardian.co.uk/uk/2005/feb/06/world.guantanamo

86. 'Note for File: MUBANGA: Background to case', 22 August 2002, *Al Rawi and others v Security Service and others*, Exhibit LC13. The redaction leaves unclear whether the desire to interrogate Mubanga was conveyed to the Kenyans or the Americans

87. 'Loose Minute: Martin Mubanga: Interviews', 2 April 2002, *Al Rawi and others v Security Service and others*, Exhibit LC14

88. Letter from Eliza Manningham-Buller to John Gieve, 27 March 2002

89. Telegram 123 from Lusaka to FCO, 22 May 2002, *Al Rawi and others v Security Service and others*, Exhibit SM20; 'Note for File: MUBANGA: Background to case', 22 August 2002

90. Telegram 123 from Lusaka to FCO, 22 May 2002; email from FCO Consular Division, 15

August 2002, *Al Rawi and others v Security Service and others,* Exhibit SM20

91. Out-Telegram, 26 March 2002, *Al Rawi and others v Security Service and others,* Exhibit LC14; ISC (2007), *Report on Rendition,* pp. 31-2

92. Email from Lusaka to FCO, 13 August 2002, *Al Rawi and others v Security Service and others,* Exhibit SM20; ISC (2007), *Report on Rendition,* p. 32

93. Stafford Smith, *Bad Men,* pp. 10, 226, 258-60 ; Patrick Barkham, 'How I fought to survive Guantánamo', *The Guardian,* 21 January 2010, see: http://www.guardian.co.uk/world/2010/jan/21/i-fought-to-survive-guantanamo

94. Out-Telegram, 21 June 2002, *Al Rawi and others v Security Service and others,* Exhibit LC15; Telegram, 26 June 2002 and Prisoner Interview Report, 5 July 2002, *Al Rawi and others v Security Service and others,* Exhibits LC13 and (one page) LC15; Stafford Smith, *Bad Men,* pp. 254-6; The Office of the Secretary of Defense and Joint Staff Reading Room, *CSRT and ARB Documents,* CSRT Summary of Evidence for Omar Deghayes, 27 September 2004, Unclassified Summary of Evidence for ARB Round One, 24 May 2005, for Round Two, 8 August 2006, and for Round Three, 14 August 2007, ARB transcript 3 June 2005

95. Out-Telegram, 21 June 2002; Barkham, 'How I fought to survive Guantánamo'

96. Telegram, 26 June 2002 and Prisoner Interview Report, 5 July 2002

97. Telegrams 5 and 12 July 2002, *Al Rawi and others v Security Service and others,* Exhibit LC13

Bibliography

Books and articles

Matthew Alexander with John R. Bruning, *How to Break a Terrorist: The U.S. Interrogators Who Used Brains, Not Brutality, to Take Down the Deadliest Man in Iraq* (New York: Free Press, 2008)

Richard A. Clarke, *Against All Enemies: Inside America's War on Terror* (New York: Free Press, 2004)

Duane R. Clarridge with Digby Diehl, *A Spy for All Seasons: My Life in the CIA* (New York: Scribner, 1997)

Steve Coll, *Ghost Wars: The Secret History of the CIA, Afghanistan and Bin Laden, from the Soviet Invasion to September 10, 2001* (New York: Penguin, 2004)

Alberto Costi, 'Problems with Current International and National Practices Concerning Extraterritorial Abductions', *Yearbook of the New Zealand Association for Comparative Law*, Volume 8 (2002)

Alan M Dershowitz, 'The Torture Warrant: A Response to Professor Strauss', *New York Law School Law Review*, Volume 48 (2003)

Jack Goldsmith, *The Terror Presidency: Law and Judgement Inside the Bush Administration* (New York: Norton, 2007)

Stephen Grey, *Ghost Plane: The True Story of the CIA Rendition and Torture Program* (New York: St Martin's Griffin, 2007)

Jane Mayer, *The Dark Side: The Inside Story of How the War on Terror turned into a War on American Ideals* (revised edition) (New York: Anchor Books, 2009)

Gregory S. McNeal and Brian J. Field, 'Snatch and Grab Ops: Justifying Extraterritorial Abduction', *University of Iowa: Journal of Transnational Law and Contemporary Problems* 16.9 (2007)

Philippe Sands, *Torture Team: Deception, cruelty and the compromise of law* (London: Penguin, 2008)

Margaret L. Satterthwaite, 'The Legal Regime Governing Transfer of Persons in the Fight Against Terrorism', *NYU School of Law, Public Law Research Paper No. 10-27* (2010)

George P. Shultz, *Turmoil and Triumph: My Years as Secretary of State* (New York: Scribner, 1993)

Clive Stafford Smith, *Bad Men: Guantanamo Bay And The Secret Prisons* (London: Weidenfeld & Nicolson, 2007)

Ron Suskind, *The One Percent Solution* (New York: Simon & Schuster, 2006)

Benjamin Wittes, *Law and the Long War: The Future of Justice in the Age of Terror* (New York: Penguin, 2008)

Congressional and other Hearings and Reports (US)

House Committee on Foreign Affairs, Joint Hearing of subcommittees on 'Extraordinary Rendition in US counterterrorism policy: The Impact on Transatlantic Relations', 17 April 2007 (testimony by Julianne Smith and Michael Scheuer)

House Committee on the Judiciary, Hearing on 'From the Department of Justice to Guantánamo Bay: Administration lawyers and Administration interrogation rules (Part V)', 17 July 2008 (testimony by John Ashcroft, Benjamin Wittes and Walter Dellinger)

House Committee on the Judiciary, Subcommittee on the Constitution, Civil Rights, and Civil Liberties, 14 February 2008 (prepared statement of Steven G. Bradbury)

The National Commission on Terrorist Attacks Upon the United States, Eighth Public Hearing, 23-24 March 2004 (including testimony by George J. Tenet, Sandy Berger and Richard A. Clarke)

Senate Committee on Armed Forces, *Inquiry into the Treatment of Detainees in US Custody* (20 November 2008)

Senate Select Committee on Intelligence, Statement by Director of Central Intelligence George J. Tenet on 'The Worldwide Threat in 2000: Global Realities of Our National Security', 21 March 2000

—. Hearing on 'Current and projected threats to the national security of the United States', 5 February 2008 (testimony by General Michael Hayden)

Senate Select Committee on Intelligence and House Permanent Select Committee on Intelligence, Joint Inquiry on 'US Government Counterterrorism Organizations (Before September 11, 2001) and on the Evolution of the Terrorist Threat and US Response, 1986-2001' (testimony by Richard A. Clarke)

Official documents (US)

Department of Defense, Independent Panel To Review DoD Detention Operations, *Final Report* (August 2004)

Department of State, *Egypt Country Report on Human Rights Practices for 1998* (February 1999)

Departments of Justice, Defense, State, Homeland Security, Office of the Director of National Intelligence and Joint Chiefs of Staff, Guantánamo Review Task Force, *Final Report* (January 2010)

Executive Order 13440, *Interpretation of the Geneva Conventions Common Article 3 as Applied to a Program of Detention and Interrogation Operated by the Central Intelligence Agency* (President George W Bush, 20 July 2007)

Executive Order 13491, *Ensuring Lawful Interrogations* (President Barack Obama, 22 January 2009)

Executive Order 13492, *Closing Guantánamo Detention Facilities* (President Barack Obama, 22 January 2009)

Executive Order 13493, *Review of Detention Policy Options* (President Barack Obama, 22 January 2009)

Executive Order 13567, *Periodic Review of Individuals Detained at Guantánamo Bay Naval Station Pursuant to the Authorization for Use of Military Force* (President Barack Obama, 7 March 2011)

National Security Decision Directive 207 (NSDD-207), *The National Program for Combating Terrorism* (President Ronald Reagan, 20 January 1986)

Office of Inspector General, Central Intelligence Agency, *Special Review: Counterterrorism Detention and Interrogation Activities (September 2001-October 2003)* (7 May 2004)

Office of the Inspector General, US Department of Justice, *A Review of the FBI's Involvement in and Observations of Detainee Interrogations in Guantánamo Bay, Afghanistan and Iraq* (May 2008)

Presidential Decision Directive 39 (PDD-39), *U.S. Policy on Counterterrorism* (President William J. Clinton, 21 June 1995)

Presidential Decision Directive 62 (PDD-62), *Protection Against Unconventional Threats to the Homeland and Americans Overseas* (President William J. Clinton, 22 May 1998)

Lieutenant General Randall Schmidt and Brigadier General John Furlow, *Investigation into FBI Allegations of Detainee Abuse at Guantánamo Bay, Cuba Detention Facility* (9 June 2005)

Parliamentary Hearings, Reports and Official Documents (UK and Australia)

All Party Parliamentary Group on Extraordinary Rendition, *Extraordinary Rendition: Closing the Gap. A Proposal to Criminalise UK Involvement* (November 2009)

Cabinet Office, *Consolidated Guidance to Intelligence Officers and Service Personnel on the Detention and Interviewing of Detainees Overseas, and on the Passing and Receipt of Intelligence Relating to Detainees* (July 2010)

Commonwealth of Australia, Official Committee *Hansard*, Senate Foreign Affairs, Defence and Trade Legislation Committee, 31 May 2004

Foreign Affairs Select Committee, Oral Evidence (Rt Hon Jack Straw MP), 'Developments in the European Union', 13 December 2005

—. *Human Rights Annual Report 2007*, Ninth Report 2007-08 (20 July 2008)

—. *Human Rights Annual Report 2008*, Seventh Report 2008-09 (21 July 2009)

Foreign and Commonwealth Office, *Annual Report on Human Rights 2008* (March 2009)

Intelligence and Security Committee, *The Handling of Detainees by UK Intelligence Personnel in Afghanistan, Guantánamo Bay and Iraq* (March 2005)

—. *Report on Rendition* (July 2007)

—. *Annual Report 2008-09* (March 2010)

—. *Annual Report 2009-10* (March 2010)

Joint Committee on Human Rights, *Report on the UN Convention against Torture*, Nineteenth Report 2005-06 (26 May 2006)

—. *Counter-Terrorism Policy and Human Rights (Seventeenth Report): Bringing Human Rights Back In,* Sixteenth Report 2009-10 (25 March 2010)

Other reports

American Civil Liberties Union, *America Unrestored: An assessment of the Obama administration's fulfilment of ACLU recommended 'Actions for Restoring America'* (Washington: ACLU, 2010)

Amnesty International, *State of Denial: Europe's role in rendition and secret detention* (London: Amnesty International Publications, 2008)

—. *Open Secret: Mounting evidence of Europe's complicity in rendition and secret detention* (London: Amnesty International Publications, 2010)

Arar Commission (Commission of Inquiry into the Actions of Canadian Officials in Relation to Maher Arar), *Report of the Events Relating to Maher Arar: Analysis and Recommendations* (Public Works and Government Services Canada, Ottawa, 2006)

Eminent Jurists Panel, *Assessing Damage, Urging Action: Report of the Eminent Jurists Panel on Terrorism, Counter-terrorism and Human Rights* (International Commission of Jurists, Geneva, 2009)

Giovanni Claudio Fava (rapporteur), *Report on the alleged use of European countries by the CIA for the transportation and illegal detention of prisoners* (Temporary Committee of the European Parliament, 2007); European Parliament resolution based on this adopted 14 February 2007, P6_TA(2007)0032

Human Rights Watch, *'Why Am I Still Here?' The 2007 Horn of Africa Renditions and the Fate of Those Still Missing* (Human Rights Watch, New York, 2008)

International Committee of the Red Cross, *ICRC Report on The Treatment of Fourteen "High Value Detainees" in CIA Custody* (ICRC, 2007)

Dick Marty (rapporteur), *Alleged secret detentions and unlawful inter-state transfers involving Council of Europe member states: report* (Committee on Legal Affairs and Human Rights, Council of Europe, Strasbourg, 2006)

—. *Secret detentions and illegal transfers of detainees involving Council of Europe member states: second report* (Committee on Legal Affairs and Human Rights, Council of Europe, Strasbourg, 2007)

Redress, *The United Kingdom, Torture and Anti-Terrorism: Where the Problems Lie* (London: The Redress Trust, 2008)

Martin Scheinin, Manfred Nowak, the Working Group on Arbitrary Detention and the Working Group on Enforced and Involuntary Disappearances (2010), *Joint Study on Global Practices in relation to secret detention in the context of countering terrorism* (United Nations Human Rights Council, 2010)

International Treaties

Convention against Torture and Other Cruel, Inhuman or Degrading Treatment or Punishment, New York, 10 December 1984, No. 24841 United Nations, *Treaty Series*, vol. 1465, p. 85

U.S. reservations, declarations, and understandings, Convention Against Torture and Other Cruel, Inhuman or Degrading Treatment or Punishment, Cong. Rec. S17486-01

Convention for the Protection of Human Rights and Fundamental Freedoms, as amended by Protocols No. 11 and No. 14, Council of Europe, Rome, 4.XI.1950

International Covenant on Civil and Political Rights, New York, 16 December 1966, No. 14668 United Nations, *Treaty Series*, vol. 999, p. 171 and vol. 1057, p. 407

Vienna Convention on the Law of Treaties, Vienna, 23 May 1969, No. 18232, United Nations, Treaty Series, vol. 1155, p. 331

Legal cases, judgments and opinions

Aamer v. *Secretary of State for Foreign and Commonwealth Affairs* [2009] EWHC 3316 (Admin)

Adel Hassan Hamed v. *George W. Bush, Donald Rumsfeld, Jay Hood and Brice Gyurisko*, CV 05-1009 JDB US District Court for the District of Columbia

Al-Zery vs. *Sweden*, United Nations Human Rights Committee, Communication No. 1416/2005, 10/11/2006, CCPR/C/88/D/1416/2005 (Jurisprudence)

APPG on Extraordinary Rendition, Legal Opinion on Detainee Handovers by UK Forces, Michael Fordham QC and Tom Hickman, July 2008

Boumediene v. *Bush*, 553 US 723 (2008)

European Commission for Democracy through Law (Venice Commission), 'Opinion on the International legal obligations of Council of Europe member States in respect of secret detention facilities and inter-State transport of Prisoners', adopted at the 66th Plenary Session (Venice, 17-18 March 2006)

Filártiga v. *Peña-Irala*, 630 F.2d 876 (June 30 1980)

Frisbie v. *Collins* 342 U.S. 519 (1952)

Hamdan v. *Rumsfeld*, 548 US 557 (2006)

Hamdi v. *Rumsfeld*, 542 US 507 (2004)

Jamil el Banna et al v. *George W Bush et al*, 04-CV-1144 (RWR)

Johnson v. *Eisentrager* 339 U. S. 763 (1950)

Ker v. *Illinois* 119 U.S. 436 (1886)

Öcalan v. *Turkey*, 41 Eur. H.R. Rep. 985 (2005)

Prosecutor v. *Dragan Nikolic*, Decision on Interlocutory Appeal Concerning Legality of Arrest, Case No. IT-94-2-AR73, Appeals Chamber (International Criminal Tribunal for the Former Yugoslavia), 5 June 2003

R v Horseferry Road Magistrates' Court, Ex parte *Bennett* [1994] 1 AC 42

R v Nicholas Mullen [1999] EWCA Crim 278

R (Al Rawi and others) v. *Secretary of State for Foreign and Commonwealth Affairs* [2006] EWHC 972 (Admin)

R (Madni) v. *Secretary of State for Foreign and Commonwealth Affairs,* Claim No. CO/9212/2009

R (B Mohamed) v. *Secretary of State for Foreign and Commonwealth Affairs,*
[2008] EWHC 2048 (Admin)
[2008] EWHC 2100 (Admin)
[2008] EWHC 2159 (Admin)
[2009] EWHC 152 (Admin)
[2009] EWHC 2549 (Admin)
[2009] EWHC 2973 (Admin)
[2010] EWCA Civ 65
[2010] EWCA Civ 158

Rasul v. *Bush*, 542 US 466 (2004)

Sánchez Ramirez v. *France*, Eur. Commission on Human Rights, No. 28780/95 (1996)

United States v. *Álvarez-Machain*, 504 US 655 (1992)

United States v. *Toscanino*, 500 F.2d 267 (August 21 1974)

United States v. *Gengler*, 510 F.2d 62 (January 8 1975)

Broadcasts

'Bagram Airbase', BBC Radio 4, 18 May 2010 (Reporter: Hilary Andersson)

'Detained on Diego Garcia?' Newsnight, BBC 2, 31 July 2008

'Europe's Secret Prisons', *Our World*, BBC News Channel, 9 October 2010 (Reporter: Daniel Sandford)

'Extraordinary Rendition', *Frontline/World*, PBS, 4 November 2007 (Reporter: Stephen Grey)

Online document resources

American Civil Liberties Union (ACLU), 'Accountability for torture: Documents released under FOIA' collection of documents released under the Freedom of Information Act: http://www.aclu.org/accountability/released.html

APPG on Extraordinary Rendition, Document Library: http://www.extraordinaryrendition.org/index.php/document-library-mainmenu-27

Judiciary of England and Wales, 'Mohamed, R (on the application of) –v– Secretary of State for Foreign and Commonwealth Affairs', collection of judgments in the case:
http://www.judiciary.gov.uk/media/judgments/2010/binyam-mohamed-judgments

The National Commission on Terrorist Attacks Upon the United States (9/11 Commission), Report, Hearings, Staff Statements and Monographs: http://govinfo.library.unt.edu/911/

National Security Archive, 'The Torture Archive': http://www.gwu.edu/~nsarchiv/

National Security Archive and Washington Media Associates, 'Torturing Democracy' archive: http://torturingdemocracy.org/

The Office of the Secretary of Defense and Joint Staff Reading Room, *Combatant Status Review Tribunal (CSRT) and Administrative Review Board (ARB) Documents*: http://www.dod.mil/pubs/foi/detainees/csrt_arb/

PBS Frontline/World, 'Extraordinary Rendition', interviews, maps and resources: http://www.pbs.org/frontlineworld/stories/rendition701/

Reprieve, documents released (July 2010) in *Al Rawi and others v Security Service and others*: http://www.reprieve.org.uk/2010_07_14_al_rawi_court_revelations

EXTRAORDINARY RENDITION IN
DOCUMENTS

CONTENTS

The British role: policy

The British role: individual cases

The US policy background

1. Memorandum for the President from Alberto R. Gonzales concerning application of the Geneva Convention, 25 January 2002—p.132

In the wake of the invasion of Afghanistan, President Bush ruled that the Geneva Convention on Prisoners of War did not apply to al Qaeda and Taliban prisoners. The decision, a key building block of the administration's legal architecture in prosecuting the War on Terror, was strongly resisted by the State Department. In this Memorandum, the President's legal adviser argues that the Conventions should not be applied, not least because the administration found itself in 'a new kind of war', in which there was a premium on the ability to carry out successful interrogations.

2. OLC Memorandum on Standards of Conduct for Interrogation under the Torture Statute, 1 August 2002 (extracts)—p.135

This Memorandum provides the broader legal background to a view on the legality of the CIA's Enhanced Interrogation Techniques (EITs). The selected sections provide an exceptionally narrow definition of torture, while using other arguments – notably the President's Commander-in-Chief powers and a self-defence justification – to give legal cover to interrogators. Criticised even within the Bush administration for its legal reasoning, the Memorandum was withdrawn in 2004.

3. OLC Memorandum on Interrogation Methods for Abu Zubaydah, 1 August 2002—p.143

This Memorandum, addressed to the CIA's most senior legal adviser, applies the principles set out in Document 2 to the use of Enhanced Interrogation Techniques (EITs) in the case of Abu Zubaydah, whom the US administration believed to be the most senior al Qaeda figure in its custody. It concluded that the EITs, including waterboarding, are legal.

4. Guantánamo Bay interrogation memos, 11 October 2002 (extracts)—p.161

This correspondence requested permission to use coercive interrogation techniques; it included legal advice (not reproduced in these extracts) sanctioning their use. The then Secretary of Defense, Donald Rumsfeld, subsequently approved the techniques in Categories I and II, and the fourth technique listed in Category III, in a memo dated 27 November 2002.

5. Statement by Secretary of State Condoleezza Rice on her departure for Europe, 5 December 2005—p.165

A series of revelations about rendition in the autumn of 2005 triggered widespread media and political concern. Secretary of State Rice set out the official US position as she embarked on a tour of European capitals. Her argument was open to the criticism that it elided rendition to justice with the other forms of rendition used by the Bush administration. She also insisted that the US did not practise either torture or cruel, inhuman and degrading treatment.

6. Speech by President George W. Bush on the secret prisons programme, 6 September 2006 and summary of the HVD Program—p.169

Faced with growing disclosures about the rendition and secret prisons programmes, and the Supreme Court's ruling in the Hamdan *case, the President gave the first official acknowledgement of their existence. He insisted that the 'alternative set of procedures' used in the CIA programme did not amount to torture, and gave specific examples in which they had allegedly helped forestall terrorist plots. He also announced the transfer of the High Value Detainees (HVDs) to Guantánamo, stating that at that point there were no prisoners held in the CIA programme. A summary of the 'High Value Terrorist Detainee Program' was published by the Office of the Director of National Intelligence to coincide with the President's speech and is also included here.*

The US policy background

(1) Memorandum for the President from Alberto R. Gonzales concerning application of the Geneva Convention, 25 January 2002

January 25, 2002

MEMORANDUM FOR THE PRESIDENT

FROM: ALBERTO R. GONZALES

SUBJECT: DECISION RE APPLICATION OF THE GENEVA CONVENTION ON PRISONERS OF WAR TO THE CONFLICT WITH AL QAEDA AND THE TALIBAN

Purpose

On January 18, I advised you that the Department of Justice had issued a formal legal opinion concluding that the Geneva Convention III on the Treatment of Prisoners of War (GPW) does not apply to the conflict with al Qaeda. I also advised you that DOJ's opinion concludes that there are reasonable grounds for you to conclude that GPW does not apply with respect to the conflict with the Taliban. I understand that you decided that GPW does not apply and, accordingly, that al Qaeda and Taliban detainees are not prisoners of war under the GPW.

The Secretary of State has requested that you reconsider that decision. Specifically, he has asked that you conclude that GPW does apply to both al Qaeda and the Taliban. I understand, however, that he would agree that al Qaeda and Taliban fighters could be determined not to be prisoners of war (POWs) but only on a case-by-case basis following individual hearings before a military board.

This memorandum outlines the ramifications of your decision and the Secretary's request for reconsideration.

Legal Background

As an initial matter, I note that you have the constitutional authority to make the determination you made on January 18 that the GPW does not apply to al Qaeda and the Taliban. (Of course, you could nevertheless, as a matter of policy, decide to apply the principles of GPW to the conflict with al Qaeda and the Taliban.) The Office of Legal Counsel of the Department of Justice has opined that, as a matter of international and domestic law, GPW does not apply to the conflict with al Qaeda. OLC has further opined that you have the authority to determine that GPW does not apply to the Taliban. As I discussed with you, the grounds for such a determination may include:

- A determination that Afghanistan was a failed state because the Taliban did not exercise full control over the territory and people, was not recognized by the international community, and was not capable of fulfilling its international obligations (e.g., was in widespread material breach of its international obligations).
- A determination that the Taliban and its forces were, in fact, not a government, but a militant, terrorist-like group.

OLC's interpretation of this legal issue is definitive. The Attorney General is charged by statute with interpreting the law for the Executive Branch. This interpretive authority extends to both domestic and international law. He has, in turn, delegated this role to OLC. Nevertheless, you should be aware that the Legal Adviser to the Secretary of State has expressed a different view.

Ramifications of Determination that GPW Does Not Apply

The consequences of a decision to adhere to what I understood to be your earlier determination that the GPW does not apply to the Taliban include the following:

Positive:

- Preserves flexibility:
  - As you have said, the war against terrorism is a new kind of war. It is not the traditional clash between nations adhering to the laws of war that formed the backdrop for GPW. The nature of the new war places a high premium on other factors, such as the ability to quickly obtain information from captured terrorists and their sponsors in order to avoid further atrocities against American civilians, and the need to try terrorists for war crimes such as wantonly killing civilians. In my judgment, this new paradigm renders obsolete Geneva's strict limitations on questioning of enemy prisoners and renders quaint some of its provisions requiring that captured enemy be afforded such things as commissary privileges, scrip (i.e., advances of monthly pay), athletic uniforms, and scientific instruments.
  - Although some of these provisions do not apply to detainees who are not POWs, a determination that GPW does not apply to al Qaeda and the Taliban eliminates any argument regarding the need for case-by-case determinations of POW status. It also holds open options for the future conflicts in which it may be more difficult to determine whether an enemy force as a whole meets the standard for POW status.
  - By concluding that GPW does not apply to al Qaeda and the Taliban, we avoid foreclosing options for the future, particularly against nonstate actors.
- Substantially reduces the threat of domestic criminal prosecution under the War Crimes Act (18 U.S.C. 2441).
  - That statute, enacted in 1996, prohibits the commission of a "war crime" by or against a U.S. person, including U.S. officials. "War crime" for these purposes is defined to include any grave breach of GPW or any violation of common Article 3 thereof (such as "outrages against personal dignity"). Some of these provisions apply (if the GPW applies) regardless of whether the individual being detained qualifies as a POW. Punishments for violations of Section 2441 include the death penalty. A determination that the GPW is not applicable to the Taliban would mean that Section 2441 would not apply to actions taken with respect to the Taliban.
  - Adhering to your determination that GPW does not apply would guard effectively against misconstruction or misapplication of Section 2441 for several reasons.
    - First, some of the language of the GPW is undefined (it prohibits, for example, "outrages upon personal dignity" and "inhuman treatment"), and it is difficult to predict with confidence what actions might be deemed to constitute violations of the relevant provisions of GPW.
    - Second, it is difficult to predict the needs and circumstances that could arise in the course of the war on terrorism.
    - Third, it is difficult to predict the motives of prosecutors and independent counsels who may in the future decide to pursue unwarranted charges based on Section 2441. Your determination would create a reasonable basis in law that Section 2441 does not apply, which would provide a solid defense to any future prosecution.

Negative:

On the other hand, the following arguments would support reconsideration and reversal of your decision that the GPW does not apply to either al Qaeda or the Taliban:

Since the Geneva Conventions were concluded in 1949, the United States has never denied their applicability to either U.S. or opposing forces engaged in armed conflict, despite several opportunities to do so. During the last Bush Administration, the United States stated that it "has a policy of applying the Geneva Conventions of 1949 whenever armed hostilities occur with regular foreign armed forces, even if arguments could be made that the threshold standards for the applicability of the Conventions . . . are not met."

- The United States could not invoke the GPW if enemy forces threatened to mistreat or mistreated U.S. or coalition forces captured during operations in Afghanistan, or if they denied Red Cross access or other POW privileges.
- The War Crimes Act could not be used against the enemy, although other criminal statutes and the customary law of war would still be available.
- Our position would likely provoke widespread condemnation among our allies and in some domestic quarters, even if we make clear that we will comply with the core humanitarian principles of the treaty as a matter of policy.
- Concluding that the Geneva Convention does not apply may encourage other countries to look for technical "loopholes" in future conflicts to conclude that they are not bound by GPW either.
- Other countries may be less inclined to turn over terrorists or provide legal assistance to us if we do not recognize a legal obligation to comply with the GPW.
- A determination that GPW does not apply to al Qaeda and the Taliban could undermine U.S. military culture which emphasizes maintaining the highest standards of conduct in combat, and could introduce an element of uncertainty in the status of adversaries.

Response to Arguments for Applying GPW to the al Qaeda and the Taliban

On balance, I believe that the arguments for reconsideration and reversal are unpersuasive.

- The argument that the U.S. has never determined that GPW did not apply is incorrect. In at least one case (Panama in 1989) the U.S. determined that GPW did not apply even though it determined for policy reasons to adhere to the convention. More importantly, as noted above, this is a new type of warfare — one not contemplated in 1949 when the GPW was framed — and requires a new approach in our actions towards captured terrorists. Indeed, as the statement quoted from the administration of President George Bush makes clear, the U.S. will apply GPW "whenever hostilities occur *with regular foreign armed forces*." By its terms, therefore, the policy does not apply to a conflict with terrorists, or with irregular forces, like the Taliban, who are armed militants that oppressed and terrorized the people of Afghanistan.
- In response to the argument that we should decide to apply GPW to the Taliban in order to encourage other countries to treat captured U.S. military personnel in accordance with the GPW, it should be noted that your policy of providing humane treatment to enemy detainees gives us the credibility to insist on like treatment for our soldiers. Moreover, even if GPW is not applicable, we can still bring war crimes charges against anyone who mistreats U.S. personnel. Finally, I note that our adversaries in several recent conflicts have not been deterred by GPW in their mistreatment of captured U.S. personnel, and terrorists will not follow GPW rules in any event.
- The statement that other nations would criticize the U.S. because we have determined that GPW does not apply is undoubtedly true. It is even possible that some nations would point to that determination as a basis for failing to cooperate with us on specific matters in the war against terrorism. On the other hand, some international and domestic criticism is already likely to flow from your previous decision not to treat the detainees as POWs. And we can facilitate cooperation with other nations by reassuring them that we fully support GPW where it is applicable and by acknowledging that in this conflict the U.S. continues to respect other recognized standards.

- In the treatment of detainees, the U.S. will continue to be constrained by (i) its commitment to treat the detainees humanely and, to the extent appropriate and consistent with military necessity, in a manner consistent with the principles of GPW, (ii) its applicable treaty obligations, (iii) minimum standards of treatment universally recognized by the nations of the world, and (iv) applicable military regulations regarding the treatment of detainees.
- Similarly, the argument based on military culture fails to recognize that our military remain bound to apply the principles of GPW because that is what you have directed them to do.

(2)   OLC Memorandum on Standards of Conduct for Interrogation under the Torture Statute, 1 August 2002 (extracts)

U.S. Department of Justice

Office of Legal Counsel

Office of the Assistant Attorney General	*Washington, D.C. 20530*

August 1, 2002

Memorandum for Alberto R. Gonzales
Counsel to the President

Re: Standards of Conduct for Interrogation under 18 U.S.C. §§ 2340–2340A

You have asked for our Office's views regarding the standards of conduct under the Convention Against Torture and Other Cruel, Inhuman and Degrading Treatment or Punishment as implemented by Sections 2340–2340A of title 18 of the United States Code. As we understand it, this question has arisen in the context of the conduct of interrogations outside of the United States. We conclude below that Section 2340A proscribes acts inflicting, and that are specifically intended to inflict, severe pain or suffering, whether mental or physical. Those acts must be of an extreme nature to rise to the level of torture within the meaning of Section 2340A and the Convention. We further conclude that certain acts may be cruel, inhuman, or degrading, but still not produce pain and suffering of the requisite intensity to fall within Section 2340A's proscription against torture. We conclude by examining possible defenses that would negate any claim that certain interrogation methods violate the statute.

In Part I, we examine the criminal statute's text and history. We conclude that for an act to constitute torture as defined in Section 2340, it must inflict pain that is difficult to endure. Physical pain amounting to torture must be equivalent in intensity to the pain accompanying serious physical injury, such as organ failure, impairment of bodily function, or even death. For purely mental pain or suffering to amount to torture under Section 2340, it must result in significant psychological harm of significant duration, e.g., lasting for months or even years. We conclude that the mental harm also must result from one of the predicate acts listed in the statute, namely: threats of imminent death; threats of infliction of the kind of pain that would amount to physical torture; infliction of such physical pain as a means of psychological torture; use of drugs or other procedures designed to deeply disrupt the senses, or fundamentally alter an individual's personality; or threatening to do any of these things to a third party. The legislative history simply reveals that Congress intended for the statute's definition to track the Convention's definition of torture and the reservations, understandings, and declarations that the United States submitted with its ratification. We conclude that the statute, taken as a whole, makes plain that it prohibits only extreme acts.

[...]

B. "Severe Pain or Suffering"

The key statutory phrase in the definition of torture is the statement that acts amount to torture if they cause "severe physical or mental pain or suffering." In examining the meaning of a statute, its text must be the starting point. *See INS v. Phinpathya*, 464 U.S. 183, 189 (1984) ("This Court has noted on numerous occasions that in all cases involving statutory construction, our starting point must be the language employed by Congress, . . . and we assume that the legislative purpose is expressed by the ordinary meaning of the words used.") (internal quotations and citations omitted). Section 2340 makes plain that the infliction of pain or suffering per se, whether it is physical or mental, is insufficient to amount to torture. Instead, the text provides that pain or suffering must be "severe." The statute does not, however, define the term "severe." "In the absence of such a definition, we construe a statutory term in accordance with its ordinary or natural meaning." *FDIC v. Meyer*, 510 U.S. 471, 476 (1994). The dictionary defines "severe" as "[u]nsparing in exaction, punishment, or censure" or "[I]nflicting discomfort or pain hard to endure; sharp; afflictive; distressing; violent; extreme; as *severe* pain, anguish, torture." Webster's New International Dictionary 2295 (2d ed. 1935); *see* American Heritage Dictionary of the English Language 1653 (3d ed. 1992) ("extremely violent or grievous: *severe* pain") (emphasis in original); IX The Oxford English Dictionary 572 (1978) ("Of pain, suffering, loss, or the like: Grievous, extreme" and "of circumstances . . .: hard to sustain or endure"). Thus, the adjective "severe" conveys that the pain or suffering must be of such a high level of intensity that the pain is difficult for the subject to endure.

Congress's use of the phrase "severe pain" elsewhere in the United States Code can shed more light on its meaning. *See, e.g., West Va. Univ. Hosps., Inc. v. Casey*, 499 U.S. 83, 100 (1991) ("[W]e construe [a statutory term] to contain that permissible meaning which fits most logically and comfortably into the body of both previously and subsequently enacted law."). Significantly, the phrase "severe pain" appears in statutes defining an emergency medical condition for the purpose of providing health benefits. *See, e.g.,* 8 U.S.C. § 1369 (2000); 42 U.S.C § 1395w-22 (2000); *id.* § 1395x (2000); *id.* §

1395dd (2000); *id.* § 1396b (2000); *id.* § 1396u-2 (2000). These statutes define an emergency condition as one "manifesting itself by acute symptoms of sufficient severity (including *severe pain*) such that a prudent lay person, who possesses an average knowledge of health and medicine, could reasonably expect the absence of immediate medical attention to result in—placing the health of the individual . . . (i) in serious jeopardy, (ii) serious impairment to bodily functions, or (iii) serious dysfunction of any bodily organ or part." *Id.* § 1395w-22(d)(3)(B) (emphasis added). Although these statutes address a substantially different subject from Section 2340, they are nonetheless helpful for understanding what constitutes severe physical pain. They treat severe pain as an indicator of ailments that are likely to result in permanent and serious physical damage in the absence of immediate medical treatment. Such damage must rise to the level of death, organ failure, or the permanent impairment of a significant body function. These statutes suggest that "severe pain," as used in Section 2340, must rise to a similarly high level—the level that would ordinarily be associated with a sufficiently serious physical condition or injury such as death, organ failure, or serious impairment of body functions—in order to constitute torture.

C. "Severe mental pain or suffering"

[...]

4. Summary

Section 2340's definition of torture must be read as a sum of these component parts. *See Argentine Rep. v. Amerada Hess Shipping Corp.*, 488 U.S. 428, 434–35 (1989) (reading two provisions together to determine statute's meaning); *Bethesda Hosp. Ass'n v. Bowen*, 485 U.S. 399, 405 (1988) (looking to "the language and design of the statute as a whole" to ascertain a statute's meaning). Each component of the definition emphasizes that torture is not the mere infliction of pain or suffering on another, but is instead a step well removed. The victim must experience intense pain or suffering of the kind that is equivalent to the pain that would be associated with serious physical injury so severe that death, organ failure, or permanent damage resulting in a loss of significant body function will likely result. If that pain or suffering is psychological, that suffering must result from one of the acts set forth in the statute. In addition, these acts must cause long-term mental harm. Indeed, this view of the criminal act of torture is consistent with the term's common meaning. Torture is generally understood to involve "intense pain" or "excruciating pain," or put another way, "extreme anguish of body or mind." Black's Law Dictionary at 1498 (7th Ed. 1999); Random House Webster's Unabridged Dictionary 1999 (1999); Webster's New International Dictionary 2674 (2d ed. 1935). In short, reading the definition of torture as a whole, it is plain that the term encompasses only extreme acts.[6]

---

[6] Torture is a term also found in state law. Some states expressly proscribe "murder by torture." *See, e.g.*, Idaho Code § 18-4001 (Michie 1997); N.C. Gen. Stat. Ann. § 14-17 (1999) ; *see also* Me. Rev. Stat. Ann. tit. 17-A, § 152-A (West Supp. 2001) (aggravated attempted murder is "[t]he attempted murder . . . accompanied by torture, sexual assault or other extreme cruelty inflicted upon the victim"). Other states have made torture an aggravating factor supporting imposition of the death penalty. *See, e.g.*, Ark. Code Ann. § 5-4-604(8)(B); Del. Code Ann. tit. 11, § 4209(e)(1)(*l*) (1995); Ga. Code Ann. § 17-10-30(b)(7) (1997); ; 720 Ill. Comp. Stat. Ann. 5/9-1(b)(14) (West Supp. 2002); Mass. Ann. Laws ch. 279, § 69(a) (Law. Co-op. 1992); Mo. Ann. Stat. § 565.032(2)(7) (West 1999); Nev. Rev. Stat. Ann. 200-033(8) (Michie 2001); N.J. Stat. Ann. § 2C:11-3 (West Supp. 2002) (same); Tenn. Code Ann. § 39-13-204(i)(5) (Supp. 2001); *see also* Alaska Stat. § 12.55.125(a)(3) (2000) (term of 99 years' imprisonment mandatory where defendant subjected victim to "substantial physical torture"). *All of these laws support the conclusion that torture is generally an extreme act far beyond the infliction of pain or suffering alone.*

California law is illustrative on this point. The California Penal Code not only makes torture itself an offense, see Cal. Penal Code § 206 (West Supp. 2002), it also prohibits murder by torture, see Cal. Penal Code § 189 (West Supp. 2002), and provides that torture is an aggravating circumstance supporting the imposition of the death penalty, see Cal. Penal Code § 190.2 (West Supp. 2002). California's definitions of torture demonstrate that the term is reserved for especially cruel acts inflicting serious injury. Designed to "fill[] a gap in existing law dealing with extremely violent and callous criminal conduct[,]" *People v. Hale*, 88 Cal. Rptr. 2d 904, 913 (1999) (internal quotation marks and citation omitted), Section 206 defines the offense of torture as:

[e]very person who, with the intent to cause *cruel* or *extreme* pain and suffering for the purpose of revenge, extortion, persuasion, or for any sadistic purpose, inflicts great bodily

138

II.   U.N. Convention Against Torture and Other Cruel Inhuman or Degrading Treatment or Punishment.

Because Congress enacted the criminal prohibition against torture to implement CAT, we also examine the treaty's text and history to develop a fuller understanding of the context of Sections 2340–2340A. As with the statute, we begin our analysis with the treaty's text. *See Eastern Airlines Inc. v. Floyd*, 499 U.S. 530, 534–35 (1991) ("When interpreting a treaty, we begin with the text of the treaty and the context in which the written words are used.) (quotation marks and citations omitted). CAT defines torture as:

> any act by which *severe* pain or suffering, whether physical or mental, is intentionally inflicted on a person for such purposes as obtaining from him or a third person information or a confession, punishing him for an act he or a third person has committed or is suspected of having committed, or intimidating or coercing him or a third person, or for any reason based on discrimination of any kind, when such pain or suffering is inflicted by or at the instigation of or with the consent or acquiescence of a public official or other person acting in an official capacity.

Article 1(1) (emphasis added). Unlike Section 2340, this definition includes a list of purposes for which such pain and suffering is inflicted. The prefatory phrase "such purposes as" makes clear that this list is, however, illustrative rather than exhaustive. Accordingly, severe pain or suffering need not be inflicted for those specific purposes to constitute torture; instead, the perpetrator must simply have a purpose of the same kind.

---

injury . . . upon the person of another, is guilty of torture. The crime of torture does not require any proof that the victim suffered pain.

(Emphasis added). With respect to sections190.2 and 189, neither of which are statutorily defined, California courts have recognized that torture generally means an "[a]ct or process of inflicting severe pain, esp[ecially] as a punishment to extort confession, or in revenge. . . . Implicit in that definition is the requirement of an intent to cause pain and suffering in addition to death." *People v. Barrera*, 18 Cal. Rptr. 2d 395, 399 (Ct. App. 1993) (quotation marks and citation omitted). Further, "'murder by torture was and is considered among the most reprehensible types of murder because of the calculated nature of the acts causing death." *Id.* at 403 (quoting *People v. Wiley*, 133 Cal. Rptr. 135, 138 (1976) (in bank)). The definition of murder by torture special circumstance, proscribed under Cal. Penal Code § 190.2, likewise shows an attempt to reach the most heinous acts imposing pain beyond that which a victim suffers through death alone. To establish murder by torture special circumstance, the "intent to kill, intent to torture, and infliction of an extremely painful act upon a living victim" must be present. *People v. Bemore*, 94 Cal. Rptr. 2d 840, 861 (2000). The intent to torture is characterized by a "'sadistic intent to cause the victim to suffer pain in addition to the pain of death.'" *Id.* at 862 (quoting *People v. Davenport*, 221 Cal. Rptr. 794, 875 (1985)). Like the Torture Victims Protection Act and the Convention Against Torture, discussed *infra* at Parts II and III, each of these California prohibitions against torture require an evil intent—such as cruelty, revenge or even sadism. Section 2340 does not require this additional intent, but as discussed *supra* pp. 2–3, requires that the individual specifically intended to cause severe pain or suffering. Furthermore, unlike Section 2340, neither section 189 nor section 206 appear to require proof of actual pain to establish torture.

14

More importantly, like Section 2340, the pain and suffering must be severe to reach the threshold of torture. Thus, the text of CAT reinforces our reading of Section 2340 that torture must be an extreme act.[7]

CAT also distinguishes between torture and other acts of cruel, inhuman, or degrading treatment or punishment.[8] Article 16 of CAT requires state parties to "undertake to prevent . . . other acts of cruel, inhuman or degrading treatment or punishment *which do not amount to torture* as defined in article 1." (Emphasis added). CAT thus establishes a category of acts that are not to be committed and that states must endeavor to prevent, but that states need not criminalize, leaving those acts without the stigma of criminal penalties. CAT reserves criminal penalties and the stigma attached to those penalties for torture alone. In so doing, CAT makes clear that torture is at the farthest end of impermissible actions, and that it is distinct and separate from the lower level of "cruel, inhuman, or degrading treatment or punishment." This approach is in keeping with CAT's predecessor, the U.N. Declaration on the Protection from Torture. That declaration defines torture as "an aggravated and deliberate form of cruel, inhuman or degrading treatment or punishment." Declaration on Protection from Torture, UN Res. 3452, Art. 1(2) (Dec. 9, 1975).

---

[7] To be sure, the text of the treaty requires that an individual act "intentionally." This language might be read to require only general intent for violations of the Torture Convention. We believe, however, that the better interpretation is that that the use of the phrase "intentionally" also created a specific intent-type standard. In that event, the Bush administration's understanding represents only an explanation of how the United States intended to implement the vague language of the Torture Convention. If, however, the Convention established a general intent standard, then the Bush understanding represents a modification of the obligation undertaken by the United States.

[8] Common article 3 of Geneva Convention on prisoners of war, Convention Relative to the Treatment of Prisoners of War, 6 U.S.T. 3517 ("Geneva Convention III") contains somewhat similar language. Article 3(1)(a) prohibits "violence to life and person, in particular murder of all kinds, mutilation, *cruel treatment and torture*." (Emphasis added). Article 3(1)(c) additionally prohibits "outrages upon personal dignity, in particular, humiliating and degrading treatment." Subsection (c) must forbid more conduct than that already covered in subsection (a) otherwise subsection (c) would be superfluous. Common article 3 does not, however, define either of the phrases "outrages upon personal dignity" or "humiliating and degrading treatment." International criminal tribunals, such as those respecting Rwanda and former Yugoslavia have used common article 3 to try individuals for committing inhuman acts lacking any military necessity whatsoever. Based on our review of the case law, however, these tribunals have not yet articulated the full scope of conduct prohibited by common article 3. Memorandum for John C. Yoo, Deputy Assistant Attorney General, Office of Legal Counsel, from James C. Ho, Attorney-Advisor, Office of Legal Counsel, *Re: Possible Interpretations of Common Article 3 of the 1949 Geneva Convention Relative to the Treatment of Prisoners of War* (Feb. 1, 2002).

We note that Section 2340A and CAT protect any individual from torture. By contrast, the standards of conduct established by common article 3 of Convention III, do not apply to "an armed conflict between a nation-state and a transnational terrorist organization." Memorandum for Alberto R. Gonzales, Counsel to the President and William J. Haynes, II, General Counsel, Department of Defense, from Jay S. Bybee, Assistant Attorney General, Office of Legal Counsel, *Re: Application of Treaties and Laws to al Qaeda and Taliban Detainees* at 8 (Jan. 22, 2002).

140

A.   Ratification History

[...]

Although the Reagan administration relied on CAT's distinction between torture and "cruel, inhuman, or degrading treatment or punishment," it viewed the phrase "cruel, inhuman, or degrading treatment or punishment" as vague and lacking in a universally accepted meaning. Of even greater concern to the Reagan administration was that because of its vagueness this phrase could be construed to bar acts not prohibited by the U.S. Constitution. The administration pointed to *Case of X v. Federal Republic of Germany* as the basis for this concern. In that case, the European Court of Human Rights determined that the prison officials' refusal to recognize a prisoner's sex change might constitute degrading treatment. *See* S. Treaty Doc. No. 100-20, at 15 (citing European Commission on Human Rights, *Dec. on Adm.*, Dec. 15, 1977, *Case of X v. Federal Republic of Germany* (No. 6694/74), 11 Dec. & Rep. 16)). As a result of this concern, the Administration added the following understanding:

> The United States understands the term, 'cruel, inhuman or degrading treatment or punishment,' as used in Article 16 of the Convention, to mean the cruel, unusual, and inhumane treatment or punishment prohibited by the Fifth, Eighth and/or Fourteenth Amendments to the Constitution of the United States."

S. Treaty Doc. No. 100-20, at 15–16. Treatment or punishment must therefore rise to the level of action that U.S. courts have found to be in violation of the U.S. Constitution in order to constitute cruel, inhuman, or degrading treatment or punishment. That which fails to rise to this level must fail, *a fortiori*, to constitute torture under Section 2340.[9]

---

[9] The vagueness of "cruel, inhuman and degrading treatment" enables the term to have a far-ranging reach. Article 3 of the European Convention on Human Rights similarly prohibits such treatment. The European Court of Human Rights has construed this phrase broadly, even assessing whether such treatment has occurred from the subjective stand point of the victim. *See* Memorandum from James C. Ho, Attorney-Advisor to John C. Yoo, Deputy Assistant Attorney General, *Re: Possible Interpretations of Common Article 3 of the 1949 Geneva Convention Relative to the Treatment of Prisoners of War* (Feb. 1, 2002) (finding that European Court of Human Right's construction of inhuman or degrading treatment "is broad enough to arguably forbid even standard U.S. law enforcement interrogation techniques, which endeavor to break down a detainee's 'moral resistance' to answering questions.").

17

[...]

V.   The President's Commander-in-Chief Power

Even if an interrogation method arguably were to violate Section 2340A, the statute would be unconstitutional if it impermissibly encroached on the President's constitutional power to conduct a military campaign. As Commander-in-Chief, the President has the constitutional authority to order interrogations of enemy combatants to gain intelligence information concerning the military plans of the enemy. The demands of the Commander-in-Chief power are especially pronounced in the middle of a war in which the nation has already suffered a direct attack. In such a case, the information gained from interrogations may prevent future attacks by foreign enemies. Any effort to apply Section 2340A in a manner that interferes with the President's direction of such core war matters as the detention and interrogation of enemy combatants thus would be unconstitutional.

[...]

VI. Defenses

[...]

B. Self-Defense

[...]

Under the current circumstances, we believe that a defendant accused of violating Section 2340A could have, in certain circumstances, grounds to properly claim the defense of another. The threat of an impending terrorist attack threatens the lives of hundreds if not thousands of American citizens. Whether such a defense will be upheld depends on the specific context within which the interrogation decision is made. If an attack appears increasingly likely, but our intelligence services and armed forces cannot prevent it without the information from the interrogation of a specific individual, then the more likely it will appear that the conduct in question will be seen as necessary. If intelligence and other information support the conclusion that an attack is increasingly certain, then the necessity for the interrogation will be reasonable. The increasing certainty of an attack will also satisfy the imminence requirement. Finally, the fact that previous al Qaeda attacks have had as their aim the deaths of American citizens, and that evidence of other plots have had a similar goal in mind, would justify proportionality of interrogation methods designed to elicit information to prevent such deaths.

To be sure, this situation is different from the usual self-defense justification, and, indeed, it overlaps with elements of the necessity defense. Self-defense as usually discussed involves using force against an individual who is about to conduct the attack. In the current circumstances, however, an enemy combatant in detention does not himself present a threat of harm. He is not actually carrying out the attack; rather, he has participated in the planning and preparation for the attack, or merely has knowledge of the attack through his membership in the terrorist organization. Nonetheless, leading scholarly commentators believe that interrogation of such individuals using methods that might violate Section 2340A would be justified under the doctrine of self-defense, because the combatant by aiding and promoting the terrorist plot "has culpably caused the situation where someone might get hurt. If hurting him is the only means to prevent the death or injury of others put at risk by his actions, such torture should be permissible, and on the same basis that self-defense is permissible." Michael S. Moore, *Torture and the Balance of Evils*, 23 Israel L. Rev. 280, 323 (1989) (symposium on Israel's Landau Commission Report).   Thus, some commentators believe that by helping to create the threat of loss of life, terrorists become culpable for the threat even though they do not actually carry out the attack itself. They may be hurt in an interrogation because they are part of the mechanism that has set the attack in motion, *id.* at 323, just as is someone who feeds ammunition or targeting information to an attacker.   Under the present circumstances, therefore, even though a detained enemy combatant may not be the exact attacker—he is not planting the bomb, or piloting a hijacked plane to kill civilians—he still may be harmed in self-defense if he has knowledge of future attacks because he has assisted in their planning and execution.

[...]

Conclusion

For the foregoing reasons, we conclude that torture as defined in and proscribed by Sections 2340–2340A, covers only extreme acts. Severe pain is generally of the kind difficult for the victim to endure. Where the pain is physical, it must be of an intensity akin to that which accompanies serious physical injury such as death or organ failure. Severe mental pain requires suffering not just at the moment of infliction but it also requires lasting psychological harm, such as seen in mental disorders like posttraumatic stress disorder. Additionally, such severe mental pain can arise only from the predicate acts listed in Section 2340. Because the acts inflicting torture are extreme, there is significant range of acts that though they might constitute cruel, inhuman, or degrading treatment or punishment fail to rise to the level of torture.

Further, we conclude that under the circumstances of the current war against al Qaeda and its allies, application of Section 2340A to interrogations undertaken pursuant to the President's Commander-in-Chief powers may be unconstitutional. Finally, even if an interrogation method might violate Section 2340A, necessity or self-defense could provide justifications that would eliminate any criminal liability.

Please let us know if we can be of further assistance.

Jay S. Bybee
Assistant Attorney General

(3)   OLC Memorandum on Interrogation Methods for Abu Zubaydah, 1 August 2002

U.S. Department of Justice

Office of Legal Counsel

Office of the Assistant Attorney General   *Washington, D.C. 20530*

August 1, 2002

Memorandum for John Rizzo
Acting General Counsel of the Central Intelligence Agency

Interrogation of al Qaeda Operative

You have asked for this Office's views on whether certain proposed conduct would violate the prohibition against torture found at Section 2340A of title 18 of the United States Code. You have asked for this advice in the course of conducting interrogations of Abu Zubaydah. As we understand it, Zubaydah is one of the highest ranking members of the al Qaeda terrorist organization, with which the United States is currently engaged in an international armed conflict following the attacks on the World Trade Center and the Pentagon on September 11, 2001. This letter memorializes our previous oral advice, given on July 24, 2002 and July 26, 2002, that the proposed conduct would not violate this prohibition.

I.

Our advice is based upon the following facts, which you have provided to us. We also understand that you do not have any facts in your possession contrary to the facts outlined here, and this opinion is limited to these facts. If these facts were to change, this advice would not necessarily apply. Zubaydah is currently being held by the United States. The interrogation team is certain that he has additional information that he refuses to divulge. Specifically, he is withholding information regarding terrorist networks in the United States or in Saudi Arabia and information regarding plans to conduct attacks within the United States or against our interests overseas. Zubaydah has become accustomed to a certain level of treatment and displays no signs of willingness to disclose further information. Moreover, your intelligence indicates that there is currently a level of "chatter" equal to that which preceded the September 11 attacks. In light of the information you believe Zubaydah has and the high level of threat you believe now exists, you wish to move the interrogations into what you have described as an "increased pressure phase."

As part of this increased pressure phase, Zubaydah will have contact only with a new interrogation specialist, whom he has not met previously, and the Survival, Evasion, Resistance, Escape ("SERE") training psychologist who has been involved with the interrogations since they began. This phase will likely last no more than several days but could last up to thirty days. In this phase, you would like to employ ten techniques that you believe will dislocate his

144

expectations regarding the treatment he believes he will receive and encourage him to disclose the crucial information mentioned above. These ten techniques are: (1) attention grasp, (2) walling, (3) facial hold, (4) facial slap (insult slap), (5) cramped confinement, (6) wall standing, (7) stress positions, (8) sleep deprivation, (9) insects placed in a confinement box, and (10) the waterboard. You have informed us that the use of these techniques would be on an as-needed basis and that not all of these techniques will necessarily be used. The interrogation team would use these techniques in some combination to convince Zubaydah that the only way he can influence his surrounding environment is through cooperation. You have, however, informed us that you expect these techniques to be used in some sort of escalating fashion, culminating with the waterboard, though not necessarily ending with this technique. Moreover, you have also orally informed us that although some of these techniques may be used with more than once, that repetition will not be substantial because the techniques generally lose their effectiveness after several repetitions. You have also informed us that Zabaydah sustained a wound during his capture, which is being treated.

Based on the facts you have given us, we understand each of these techniques to be as follows. The attention grasp consists of grasping the individual with both hands, one hand on each side of the collar opening, in a controlled and quick motion. In the same motion as the grasp, the individual is drawn toward the interrogator.

For walling, a flexible false wall will be constructed. The individual is placed with his heels touching the wall. The interrogator pulls the individual forward and then quickly and firmly pushes the individual into the wall. It is the individual's shoulder blades that hit the wall. During this motion, the head and neck are supported with a rolled hood or towel that provides a c-collar effect to help prevent whiplash. To further reduce the probability of injury, the individual is allowed to rebound from the flexible wall. You have orally informed us that the false wall is in part constructed to create a loud sound when the individual hits it, which will further shock or surprise in the individual. In part, the idea is to create a sound that will make the impact seem far worse than it is and that will be far worse than any injury that might result from the action.

The facial hold is used to hold the head immobile. One open palm is placed on either side of the individual's face. The fingertips are kept well away from the individual's eyes.

With the facial slap or insult slap, the interrogator slaps the individual's face with fingers slightly spread. The hand makes contact with the area directly between the tip of the individual's chin and the bottom of the corresponding earlobe. The interrogator invades the individual's personal space. The goal of the facial slap is not to inflict physical pain that is severe or lasting. Instead, the purpose of the facial slap is to induce shock, surprise, and/or humiliation.

Cramped confinement involves the placement of the individual in a confined space, the dimensions of which restrict the individual's movement. The confined space is usually dark.

TOP SECRET

The duration of confinement varies based upon the size of the container. For the larger confined space, the individual can stand up or sit down; the smaller space is large enough for the subject to sit down. Confinement in the larger space can last up to eighteen hours; for the smaller space, confinement lasts for no more than two hours.

Wall standing is used to induce muscle fatigue. The individual stands about four to five feet from a wall, with his feet spread approximately to shoulder width. His arms are stretched out in front of him, with his fingers resting on the wall. His fingers support all of his body weight. The individual is not permitted to move or reposition his hands or feet.

A variety of stress positions may be used. You have informed us that these positions are not designed to produce the pain associated with contortions or twisting of the body. Rather, somewhat like walling, they are designed to produce the physical discomfort associated with muscle fatigue. Two particular stress positions are likely to be used on Zubaydah: (1) sitting on the floor with legs extended straight out in front of him with his arms raised above his head; and (2) kneeling on the floor while leaning back at a 45 degree angle. You have also orally informed us that through observing Zubaydah in captivity, you have noted that he appears to be quite flexible despite his wound.

Sleep deprivation may be used. You have indicated that your purpose in using this technique is to reduce the individual's ability to think on his feet and, through the discomfort associated with lack of sleep, to motivate him to cooperate. The effect of such sleep deprivation will generally remit after one or two nights of uninterrupted sleep. You have informed us that your research has revealed that, in rare instances, some individuals who are already predisposed to psychological problems may experience abnormal reactions to sleep deprivation. Even in those cases, however, reactions abate after the individual is permitted to sleep. Moreover, personnel with medical training are available to and will intervene in the unlikely event of an abnormal reaction. You have orally informed us that you would not deprive Zubaydah of sleep for more than eleven days at a time and that you have previously kept him awake for 72 hours, from which no mental or physical harm resulted.

You would like to place Zubaydah in a cramped confinement box with an insect. You have informed us that he appears to have a fear of insects. In particular, you would like to tell Zubaydah that you intend to place a stinging insect into the box with him. You would, however, place a harmless insect in the box. You have orally informed us that you would in fact place a harmless insect such as a caterpillar in the box with him.

Finally, you would like to use a technique called the "waterboard." In this procedure, the individual is bound securely to an inclined bench, which is approximately four feet by seven feet. The individual's feet are generally elevated. A cloth is placed over the forehead and eyes. Water

146

is then applied to the cloth in a controlled manner. As this is done, the cloth is lowered until it covers both the nose and mouth. Once the cloth is saturated and completely covers the mouth and nose, air flow is slightly restricted for 20 to 40 seconds due to the presence of the cloth. This causes an increase in carbon dioxide level in the individual's blood. This increase in the carbon dioxide level stimulates increased effort to breathe. This effort plus the cloth produces the perception of "suffocation and incipient panic," i.e., the perception of drowning. The individual does not breathe any water into his lungs. During those 20 to 40 seconds, water is continuously applied from a height of twelve to twenty-four inches. After this period, the cloth is lifted, and the individual is allowed to breathe unimpeded for three or four full breaths. The sensation of drowning is immediately relieved by the removal of the cloth. The procedure may then be repeated. The water is usually applied from a canteen cup or small watering can with a spout. You have orally informed us that this procedure triggers an automatic physiological sensation of drowning that the individual cannot control even though he may be aware that he is in fact not drowning. You have also orally informed us that it is likely that this procedure would not last more than 20 minutes in any one application.

We also understand that a medical expert with SERE experience will be present throughout this phase and that the procedures will be stopped if deemed medically necessary to prevent severe mental or physical harm to Zubaydah. As mentioned above, Zubaydah suffered an injury during his capture. You have informed us that steps will be taken to ensure that this injury is not in any way exacerbated by the use of these methods and that adequate medical attention will be given to ensure that it will heal properly.

II.

In this part, we review the context within which these procedures will be applied. You have informed us that you have taken various steps to ascertain what effect, if any, these techniques would have on Zubaydah's mental health. These same techniques, with the exception of the insect in the cramped confined space, have been used and continue to be used on some members of our military personnel during their SERE training. Because of the use of these procedures in training our own military personnel to resist interrogations, you have consulted with various individuals who have extensive experience in the use of these techniques. You have done so in order to ensure that no prolonged mental harm would result from the use of these proposed procedures.

Through your consultation with various individuals responsible for such training, you have learned that these techniques have been used as elements of a course of conduct without any reported incident of prolonged mental harm. ██████████████ of the SERE school, ██████████ has reported that, during the seven-year period that he spent in those positions, there were two requests from Congress for information concerning alleged injuries resulting from the training. One of these inquiries was prompted by the temporary physical injury a trainee sustained as result of being placed in a confinement box. The other inquiry involved claims that the SERE training caused two individuals to engage in criminal behavior, namely, felony shoplifting and downloading child pornography onto a military computer. According to this official, these claims were found to be baseless. Moreover, he has indicated that during the three and a half years he spent as ███ ██████ of the SERE program, he trained 10,000 students. Of those students, only two dropped out of the training following the use of these techniques. Although on rare occasions some students temporarily postponed the remainder of their training and received psychological counseling, those students were able to finish the program without any indication of subsequent mental health effects.

You have informed us that you have consulted with ████████████ who has ten years of experience with SERE training ██████████████████████████████ ████████████████████████████████ He stated that, during those ten years, insofar as he is aware, none of the individuals who completed the program suffered any adverse mental health effects. He informed you that there was one person who did not complete the training. That person experienced an adverse mental health reaction that lasted only two hours. After those two hours, the individual's symptoms spontaneously dissipated without requiring treatment or counseling and no other symptoms were ever reported by this individual. According to the information you have provided to us, this assessment of the use of these procedures includes the use of the waterboard.

Additionally, you received a memorandum from the ██████████████████████ ████████████████████████████ which you supplied to us. ████████████████ has experience with the use of all of these procedures in a course of conduct, with the exception of the insect in the confinement box and the waterboard. This memorandum confirms that the use of these procedures has not resulted in any reported instances of prolonged mental harm, and very few instances of immediate and temporary adverse psychological responses to the training. ██████████████ reported that a small minority of students have had temporary adverse psychological reactions during training. Of the 26,829 students trained from 1992 through 2001 in the Air Force SERE training, 4.3 percent of those students had contact with psychology services. Of those 4.3 percent, only 3.2 percent were pulled from the program for psychological reasons. Thus, out of the students trained overall, only 0.14 percent were pulled from the program for psychological reasons. Furthermore, although ██████████████ indicated that surveys of students having completed this training are not done, he expressed confidence that the training did not cause any long-term psychological impact. He based his conclusion on the debriefing of students that is done after the training. More importantly, he based this assessment on the fact that although training is required to be extremely stressful in order to be effective, very few complaints have been made regarding the training. During his tenure, in which 10,000 students were trained, no congressional complaints have been made. While there was one Inspector General complaint, it was not due to psychological concerns. Moreover, he was aware of only one letter inquiring about the long-term impact of these techniques from an individual trained

148

TOP SECRET

over twenty years ago. He found that it was impossible to attribute this individual's symptoms to his training. ▓▓▓▓▓▓▓ concluded that if there are any long-term psychological effects of the United States Air Force training using the procedures outlined above they "are certainly minimal."

With respect to the waterboard, you have also orally informed us that the Navy continues to use it in training. You have informed us that your on-site psychologists, who have extensive experience with the use of the waterboard in Navy training, have not encountered any significant long-term mental health consequences from its use. Your on-site psychologists have also indicated that JPRA has likewise not reported any significant long-term mental health consequences from the use of the waterboard. You have informed us that other services ceased use of the waterboard because it was so successful as an interrogation technique, but not because of any concerns over any harm, physical or mental, caused by it. It was also reported to be almost 100 percent effective in producing cooperation among the trainees. ▓▓▓▓▓▓▓ also indicated that he had observed the use of the waterboard in Navy training some ten to twelve times. Each time it resulted in cooperation but it did not result in any physical harm to the student.

You have also reviewed the relevant literature and found no empirical data on the effect of these techniques, with the exception of sleep deprivation. With respect to sleep deprivation, you have informed us that is not uncommon for someone to be deprived of sleep for 72 hours and still perform excellently on visual-spatial motor tasks and short-term memory tests. Although some individuals may experience hallucinations, according to the literature you surveyed, those who experience such psychotic symptoms have almost always had such episodes prior to the sleep deprivation. You have indicated the studies of lengthy sleep deprivation showed no psychosis, loosening of thoughts, flattening of emotions, delusions, or paranoid ideas. In one case, even after eleven days of deprivation, no psychosis or permanent brain damaged occurred. In fact the individual reported feeling almost back to normal after one night's sleep. Further, based on the experiences with its use in military training (where it is induced for up to 48 hours), you found that rarely, if ever, will the individual suffer harm after the sleep deprivation is discontinued. Instead, the effects remit after a few good nights of sleep.

You have taken the additional step of consulting with U.S. interrogations experts, and other individuals with oversight over the SERE training process. None of these individuals was aware of any prolonged psychological effect caused by the use of any of the above techniques either separately or as a course of conduct. Moreover, you consulted with outside psychologists who reported that they were unaware of any cases where long-term problems have occurred as a result of these techniques.

Moreover, in consulting with a number of mental health experts, you have learned that the effect of any of these procedures will be dependant on the individual's personal history, cultural history and psychological tendencies. To that end, you have informed us that you have

TOP SECRET

6

completed a psychological assessment of Zubadyah. This assessment is based on interviews with Zubaydah, observations of him, and information collected from other sources such as intelligence and press reports. Our understanding of Zubaydah's psychological profile, which we set forth below, is based on that assessment.

According to this assessment, Zubaydah, though only 31, rose quickly from very low level mujahedin to third or fourth man in al Qaeda. He has served as Usama Bin Laden's senior lieutenant. In that capacity, he has managed a network of training camps. He has been instrumental in the training of operatives for al Qaeda, the Egyptian Islamic Jihad, and other terrorist elements inside Pakistan and Afghanistan. He acted as the Deputy Camp Commander for al Qaeda training camp in Afghanistan, personally approving entry and graduation of all trainees during 1999-2000. From 1996 until 1999, he approved all individuals going in and out of Afghanistan to the training camps. Further, no one went in and out of Peshawar, Pakistan without his knowledge and approval. He also acted as al Qaeda's coordinator of external contacts and foreign communications. Additionally, he has acted as al Qaeda's counter-intelligence officer and has been trusted to find spies within the organization.

Zubaydah has been involved in every major terrorist operation carried out by al Qaeda. He was a planner for the Millennium plot to attack U.S. and Israeli targets during the Millennium celebrations in Jordan. Two of the central figures in this plot who were arrested have identified Zubaydah as the supporter of their cell and the plot. He also served as a planner for the Paris Embassy plot in 2001. Moreover, he was one of the planners of the September 11 attacks. Prior to his capture, he was engaged in planning future terrorist attacks against U.S. interests.

Your psychological assessment indicates that it is believed Zubaydah wrote al Qaeda's manual on resistance techniques. You also believe that his experiences in al Qaeda make him well-acquainted with and well-versed in such techniques. As part of his role in al Qaeda, Zubaydah visited individuals in prison and helped them upon their release. Through this contact and activities with other al Qaeda mujahedin, you believe that he knows many stories of capture, interrogation, and resistance to such interrogation. Additionally, he has spoken with Ayman al-Zawahiri, and you believe it is likely that the two discussed Zawahiri's experiences as a prisoner of the Russians and the Egyptians.

Zubaydah stated during interviews that he thinks of any activity outside of jihad as "silly." He has indicated that his heart and mind are devoted to serving Allah and Islam through jihad and he has stated that he has no doubts or regrets about committing himself to jihad. Zubaydah believes that the global victory of Islam is inevitable. You have informed us that he continues to express his unabated desire to kill Americans and Jews.

Your psychological assessment describes his personality as follows. He is "a highly self-directed individual who prizes his independence." He has "narcissistic features," which are evidenced in the attention he pays to his personal appearance and his "obvious 'efforts' to demonstrate that he is really a rather 'humble and regular guy.'" He is "somewhat compulsive" in how he organizes his environment and business. He is confident, self-assured, and possesses an air of authority. While he admits to at times wrestling with how to determine who is an "innocent," he has acknowledged celebrating the destruction of the World Trade Center. He is intelligent and intellectually curious. He displays "excellent self-discipline." The assessment describes him as a perfectionist, persistent, private, and highly capable in his social interactions. He is very guarded about opening up to others and your assessment repeatedly emphasizes that he tends not to trust others easily. He is also "quick to recognize and assess the moods and motivations of others." Furthermore, he is proud of his ability to lie and deceive others successfully. Through his deception he has, among other things, prevented the location of al Qaeda safehouses and even acquired a United Nations refugee identification card.

According to your reports, Zubaydah does not have any pre-existing mental conditions or problems that would make him likely to suffer prolonged mental harm from your proposed interrogation methods. Through reading his diaries and interviewing him, you have found no history of "mood disturbance or other psychiatric pathology[,]" "thought disorder[,] . . . enduring mood or mental health problems." He is in fact "remarkably resilient and confident that he can overcome adversity." When he encounters stress or low mood, this appears to last only for a short time. He deals with stress by assessing its source, evaluating the coping resources available to him, and then taking action. Your assessment notes that he is "generally self-sufficient and relies on his understanding and application of religious and psychological principles, intelligence and discipline to avoid and overcome problems." Moreover, you have found that he has a "reliable and durable support system" in his faith, "the blessings of religious leaders, and camaraderie of like-minded mujahedin brothers." During detention, Zubaydah has managed his mood, remaining at most points "circumspect, calm, controlled, and deliberate." He has maintained this demeanor during aggressive interrogations and reductions in sleep. You describe that in an initial confrontational incident, Zubaydah showed signs of sympathetic nervous system arousal, which you think was possibly fear. Although this incident led him to disclose intelligence information, he was able to quickly regain his composure, his air of confidence, and his "strong resolve" not to reveal any information.

Overall, you summarize his primary strengths as the following: ability to focus, goal-directed discipline, intelligence, emotional resilience, street savvy, ability to organize and manage people, keen observation skills, fluid adaptability (can anticipate and adapt under duress and with minimal resources), capacity to assess and exploit the needs of others, and ability to adjust goals to emerging opportunities.

You anticipate that he will draw upon his vast knowledge of interrogation techniques to cope with the interrogation. Your assessment indicates that Zubaydah may be willing to die to protect the most important information that he holds. Nonetheless, you are of the view that his belief that Islam will ultimately dominate the world and that this victory is inevitable may provide the chance that Zubaydah will give information and rationalize it solely as a temporary setback. Additionally, you believe he may be willing to disclose some information, particularly information he deems to not be critical, but which may ultimately be useful to us when pieced together with other intelligence information you have gained.

III.

Section 2340A makes it a criminal offense for any person "outside of the United States [to] commit[] or attempt[] to commit torture." Section 2340(1) defines torture as:

> an act committed by a person acting under the color of law specifically intended to inflict severe physical or mental pain or suffering (other than pain or suffering incidental to lawful sanctions) upon another person within his custody of physical control.

18 U.S.C. § 2340(1). As we outlined in our opinion on standards of conduct under Section 2340A, a violation of 2340A requires a showing that: (1) the torture occurred outside the United States; (2) the defendant acted under the color of law; (3) the victim was within the defendant's custody or control; (4) the defendant specifically intended to inflict severe pain or suffering; and (5) that the acted inflicted severe pain or suffering. *See* Memorandum for John Rizzo, Acting General Counsel for the Central Intelligence Agency, from Jay S. Bybee, Assistant Attorney General, Office of Legal Counsel, *Re: Standards of Conduct for Interrogation under 18 U.S.C. §§ 2340–2340A* at 3 (August 1, 2002) ("Section 2340A Memorandum"). You have asked us to assume that Zubayadah is being held outside the United States, Zubayadah is within U.S. custody, and the interrogators are acting under the color of law. At issue is whether the last two elements would be met by the use of the proposed procedures, namely, whether those using these procedures would have the requisite mental state and whether these procedures would inflict severe pain or suffering within the meaning of the statute.

Severe Pain or Suffering. In order for pain or suffering to rise to the level of torture, the statute requires that it be severe. As we have previously explained, this reaches only extreme acts. *See id.* at 13. Nonetheless, drawing upon cases under the Torture Victim Protection Act (TVPA), which has a definition of torture that is similar to Section 2340's definition, we found that a single event of sufficiently intense pain may fall within this prohibition. *See id.* at 26. As a result, we have analyzed each of these techniques separately. In further drawing upon those cases, we also have found that courts tend to take a totality-of-the-circumstances approach and consider an entire course of conduct to determine whether torture has occurred. *See id.* at 27. Therefore, in addition to considering each technique separately, we consider them together as a course of conduct.

Section 2340 defines torture as the infliction of severe physical or mental pain or suffering. We will consider physical pain and mental pain separately. *See* 18 U.S.C. § 2340(1). With respect to *physical* pain, we previously concluded that "severe pain" within the meaning of

152

Section 2340 is pain that is difficult for the individual to endure and is of an intensity akin to the pain accompanying serious physical injury. *See* Section 2340A Memorandum at 6. Drawing upon the TVPA precedent, we have noted that examples of acts inflicting severe pain that typify torture are, among other things, severe beatings with weapons such as clubs, and the burning of prisoners. *See id.* at 24. We conclude below that none of the proposed techniques inflicts such pain.

The facial hold and the attention grasp involve no physical pain. In the absence of such pain it is obvious that they cannot be said to inflict severe physical pain or suffering. The stress positions and wall standing both may result in muscle fatigue. Each involves the sustained holding of a position. In wall standing, it will be holding a position in which all of the individual's body weight is placed on his finger tips. The stress positions will likely include sitting on the floor with legs extended straight out in front and arms raised above the head, and kneeling on the floor and leaning back at a 45 degree angle. Any pain associated with muscle fatigue is not of the intensity sufficient to amount to "severe physical pain or suffering" under the statute, nor, despite its discomfort, can it be said to be difficult to endure. Moreover, you have orally informed us that no stress position will be used that could interfere with the healing of Zubaydah's wound. Therefore, we conclude that these techniques involve discomfort that falls far below the threshold of severe physical pain.

Similarly, although the confinement boxes (both small and large) are physically uncomfortable because their size restricts movement, they are not so small as to require the individual to contort his body to sit (small box) or stand (large box). You have also orally informed us that despite his wound, Zubaydah remains quite flexible, which would substantially reduce any pain associated with being placed in the box. We have no information from the medical experts you have consulted that the limited duration for which the individual is kept in the boxes causes any substantial physical pain. As a result, we do not think the use of these boxes can be said to cause pain that is of the intensity associated with serious physical injury.

The use of one of these boxes with the introduction of an insect does not alter this assessment. As we understand it, no actually harmful insect will be placed in the box. Thus, though the introduction of an insect may produce trepidation in Zubaydah (which we discuss below), it certainly does not cause physical pain.

As for sleep deprivation, it is clear that depriving someone of sleep does not involve severe physical pain within the meaning of the statute. While sleep deprivation may involve some physical discomfort, such as the fatigue or the discomfort experienced in the difficulty of keeping one's eyes open, these effects remit after the individual is permitted to sleep. Based on the facts you have provided us, we are not aware of any evidence that sleep deprivation results in severe physical pain or suffering. As a result, its use does not violate Section 2340A.

Even those techniques that involve physical contact between the interrogator and the individual do not result in severe pain. The facial slap and walling contain precautions to ensure that no pain even approaching this level results. The slap is delivered with fingers slightly spread, which you have explained to us is designed to be less painful than a closed-hand slap. The slap is also delivered to the fleshy part of the face, further reducing any risk of physical damage or serious pain. The facial slap does not produce pain that is difficult to endure. Likewise, walling involves quickly pulling the person forward and then thrusting him against a flexible false wall. You have informed us that the sound of hitting the wall will actually be far worse than any possible injury to the individual. The use of the rolled towel around the neck also reduces any risk of injury. While it may hurt to be pushed against the wall, any pain experienced is not of the intensity associated with serious physical injury.

As we understand it, when the waterboard is used, the subject's body responds as if the subject were drowning—even though the subject may be well aware that he is in fact not drowning. You have informed us that this procedure does not inflict actual physical harm. Thus, although the subject may experience the fear or panic associated with the feeling of drowning, the waterboard does not inflict physical pain. As we explained in the Section 2340A Memorandum, "pain and suffering" as used in Section 2340 is best understood as a single concept, not distinct concepts of "pain" as distinguished from "suffering." *See* Section 2340A Memorandum at 6 n.3. The waterboard, which inflicts no pain or actual harm whatsoever, does not, in our view inflict "severe pain or suffering." Even if one were to parse the statute more finely to attempt to treat "suffering" as a distinct concept, the waterboard could not be said to inflict severe suffering. The waterboard is simply a controlled acute episode, lacking the connotation of a protracted period of time generally given to suffering.

Finally, as we discussed above, you have informed us that in determining which procedures to use and how you will use them, you have selected techniques that will not harm Zubaydah's wound. You have also indicated that numerous steps will be taken to ensure that none of these procedures in any way interferes with the proper healing of Zubaydah's wound. You have also indicated that, should it appear at any time that Zubaydah is experiencing severe pain or suffering, the medical personnel on hand will stop the use of any technique.

Even when all of these methods are considered combined in an overall course of conduct, they still would not inflict severe physical pain or suffering. As discussed above, a number of these acts result in no physical pain, others produce only physical discomfort. You have indicated that these acts will not be used with substantial repetition, so that there is no possibility that severe physical pain could arise from such repetition. Accordingly, we conclude that these acts neither separately nor as part of a course of conduct would inflict severe physical pain or suffering within the meaning of the statute.

We next consider whether the use of these techniques would inflict severe *mental* pain or suffering within the meaning of Section 2340. Section 2340 defines severe mental pain or suffering as "the prolonged mental harm caused by or resulting from" one of several predicate

154

acts. 18 U.S.C. § 2340(2). Those predicate acts are: (1) the intentional infliction or threatened infliction of severe physical pain or suffering; (2) the administration or application, or threatened administration or application of mind-altering substances or other procedures calculated to disrupt profoundly the senses or the personality; (3) the threat of imminent death; or (4) the threat that any of the preceding acts will be done to another person. *See* 18 U.S.C. § 2340(2)(A)–(D). As we have explained, this list of predicate acts is exclusive. *See* Section 2340A Memorandum at 8. No other acts can support a charge under Section 2340A based on the infliction of severe mental pain or suffering. *See id.* Thus, if the methods that you have described do not either in and of themselves constitute one of these acts or as a course of conduct fulfill the predicate act requirement, the prohibition has not been violated. *See id.* Before addressing these techniques, we note that it is plain that none of these procedures involves a threat to any third party, the use of any kind of drugs, or for the reasons described above, the infliction of severe physical pain. Thus, the question is whether any of these acts, separately or as a course of conduct, constitutes a threat of severe physical pain or suffering, a procedure designed to disrupt profoundly the senses, or a threat of imminent death. As we previously explained, whether an action constitutes a threat must be assessed from the standpoint of a reasonable person in the subject's position. *See id.* at 9.

No argument can be made that the attention grasp or the facial hold constitute threats of imminent death or are procedures designed to disrupt profoundly the senses or personality. In general the grasp and the facial hold will startle the subject, produce fear, or even insult him. As you have informed us, the use of these techniques is not accompanied by a specific verbal threat of severe physical pain or suffering. To the extent that these techniques could be considered a threat of severe physical pain or suffering, such a threat would have to be inferred from the acts themselves. Because these actions themselves involve no pain, neither could be interpreted by a reasonable person in Zubaydah's position to constitute a threat of severe pain or suffering. Accordingly, these two techniques are not predicate acts within the meaning of Section 2340.

The facial slap likewise falls outside the set of predicate acts. It plainly is not a threat of imminent death, under Section 2340(2)(C), or a procedure designed to disrupt profoundly the senses or personality, under Section 2340(2)(B). Though it may hurt, as discussed above, the effect is one of smarting or stinging and surprise or humiliation, but not severe pain. Nor does it alone constitute a threat of severe pain or suffering, under Section 2340(2)(A). Like the facial hold and the attention grasp, the use of this slap is not accompanied by a specific verbal threat of further escalating violence. Additionally, you have informed us that in one use this technique will typically involve at most two slaps. Certainly, the use of this slap may dislodge any expectation that Zubaydah had that he would not be touched in a physically aggressive manner. Nonetheless, this alteration in his expectations could hardly be construed by a reasonable person in his situation to be tantamount to a threat of severe physical pain or suffering. At most, this technique suggests that the circumstances of his confinement and interrogation have changed. Therefore, the facial slap is not within the statute's exclusive list of predicate acts.

Walling plainly is not a procedure calculated to disrupt profoundly the senses or personality. While walling involves what might be characterized as rough handling, it does not involve the threat of imminent death or, as discussed above, the infliction of severe physical pain. Moreover, once again we understand that use of this technique will not be accompanied by any specific verbal threat that violence will ensue absent cooperation. Thus, like the facial slap, walling can only constitute a threat of severe physical pain if a reasonable person would infer such a threat from the use of the technique itself. Walling does not in and of itself inflict severe pain or suffering. Like the facial slap, walling may alter the subject's expectation as to the treatment he believes he will receive. Nonetheless, the character of the action falls so far short of inflicting severe pain or suffering within the meaning of the statute that even if he inferred that greater aggressiveness was to follow, the type of actions that could be reasonably be anticipated would still fall below anything sufficient to inflict severe physical pain or suffering under the statute. Thus, we conclude that this technique falls outside the proscribed predicate acts.

Like walling, stress positions and wall-standing are not procedures calculated to disrupt profoundly the senses, nor are they threats of imminent death. These procedures, as discussed above, involve the use of muscle fatigue to encourage cooperation and do not themselves constitute the infliction of severe physical pain or suffering. Moreover, there is no aspect of violence to either technique that remotely suggests future severe pain or suffering from which such a threat of future harm could be inferred. They simply involve forcing the subject to remain in uncomfortable positions. While these acts may indicate to the subject that he may be placed in these positions again if he does not disclose information, the use of these techniques would not suggest to a reasonable person in the subject's position that he is being threatened with severe pain or suffering. Accordingly, we conclude that these two procedures do not constitute any of the predicate acts set forth in Section 2340(2).

As with the other techniques discussed so far, cramped confinement is not a threat of imminent death. It may be argued that, focusing in part on the fact that the boxes will be without light, placement in these boxes would constitute a procedure designed to disrupt profoundly the senses. As we explained in our recent opinion, however, to "disrupt profoundly the senses" a technique must produce an extreme effect in the subject. *See* Section 2340A Memorandum at 10–12. We have previously concluded that this requires that the procedure cause substantial interference with the individual's cognitive abilities or fundamentally alter his personality. *See id.* at 11. Moreover, the statute requires that such procedures must be calculated to produce this effect. *See id.* at 10; 18 U.S.C. § 2340(2)(B).

With respect to the small confinement box, you have informed us that he would spend at most two hours in this box. You have informed us that your purpose in using these boxes is not to interfere with his senses or his personality, but to cause him physical discomfort that will encourage him to disclose critical information. Moreover, your imposition of time limitations on the use of either of the boxes also indicates that the use of these boxes is not designed or calculated to disrupt profoundly the senses or personality. For the larger box, in which he can

156

both stand and sit, he may be placed in this box for up to eighteen hours at a time, while you have informed us that he will never spend more than an hour at time in the smaller box. These time limits further ensure that no profound disruption of the senses or personality, were it even possible, would result. As such, the use of the confinement boxes does not constitute a procedure calculated to disrupt profoundly the senses or personality.

Nor does the use of the boxes threaten Zubaydah with severe physical pain or suffering. While additional time spent in the boxes may be threatened, their use is not accompanied by any express threats of severe physical pain or suffering. Like the stress positions and walling, placement in the boxes is physically uncomfortable but any such discomfort does not rise to the level of severe physical pain or suffering. Accordingly, a reasonable person in the subject's position would not infer from the use of this technique that severe physical pain is the next step in his interrogator's treatment of him. Therefore, we conclude that the use of the confinement boxes does not fall within the statute's required predicate acts.

In addition to using the confinement boxes alone, you also would like to introduce an insect into one of the boxes with Zubaydah. As we understand it, you plan to inform Zubaydah that you are going to place a stinging insect into the box, but you will actually place a harmless insect in the box, such as a caterpillar. If you do so, to ensure that you are outside the predicate act requirement, you must inform him that the insects will not have a sting that would produce death or severe pain. If, however, you were to place the insect in the box without informing him that you are doing so, then, in order to not commit a predicate act, you should not affirmatively lead him to believe that any insect is present which has a sting that could produce severe pain or suffering or even cause his death. ▮▮▮▮▮▮▮▮▮▮▮ so long as you take either of the approaches we have described, the insect's placement in the box would not constitute a threat of severe physical pain or suffering to a reasonable person in his position. An individual placed in a box, even an individual with a fear of insects, would not reasonably feel threatened with severe physical pain or suffering if a caterpillar was placed in the box. Further, you have informed us that you are not aware that Zubaydah has any allergies to insects, and you have not informed us of any other factors that would cause a reasonable person in that same situation to believe that an unknown insect would cause him severe physical pain or death. Thus, we conclude that the placement of the insect in the confinement box with Zubaydah would not constitute a predicate act.

Sleep deprivation also clearly does not involve a threat of imminent death. Although it produces physical discomfort, it cannot be said to constitute a threat of severe physical pain or suffering from the perspective of a reasonable person in Zubaydah's position. Nor could sleep deprivation constitute a procedure calculated to disrupt profoundly the senses, so long as sleep deprivation (as you have informed us is your intent) is used for limited periods, before hallucinations or other profound disruptions of the senses would occur. To be sure, sleep deprivation may reduce the subject's ability to think on his feet. Indeed, you indicate that this is

14

the intended result. His mere reduced ability to evade your questions and resist answering does not, however, rise to the level of disruption required by the statute. As we explained above, a disruption within the meaning of the statute is an extreme one, substantially interfering with an individual's cognitive abilities, for example, inducing hallucinations, or driving him to engage in uncharacteristic self-destructive behavior. *See infra* 13; Section 2340A Memorandum at 11. Therefore, the limited use of sleep deprivation does not constitute one of the required predicate acts.

We find that the use of the waterboard constitutes a threat of imminent death. As you have explained the waterboard procedure to us, it creates in the subject the uncontrollable physiological sensation that the subject is drowning. Although the procedure will be monitored by personnel with medical training and extensive SERE school experience with this procedure who will ensure the subject's mental and physical safety, the subject is not aware of any of these precautions. From the vantage point of any reasonable person undergoing this procedure in such circumstances, he would feel as if he is drowning at very moment of the procedure due to the uncontrollable physiological sensation he is experiencing. Thus, this procedure cannot be viewed as too uncertain to satisfy the imminence requirement. Accordingly, it constitutes a threat of imminent death and fulfills the predicate act requirement under the statute.

Although the waterboard constitutes a threat of imminent death, prolonged mental harm must nonetheless result to violate the statutory prohibition on infliction of severe mental pain or suffering. *See* Section 2340A Memorandum at 7. We have previously concluded that prolonged mental harm is mental harm of some lasting duration, e.g., mental harm lasting months or years. *See id.* Prolonged mental harm is not simply the stress experienced in, for example, an interrogation by state police. *See id.* Based on your research into the use of these methods at the SERE school and consultation with others with expertise in the field of psychology and interrogation, you do not anticipate that any prolonged mental harm would result from the use of the waterboard. Indeed, you have advised us that the relief is almost immediate when the cloth is removed from the nose and mouth. In the absence of prolonged mental harm, no severe mental pain or suffering would have been inflicted, and the use of these procedures would not constitute torture within the meaning of the statute.

When these acts are considered as a course of conduct, we are unsure whether these acts may constitute a threat of severe physical pain or suffering. You have indicated to us that you have not determined either the order or the precise timing for implementing these procedures. It is conceivable that these procedures could be used in a course of escalating conduct, moving incrementally and rapidly from least physically intrusive, e.g., facial hold, to the most physical contact, e.g., walling or the waterboard. As we understand it, based on his treatment so far, Zubaydah has come to expect that no physical harm will be done to him. By using these techniques in increasing intensity and in rapid succession, the goal would be to dislodge this expectation. Based on the facts you have provided to us, we cannot say definitively that the entire course of conduct would cause a reasonable person to believe that he is being threatened with severe pain or suffering within the meaning of section 2340. On the other hand, however, under certain circumstances—for example, rapid escalation in the use of these techniques culminating in the waterboard (which we acknowledge constitutes a threat of imminent death) accompanied by verbal or other suggestions that physical violence will follow—might cause a reasonable person to believe that they are faced with such a threat. Without more information, we are uncertain whether the course of conduct would constitute a predicate act under Section 2340(2).

Even if the course of conduct were thought to pose a threat of physical pain or suffering, it would nevertheless—on the facts before us—not constitute a violation of Section 2340A. Not only must the course of conduct be a predicate act, but also those who use the procedure must actually cause prolonged mental harm. Based on the information that you have provided to us, indicating that no evidence exists that this course of conduct produces any prolonged mental harm, we conclude that a course of conduct using these procedures and culminating in the waterboard would not violate Section 2340A.

Specific Intent. To violate the statute, an individual must have the specific intent to inflict severe pain or suffering. Because specific intent is an element of the offense, the absence of specific intent negates the charge of torture. As we previously opined, to have the required specific intent, an individual must expressly intend to cause such severe pain or suffering. *See* Section 2340A Memorandum at 3 *citing Carter v. United States*, 530 U.S. 255, 267 (2000). We have further found that if a defendant acts with the good faith belief that his actions will not cause such suffering, he has not acted with specific intent. *See id.* at 4 *citing South Atl. Lmtd. Ptrshp. of Tenn. v. Reise*, 218 F.3d 518, 531 (4th Cir. 2002). A defendant acts in good faith when he has an honest belief that his actions will not result in severe pain or suffering. *See id. citing Cheek v. United States*, 498 U.S. 192, 202 (1991). Although an honest belief need not be reasonable, such a belief is easier to establish where there is a reasonable basis for it. *See id.* at 5. Good faith may be established by, among other things, the reliance on the advice of experts. *See id.* at 8.

Based on the information you have provided us, we believe that those carrying out these procedures would not have the specific intent to inflict severe physical pain or suffering. The objective of these techniques is not to cause severe physical pain. First, the constant presence of personnel with medical training who have the authority to stop the interrogation should it appear it is medically necessary indicates that it is not your intent to cause severe physical pain. The personnel on site have extensive experience with these specific techniques as they are used in SERE school training. Second, you have informed us that you are taking steps to ensure that Zubaydah's injury is not worsened or his recovery impeded by the use of these techniques.

Third, as you have described them to us, the proposed techniques involving physical contact between the interrogator and Zubaydah actually contain precautions to prevent any serious physical harm to Zubaydah. In "walling," a rolled hood or towel will be used to prevent whiplash and he will be permitted to rebound from the flexible wall to reduce the likelihood of injury. Similarly, in the "facial hold," the fingertips will be kept well away from the his eyes to ensure that there is no injury to them. The purpose of that facial hold is not injure him but to hold the head immobile. Additionally, while the stress positions and wall standing will undoubtedly result in physical discomfort by tiring the muscles, it is obvious that these positions are not intended to produce the kind of extreme pain required by the statute.

Furthermore, no specific intent to cause severe mental pain or suffering appears to be present. As we explained in our recent opinion, an individual must have the specific intent to cause prolonged mental harm in order to have the specific intent to inflict severe mental pain or suffering. *See* Section 2340A Memorandum at 8. Prolonged mental harm is substantial mental harm of a sustained duration, e.g., harm lasting months or even years after the acts were inflicted upon the prisoner. As we indicated above, a good faith belief can negate this element. Accordingly, if an individual conducting the interrogation has a good faith belief that the procedures he will apply, separately or together, would not result in prolonged mental harm, that individual lacks the requisite specific intent. This conclusion concerning specific intent is further bolstered by the due diligence that has been conducted concerning the effects of these interrogation procedures.

The mental health experts that you have consulted have indicated that the psychological impact of a course of conduct must be assessed with reference to the subject's psychological history and current mental health status. The healthier the individual, the less likely that the use of any one procedure or set of procedures as a course of conduct will result in prolonged mental harm. A comprehensive psychological profile of Zubaydah has been created. In creating this profile, your personnel drew on direct interviews, Zubaydah's diaries, observation of Zubaydah since his capture, and information from other sources such as other intelligence and press reports.

As we indicated above, you have informed us that your proposed interrogation methods have been used and continue to be used in SERE training. It is our understanding that these techniques are not used one by one in isolation, but as a full course of conduct to resemble a real interrogation. Thus, the information derived from SERE training bears both upon the impact of the use of the individual techniques and upon their use as a course of conduct. You have found that the use of these methods together or separately, including the use of the waterboard, has not resulted in any negative long-term mental health consequences. The continued use of these methods without mental health consequences to the trainees indicates that it is highly improbable

160

that such consequences would result here. Because you have conducted the due diligence to determine that these procedures, either alone or in combination, do not produce prolonged mental harm, we believe that you do not meet the specific intent requirement necessary to violate Section 2340A.

You have also informed us that you have reviewed the relevant literature on the subject, and consulted with outside psychologists. Your review of the literature uncovered no empirical data on the use of these procedures, with the exception of sleep deprivation for which no long-term health consequences resulted. The outside psychologists with whom you consulted indicated were unaware of any cases where long-term problems have occurred as a result of these techniques.

As described above, it appears you have conducted an extensive inquiry to ascertain what impact, if any, these procedures individually and as a course of conduct would have on Zubaydah. You have consulted with interrogation experts, including those with substantial SERE school experience, consulted with outside psychologists, completed a psychological assessment and reviewed the relevant literature on this topic. Based on this inquiry, you believe that the use of the procedures, including the waterboard, and as a course of conduct would not result in prolonged mental harm. Reliance on this information about Zubaydah and about the effect of the use of these techniques more generally demonstrates the presence of a good faith belief that no prolonged mental harm will result from using these methods in the interrogation of Zubaydah. Moreover, we think that this represents not only an honest belief but also a reasonable belief based on the information that you have supplied to us. Thus, we believe that the specific intent to inflict prolonged mental is not present, and consequently, there is no specific intent to inflict severe mental pain or suffering. Accordingly, we conclude that on the facts in this case the use of these methods separately or a course of conduct would not violate Section 2340A.

Based on the foregoing, and based on the facts that you have provided, we conclude that the interrogation procedures that you propose would not violate Section 2340A. We wish to emphasize that this is our best reading of the law; however, you should be aware that there are no cases construing this statute; just as there have been no prosecutions brought under it.

Please let us know if we can be of further assistance.

Jay S. Bybee
Assistant Attorney General

(4) Guantánamo Bay interrogation memos, 11 October 2002 (extracts)

DEPARTMENT OF DEFENSE
JOINT TASK FORCE 170
GUANTANAMO BAY, CUBA
APO AE 09860

JTF 170-CG   11 October 2002

MEMORANDUM FOR Commander, United States Southern Command, 3511 NW 91st Avenue, Miami, Florida 33172-1217

SUBJECT: Counter-Resistance Strategies

1. Request that you approve the interrogation techniques delineated in the enclosed Counter-Resistance Strategies memorandum. I have reviewed this memorandum and the legal review provided to me by the JTF-170 Staff Judge Advocate and concur with the legal analysis provided.

2. I am fully aware of the techniques currently employed to gain valuable intelligence in support of the Global War on Terrorism. Although these techniques have resulted in significant exploitable intelligence, the same methods have become less effective over time. I believe the methods and techniques delineated in the accompanying J-2 memorandum will enhance our efforts to extract additional information. Based on the analysis provided by the JTF-170 SJA, I have concluded that these techniques do not violate U.S. or international laws.

3. My point of contact for this issue is LTC Jerald Phifer at DSN 660-3476.

MICHAEL E. DUNLAVEY
Major General, USA
Commanding

2 Encls
1. JTF 170-J2 Memo,
   11 Oct 02
2. JTF 170-SJA Memo,
   11 Oct 02

UNCLASSIFIED

DEPARTMENT OF DEFENSE
JOINT TASK FORCE 170
GUANTANAMO BAY, CUBA
APO AE 09360

JTF-J2   11 October 2002

MEMORANDUM FOR Commander, Joint Task Force 170

SUBJECT: Request for Approval of Counter-Resistance Strategies

1. (S/NF) PROBLEM: The current guidelines for interrogation procedures at GTMO limit the ability of interrogators to counter advanced resistance.

2. (S/NF) Request approval for use of the following interrogation plan.

   a. Category I techniques. During the initial category of interrogation the detainee should be provided a chair and the environment should be generally comfortable. The format of the interrogation is the direct approach. The use of rewards like cookies or cigarettes may be helpful. If the detainee is determined by the interrogator to be uncooperative, the interrogator may use the following techniques.

      (1) Yelling at the detainee (not directly in his ear or to the level that it would cause physical pain or hearing problems)

      (2) Techniques of deception:

      (a) Multiple interrogator techniques.

      (b) Interrogator identity. The interviewer may identify himself as a citizen of a foreign nation or as an interrogator from a country with a reputation for harsh treatment of detainees.

   b. Category II techniques. With the permission of the OIC, Interrogation Section, the interrogator may use the following techniques.

      (1) The use of stress positions (like standing), for a maximum of four hours.

      (2) The use of falsified documents or reports.

      (3) Use of the isolation facility for up to 30 days. Request must be made to through the OIC, Interrogation Section, to the Director, Joint Interrogation Group (JIG). Extensions beyond the initial 30 days must be approved by the Commanding General. For selected

Declassify Under the Authority of Executive Order 12958
By Executive Secretary, Office of the Secretary of Defense
By William P. Marriott, CAPT, USN
June 21, 2004

SECRET//NOFORN **UNCLASSIFIED**

SECRET/NOFORN

JTF 170-J2
SUBJECT: Request for Approval of Counter-Resistance Strategies

detainees, the OIC, Interrogation Section, will approve all contacts with the detainee, to include medical visits of a non-emergent nature.

(4) Interrogating the detainee in an environment other than the standard interrogation booth.

(5) Deprivation of light and auditory stimuli.

(6) The detainee may also have a hood placed over his head during transportation and questioning. The hood should not restrict breathing in any way and the detainee should be under direct observation when hooded.

(7) The use of 20-hour interrogations.

(8) Removal of all comfort items (including religious items).

(9) Switching the detainee from hot rations to MREs.

(10) Removal of clothing.

(11) Forced grooming (shaving of facial hair etc..)

(12) Using detainees individual phobias (such as fear of dogs) to induce stress.

c. Category III techniques. Techniques in this category may be used only by submitting a request through the Director, JIG, for approval by the Commanding General with appropriate legal review and information to Commander, USSOUTHCOM. These techniques are required for a very small percentage of the most uncooperative detainees (less than 3%). The following techniques and other aversive techniques, such as those used in U.S. military interrogation resistance training or by other U.S. government agencies, may be utilized in a carefully coordinated manner to help interrogate exceptionally resistant detainees. Any or these techniques that require more than light grabbing, poking, or pushing, will be administered only by individuals specifically trained in their safe application.

(1) The use of scenarios designed to convince the detainee that death or severely painful consequences are imminent for him and/or his family.

(2) Exposure to cold weather or water (with appropriate medical monitoring).

(3) Use of a wet towel and dripping water to induce the misperception of suffocation.

SECRET/NOFORN   UNCLASSIFIED
2

UNCLASSIFIED

~~SECRET/NOFORN~~

JTF 170-J2
SUBJECT: Request for Approval of Counter-Resistance Strategies

(4) Use of mild, non-injurous physical contact such as grabbing, poking in the chest with the finger, and light pushing.

3. (U) The POC for this memorandum is the undersigned at 23476.

JERALD PHIFER
LTC, USA
Director, J2

~~SECRET/NOFORN~~   UNCLASSIFIED

3

(5)   Statement by Secretary of State Condoleezza Rice on her departure for Europe, 5 December 2005

We have received enquiries from the European Union, the Council of Europe, and from several individual countries about media reports concerning US conduct in the war on terror.

I am going to respond now to those enquiries, as I depart today for Europe.

And this will also essentially form the text of the letter that I will send to [British Foreign] Secretary [Jack] Straw, who wrote on behalf of the European Union as the European Union president.

The United States and many other countries are waging a war against terrorism. For our country this war often takes the form of conventional military operations in places like Afghanistan and Iraq.

Sometimes this is a political struggle, a war of ideas. It is a struggle waged also by our law enforcement agencies. Often we engage the enemy through the co-operation of our intelligence services with their foreign counterparts.

We must track down terrorists who seek refuge in areas where governments cannot take effective action, including where the terrorists cannot in practice be reached by the ordinary processes of law.

In such places, terrorists have planned the killings of thousands of innocents - in New York City or Nairobi, in Bali or London, in Madrid or Beslan, in Casablanca or Istanbul.

Just two weeks ago I also visited a hotel ballroom in Amman, viewing the silent, shattered aftermath of one of those attacks.

The United States, and those countries that share the commitment to defend their citizens, will use every lawful weapon to defeat these terrorists. Protecting citizens is the first and oldest duty of any government.

Sometimes these efforts are misunderstood. I want to help all of you understand the hard choices involved, and some of the responsibilities that go with them.

One of the difficult issues in this new kind of conflict is what to do with captured individuals who we know or believe to be terrorists. The individuals come from many countries and are often captured far from their original homes.

Among them are those who are effectively stateless, owing allegiance only to the extremist cause of transnational terrorism. Many are extremely dangerous. And some have information that may save lives, perhaps even thousands of lives.

The captured terrorists of the 21st Century do not fit easily into traditional systems of criminal or military justice, which were designed for different needs. We have to adapt. Other governments are now also facing this challenge.

We consider the captured members of al-Qaeda and its affiliates to be unlawful combatants who may be held, in accordance with the law of war, to keep them from killing innocents.

We must treat them in accordance with our laws, which reflect the values of the American people. We must question them to gather potentially significant, life-saving, intelligence. We must bring terrorists to justice wherever possible.

For decades, the United States and other countries have used 'renditions' to transport terrorist suspects from the country where they were captured to their home country or to other countries where they can be questioned, held or brought to justice.

In some situations a terrorist suspect can be extradited according to traditional judicial procedures. But there have long been many other cases where, for some reason, the local government cannot detain or prosecute a suspect, and traditional extradition is not a good option.

In those cases the local government can make the sovereign choice to co-operate in a rendition. Such renditions are permissible under international law and are consistent with the responsibilities of those governments to protect their citizens.

Rendition is a vital tool in combating transnational terrorism. Its use is not unique to the United States, or to the current administration. Last year, then director of Central Intelligence, George Tenet, recalled that our earlier counterterrorism successes included 'the rendition of many dozens of terrorists prior to September 11, 2001'.

Ramzi Yousef masterminded the 1993 bombing of the World Trade Center and plotted to blow up airlines over the Pacific Ocean, killing a Japanese airline passenger in a test of one of his bombs. Once tracked down, a rendition brought him to the United States, where he now serves a life sentence.

One of history's most infamous terrorists, best known as Carlos the Jackal, had participated in murders in Europe and the Middle East. He was finally captured in Sudan in 1994. A rendition by the French government brought him to justice in France, where he is now imprisoned. Indeed, the European Commission of Human Rights rejected Carlos' claim that his rendition from Sudan was unlawful.

Renditions take terrorists out of action, and save lives. In conducting such renditions, it is the policy of the United States, and I presume of any other democracies who use this procedure, to comply with its laws and comply with its treaty obligations, including those under the Convention Against Torture.

Torture is a term that is defined by law. We rely on our law to govern our operations. The United States does not permit, tolerate, or condone torture under any circumstances.

Moreover, in accordance with the policy of this administration:

•   The United States has respected - and will continue to respect - the sovereignty of other countries

•   The United States does not transport, and has not transported, detainees from one country to another for the purpose of interrogation using torture

•   The United States does not use the airspace or the airports of any country for the purpose of transporting a detainee to a country where he or she will be tortured

•   The United States has not transported anyone, and will not transport anyone, to a country when we believe he will be tortured. Where appropriate, the United States seeks assurances that transferred persons will not be tortured.

International law allows a state to detain enemy combatants for the duration of hostilities.

Detainees may only be held for an extended period if the intelligence or other evidence against them has been carefully evaluated and supports a determination that detention is lawful.

The US does not seek to hold anyone for a period beyond what is necessary to evaluate the intelligence or other evidence against them, prevent further acts of terrorism, or hold them for legal proceedings.

With respect to detainees, the United States government complies with its constitution, its laws, and its treaty obligations.

Acts of physical or mental torture are expressly prohibited.

The United States government does not authorise or condone torture of detainees. Torture, and conspiracy to commit torture, are crimes under US law, wherever they may occur in the world.

Violations of these and other detention standards have been investigated and punished. There have been cases of unlawful treatment of detainees, such as the abuse of a detainee by an intelligence agency contractor in Afghanistan or the horrible mistreatment of some prisoners at Abu Ghraib that sickened us all and which arose under the different legal framework that applies to armed conflict in Iraq.

In such cases the United States has vigorously investigated, and where appropriate, prosecuted and punished those responsible.

Some individuals have already been sentenced to lengthy terms in prison; others have been demoted or reprimanded.

As CIA Director [Porter] Goss recently stated, our intelligence agencies have handled the gathering of intelligence from a very small number of extremely dangerous detainees, including the individuals who planned the 9/11 attacks in the United States, the attack on the USS Cole, and many other murders and attempted murders.

It is the policy of the United States that this questioning is to be conducted within US law and treaty obligations, without using torture.

It is also US policy that authorised interrogation will be consistent with US obligations under the Convention Against Torture, which prohibit cruel, inhuman, or degrading treatment.

The intelligence so gathered has stopped terrorist attacks and saved innocent lives - in Europe as well as in the United States and other countries.

The United States has fully respected the sovereignty of other countries that co-operate in these matters.

Because this war on terrorism challenges traditional norms and precedents of previous conflicts, our citizens have been discussing and debating the proper legal standards that should apply.

President Bush is working with the US Congress to come up with good solutions. I want to emphasise a few key points:

168

- The United States is a country of laws. My colleagues and I have sworn to support and defend the constitution of the United States. We believe in the rule of law.
- The United States government must protect its citizens. We and our friends around the world have the responsibility to work together in finding practical ways to defend ourselves against ruthless enemies. And these terrorists are some of the most ruthless enemies we face.
- We cannot discuss information that would compromise the success of intelligence, law enforcement, and military operations. We expect that other nations share this view.

Some governments choose to co-operate with the United States in intelligence, law enforcement, or military matters. That co-operation is a two-way street. We share intelligence that has helped protect European countries from attack, helping save European lives.

It is up to those governments and their citizens to decide if they wish to work with us to prevent terrorist attacks against their own country or other countries, and decide how much sensitive information they can make public. They have a sovereign right to make that choice.

Debate in and among democracies is natural and healthy. I hope that that debate also includes a healthy regard for the responsibilities of governments to protect their citizens.

Four years after 11 September, most of our populations are asking us if we are doing all that we can to protect them.

I know what it is like to face an inquiry into whether everything was done that could have been done. So now, before the next attack, we should all consider the hard choices that democratic governments must face.

And we can all best meet this danger if we work together

(6) Speech by President George W. Bush on the secret prisons programme, 6 September 2006 and summary of the HVD Program

THE WHITE HOUSE
Office of the Press Secretary
September 6, 2006

REMARKS BY THE PRESIDENT ON THE GLOBAL WAR ON TERROR
The East Room
1:45 P.M. EDT

THE PRESIDENT: Thank you. Thanks for the warm welcome. Welcome to the White House. Mr. Vice President, Secretary Rice, Attorney General Gonzales, Ambassador Negroponte, General Hayden, members of the United States Congress, families who lost loved ones in the terrorist attacks on our nation, and my fellow citizens: Thanks for coming.

On the morning of September the 11th, 2001, our nation awoke to a nightmare attack. Nineteen men, armed with box cutters, took control of airplanes and turned them into missiles. They used them to kill nearly 3,000 innocent people. We watched the Twin Towers collapse before our eyes -- and it became instantly clear that we'd entered a new world, and a dangerous new war.

The attacks of September the 11th horrified our nation. And amid the grief came new fears and urgent questions: Who had attacked us? What did they want? And what else were they planning? Americans saw the destruction the terrorists had caused in New York, and Washington, and Pennsylvania, and they wondered if there were other terrorist cells in our midst poised to strike; they wondered if there was a second wave of attacks still to come.

With the Twin Towers and the Pentagon still smoldering, our country on edge, and a stream of intelligence coming in about potential new attacks, my administration faced immediate challenges: We had to respond to the attack on our country. We had to wage an unprecedented war against an enemy unlike any we had fought before. We had to find the terrorists hiding in America and across the world, before they were able to strike our country again. So in the early days and weeks after 9/11, I directed our government's senior national security officials to do everything in their power, within our laws, to prevent another attack.

Nearly five years have passed since these -- those initial days of shock and sadness -- and we are thankful that the terrorists have not succeeded in launching another attack on our soil. This is not for the lack of desire or determination on the part of the enemy. As the recently foiled plot in London shows, the terrorists are still active, and they're still trying to strike America, and they're still trying to kill our people. One reason the terrorists have not succeeded is because of the hard work of thousands of dedicated men and women in our government, who have toiled day and night, along with our allies, to stop the enemy from carrying out their plans.

And we are grateful for these hardworking citizens of ours.

Another reason the terrorists have not succeeded is because our government has changed its policies -- and given our military, intelligence, and law enforcement personnel the tools they need to fight this enemy and protect our people and preserve our freedoms.

The terrorists who declared war on America represent no nation, they defend no territory, and they wear no uniform. They do not mass armies on borders, or flotillas of warships on the high seas. They operate in the shadows of society; they send small teams of operatives to infiltrate free nations; they live quietly among their victims; they conspire in secret, and then they strike without warning. In this new war, the most important source of information on where the terrorists are hiding and what they are planning is the terrorists, themselves. Captured terrorists have unique knowledge about how terrorist networks operate. They have knowledge of where their operatives are deployed, and knowledge about what plots are underway. This intelligence -- this is intelligence that cannot be found any other place. And our security depends on getting this kind of information. To win the war on terror, we must be able to detain, question, and, when appropriate, prosecute terrorists captured here in America, and on the battlefields around the world.

After the 9/11 attacks, our coalition launched operations across the world to remove terrorist safe havens, and capture or kill terrorist operatives and leaders. Working with our allies, we've captured and detained thousands of terrorists and enemy fighters in Afghanistan, in Iraq, and other fronts of this war on terror. These enemy -- these are enemy combatants, who were waging war on our nation. We have a right under the laws of war, and we have an obligation to the American people, to detain these enemies and stop them from rejoining the battle.

Most of the enemy combatants we capture are held in Afghanistan or in Iraq, where they're questioned by our military personnel. Many are released after questioning, or turned over to local authorities -- if we determine that they do not pose a continuing threat and no longer have significant intelligence value. Others remain in American custody near the battlefield, to ensure that they don't return to the fight.

In some cases, we determine that individuals we have captured pose a significant threat, or may have intelligence that we and our allies need to have to prevent new attacks. Many are al Qaeda operatives or Taliban fighters trying to conceal their identities, and they withhold information that could save American lives. In these cases, it has been necessary to move these individuals to an environment where they can be held secretly [sic], questioned by experts, and -- when appropriate -- prosecuted for terrorist acts.

Some of these individuals are taken to the United States Naval Base at Guantánamo Bay, Cuba. It's important for Americans and others across the world to understand the kind of people held at Guantánamo. These aren't common criminals, or bystanders accidentally swept up on the battlefield -- we have in place a rigorous process to ensure those held at Guantánamo Bay belong at Guantánamo. Those held at Guantánamo include suspected bomb makers, terrorist trainers, recruiters and facilitators, and potential suicide bombers. They are in our custody so they cannot murder our people. One detainee held at Guantánamo told a questioner questioning him -- he said this: "I'll never forget your face. I will kill you, your brothers, your mother, and sisters."

In addition to the terrorists held at Guantánamo, a small number of suspected terrorist leaders and operatives captured during the war have been held and questioned outside the United States, in a separate program operated by the Central Intelligence Agency. This group includes individuals believed to be the key architects of the September the 11th attacks, and attacks on the USS Cole, an operative involved in the bombings of our embassies in Kenya and Tanzania, and individuals involved in other attacks that have taken the lives of innocent civilians across the world. These are dangerous men with unparalleled knowledge about terrorist networks and their plans for new attacks. The security of our nation and the lives of our citizens depend on our ability to learn what these terrorists know.

Many specifics of this program, including where these detainees have been held and the details of their confinement, cannot be divulged. Doing so would provide our enemies with information they could use to take retribution against our allies and harm our country. I can say that questioning the detainees in this program has given us information that has saved innocent lives by helping us stop new attacks -- here in the United States and across the world. Today, I'm going to share with you some of the examples provided by our intelligence community of how this program has saved lives; why it remains vital to the security of the United States, and our friends and allies; and why it deserves the support of the United States Congress and the American people.

Within months of September the 11th, 2001, we captured a man known as Abu Zubaydah. We believe that Zubaydah was a senior terrorist leader and a trusted associate of Osama bin Laden. Our intelligence community believes he had run a terrorist camp in Afghanistan where some of the 9/11 hijackers trained, and that he helped smuggle al Qaeda leaders out of Afghanistan after coalition forces arrived to liberate that country. Zubaydah was severely wounded during the firefight that brought him into custody -- and he survived only because of the medical care arranged by the CIA.

After he recovered, Zubaydah was defiant and evasive. He declared his hatred of America. During questioning, he at first disclosed what he thought was nominal information -- and then stopped all cooperation. Well, in fact, the "nominal" information he gave us turned out to be quite important. For example, Zubaydah disclosed Khalid Sheikh Mohammed -- or KSM -- was the mastermind behind the 9/11 attacks, and used the alias "Muktar." This was a vital piece of the puzzle that helped our intelligence community pursue KSM. Abu Zubaydah also provided information that helped stop a terrorist attack being planned for inside the United States -- an attack about which we had no previous information. Zubaydah told us that al Qaeda operatives were planning to launch an attack in the U.S., and provided physical descriptions of the operatives and information on their general location. Based on the information he provided, the operatives were detained --

172

one while traveling to the United States.

We knew that Zubaydah had more information that could save innocent lives, but he stopped talking. As his questioning proceeded, it became clear that he had received training on how to resist interrogation. And so the CIA used an alternative set of procedures. These procedures were designed to be safe, to comply with our laws, our Constitution, and our treaty obligations. The Department of Justice reviewed the authorized methods extensively and determined them to be lawful. I cannot describe the specific methods used -- I think you understand why -- if I did, it would help the terrorists learn how to resist questioning, and to keep information from us that we need to prevent new attacks on our country. But I can say the procedures were tough, and they were safe, and lawful, and necessary.

Zubaydah was questioned using these procedures, and soon he began to provide information on key al Qaeda operatives, including information that helped us find and capture more of those responsible for the attacks on September the 11th. For example, Zubaydah identified one of KSM's accomplices in the 9/11 attacks -- a terrorist named Ramzi bin al Shibh. The information Zubaydah provided helped lead to the capture of bin al Shibh. And together these two terrorists provided information that helped in the planning and execution of the operation that captured Khalid Sheikh Mohammed.

Once in our custody, KSM was questioned by the CIA using these procedures, and he soon provided information that helped us stop another planned attack on the United States. During questioning, KSM told us about another al Qaeda operative he knew was in CIA custody -- a terrorist named Majid Khan. KSM revealed that Khan had been told to deliver $50,000 to individuals working for a suspected terrorist leader named Hambali, the leader of al Qaeda's Southeast Asian affiliate known as "J-I". CIA officers confronted Khan with this information. Khan confirmed that the money had been delivered to an operative named Zubair, and provided both a physical description and contact number for this operative.

Based on that information, Zubair was captured in June of 2003, and he soon provided information that helped lead to the capture of Hambali. After Hambali's arrest, KSM was questioned again. He identified Hambali's brother as the leader of a "J-I" cell, and Hambali's conduit for communications with al Qaeda. Hambali's brother was soon captured in Pakistan, and, in turn, led us to a cell of 17 Southeast Asian "J-I" operatives. When confronted with the news that his terror cell had been broken up, Hambali admitted that the operatives were being groomed at KSM's request for attacks inside the United States -- probably [sic] using airplanes.

During questioning, KSM also provided many details of other plots to kill innocent Americans. For example, he described the design of planned attacks on buildings inside the United States, and how operatives were directed to carry them out. He told us the operatives had been instructed to ensure that the explosives went off at a point that was high enough to prevent the people trapped above from escaping out the windows.

KSM also provided vital information on al Qaeda's efforts to obtain biological weapons. During questioning, KSM admitted that he had met three individuals involved in al Qaeda's efforts to produce anthrax, a deadly biological agent -- and he identified one of the individuals as a terrorist named Yazid. KSM apparently believed we already had this information, because Yazid had been captured and taken into foreign custody before KSM's arrest. In fact, we did not know about Yazid's role in al Qaeda's anthrax program. Information from Yazid then helped lead to the capture of his two principal assistants in the anthrax program. Without the information provided by KSM and Yazid, we might not have uncovered this al Qaeda biological weapons program, or stopped this al Qaeda cell from developing anthrax for attacks against the United States.

These are some of the plots that have been stopped because of the information of this vital program. Terrorists held in CIA custody have also provided information that helped stop a planned strike on U.S. Marines at Camp Lemonier in Djibouti -- they were going to use an explosive laden water tanker. They helped stop a planned attack on the U.S. consulate in Karachi using car bombs and motorcycle bombs, and they helped stop a plot to hijack passenger planes and fly them into Heathrow or the Canary Wharf in London.

We're getting vital information necessary to do our jobs, and that's to protect the American people and our allies.

Information from the terrorists in this program has helped us to identify individuals that al Qaeda deemed suitable for Western operations, many of whom we had never heard about before. They include terrorists who were set to case targets inside the United States, including financial buildings in major cities on the East Coast. Information from terrorists in CIA custody has played a role in the capture or questioning of nearly every senior al Qaeda member or associate detained by the U.S. and its allies since this program began. By providing everything from initial leads to photo identifications, to precise locations of where terrorists were hiding, this program has helped us to take potential mass murderers off the streets before they were able to kill.

This program has also played a critical role in helping us understand the enemy we face in this war. Terrorists in this program have painted a picture of al Qaeda's structure and financing, and communications and logistics. They identified al Qaeda's travel routes and safe havens, and explained how al Qaeda's senior leadership communicates with its operatives in places like Iraq. They provided information that allows us -- that has allowed us to make sense of documents and computer records that we have seized in terrorist raids. They've identified voices in recordings of intercepted calls, and helped us understand the meaning of potentially critical terrorist communications.

The information we get from these detainees is corroborated by intelligence, and we've received -- that we've received from other sources -- and together this intelligence has helped us connect the dots and stop attacks before they occur. Information from the terrorists questioned in this program helped unravel plots and terrorist cells in Europe and in other places. It's helped our allies protect their people from deadly enemies. This program has been, and remains, one of the most vital tools in our war against the terrorists. It is invaluable to America and to our allies. Were it not for this program, our intelligence community believes that al Qaeda and its allies would have succeeded in launching another attack against the American homeland. By giving us information about terrorist plans we could not get anywhere else, this program has saved innocent lives.

This program has been subject to multiple legal reviews by the Department of Justice and CIA lawyers; they've determined it complied with our laws. This program has received strict oversight by the CIA's Inspector General. A small number of key leaders from both political parties on Capitol Hill were briefed about this program. All those involved in the questioning of the terrorists are carefully chosen and they're screened from a pool of experienced CIA officers. Those selected to conduct the most sensitive questioning had to complete more than 250 additional hours of specialized training before they are allowed to have contact with a captured terrorist.

I want to be absolutely clear with our people, and the world: The United States does not torture. It's against our laws, and it's against our values. I have not authorized it -- and I will not authorize it. Last year, my administration worked with Senator John McCain, and I signed into law the Detainee Treatment Act, which established the legal standard for treatment of detainees wherever they are held. I support this act. And as we implement this law, our government will continue to use every lawful method to obtain intelligence that can protect innocent people, and stop another attack like the one we experienced on September the 11th, 2001.

The CIA program has detained only a limited number of terrorists at any given time -- and once we've determined that the terrorists held by the CIA have little or no additional intelligence value, many of them have been returned to their home countries for prosecution or detention by their governments. Others have been accused of terrible crimes against the American people, and we have a duty to bring those responsible for these crimes to justice. So we intend to prosecute these men, as appropriate, for their crimes.

Soon after the war on terror began, I authorized a system of military commissions to try foreign terrorists accused of war crimes. Military commissions have been used by Presidents from George Washington to Franklin Roosevelt to prosecute war criminals, because the rules for trying enemy combatants in a time of conflict must be different from those for trying common criminals or members of our own military. One of the first suspected terrorists to be put on trial by military commission was one of Osama bin Laden's bodyguards -- a man named Hamdan. His lawyers challenged the legality of the military commission system. It took more than two years for this case to make its way through the courts. The Court of Appeals for the District of Columbia Circuit upheld the military commissions we had designed, but this past June, the Supreme Court overturned that decision. The Supreme Court determined that military commissions are an appropriate venue for trying terrorists, but ruled that military commissions needed to be explicitly authorized by the United States Congress.

So today, I'm sending Congress legislation to specifically authorize the creation of military commissions to try terrorists for war crimes. My administration has been working with members of both parties in the House and Senate on this legislation.

We put forward a bill that ensures these commissions are established in a way that protects our national security, and ensures a full and fair trial for those accused. The procedures in the bill I am sending to Congress today reflect the reality that we are a nation at war, and that it's essential for us to use all reliable evidence to bring these people to justice.

We're now approaching the five-year anniversary of the 9/11 attacks -- and the families of those murdered that day have waited patiently for justice. Some of the families are with us today -- they should have to wait no longer. So I'm announcing today that Khalid Sheikh Mohammed, Abu Zubaydah, Ramzi bin al-Shibh, and 11 other terrorists in CIA custody have been transferred to the United States Naval Base at Guantánamo Bay. (Applause.) They are being held in the custody of the Department of Defense. As soon as Congress acts to authorize the military commissions I have proposed, the men our intelligence officials believe orchestrated the deaths of nearly 3,000 Americans on September the 11th, 2001, can face justice. (Applause.)

We'll also seek to prosecute those believed to be responsible for the attack on the USS Cole, and an operative believed to be involved in the bombings of the American embassies in Kenya and Tanzania. With these prosecutions, we will send a clear message to those who kill Americans: No longer -- how long it takes, we will find you and we will bring you to justice. (Applause.)

These men will be held in a high-security facility at Guantánamo. The International Committee of the Red Cross is being advised of their detention, and will have the opportunity to meet with them. Those charged with crimes will be given access to attorneys who will help them prepare their defense -- and they will be presumed innocent. While at Guantánamo, they will have access to the same food, clothing, medical care, and opportunities for worship as other detainees. They will be questioned subject to the new U.S. Army Field Manual, which the Department of Defense is issuing today. And they will continue to be treated with the humanity that they denied others.

As we move forward with the prosecutions, we will continue to urge nations across the world to take back their nationals at Guantánamo who will not be prosecuted by our military commissions. America has no interest in being the world's jailer. But one of the reasons we have not been able to close Guantánamo is that many countries have refused to take back their nationals held at the facility. Other countries have not provided adequate assurances that their nationals will not be mistreated -- or they will not return to the battlefield, as more than a dozen people released from Guantánamo already have. We will continue working to transfer individuals held at Guantánamo, and ask other countries to work with us in this process. And we will move toward the day when we can eventually close the detention facility at Guantánamo Bay.

I know Americans have heard conflicting information about Guantánamo. Let me give you some facts. Of the thousands of terrorists captured across the world, only about 770 have ever been sent to Guantánamo. Of these, about 315 have been returned to other countries so far -- and about 455 remain in our custody. They are provided the same quality of medical care as the American service members who guard them. The International Committee of the Red Cross has the opportunity to meet privately with all who are held there. The facility has been visited by government officials from more than 30 countries, and delegations from international organizations, as well. After the Organization for Security and Cooperation in Europe came to visit, one of its delegation members called Guantánamo "a model prison" where people are treated better than in prisons in his own country. Our troops can take great pride in the work they do at Guantánamo Bay -- and so can the American people.

As we prosecute suspected terrorist leaders and operatives who have now been transferred to Guantánamo, we'll continue searching for those who have stepped forward to take their places. This nation is going to stay on the offense to protect the American people. We will continue to bring the world's most dangerous terrorists to justice -- and we will continue working to collect the vital intelligence we need to protect our country. The current transfers mean that there are now no terrorists in the CIA program. But as more high-ranking terrorists are captured, the need to obtain intelligence from them will remain critical -- and having a CIA program for questioning terrorists will continue to be crucial to getting life-saving information.

Some may ask: Why are you acknowledging this program now? There are two reasons why I'm making these limited disclosures today. First, we have largely completed our questioning of the men -- and to start the process for bringing them to trial, we must bring them into the open. Second, the Supreme Court's recent decision has impaired our ability to prosecute terrorists through military commissions, and has put in question the future of the CIA program. In its ruling on military commissions, the Court determined that a provision of the Geneva Conventions known as "Common Article Three" applies to our war with al Qaeda. This article includes provisions that prohibit "outrages upon personal dignity" and "humiliating and degrading treatment." The problem is that these and other provisions of Common Article Three are vague and undefined, and each could be interpreted in different ways by American or foreign judges. And some believe our military and intelligence personnel involved in capturing and questioning terrorists could now be at risk of prosecution under the War Crimes Act -- simply for doing their jobs in a thorough and professional way.

This is unacceptable. Our military and intelligence personnel go face to face with the world's most dangerous men every day. They have risked their lives to capture some of the most brutal terrorists on Earth. And they have worked day and night to find out what the terrorists know so we can stop new attacks. America owes our brave men and women some things in return. We owe them their thanks for saving lives and keeping America safe. And we owe them clear rules, so they can continue to do their jobs and protect our people.

So today, I'm asking Congress to pass legislation that will clarify the rules for our personnel fighting the war on terror. First, I'm asking Congress to list the specific, recognizable offenses that would be considered crimes under the War Crimes Act -- so our personnel can know clearly what is prohibited in the handling of terrorist enemies. Second, I'm asking that Congress make explicit that by following the standards of the Detainee Treatment Act our personnel are fulfilling America's obligations under Common Article Three of the Geneva Conventions. Third, I'm asking that Congress make it clear that captured terrorists cannot use the Geneva Conventions as a basis to sue our personnel in courts -- in U.S. courts. The men and women who protect us should not have to fear lawsuits filed by terrorists because they're doing their jobs.

The need for this legislation is urgent. We need to ensure that those questioning terrorists can continue to do everything within the limits of the law to get information that can save American lives. My administration will continue to work with the Congress to get this legislation enacted -- but time is of the essence. Congress is in session just for a few more weeks, and passing this legislation ought to be the top priority. (Applause.)

As we work with Congress to pass a good bill, we will also consult with congressional leaders on how to ensure that the CIA program goes forward in a way that follows the law, that meets the national security needs of our country, and protects the brave men and women we ask to obtain information that will save innocent lives. For the sake of our security, Congress needs to act, and update our laws to meet the threats of this new era. And I know they will.

We're engaged in a global struggle -- and the entire civilized world has a stake in its outcome. America is a nation of law. And as I work with Congress to strengthen and clarify our laws here at home, I will continue to work with members of the international community who have been our partners in this struggle. I've spoken with leaders of foreign governments, and worked with them to address their concerns about Guantánamo and our detention policies. I'll continue to work with the international community to construct a common foundation to defend our nations and protect our freedoms.

Free nations have faced new enemies and adjusted to new threats before -- and we have prevailed. Like the struggles of the last century, today's war on terror is, above all, a struggle for freedom and liberty. The adversaries are different, but the stakes in this war are the same: We're fighting for our way of life, and our ability to live in freedom. We're fighting for the cause of humanity, against those who seek to impose the darkness of tyranny and terror upon the entire world. And we're fighting for a peaceful future for our children and our grandchildren.

May God bless you all. (Applause.)

END   2:22 P.M. EDT.

The High Value Detainee Program

OFFICE OF THE DIRECTOR OF NATIONAL INTELLIGENCE
WASHINGTON, DC 20511

Summary of the High Value Terrorist Detainee Program

Since 9/11, we have been engaged in a struggle against an elusive enemy; terrorists work in the shadows, relying on secrecy and the element of surprise to maximize the impact of their attacks. Timely and accurate intelligence is crucial to success in the War on Terrorism. One of the key tools in this war has been the information we have gleaned from the terrorists themselves. Detainees who have been in the inner circle of al-Qa'ida, occupying some of the most important positions in that organization, hold information that simply cannot be obtained from any other source.

- *In the last five years, reporting from terrorist detainees has become a crucial pillar of US counterterrorism efforts, representing the single largest source of insight into al-Qa'ida for the US and its CT partners.*

- *Detainees have confirmed that al-Qa'ida continues to work on operations against the US and its CT allies; a fact underscored by the recent foiled plot in the United Kingdom. Detainee reporting will remain a critical tool if we and our allies are to continue to protect ourselves against these terrorists.*

A Program with Safeguards and Oversight

In March 2002, the CIA and our Coalition partners captured Abu Zubaydah—a terrorist leader and trainer and a key associate of Usama Bin Ladin. A dedicated terrorist, Abu Zubaydah was wounded in the capture operation and likely would have died had it not been for the medical attention arranged by the CIA. During initial interrogation, Abu Zubaydah gave some information that he probably viewed as nominal. Some was important, however, including that Khalid Shaykh Mohammad (KSM) was the 9/11 mastermind and used the moniker "Mukhtar." This identification allowed us to comb previously collected intelligence for both names, opening up new leads to this terrorist plotter—leads that eventually resulted in his capture. **It was clear to his interrogators that Abu Zubaydah possessed a great deal of information about al-Qa'ida; however, he soon stopped all cooperation. Over the ensuing months, the CIA designed a new interrogation program that would be safe, effective, and legal.**

- The CIA sought and obtained legal guidance from the Department of Justice that none of the new procedures violated the US statutes prohibiting torture. Policymakers were also briefed and approved the use of the procedures.

- The procedures proved highly effective. Abu Zubaydah soon began providing accurate and timely actionable intelligence, including information that led to the capture of 9/11 plotter Ramzi bin al-Shibh.

CIA's interrogation program is designed to ensure that intelligence is collected in a manner that does not violate the US Constitution, any US statute, or US treaty obligations.

- **Shortly after 11 September 2001, the majority and minority leaders of the Senate, the Speaker and the minority leader of the House, and the chairs and ranking members of the intelligence committees were briefed on the authorities for CIA's detention and interrogation program, in accordance with established procedures for sensitive intelligence programs. Within weeks of that time, the authorities were also briefed to the full intelligence committee.**

- **As CIA's efforts to implement these authorities got underway in 2002, the chairs, ranking members, and majority and minority staff directors of the intelligence committees were fully briefed on the interrogation procedures. Briefings to the chairs, ranking members, and majority an minority staff directors have been given on multiple occasions since that time, and in the fall of 2005, in connection with discussion on the Detainee Treatment Act, several other Members were briefed on the program, including the interrogation procedures.**

- **The Department of Justice has reviewed procedures proposed by the CIA on more than one occasion and determined them to be lawful.**

- **The program has been investigated and audited by the CIA's Office of the Inspector General (OIG), which was given full and complete access to all aspects of the program.**

Multiple safeguards have been built into the program to assure its professionalism. All those involved in the questioning of detainees are carefully chosen and screened for demonstrated professional judgment and maturity; the average age of officers interrogating detainees is 43. Once selected, they must complete more than 250 hours of specialized training before they are allowed to come face-to-face with a terrorist. Additional fieldwork under the direct supervision of an experienced officer is required before they can direct an interrogation.

- Specific senior CIA officers, and currently only the Director of the CIA, must approve—prior to use—each and every one of the lawful interrogation procedures to be used. No deviation from the approved procedures and methods is permitted.

- All interrogation sessions in which one of these lawful procedures is authorized for use must be observed by non-participants to ensure the procedures are applied appropriately and safely. These observers are authorized to terminate an interrogation immediately should they believe anything unauthorized is occurring.

- Any deviations from approved program procedures and practices are to be immediately reported and immediate corrective action taken, including referral to CIA's Office of the Inspector General and the Department of Justice, as appropriate.

2

Another key to the success of CIA's program is the involvement of CIA's substantive terrorism experts, who work together with the full spectrum of CIA's operations officers. In addition to interrogators, detainees are questioned by subject matter experts with years of experience studying and tracking al-Qa'ida members and plots whose expertise contributed to the capture of the detainees. These debriefers are also carefully selected and trained before being permitted to come face-to-face with a detainee. Their expertise helps to maintain a fast pace of questions and answers: they know the detainee's history and what information he should know; they can direct the questions to obtain the most critical information a detainee possesses; and they can quickly verify the truthfulness of a response.

- Debriefers with in-depth knowledge of al-Qa'ida are able to confront the terrorists with multiple sources of information about their activities, including reporting from other detainees. Debriefers use all source information not only to develop questions for detainees but to corroborate the information the detainees supply.

Proven Effectiveness

Captured al-Qa'ida training manuals indicate that al-Qa'ida operatives receive counter-interrogation training; detainees in CIA's program have provided valuable information despite their efforts to apply this training. **Detainees have provided lead information that has aided the US and its allies in capturing al-Qa'ida operatives who pose a serious threat.**

- **Unraveling the network of Jemaah Islamiyah (JI) leader and al-Qa'ida's South Asia representative Hambali and foiling future US operations.** This network's unraveling is an example of how detainees all held by CIA can be more effectively debriefed than if they were held by a variety of different governments. Quickly using information from one detainee in the questioning of another would be practically impossible if the detainees were in the custody of multiple foreign states. In March 2003, al-Qa'ida operations chief KSM provided the first information on his use of the Hambali network for Western operations, setting off a chain of detentions and reporting that ultimately led to the capture not only of Hambali, but of his brother and a cell of JI operatives. **Hambali admitted that the cell was intended for KSM's future US operations.**

Terrorists taken off the street with the help of detainee reporting include some who were involved in casing targets in the US:

1. **US Government and Tourist Sites:** In 2003 and 2004, an individual was tasked by al-Qa'ida to case important US Government and tourist targets within the United States. He is in the custody of a foreign state.

2. **Iyman Faris and the Brooklyn Bridge:** In 2003, a senior al-Qa'ida plotter described an Ohio based truck driver who had taken operational tasking from al-

Qa'ida and who the FBI identified as Iyman Faris. Faris was located and acknowledged discussing the destruction of the Brooklyn Bridge in New York. Faris ultimately pled guilty to providing material support to al-Qa'ida and is now in a federal corrections facility.

3. **Financial Institutions:** KSM and other detainees provided key leads to an elusive operative who had been tasked prior to 9/11 to case financial buildings in major cities along the East Coast. He is in the custody of a foreign state.

Other Operatives for Attacks Against the US and Its Allies. Detainees have provided names approximately 86 individuals—many of whom we had never heard of before—that al-Qa'ida has deemed suitable for Western operations. We have shared these names broadly within the US intelligence and law enforcement communities and with key partners overseas. Nearly half these individuals have been removed from the battlefield by the US and its allies.

- Jafar al-Tayyar was described by Abu Zubaydah who named him as one of the most likely individuals to be used by al-Qa'ida for operations in the United States or Europe. Other detainees added more details, helping us confirm that he is an al-Qa'ida operative and uncover his true name. As a result, a $5 million reward has been posted for information leading to the capture of Adnan El Shukrijumah, who remains at large.

The detention of terrorists disrupts—at least temporarily—the plots they were involved in, saving the lives not only of Americans but also of countless of men, women, and children around the globe:

1. **The West Coast Airliner Plot:** In mid-2002, thanks to leads from a variety of detainees, the US disrupted a plot by 9/11 mastermind KSM to attack targets on the West Coast of the United States using hijacked airplanes.

2. **The 2004 UK Urban Targets Plot:** In mid-2004, the US and its counterterrorism partners disrupted a plot that involved attacking urban targets in the United Kingdom with explosive devices. Some of the key leads to these plotters came from detainees.

3. **The 2003 Karachi Plot:** In the spring of 2003, the US and a partner detained key al-Qa'ida operatives who were in the advanced stages of plotting an attack against several targets in Karachi, Pakistan that would have killed hundreds of innocent men, women, and children.

4. **The Heathrow Airport Plot:** In 2003, the US and several partners—acting on information from several detainees—disrupted a plot to attack Heathrow Airport using hijacked commercial airliners. KSM and his network were behind the planning for this attack.

4

5. **The 2002 Arabian Gulf Shipping Plot:** In late 2002 and early 2003, the work of the US and partner nations to detain two senior al-Qa'ida operatives thwarted these operatives' plot to attack ships in the Arabian Gulf.

6. **The Straits of Hormuz Plot:** One of the Arabian Gulf shipping plotters was also working on a plot to attack ships transiting the Straits of Hormuz. His detention disrupted this plot.

7. **The Tall Buildings Plot.** Working with information from detainees, the US disrupted a plot to blow up tall buildings in the United States. KSM later described how he had directed operatives to ensure the buildings were high enough to prevent the people trapped above from escaping out of the windows, thus ensuring their deaths from smoke inhalation.

8. **Camp Lemonier Plot:** In early 2004, shortly after his capture, al-Qa'ida facilitator Gouled Hassan Dourad revealed that in mid-2003 al-Qa'ida East Africa cell leader Abu Talha al-Sudani sent him from Mogadishu to Djibouti to case the US Marine base at Camp Lemonier, as part of a plot to send suicide bombers with a truck bomb into the base. His information—including identifying operatives associated with the plot—helped us to enhance the security at the camp.

In the years since 9/11, successive detainees have helped us and our allies gauge our progress in the fight against al-Qa'ida by providing updated information on the changing structure and health of the organization. They also have given the US and its CT partners context to understand new threat information as it becomes available—insights that illuminate activity we and our allies see in reporting on current threats and plotting. In addition, detainees have provided us locational information on al-Qa'ida managers and operatives.

- **As a result, we have been able to provide leads to our CT partners around the world that have helped them root out al-Qa'ida safehavens. Subsequent detainees have reported that attempts to mount additional attacks in the US Homeland have been set back by these counterterrorism operations.**

Rendition and detention: the realities

7. CIA background paper sent to acting OLC head Dan Levin, 30 December 2004—p.185

The 'torture memos' (see Documents 2 and 3) were scrapped by Jack Goldsmith, head of the OLC, in mid-2004. His acting successor, Dan Levin, sought to draw up a replacement document. As part of his research – which, remarkably, appears to have included subjecting himself to waterboarding and other 'enhanced techniques' – Levin was sent this background paper by the CIA. The message on the fax cover sheet reads, 'Dan, a generic description of the process. Thank you.'

8. International Committee of the Red Cross, 'Report on the Treatment of Fourteen "High Value Detainees" in CIA Custody', 14 February 2007 (extracts)—p.203

When fourteen High Value Detainees were transferred to Guantánamo (Document 6), the ICRC was given access to them for the first time since their arrest. Its account, drawing on interviews with the detainees, details the same methods of ill-treatment described in US government papers (Documents 2 and 3). It was presented to the US authorities on a confidential basis, but was leaked in March 2009.

9. CIA Office of the Inspector General report, 'Special Review' on Counterterrorism and Interrogation Activities, 7 May 2004 (extracts)—p.208

This internal CIA report, released in highly redacted form in 2009, makes clear that on a number of occasions interrogators went beyond the guidelines set out in the OLC's advice (Document 3). The section on waterboarding indicates that it was to be used in something close to the 'ticking bomb' scenario, but also that its use was much more intensive than had originally been envisaged. The report also makes clear the growing alarm within the CIA at the potential legal and political repercussions of the HVD programme.

10. United Nations Human Rights Committee Views in case of *Alzery v. Sweden*, 25 October 2006 (extracts)—p.212

The rendition of Mohammed al-Zery and Ahmed Agiza from Sweden to Egypt in December 2001, after which they were allegedly tortured, became the subject of a number of inquiries both in Sweden and internationally. In 2004, the Committee Against Torture of the United Nations' Office of the High Commissioner for Human Rights found (in Agiza v. Sweden) that Sweden had violated its obligations under the CAT with respect to one of the men involved. In this subsequent finding, the Human Rights Committee (operating under the auspices of the ICCPR) examined the case of al-Zery. These extracts from the Committee's report describe the rendition, the allegations of how al-Zery was tortured after he reached Egypt, the weaknesses of the assurances that Sweden secured from the Egyptian authorities and the role of a CIA aircraft in the hasty transfer of the men. The Committee found against Sweden on most counts.

11. Council of Europe report, 'Alleged secret detentions and inter-state transfers of detainees involving Council of Europe member states', 12 June 2006 (extracts)—p.216

This initial report by the Council of Europe's Parliamentary Assembly, led by its rapporteur Dick Marty, described the rendition network (colourfully characterised as a 'spider's web'). It gave indications as to how European countries had been involved in rendition and drew attention to a number of individual cases, including those of Bisher al-Rawi, Jamil el-Banna and Binyam Mohamed. Significant further detail was added in a second report published in June 2007.

12. European Parliament Resolution adopting Report by Temporary Committee, 14 February 2007 (extracts)—p.227

A report by the Temporary Committee on the alleged use of European countries by the CIA for the transportation and illegal detention of prisoners (TIDP) was strongly critical of many member states, in particular for their failure to cooperate with the Committee's work. This extract refers to the approach of the British government. The wording of the Committee's original draft was somewhat harsher in its criticisms than the Resolution adopted by the Parliament.

(7)   CIA background paper sent to acting OLC head Dan Levin, 30 December 2004

<u>Background Paper on CIA's Combined Use of Interrogation Techniques</u>

Note: This paper provides further background information and details on High-Value Detainee (HVD) interrogation techniques to support documents CIA has previously provided the Department of Justice.

This paper focuses strictly on the topic of combined use of interrogation techniques.

The purpose of interrogation is to persuade High-Value Detainees (HVD) to provide threat information and terrorist intelligence in a timely manner, to allow the US Government to identify and disrupt terrorist plots
                    and to collect critical intelligence on al-Qa'ida

                                                    In support
of information previously sent to the Department of Justice, this paper provides additional background on how interrogation techniques are used, in combination and separately, to achieve interrogation objectives.   Effective interrogation is based on the concept of using both physical and psychological pressures in a comprehensive, systematic, and cumulative manner to influence HVD behavior, to overcome a detainee's resistance posture.   The goal of interrogation is to create a state of learned helplessness and dependence conducive to the collection of intelligence in a predictable, reliable, and sustainable manner.   For the purpose of this paper, the interrogation process can be broken into three separate phases: Initial Conditions; Transition to Interrogation; and Interrogation.

    A.   <u>Initial Conditions.</u>   Capture,
                 contribute to the physical and psychological condition of the HVD prior to the start of interrogation.   Of these, "capture shock" and detainee reactions   are factors that may vary significantly between detainees

DEC.30.2004 10:17AM

Regardless of their previous environment and experiences, once an HVD is turned over to CIA a predictable set of events occur:

1) Rendition.

a. The HVD is flown to a Black Site
A medical examination is conducted prior to the flight. During the flight, the detainee is securely shackled and is deprived of sight and sound through the use of blindfolds, earmuffs, and hoods.
There is no interaction with the HVD during this rendition movement except for periodic, discreet assessments by the on-board medical officer.

b. Upon arrival at the destination airfield, the HVD is moved to the Black Site under the same conditions and using appropriate security procedures.

2) Reception at Black Site. The HVD is subjected to administrative procedures and medical assessment upon arrival at the Black Site.

the HVD finds himself in the complete control of Americans;

the procedures he is subjected to are precise, quiet, and almost clinical; and no one is mistreating him. While each HVD is different, the rendition and reception process generally creates significant apprehension in the HVD because of the enormity and suddenness of the change in environment, the uncertainty about what will happen next, and the potential dread an HVD might have of US custody. Reception procedures include:

a. The HVD's head and face are shaved.

2

b. A series of photographs are taken of the HVD while nude to document the physical condition of the HVD upon arrival.

c. A Medical Officer interviews the HVD and a medical evaluation is conducted to assess the physical condition of the HVD. The medical officer also determines if there are any contraindications to the use of interrogation techniques.

d. A Psychologist interviews the HVD to assess his mental state. The psychologist also determines if there are any contraindications to the use of interrogation techniques.

Transitioning to Interrogation - The Initial Interview.
Interrogators use the Initial Interview to assess the initial resistance posture of the HVD and to determine--in a relatively benign environment--if the HVD intends to willingly participate with CIA interrogators. The standard on participation is set very high during the Initial Interview. The HVD would have to willingly provide information on actionable threats and location information on High-Value Targets at large--not lower level information--for interrogators to continue with the neutral approach.

3

to HQS. Once approved, the interrogation process begins provided the required medical and psychological assessments contain no contraindications to interrogation

C.   Interrogation.

For descriptive purposes, these techniques can be separated into three categories: Conditioning Techniques; Corrective Techniques; and Coercive Techniques. To more completely describe the three categories of techniques and their effects, we begin with a summary of the detention conditions that are used in all CIA HVD facilities and that may be a factor in interrogations.

1)   Existing detention conditions. Detention conditions are not interrogation techniques, but they have an impact on the detainee undergoing interrogation. Specifically, the HVD will be exposed to white noise/loud sounds (not to exceed 79 decibels) and constant light during portions of the interrogation process. These conditions provide additional operational security: white noise/loud sounds mask conversations of staff members and deny the HVD any auditory clues about his surroundings and deter and disrupt the HVD's potential efforts to communicate with other detainees. Constant light provides an improved environment for Black Site security, medical, psychological, and interrogator staff to monitor the HVD.

2)   Conditioning Techniques. The HVD is typically reduced to a baseline, dependent state using the three interrogation techniques discussed below in combination. Establishing this baseline state is important to demonstrate to the HVD that he has no control over basic human needs. The baseline state also creates in the detainee a mindset in which he learns to perceive and value his personal welfare, comfort, and immediate needs more than the information he is protecting. The use of these

4

TOP SECRET/ ..... /NOFORN,ORCON//MR1

conditioning techniques do not generally bring immediate results; rather, it is the cumulative effect of these techniques, used over time and in combination with other interrogation techniques and intelligence exploitation methods, which achieve interrogation objectives. These conditioning techniques require little to no physical interaction between the detainee and the interrogator. The specific conditioning interrogation techniques are:

    a. Nudity. The HVD's clothes are taken and he remains nude until the interrogators provide clothes to him.

    b. Sleep Deprivation. The HVD is placed in the vertical shackling position to begin sleep deprivation. Other shackling procedures may be used during interrogations. The detainee is diapered for sanitary purposes, although the diaper is not used at all times.

    c. Dietary manipulation. The HVD is fed Ensure Plus or other food at regular intervals. The HVD receives a target of 1500 calories per day per OMS guidelines.

    3) Corrective Techniques. Techniques that require physical interaction between the interrogator and detainee are used principally to correct, startle, or to achieve another enabling objective with the detainee. These techniques-the insult slap, abdominal slap, facial hold, and attention grasp-are not used simultaneously but are often used interchangeably during an individual interrogation session. These techniques generally are used while the detainee is subjected to the conditioning techniques outlined above (nudity, sleep deprivation, and dietary manipulation). Examples of application include:

    a. Insult Slap. The insult slap often is the first physical technique used with an HVD once an interrogation begins. As noted, the HVD may already be nude, in sleep deprivation, and subject to dietary manipulation, even though the detainee will likely feel little effect from these techniques early in the interrogation. The insult slap is used sparingly but periodically throughout the interrogation process when the interrogator needs to immediately correct the

5

190

detainee or provide a consequence to a detainee's
response or non-response. The interrogator will
continually assess the effectiveness of the insult
slap and continue to employ it so long as it has the
desired effect on the detainee. Because of the
physical dynamics of the various techniques, the
insult slap can be used in combination with water
dousing or kneeling stress positions. Other
combinations are possible but may not be practical.

　　　b. Abdominal Slap. The abdominal slap is
similar to the insult slap in application and desired
result. It provides the variation necessary to keep a
high level of unpredictability in the interrogation
process. The abdominal slap will be used sparingly
and periodically throughout the interrogation process
when the interrogator wants to immediately correct the
detainee

　　　　　　　　　　　　　, and the interrogator will
continually assess its effectiveness. Because of the
physical dynamics of the various techniques, the
abdominal slap can be used in combination with water
dousing, stress positions, and wall standing. Other
combinations are possible but may not be practical.

　　　c. Facial Hold. The facial hold is a
corrective technique and is used sparingly throughout
interrogation. The facial hold is not painful and is
used to correct the detainee in a way that
demonstrates the interrogator's control over the HVD.

Because of the physical dynamics of the various
techniques, the facial hold can be used in combination
with water dousing, stress positions, and wall
standing. Other combinations are possible but may not
be practical.

　　　d. Attention Grasp.

　　　　　　　It may be used several times in the
same interrogation. This technique is usually applied

　　　　　　　　　　grasp the HVD and pull him

6

into close proximity of the interrogator (face to face). Because of the physical dynamics of the various techniques, the attention grasp can be used in combination with water dousing or kneeling stress positions. Other combinations are possible but may not be practical.

4) Coercive Techniques. Certain interrogation techniques place the detainee in more physical and psychological stress and, therefore, are considered more effective tools in persuading a resistant HVD to participate with CIA interrogators. These techniques-- walling, water dousing, stress positions, wall standing, and cramped confinement--are typically not used in combination, although some combined use is possible. For example, an HVD in stress positions or wall standing can be water doused at the same time. Other combinations of these techniques may be used while the detainee is being subjected to the conditioning techniques discussed above (nudity, sleep deprivation, and dietary manipulation). Examples of coercive techniques include:

a. Walling. Walling is one of the most effective interrogation techniques because it wears down the HVD physically, heightens uncertainty in the detainee about what the interrogator may do to him, and creates a sense of dread when the HVD knows he is about to be walled again.

interrogator

An HVD may be walled one time (one impact with the wall) to make a point or twenty to thirty times consecutively when the interrogator requires a more significant response to a question. During an interrogation session that is designed to be intense, an HVD will be walled multiple times in the session. Because of the physical dynamics of walling, it is impractical to use it simultaneously with other corrective or coercive techniques.

b. Water Dousing. The frequency and duration of water dousing applications are based on water temperature and other safety considerations as

7

192

established by OMS guidelines. It is an effective
interrogation technique and may be used frequently
within those guidelines. The physical dynamics of
water dousing are such that it can be used in
combination with other corrective and coercive
techniques. As noted above, an HVD in stress
positions or wall standing can be water doused.
Likewise, it is possible to use the insult slap or
abdominal slap with an HVD during water dousing.

c. Stress Positions. The frequency and duration
of use of the stress positions are based on the
interrogator's assessment of their continued
effectiveness during interrogation. These techniques
are usually self-limiting in that temporary muscle
fatigue usually leads to the HVD being unable to
maintain the stress position after a period of time.
Stress positions requiring the HVD to be in contact
with the wall can be used in combination with water
dousing and abdominal slap. Stress positions
requiring the HVD to kneel can be used in combination
with water dousing, insult slap, abdominal slap,
facial hold, and attention grasp.

d. Wall Standing. The frequency and duration of
wall standing are based on the interrogator's
assessment of its continued effectiveness during
interrogation. Wall standing is usually self-limiting
in that temporary muscle fatigue usually leads to the
HVD being unable to maintain the position after a
period of time. Because of the physical dynamics of
the various techniques, wall standing can be used in
combination with water dousing and abdominal slap.
While other combinations are possible, they may not be
practical.

e. Cramped Confinement. Current OMS guidance on
the duration of cramped confinement limits confinement
in the large box to no more than 8 hours at a time for
no more than 18 hours a day, and confinement in the
small box to 2 hours.

Because of the unique
aspects of cramped confinement, it cannot be used in

8

. combination with other corrective or coercive
techniques.

D. Interrogation - A day-to-day look. This section
provides a look at a prototypical interrogation with an emphasis
on the application of interrogation techniques, in combination
and separately.

_2)_ _Session One._

    a. The HVD is brought into the interrogation
room, and under the direction of the interrogators,
stripped of his clothes, and placed into shackles

9

194

b. The HVD is placed standing with his back to
the walling wall. The HVD remains hooded.

c. Interrogators approach the HVD, place the
walling collar over his head and around his neck, and
stand in front of the HVD.

d. The interrogators remove the HVD's hood and

explain the HVD's situation to him, tell
him that the interrogators will do what it takes to
get important information, and that he can improve his
conditions immediately by participating with the
interrogators. The insult slap is normally used as
soon as the HVD does or says anything inconsistent
with the interrogators' instructions.

e.

If appropriate, an
insult slap or abdominal slap will follow.

f. The interrogators will likely use walling
once it becomes clear that the HVD is lying,
withholding information, or using other resistance
techniques.

g. The sequence
may continue for several more iterations as the
interrogators continue to measure the HVD's resistance
posture and apply a negative consequence to the HVD's
resistance efforts.

h. The interrogators, assisted by security
officers (for security purposes) will place the HVD in
the center of the interrogation room in the vertical
shackling position and diaper the HVD to begin sleep
deprivation. The HVD will be provided with Ensure
Plus (liquid dietary supplement) to begin dietary
manipulation. The HVD remains nude-. White noise
(not to exceed 79db) is used in the interrogation

10

room. The first interrogation session terminates at
this point.

    i.

    j. This first interrogation session may last
from 30 minutes to several hours based on the
interrogators' assessment of the HVD's resistance
posture.

    The three Conditioning Techniques were used to
bring the HVD to a baseline, dependent state
conductive to meeting interrogation objectives in a
timely manner.

3) Session Two.

    a. The time period between Session One and
Session Two could be as brief as one hour or more than
24 hours

11

196

In addition, the
medical and psychological personnel observing the
interrogations must advise there are no
contraindications to another interrogation session.

    b.

    c. Like the first session, interrogators
approach the HVD, place the walling collar over his
head and around his neck, and stand in front of the
HVD.

    d.

Should the HVD not respond
appropriately to the first questions, the
interrogators will respond with an <u>insult slap</u> or
<u>abdominal slap</u> to set the stage for further
questioning.

12

e.

The interrogators will likely use walling once interrogators determine the HVD is intent on maintaining his resistance posture.

f. The sequence may continue for multiple iterations as the interrogators continue to measure the HVD's resistance posture.

g. To increase the pressure on the HVD,

water douse the HVD for several minutes.

h. The interrogators, assisted by security officers, will place the HVD back into the vertical shackling position to resume sleep deprivation. Dietary manipulation also continues, and the HVD remains nude. White noise (not to exceed 79db) is used in the interrogation room. The interrogation session terminates at this point.

i. As noted above, the duration of this session may last from 30 minutes to several hours based on the interrogators' assessment of the HVD's resistance posture. In this example of the second session, the following techniques were used: sleep deprivation, nudity, dietary manipulation, walling, water dousing, attention grasp, insult slap, and abdominal slap. The three Conditioning Techniques were used to keep the HVD at a baseline, dependent state and to weaken his resolve and will to resist. In combination with these three techniques, other Corrective and Coercive Techniques were used throughout the interrogation session based on interrogation objectives and the interrogators' assessment of the HVD's resistance posture.

198

4) Session Three.

      a.

                  In addition, the medical and psychological personnel observing the interrogations must find no contraindications to continued interrogation.

      b. The HVD remains in <u>sleep deprivation</u>, <u>dietary manipulation</u> and is <u>nude</u>.

      c. Like the earlier sessions, the HVD begins the session standing against the walling wall with the walling collar around his neck.

      d. If the HVD is still maintaining a resistance posture, interrogators will continue to use <u>walling</u> and <u>water dousing</u>. All of the Corrective Techniques (<u>insult slap</u>, <u>abdominal slap</u>, <u>facial hold</u>, <u>attention grasp</u>) may be used several times during this session based on the responses and actions of the HVD. <u>Stress positions</u> and <u>wall standing</u> will be integrated into interrogations

Intense questioning and walling would be repeated multiple times.

Interrogators will often use one technique to support another. As an example, interrogators would tell an HVD in a stress position that he (HVD) is going back to the walling wall (for walling) if he fails to hold the stress position until told otherwise by the HVD. This places additional stress on the HVD who typically will try to hold the stress position for as long as possible to avoid the walling wall.

                                  the

14

TOP SECRET/;   /NOFORN, ORCON//MR1

interrogators will remind the HVD that he is
responsible for this treatment and can stop it at any
time by cooperating with the interrogators.

e.   The interrogators, assisted by security
officers, will place the HVD back into the vertical
shackling position to resume sleep deprivation.
Dietary manipulation also continues, and the HVD
remains nude. White noise (not to exceed 79db) is
used in the interrogation room. The interrogation
session terminates at this point. In this example of
the third session, the following techniques were used:
sleep deprivation, nudity, dietary manipulation,
walling, water dousing, attention grasp, insult slap,
abdominal slap, stress positions, and wall standing.

5) Continuing Sessions.

Interrogation techniques assessed as being the most
effective will be emphasized while techniques will little
assessed effectiveness will be minimized.

     a.

     b.   The use of cramped confinement may be
introduced if interrogators assess that it will have
the appropriate effect on the HVD.

          c.

     d.   Sleep deprivation may continue to the 70 to
120 hour range, or possibly beyond for the hardest
resisters, but in no case exceed the 180-hour time
limit. Sleep deprivation will end sooner if the
medical or psychologist observer finds

TOP SECRET/,   /NOFORN, ORCON//MR1

contraindications to continued sleep deprivation.

     e.

     f

     g. The interrogators' objective is to transition
the HVD to a point where he is participating in a
predictable, reliable, and sustainable manner.
Interrogation techniques may still be applied as
required, but become less frequent.

     . This transition period lasts
from several days to several weeks based on the HVDs
responses and actions.

     h. The entire interrogation process outlined
above, including transition, may last for thirty days

16

On average, the actual use of interrogation technique can vary upwards to fifteen days based on the resilience of the HVD.

If the interrogation team anticipates the potential need to use interrogation techniques beyond the 30-day approval period, it will submit a new interrogation plan to HQS for evaluation and approval.

2. Summary.

* Since the start of this program, interrogation techniques have been used in combination and separately to achieve critical intelligence collection objectives.

* The use of interrogation techniques in combination is essential to the creation of an interrogation environment conducive to intelligence collection. HVDs are well-trained, often battle-hardened terrorist operatives, and highly committed to jihad. They are intelligent and resourceful leaders and able to resist standard interrogation approaches.

*

*

However, there is no template or script that states with certainty when and how these techniques will be used in combination during interrogation. However, the exemplar above is a fair representation of how these techniques are actually employed.

17

* All CIA interrogations are conducted on the basis of the "least coercive measure" principle. Interrogators employ interrogation techniques in an escalating manner consistent with the HVD's responses and actions. Intelligence production is more sustainable over the long term if the actual use of interrogation techniques diminishes steadily and the interrogation environment improves in accordance with the HVD's demonstrated consistent participation with the interrogators.

(8) International Committee of the Red Cross Report on the Treatment of Fourteen "High Value Detainees" in CIA Custody, 14 February 2007 (extracts)

[...]

2. ARREST AND TRANSFER

The following fourteen persons are referred to in this report, in chronological order according to date of arrest:

Name	Nationality	Place of arrest	Date of arrest
1) Abu Zubaydah	Palestinian	Faisalabad, Pakistan	28 March 2002
2) Ramzi Mohammed Binalshib	Yemeni	Karachi, Pakistan	11 September 2002
3) Abdelrahim Hussein Abdul Nashiri	Saudi	Dubai	October 2002
4) Mustafha Ahmad Al Hawsawi	Saudi	Rawalpindi, Pakistan	01 March 2003
5) Khaled Shaik Mohammed	Pakistani	Rawalpindi, Pakistan	01 March 2003
6) Majid Khan	Pakistani	Karachi, Pakistan	05 March 2003
7) Ali Abdul Aziz Mohammed	Pakistani	Karachi, Pakistan	29 April 2003
8) Walid Bin Attash	Yemeni	Karachi, Pakistan	29 April 2003
9) Mohammed Farik Bin Amin	Malaysian	Bangkok, Thailand	08 June 2003
10) Mohammed Nazir Bin Lep	Malaysian	Bangkok, Thailand	11 August 2003
11) Encep Nuraman (aka Hambali)	Indonesian	Ayutthaya, Thailand	11 August 2003
12) Haned Hassan Ahmad Guleed	Somali	Djibouti	04 March 2004
13) Ahmed Khalafan Ghailani	Tanzanian	Gujarat, Pakistan	25 July 2004
14) Mustafah Faraj Al-Azibi	Libyan	Mardan, Pakistan	02 May 2005

The fourteen were arrested in four different countries. In each case, they were reportedly arrested by the national police or security forces of the country in which they were arrested.

In some cases US agents were present at the time of arrest. All fourteen were detained in the country of arrest for periods ranging from a few days up to one month before their first transfer to a third country (reportedly Afghanistan, see below) and from there on to other countries. Interrogation in the country of arrest was conducted by US agents in nearly all cases. In two cases, however, detainees reported having been interrogated by the national authorities, either alone or jointly with US agents: Mr Abdelrahim Hussein Abdul Nashiri was allegedly interrogated for the first month after arrest by Dubai agents, and one detainee who did not wish his name to be transmitted to the authorities was allegedly interrogated by both Pakistani and US agents. During their subsequent detention, outlined below, detainees sometimes reported the presence of non-US personnel (believed to be personnel of the country in which they were held), even though the overall control of the facility appeared to remain under the control of the US authorities.

Throughout their detention, the fourteen were moved from one place to another and were allegedly kept in several different places of detention, probably in several different countries. The number of locations reported by the detainees varied, however ranged from three to ten locations prior to their arrival in Guantanamo in September 2006.

The transfer procedure was fairly standardised in most cases. The detainee would be photographed, both clothed and naked prior to and again after transfer. A body cavity check (rectal examination) would be carried out and some detainees alleged that a suppository (the type and the effect of such suppositories was unknown by the detainees), was also administered at that moment.

The detainee would be made to wear a diaper and dressed in a tracksuit. Earphones would be placed over his ears, through which music would sometimes be played. He would be blindfolded with at least a cloth tied around the head and black goggles. In addition, some detainees alleged that cotton wool was also taped over their eyes prior to the blindfold and goggles being applied. Mr Abu Zubaydah alleged that during one transfer operation the blindfold was tied very tightly resulting in wounds to his nose and ears. He does not know how long the transfer took but, prior to the transfer, he reported being told by his detaining authorities that he would be going on a journey that would last twenty-four to thirty hours.

The detainee would be shackled by hands and feet and transported to the airport by road and loaded onto a plane. He would usually be transported in a reclined sitting position with his hands shackled in front. The journey times obviously varied considerably and ranged from one hour to over twenty-four to thirty hours. The detainee was not allowed to go to the toilet and if necessary was obliged to urinate or defecate into the diaper.

On some occasions the detainees were transported lying flat on the floor of the plane and/or with their hands cuffed behind their backs. When transported in this position the detainees complained of severe pain and discomfort.

In addition to causing severe physical pain, these transfers to unknown locations and unpredictable conditions of detention and treatment placed mental strain on the fourteen, increasing their sense of disorientation and isolation. The ability of the detaining authority to transfer persons over apparently significant distances to secret locations in foreign countries acutely increased the detainees' feeling of futility and helplessness, making them more vulnerable to the methods of ill-treatment described below.

The ICRC was informed by the US authorities that the practice of transfers was linked specifically to issues that included national security and logistics, as opposed to being an integral part of the program, for example to maintain compliance. However, in practice, these transfers increased the vulnerability of the fourteen to their interrogation, and was performed in a manner (goggles, earmuffs, use of diapers, strapped to stretchers, sometimes rough handling) that was intrusive and humiliating and that challenged the dignity of the persons concerned.

As their detention was specifically designed to cut off contact with the outside world and emphasise a feeling of disorientation and isolation, some of the time periods referred to in the report are approximate estimates made by the detainees concerned. For the same reasons, the detainees were usually unaware of their exact location beyond the first place of detention in the country of arrest and the second country of detention, which was identified by all fourteen as being Afghanistan. This report will not enter into conjecture by referring to possible countries or locations of places of detention beyond the first and second countries of detention, which are named, and will refer, where necessary, to subsequent places of detention by their position in the sequence for the detainee concerned (eg. third place of detention, fourth place of detention). The ICRC is confident that the concerned authorities will be able to identify from their records which place of detention is being referred to and the relevant period of detention.

Moreover, the ICRC notes that four detainees believed that they had previously been held in Guantanamo, for periods ranging from one week to one year during 2003/4. They reported recognising this location upon return there in September 2006, as each had been allowed outdoors on a daily basis during their earlier time there. The ICRC has been assured by DoD that it was given full notification of and access to all persons held in Guantanamo during its regular detention visits. The ICRC is concerned, if the allegations are confirmed, it had in fact been denied access to these persons during the period in which they were detained there.

1.2. CONTINUOUS SOLITARY CONFINEMENT AND INCOMMUNICADO DETENTION

Throughout the entire period during which they were held in the CIA detention program—which ranged from sixteen months up to almost four and a half years and which, for eleven of the fourteen was over three years—the detainees were kept in continuous solitary confinement[8] and incommunicado detention. They had no knowledge of where they were being held, no contact with persons other than their interrogators or guards. Even their guards were usually masked and, other than the absolute minimum, did not communicate in any way with the detainees. None had any real—let alone regular—contact with other persons detained, other than occasionally for the purposes of inquiry when they were confronted with another detainee. None had any contact with legal representation. The fourteen had no access to news from the outside world, apart from in the later stages of their detention when some of them occasionally received printouts of sports news from the internet and one reported receiving newspapers.

None of the fourteen had any contact with their families, either in written form or through family visits or telephone calls. They were therefore unable to inform their families of their fate. As such, the fourteen had become missing persons. In any context, such a situation, given its prolonged duration, is clearly a cause of extreme distress for both the detainees and families concerned and itself constitutes a form of ill-treatment.

In addition, the detainees were denied access to an independent third party. In order to ensure accountability, there is a need for a procedure of notification to families, and of notification and access to detained persons, under defined modalities, for a third party, such as the ICRC. That this was not practiced, to the knowledge of the ICRC, neither for the fourteen nor for any other detainee who passed through the CIA detention program, is a matter of serious concern.

1.3. OTHER METHODS OF ILL-TREATMENT

As noted above, the fourteen were subjected to an extremely harsh detention regime, characterised by ill-treatment. The initial period of interrogation, lasting from a few days up to several months was the harshest, where compliance was secured by the infliction of various forms of physical and psychological ill-treatment. This appeared to be followed by a reward based interrogation approach with gradually improving conditions of detention, albeit reinforced by the threat of returning to former methods.

The methods of ill-treatment alleged to have been used include the following:

- **Suffocation by water** poured over a cloth placed over the nose and mouth, alleged by three of the fourteen.
- **Prolonged stress standing position**, naked, held with the arms extended and chained above the head, as alleged by ten of the fourteen, for periods from two or three days continuously, and for up to two or three months intermittently, during which period toilet access was sometimes denied resulting in allegations from four detainees that they had to defecate and urinate over themselves.
- **Beatings by use of a collar** held around the detainees neck and used to forcefully bang the head and body against the wall, alleged by six of the fourteen.
- **Beating and kicking**, including slapping, punching, kicking to the body and face, alleged by nine of the fourteen.

- **Confinement in a box** to severely restrict movement alleged in the case of one detainee.
- **Prolonged nudity** alleged by eleven of the fourteen during detention, interrogation and ill-treatment; this enforced nudity lasted for periods ranging from several weeks to several months.
- **Sleep deprivation** was alleged by eleven of the fourteen through days of interrogation, through use of forced stress positions (standing or sitting), cold water and use of repetitive loud noise or music. One detainee was kept sitting on a chair for prolonged periods of time.
- **Exposure to cold temperature** was alleged by most of the fourteen, especially via cold cells and interrogation rooms, and for seven of them, by the use of cold water poured over the body or, as alleged by three of the detainees, held around the body by means of a plastic sheet to create an immersion bath with just the head out of the water.
- **Prolonged shackling** of hands and/or feet was alleged by many of the fourteen.
- **Threats of ill-treatment** to the detainee and/or his family, alleged by nine of the fourteen.
- **Forced shaving** of the head and beard, alleged by two of the fourteen.
- **Deprivation/restricted provision of solid food** from 3 days to 1 month after arrest, alleged by eight of the fourteen.

In addition, the fourteen were subjected for longer periods to a deprivation of access to open air, exercise, appropriate hygiene facilities and basic items in relation to interrogation, and restricted access to the Koran linked with interrogation (see Section 1.4 Other Aspects of the Detention Regime).

[...]

(9) CIA Office of the Inspector General report, 'Special Review' on Counterterrorism and Interrogation Activities, 7 May 2004 (extracts)

[...]

220. (TS███████████) Inasmuch as EITs have been used only since August 2002, and they have not all been used with every high value·detainee, there is limited data on which to assess their individual effectiveness. This Review identified concerns about the use of the waterboard, specifically whether the risks of its use were justified by the results, whether it has been unnecessarily used in some instances, and whether the fact that it is being applied in a manner different from its use in SERE training brings into question the continued applicability of the DoJ opinion to its use. Although the waterboard is the most intrusive of the EITs, the fact that precautions have been taken to provide on-site medical oversight in the use of all EITs is evidence that their use poses risks.

221. (TS███████) Determining the effectiveness of each EIT is important in facilitating Agency management's decision as to which techniques should be used and for how long. Measuring the overall effectiveness of EITs is challenging for a number of reasons including: (1) the Agency cannot determine with any certainty the totality of the intelligence the detainee actually possesses; (2) each detainee has different fears of and tolerance for EITs; (3) the application of the same EITs by different interrogators may have

209

different results; and ██████████████████████████
████████████████████████████████████

222. (TS/ ██████████) The waterboard has been used on three detainees: Abu Zubaydah, Al-Nashiri, and Khalid Shaykh Muhammad. ████████████████████████

████████████████with the belief that each of the three detainees possessed perishable information about imminent threats against the United States.

223. (TS/ ██████████) Prior to the use of EITs, Abu Zubaydah provided information for ██████ intelligence reports. Interrogators applied the waterboard to Abu Zubaydah at least 83 times during August 2002. During the period between the end of the use of the waterboard and 30 April 2003, he provided information for approximately ████ additional reports. It is not possible to say definitively that the waterboard is the reason for Abu Zubaydah's increased production, or if another factor, such as the length of detention, was the catalyst. Since the use of the waterboard, however, Abu Zubaydah has appeared to be cooperative,█

████████████████████████████████
████████████████████████████████
████████████████████████████████

224. (TS/ ██████████) With respect to Al-Nashiri,██████
██████ reported two waterboard sessions in November 2002, after which the psychologist/interrogators determined that Al-Nashiri was compliant. However, after being moved█████████
████████████████ Al-Nashiri was thought to be withholding information. Al-Nashiri subsequently received additional EITs, ████████████████████ but not the waterboard. The Agency then determined Al-Nashiri to be "compliant." Because of the litany of

90
TOP SECRET

TOP SECRET ██████████████████████

techniques used by different interrogators over a relatively short period of time, it is difficult to identify exactly why Al-Nashiri became more willing to provide information. However, following the use of EITs, he provided information about his most current operational planning and ████████████████████ as opposed to the historical information he provided before the use of EITs.

225. (TS ██████████) On the other hand, Khalid Shaykh Muhammad, an accomplished resistor, provided only a few intelligence reports prior to the use of the waterboard, and analysis of that information revealed that much of it was outdated, inaccurate, or incomplete. As a means of less active resistance, at the beginning of their interrogation, detainees routinely provide information that they know is already known. Khalid Shaykh Muhammad received 183 applications of the waterboard in March 2003 ████████████

██
██
██
██

POLICY CONSIDERATIONS AND CONCERNS REGARDING THE DETENTION AND INTERROGATION PROGRAM

226. (TS ██████████) The EITs used by the Agency under the CTC Program are inconsistent with the public policy positions that the United States has taken regarding human rights. This divergence has been a cause of concern to some Agency personnel involved with the Program.

[...]

Concerns Over Participation in the CTC Program

231. (S//NF) During the course of this Review, a number of
Agency officers expressed unsolicited concern about the possibility of
recrimination or legal action resulting from their participation in the
CTC Program. A number of officers expressed concern that a human
rights group might pursue them for activities ███████████
██████████████ Additionally, they feared that the Agency
would not stand behind them if this occurred.

232. (S//NF) One officer expressed concern that one day,
Agency officers will wind up on some "wanted list" to appear before
the World Court for war crimes stemming from activities █
██████ Another said, "Ten years from now we're going to be sorry
we're doing this . . . [but] it has to be done." He expressed concern
that the CTC Program will be exposed in the news media and cited
particular concern about the possibility of being named in a leak.

[...]

(10) United Nations Human Rights Committee Views in case of *Alzery* v. *Sweden*, 25 October 2006 (extracts)

[...]

3.4 The Swedish Migration Board considered the author's application for asylum and permanent residence on first instance. On 31 January 2001, a statement was requested from the Swedish Security Police, whose functions include assessment of whether asylum cases are of a nature that consideration must be given to national security before a residence permit is granted. In April 2001, the Security Police commenced an investigation, and interviewed the author in June 2001. During the interview, he stated that he had never been involved with the movement he was accused of being involved in, and that he strongly rejected any violence as a mean to reach any political goal. He however believed that he would be arrested and tortured if returned to Egypt because of these wrongful accusations. The author was allowed to read the transcript of the hearing in September 2001, but was not informed of the conclusions drawn from this interview.

3.5 On 30 October 2001, the Security Police submitted its report, recommending that the application for permanent residence permit be rejected "for security reasons". On 12 November 2001, the Migration Board, while of the view that the author could be considered in need of protection, referred the matter to the Government for a decision pursuant to the Aliens Act, given the security issues involved. Having received the Migration Board's case file, the Aliens Appeals Board, while sharing the Migration Board's view of the merits, also considered that the Government should decide the case.

3.6 On 12 December 2001, a senior official of the Swedish Ministry for Foreign Affairs met with a representative of the Egyptian government. The purpose was to determine whether it would be possible, without violating Sweden's international obligations, including under the

Covenant, to order the author's return to Egypt. Having considered the option of obtaining assurances from the Egyptian authorities in respect of his future treatment, the Government had made the assessment that it was both possible and meaningful to inquire whether guarantees could be obtained that the author would be treated in accordance with international law upon his return to Egypt. Without such guarantees, his expulsion to Egypt would not have been an alternative. The state secretary of the Swedish Ministry for Foreign Affairs presented an Aide-Mémoire to the official which read:

"It is the understanding of the Government of the Kingdom of Sweden that [the author and another individual] will be awarded a fair trial in the Arab Republic of Egypt. It is further the understanding of the Government of the Kingdom of Sweden that these persons will not be subjected to inhuman treatment or punishment of any kind by any authority of the Arab Republic of Egypt and further that they will not be sentenced to death or if such a sentence has been imposed that it will not be executed by any competent authority of the Arab Republic of Egypt. Finally, it is the understanding of the Government of the Kingdom if Sweden that the wife and children of [another individual] will not in anyway be persecuted or harassed by any authority of the Arab Republic of Egypt."

3.7 The Egyptian Government responded in writing: "We herewith assert our full understanding to all items of this memoire, concerning the way of treatment upon repatriate from your government, with full respect to their personal and human rights. This will be done according to what the Egyptian constitution and law stipulates." In oral discussions with representatives from the Egyptian government, the Swedish Government also requested that the Embassy would be allowed to attend the trial. The author states that it remains unclear what other kind of follow-up mechanisms were discussed and decided upon prior to the expulsion. While the Swedish Government had since indicated that there had been discussions about the right to visit the author in prison, this remained unconfirmed. .

3.8 On 18 December 2001, the Government decided that the author should not be granted a residence permit in Sweden on security grounds. The Government noted the content of the guarantees that had been issued by a senior representative of the Egyptian government. Although in the light of the circumstances and the author's contentions as to his past conduct, his fear of persecution was considered to be well founded, entitling him protection in Sweden, the Government considered that he could be excluded from refugee status. In its decision, the Government concluded on the basis of intelligence services information that the author was involved, in a leading position and role, in the activities of an organization implicated in terrorist activities, and that he should be refused protection.

3.9 The Government separately assessed whether there was a risk that the author would be persecuted, sentenced to death, tortured or severely ill treated if returned, such circumstances constituting an absolute statutory bar to removal. The Government was of the view in this respect that the assurances procured were sufficient to comply with Sweden's obligations of *non-refoulement*. The Government ordered the author's immediate expulsion.

3.10 In the afternoon of 18 December 2001, a few hours after the decision to expel was taken, Swedish Security Police detained the author. According to the State party, no force was used in the arrest. He was informed that his application for asylum had been rejected and was then brought to a Stockholm remand prison. At the time of his arrest, the author was on the phone with (then) legal counsel, but the call was cut short. In the detention centre, he allegedly asked permission to call his lawyer but this request was rejected. After a few hours in detention, he was transferred by vehicle to Bromma airport. He was then escorted to the police station at the airport, where he was handed over to some ten foreign agents in civilian clothes and hoods. Later investigations by the Swedish Parliamentary Ombudsman, disclosed that the hooded individuals were United States' and Egyptian security agents.

3.11 The author states that the hooded agents forced him into a small locker room where they exposed him to what was termed a "security search", although Swedish police had already carried out a less intrusive search. The hooded agents slit the author's clothes with a pair of scissors and examined each piece of cloth before placing it in a plastic bag. Another agent checked his hair, mouths and lips, while a third agent took photographs, according to Swedish officers who witnessed the searches. When his clothes were cut off his body, he was handcuffed and chained to his feet. He was then drugged per rectum with some form of tranquilliser and placed in diapers. He was then dressed in overalls and escorted to the plane blindfolded, hooded and barefooted. Two representatives from the Embassy of the United States of America were also present during the apprehension and treatment of the applicant. In an aircraft registered abroad, he was placed on the floor in an awkward and painful position, with chains restricting further movement. The blindfold and hood stayed on throughout the transfer including when he was handed over to Egyptian military security at Cairo airport some five hours later. According to his (then) Swedish counsel, the blindfold remained on until 20 February 2002, and was only removed for a few days in connection with visits by the Swedish Ambassador on 23 January 2002 and an interview with a Swedish journalist in February 2002.

[...]

3.15 After the January meeting, the author was transferred to another section of the Tora prison controlled by the Egyptian Security Services (rather than General Intelligence). He states that for a further five weeks he was interrogated and this time harshly ill-treated, including electric shocks applied to genitals, nipples and ears. The torture was monitored by doctors who also put ointment on the skin after torture in order not to leave any scars. He was forced to confess to crimes he had not committed, and was questioned about activities such as arranging meetings for the forbidden organization he was active for and opposing "the system".

[...]

3.16 The author states that, for an extended period, he and the other individual were not allowed to meet other prisoners and were kept in isolation in cells continually deprived of light. On 20 February 2002, he was moved to another correction centre where he was kept in small isolation cell measuring 1.5 by 1.5 metres until the second week of December 2002.

[...]

3.28 On 21 September 2005, Parliament's Standing Committee on the Constitution reported on an investigation that had been initiated in May 2004 at the request of five members of Parliament

that the Committee examine the Government's handling of the matter that lead to, *inter alia*, Mr. Alzery's expulsion to Egypt. With respect to the assurances procured, the Committee was of the view that a more detailed plan for a monitoring mechanism had not been agreed with the Egyptian authorities and appears not to have existed at all prior to the decision to expel. This shortcoming was reflected in the actual monitoring of the guarantee, which was not consistent with the recommendations issued later on by the UN Special Rapporteur on issues relating to torture or the practice established by the Red Cross. A major flaw was naturally that the first visit to the men was not carried out earlier. However, the shortcomings in the actual monitoring were, in the Committee's opinion, mainly a consequence of the lack of planning in advance.

[...]

3.30 With respect to events at Bromma airport, the competence of the Committee did not extend to investigation of the actions of the Security Police; rather, the Committee focused on whether the (then) Foreign Minister, Anna Lindh, exerted undue influence on the Security Police at the time of the expulsion by indicating a preference for a certain course of action. The Committee noted that the Foreign Minister, at the presentation of the matter at the Foreign Ministry on 17 December 2001, was informed of the alternative that entailed that an American aircraft was used in the enforcement, and the Security Police, when deciding on the choice of transport, also took into account what they had come to believe was the Foreign Minister's position in that regard. It had not been possible to establish with complete clarity whether the Foreign Minister was provided with the said information during the presentation, or whether the information was available at that time in other parts of the Government Offices. The Security Police had kept a journal of its meetings with the Ministries. No corresponding documentation existed within the Government Offices.

[...]

4.29 The author argues that the execution of the Government's decision within a matter of hours, and without advice to either the author or counsel, both denied him the effective exercise of the right of complaint, including seeking interim measures of protection, guaranteed by article 1 of the Optional Protocol. In consequence, irreparable harm resulted. The author points out that on 14 December 2001 his (then) Swedish counsel had advised the Government of his intention to pursue international remedies in the event of an adverse decision. He argues that the precipitate haste of the expulsion was intended to avoid such an eventuality. He adds that in the days prior to expulsion, counsel was not provided with full security reports, any detail as to the negotiations with Egypt or the timetabling of the Government's decision; indeed, officials specifically declined to acquiesce to counsel's requests for relevant records. When counsel's call with the author was cut off on 18 December 2001, the former was advised upon contacting the Ministry of Foreign Affairs that no decision had been taken. Advice by certified letter of the decision only reached counsel after the expulsion.

4.30 The Security Police, for its part, had also planned the swiftest possible execution of the expulsion order. Although the Security Police had informed the Ministry of Foreign Affairs that it had an aircraft ready to transport the author to Egypt on 19 December 2001, this was rejected by Government as not prompt enough. The Security Police then presented the Government with a proposal it had received from the United States, namely that the Central Intelligence Agency had an aircraft that had airspace clearance to Cairo on 18 December, which could be utilised by Sweden. The author argues that it was thus clear that the Security Police both knew that the decision to expel was going to be taken that day and were ready to act as soon as it was taken.

[...]

(11)   Council of Europe report, 'Alleged secret detentions and inter-state transfers of detainees involving Council of Europe member states', 12 June 2006 (extracts)

[...]

2.   The global "spider's web"[19]

24.   The system of targeting, apprehending and detaining terrorist suspects, which forms the focus of this report, was not created overnight. Nor has it been built up from scratch in the wake of the terrorist attacks of 11 September 2001.

25.   I have chosen to adopt the metaphor of a global "spider's web" as the *leitmotif* for my report. It is a web that has been spun out incrementally over several years, using tactics and techniques that have had to be developed in response to new theatres of war, new terms of engagement and an unpredictable threat.

26.   The chief architect of the web, the United States of America, has long possessed the capacity to capture individual targets abroad and carry them to different parts of the world. Through its Central Intelligence Agency (CIA), the United States designed a programme known as "rendition" for this purpose in the mid-1990s. The CIA aimed to take terrorist suspects in foreign countries "off the streets" by transporting them back to other countries, usually their home countries, where they were wanted for trial, or for detention without any form of due process.

2.1.   The evolution of the rendition programme

27.   During a recent mission to the United States, a member of my team came into contact with several "insider sources" in the US intelligence community. The most prominent such witness was Mr Michael Scheuer, who designed the original rendition programme in the 1990s under the Clinton Administration and remained employed by the CIA until November 2004[20]. Excerpts of Mr Scheuer's testimony are reflected verbatim in this report and, to the extent possible, have been substantiated or corroborated by a range of other source material in the account below[21].

28.   The strategic target of the CIA rendition programme has always been, and remains, the global terrorist network known as Al-Qaeda. In the conception of the United States, Al-Qaeda exists as a nebulous collection of "cells" in countries around the world, comprising "operatives" who perform various roles in the preparation of terrorist attacks. When the US National Security Council became alarmed, in 1995, at what appeared to be a serious prospect of Osama bin Laden acquiring weapons of mass destruction, it developed rendition, according to Scheuer and others, as a way of *"breaking down Al-Qaeda"*, *"taking down cells"* and *"incarcerating senior Al-Qaeda people"*.

29.   Rendition was designed, at the outset of the programme at least, to fit within the United States' interpretation of its legal obligations[22]. The prerequisites for launching a rendition operation in the pre-9/11 period included:

- an "outstanding legal process" against the suspect, usually connected to terrorist offences in his country of origin;
- a CIA "dossier", or profile of the suspect, based on prior intelligence and in principle reviewed by lawyers;
- a "country willing to help" in the apprehension of the suspect on its territory; and
- "somewhere to take him after he was arrested".

---

[19] This section should be read in conjunction with the graphic map annexed to this explanatory memorandum, entitled: *The global "spider's web" of secret detentions and unlawful inter-state transfers*

[20] Mr Michael Scheuer was Chief of the Bin Laden Unit in the CIA Counter-Terrorism Center for four years, from August 1995 to June 1999. He then served for a further three years, from September 2001 to November 2004, as Special Advisor to the Chief of the Bin Laden Unit. He is recognised as one of the most important authorities on the evolution of rendition. Mr Scheuer graciously granted my representative a three-hour personal interview in Washington, DC in May 2006. Unlike many intelligence sources with whom my team spoke, he agreed to go "on the record", talking extensively about his first-hand operational experience of the rendition programme. A transcript of the interview is on file with the Rapporteur. Excerpts are cited in this report as follows: "Michael Scheuer, former Chief of the Bin Laden Unit in the CIA Counter-Terrorism Center".

[21] I also wish to recognise the valuable work of various non-governmental organisations and academic institutions in researching the evolution of rendition and to thank them for meeting with my team to relay their insights first-hand. In particular, the following groups have produced papers that I have consulted extensively: The Center for Human Rights and Global Justice at New York University School of Law, Human Rights First, Amnesty International, Human Rights Watch and Cage Prisoners.

[22] For further detail on the United States' interpretation of its international legal obligations, see the section below entitled *The point of view of the United States*, at heading 10.1.

30.   The receiving countries were, as a matter of policy, only asked to provide diplomatic assurances to the United States that they would "treat the suspects according to their own national laws". After the transfer, the United States made no effort to assess the manner in which the detainees were subsequently treated[23].

31.   Intelligence gathering, according to Scheuer, was not considered to be a priority in the pre-9/11 programme:

> "It was never intended to talk to any of these people. Success, at least as the Agency defined it, was to get someone, who was a danger to us or our allies, 'off the street' and, when we got him, to grab whatever documents he had with him. We knew that once he was captured he had been trained to either fabricate or to give us a great deal of information that we would chase for months and it would lead nowhere. So interrogations were always a very minor concern before 9/11."[24]

32.   Several current Council of Europe member States are known to have co-operated closely with the United States in the operation of its rendition programme under the Clinton Administration[25]. Indeed, the United Kingdom Government has indicated to the Council of Europe[26] that a system of prior notification existed in the 1990s, whereby even intended stopovers or overflights were reported by the United States in advance of each rendition operation[27].

33.   The act of "rendition" may not per se constitute a breach of international human rights law. It is worth noting that other States have also asserted their right to apprehend a terrorist suspect on foreign territory in order to bring him to justice if the tool of international judicial assistance or cooperation did not attain the desired result[28].

34.   The most prominent legal authorities in the United States, including its Supreme Court, have interpreted the object of the pre-9/11 rendition programme to be within the law[29]. Indeed, several human rights NGOs have assessed the original practice under the rubric of "rendition to justice", conceding that an inter-state transfer could be lawful if its object is to bring a suspect within a recognised judicial process respectful of human rights[30]. This indicator might in fact provide a legal benchmark against which unlawful inter-state transfers can be measured[31].

---

[23] In my *Information Memorandum II* in January, I quoted several former CIA agents who indicate that the United States knew some of the treatment of detainees would flout minimum standards of protection in international law. Mr Scheuer simply told my representative: *"I check my moral qualms at the door"*.

[24] Michael Scheuer, former Chief of the Bin Laden Unit in the CIA Counter-Terrorism Center, interview carried out by the Rapporteur's representative, *supra* note 19.

[25] See Jane Mayer, *Outsourcing Torture: The secret history of America's "extraordinary rendition" program*, in The New Yorker, 14 and 21 February 2005. Mayer refers to well-documented cases of rendition in which Croatia (1995) and Albania (1998) collaborated with the United States in apprehending suspects; at pages 109-110. Mr Scheuer gave a further example involving Germany, in which a suspect named Mahmood Salim, alias Abu Hajer, was arrested by Bavarian police.

[26] See Jack Straw, Secretary of State for Foreign and Commonwealth Affairs, *Written Ministerial Statement – Enquiries in respect of rendition allegations*, appended to the Response of the United Kingdom Government to the Request of the Secretary-General for an explanation in accordance with Article 52 ECHR, available at: http://www.coe.int/T/E/Com/Files/Events/2006-cia/United-Kingdom.pdf.

[27] *Ibid.* Mr Straw states: "There were four cases in 1998 where the US requested permission to render one or more detainees through the UK or Overseas Territories. In two of these cases, records show the Government granted the request, and refused two others."

[28] See US Secretary of State Condoleeza Rice, *Remarks upon her departure for Europe*, Andrews Air Force Base, 5 December 2005. Ms Rice refers to France's actions in the case of "Carlos the Jackal": "A rendition by the French government brought him to justice in France, where he is now imprisoned."

[29] See *United States v. Alvarez-Machain*, 504 U.S. 655 (1992), in which the Supreme Court upheld the jurisdiction of a US court to try a man brought to the US from Mexico by means of abduction rather than extradition. Case law on this matter dates back to the 1886 case of *Ker v. Illinois*, 119 U.S. 436 (1886), in which the Supreme Court said: "There is nothing in the Constitution that requires a court to permit a guilty person rightfully convicted to escape justice because he was brought to trial against his will."

[30] This concept of "rendition to justice" is discussed in greater detail in: Center for Human Rights and Global Justice, NYU School of Law, *Beyond Guantanamo: Transfers to Torture One Year after Rasul v. Bush*, 28 June 2005. I am also grateful to the staff of Human Rights First for their thorough explanations, in meetings, of the contemporary legal dilemmas faced in bringing terrorist suspects to justice.

[31] For a detailed analysis of the legal parameters of inter-state transfers, see Opinion No. 363/2005 of the European Commission for Democracy through Law (Venice Commission), available at: http://www.venice.coe.int/docs/2006/CDL-AD(2006)009-e.asp. See also the section below on the point of view of the Council of Europe, at heading 10.2.1.

218

35.   However, there has clearly been a critical deviation away from notions of justice in the rendition programme. In the wake of the 9/11 attacks, the United States transformed rendition into one of a range of instruments with which to pursue its so-called "war on terror". The attacks of 9/11 genuinely signalled something of a watershed in the United States approach to overcoming the terrorist threat[32]. This new "war on terrorism" was launched by the military intervention in Afghanistan in October 2001. At the same time new importance was attached to the collection of intelligence on persons suspected of terrorism. The CIA was put under pressure to play a more proactive role in the detention and interrogation of suspects rather than just putting them "behind bars". Without appropriate preparation, a global policy of arresting and detaining "the enemies" of the United States was – still according to Scheuer – improvised hastily. It was up to the lawyers to "legitimise" these operations, whilst the CIA and the American military became the principal supervisors and operators of the system[33].

36.   Rendition operations have escalated in scale and changed in focus. The central effect of the post-9/11 rendition programme has been to place captured terrorist suspects outside the reach of any justice system and keep them there. The absence of human rights guarantees and the introduction of "enhanced interrogation techniques" have led, in several cases examined, as we shall see, to detainees being subjected to torture.

37.   The reasons behind the transformation in the character of rendition are both political and operational. First, it is clear that the United States Government has set out to combat terrorism in an aggressive and urgent fashion. The executive has applied massive political pressure on all its agencies, particularly the CIA, to step up the intensity of their counter-terrorist activities. According to Scheuer, "after 9/11, we had nothing ready to go – the military had no plans, they had no response; so the Agency felt the brunt of the executive branch's desire to show the American people victories"[34].

38.   Second, and more importantly, the key operational change has been the mandate given to the CIA to administer its own detention facilities. When it takes terrorist suspects into its custody, the CIA no longer uses rendition to transport them into the custody of countries where they are wanted. Instead, for the high-level suspects at least, rendition now leads to secret detention at the CIA's so-called "black sites"[35] in unspecified locations around the world. Rather than face any form of justice, suspects become entrapped in the spider's web.

2.2.   Components of the spider's web

39.   In addition to CIA "black sites", the spider's web also encompasses a wider network of detention facilities run by other branches of the United States Government. Examples reported in the public domain have included the US Naval Base at Guantanamo Bay and military prisons such as Bagram in Afghanistan and Abu Ghraib in Iraq. Although the existence of such facilities is known, there are many aspects of their operation that remain shrouded in secrecy too.

40.   It should also be noted that "rendition" flights by the CIA are not the only means of transporting detainees between different points on the web. Particularly in the context of transfers to Guantanamo Bay, detainees have been moved extensively on military aircraft[36], including large cargo planes. Accordingly military flights have also fallen within the ambit of my inquiry.

---

[32] See Cofer Black, former Head of the CIA Counter-Terrorism Center, testimony before the House and Senate Intelligence Committees, *Hearings on Pre-9/11 Intelligence Failures*, 26 September 2002: "All you need to know is that there was a 'before 9/11' and an 'after 9/11'. After 9/11, the gloves came off."
[33] General Nicolo Pollari, the Director of the Italian Intelligence and Security Services (SISMI), testified before the European Parliament's TDIP Temporary Committee on 6 March 2003 that "the rules of the game have changed" in terms of international co-operation in the intelligence sector: "many security activities are now carried out on the borderline of legality, albeit within the legal framework".
[34] Michael Scheuer, former Chief of the Bin Laden Unit in the CIA Counter-Terrorism Center, interview carried out by the Rapporteur's representative, *supra* note 19.
[35] For an impressive account of CIA "black sites", see: Center for Human Rights and Global Justice, NYU School of Law, *Fate and Whereabouts Unknown: Detainees in the "War on Terror"*, 17 December 2005. The term "black sites" came into the public debate largely as a result of Dana Priest, *CIA Holds Terror Suspects in Secret Prisons*, Washington Post, 2 November 2005.
[36] See, *inter alia*, US Department of Defense documents released in response to a lawsuit under the *Freedom of Information Act* by Stephen H. Oleskey, Wilmer Hale LLP (copies of all disclosed documents on file with the Rapporteur). These materials shed light on the full extent to which military planes were used to transport detainees to Guantanamo Bay: in five consecutive missions in early January 2002 alone, nearly 150 detainees were transferred there (including out from European countries).

41.   The graphic included in this report depicts only a small portion of the global spider's web. It consists of two main components.

42.   First it illustrates the flights of both civilian and military aircraft, operated by the United States, which appear to be connected to secret detentions and unlawful inter-state transfers also involving Council of Europe member States. This inquiry is based on seven separate sets of data from Eurocontrol[37], combined with specific information from about twenty national aviation authorities in response to my requests. In this way, we have obtained a hitherto unique database[38].

43.   Second, it distinguishes four categories of aircraft landing points, which indicate the different degrees of collusion on the part of the countries concerned. These landing points have been placed into their respective categories as follows on the basis of the preponderance of evidence gathered[39]:

Category A: "**Stopover points**"
(points at which aircraft land to refuel, mostly on the way home)

>   Prestwick
>   Shannon
>   Roma Ciampino
>   Athens
>   Santa Maria (Azores)
>   Bangor
>   Prague

Category B: "**Staging points**"
(points from which operations are often launched - planes and crews prepare there, or meet in clusters)

>   Washington
>   Frankfurt
>   Adana-Incirlik
>   Ramstein
>   Larnaca
>   Palma de Mallorca
>   Baku

Category C: "**One-off pick-up points**"
(points from which, according to our research, one detainee or one group of detainees was picked up for rendition or unlawful transfer, but not as part of a systematic occurrence)

>   Stockholm-Bromma
>   Banjul
>   Skopje
>   Aviano
>   Tuzla

Category D: "**Detainee transfer / Drop-off points**"
(places visited often, where flights tend to stop for just short periods, mostly far off the obvious route – either their location is close to a site of a known detention facility or a *prima facie* case can be made to indicate a detention facility in their vicinity)

>   Cairo
>   Amman
>   Islamabad
>   Rabat
>   Kabul

---

[37] Eurocontrol is the European Organisation for the Safety of Air Navigation. I am grateful to Eurocontrol's Director General, Mr Victor Aguado, and his staff for responding to my various enquires in such an efficient and collegial manner. See the section below, at heading 2.3
[38] I sent a round of letters to the Heads of National Parliamentary Delegations on 31 March 2006 in which I asked specifically for information from their respective national aviation authorities.
[39] In this regard we have gathered detainee testimonies, exhibits placed before judicial and parliamentary enquiries, information obtained under *Freedom of Information* legislation, interviews with legal representatives and insider sources, the accounts of investigative journalists and research conducted by non-governmental organisations.

Guantanamo Bay
Timisoara / Bucharest
Tashkent
Algiers
Baghdad
Szymany

2.3.   Compiling a database of aircraft movements

44.   As we began our work in November 2005, various organisations and individuals in the non-governmental sector, especially investigative journalists and NGOs, sent us lists of aircraft suspected either of belonging to the CIA or of being operated on the CIA's behalf by bogus "front companies". The lists contained details such as the type of aircraft, the registered owner and operator, and the "N-number" by which an aircraft is identified. These lists are the result of painstaking efforts to piece together information that is publicly available on certain Internet sites, observations by "planespotters" and testimony from former detainees. We subsequently received from Eurocontrol "flight plans" regarding these planes, at least in so far as the European air space is concerned, for the period between the end of 2001 and early 2005. The Eurocontrol data received in January and February 2006 include, on the one hand, the plans of flights foreseen (which can be changed even during a flight for different reasons) and, on the other hand, information that has been verified following a request for collection of route charges, and flight data obtained from aviation authorities in the United States and elsewhere.

45.   The lists requested from Eurocontrol in our original correspondence were somewhat speculative, but knowingly so. It was important for the inquiry team, in conjunction with external experts and investigators familiar with the topic, to gain a sense of how CIA-related aircraft operate in relation to the thousands of other, non-CIA aircraft that use European airspace. In other words we sought to build a profile of the characteristics of CIA flights. Additionally we hoped that by casting our net widely, we would be able to identify planes never before connected to the CIA.

46.   We subsequently reverted to Eurocontrol on several occasions to obtain additional flight records[40]. As our work has progressed, we have been able to narrow down the number of aircraft movements that are of interest to our work and develop our analysis into a more sophisticated, realistic measure of the extent of illegality in the CIA's clandestine flight operations.

47.   Based on our initial analysis, we sent a series of one-off additional requests to certain national air traffic control bodies in order to obtain records of the flights actually made in their countries; we also asked for data on the movements of military aircraft, which are not covered by Eurocontrol.

48.   I am happy to report that through this channel I received useful information from various state institutions in different Council of Europe member States, including from transport ministries, aeronautic authorities, airport operators and state airlines. In addition, I obtained official records from national parliaments directly, including papers lodged by ministries of defence in response to parliamentary questions[41]. All of these diverse sources have contributed to the database of aircraft movements relied upon in this report.

2.4.   Operations of the spider's web

49.   We believe that we have made a significant step towards a better comprehension of the system of "renditions" and secret detention centres. One observation must be made. We should not lose our sense of proportion. It would be exaggerated to talk of thousands of flights, let alone hundreds of renditions concerning Europe. On this point I share the views expressed by members of the US Department of State, who recently delivered a first-hand briefing in Washington, DC at which a member of my team was present[42]. We undermine our credibility and limit the possibility for serious discussion if we make allegations that are

---

[40] Notably, in February 2006, I met with the staff of Eurocontrol for a very constructive briefing session.
[41] See, *inter alia*, the letter of the Rt. Hon Adam Ingram, UK Minister of State for the Armed Forces, in response to parliamentary questions in the House of Commons about the use of UK military airfields by US registered aircraft, dated 2 March 2006.
[42] See John Bellinger, Chief Legal Advisor to the US Secretary of State, and Dan Fried, Assistant Secretary of State, Bureau of European and Eurasian Affairs; *Briefing to European Delegation during the visit of the TDIP Temporary Committee of the European Parliament to Washington, DC*, 11 May 2006 (transcript on file with the Rapporteur – hereinafter "Bellinger, *Briefing to European Delegation*" or "Fried, *Briefing to European Delegation*").

ambiguous, exaggerated or unsubstantiated[43]. Indeed, it is evident that not all flights of CIA aircraft participate in "renditions". As Mr John Bellinger pointed out:

"Intelligence flights are a manifestation of the co-operation that happens amongst us. They carry analysts to talk with one another, they carry evidence that has been collected... I'm sure the Director of Intelligence himself was personally on a number of those flights."[44]

Mr Scheuer gave another explanation as to the purposes of such flights:

"There are lots of reasons other than moving prisoners to have aircrafts. It all depends on what you are doing. If you are in Afghanistan and you're supplying weapons to a commander that is working with Karzai's Government, then it could be a plane load of weapons. It could be food – the CIA is co-located with the US Military in bases around the country, so it could be rations.

Also, we try to take care of our people as well as we can, so it's toiletries, it's magazines, it's video recorders, it's coffee makers. We even take up collections at Christmas, to make sure we can send out hundreds and hundreds of pounds of Starbucks Coffee. So out of a thousand flights, I would bet that 98% of those flights are about logistics!"[45]

In fact it is precisely the remaining 2% that interests us.

50.   In order to understand the notion of a "spider's web", what is important to bear in mind is not the overall numbers of flights[46]; but rather the nature and context of individual flights. Our research has covered ten case studies of alleged unlawful inter-state transfers, involving a total of seventeen individual detainees. In most of these cases it was possible to generate flight logs from the amalgamated official flight database referred to earlier. I have then matched those logs with the times, dates and places of the alleged transfer operations – according to victims themselves, lawyer's notes or other sources. Finally, where possible, I have corroborated this information with factual elements acquired from legal proceedings in Council of Europe member States or in the United States.

51.   In translating these case studies into graphic representations, I resolved to trace each flight route not individually, but as part of a circuit. Each circuit begins and ends, where possible, at the aircraft's "home base" (very often Dulles Airport in Washington, DC) in the United States. Following these flight circuits helps to better understand the different categories of aircraft landings – simple stopovers for refuelling, staging points that host clusters of CIA aircraft or serve to launch operations, and detainee drop-off points. Despite being a fairly simple analytical technique, it has also helped discover some significant new information, which we present in the following sections.

2.5.   Successive rendition operations and secret detentions

52.   We believe we are in a position to state that successive CIA rendition operations have taken place in the course of the same, single flight circuit. Two of the rendition case studies examined in this report, both involving Council of Europe member States to differing degrees, belonged to the same clandestine circuit of abductions and renditions at different points of the spider's web. The information at our disposal indicates that the renditions of Binyam Mohamed and Khaled El-Masri were carried out by the same CIA-operated aircraft, within 48 hours of one another, in the course of the same 12-day tour in January 2004. This finding appears significant for a number of reasons. First, since neither man even knows of the other – Mr Mohamed is still detained at Guantanamo Bay and Mr El-Masri has returned to his home community near Ulm in the South of Germany – their respective stories can be used to lend credence to one another. My team has received direct or indirect testimony from each of them independently.

---

[43] *Ibid.* According to Mr Bellinger: "We have been trying, from Secretary Rice down, to engage in a real dialogue with our different partners in Europe, be it the EU, be it the Council of Europe. We know your concerns and we are interested in talking to you directly, but on the basis of fact and not mere hyperbole." According to Mr Fried: "If the charges are absurd, it becomes difficult to deal with the real problems of the legal regime and the legal framework in which we have to conduct this struggle."

[44] Bellinger, *Briefing to European Delegation, supra* note 41.

[45] Michael Scheuer, former Chief of the Bin Laden Unit in the CIA Counter-Terrorism Center, interview conducted by the Rapporteur's representative, *supra* note 19.

[46] Bellinger, *Briefing to European Delegation, supra* note 41: "There really is not evidence of this. There is not evidence of a thousand detainees; there's not evidence of a hundred detainees; there's not even evidence of ten detainees."

222

53.   As they both allege having been subjected to CIA rendition, the fact that the same aircraft - operated by a CIA-linked company – carried out two transfers in such quick succession allows us to speak of the existence of a "rendition circuit" within the "spider's web".

54.   It is also possible to develop a hypothesis as to the nature of some other aircraft landings belonging to the same renditions circuit. Thus, for example, the landings which occurred directly before and directly after the El-Masri rendition bear the typical characteristics of rendition operations[47].

55.   Our analysis of the rendition programme in the post-9/11 era allows us to infer that the transfer of other detainees on this rendition circuit must have entailed detainees being transferred out of Kabul to alternative detention facilities in different countries. Thus, drawing upon official flight data, the probable existence of secret detention facilities can be inferred in Algeria and, as we will see, in Romania.

2.6.   Detention facilities in Romania and Poland

2.6.1   The case of Romania

56.   Romania is thus far the only Council of Europe member State to be located on one of the rendition circuits we believe we have identified and which bears all the characteristics of a detainee transfer or drop-off point. The N313P rendition plane landed in Timisoara at 11.51 pm on 25 January 2004 and departed just 72 minutes later, at 1.03 am on 26 January 2004. I am grateful to the Romanian Civil Aeronautic Authority for confirming these flight movements[48].

57.   It is known that detainee transport flights are customarily night flights, as is the case of the other rendition flights already documented. The only other points on this rendition circuit from which the plane took off at a similar hour of the morning were Rabat, Morocco (departure at 2.05 am) and Skopje, "the former Yugoslav Republic of Macedonia" (hereinafter "Macedonia") (departure at 1.30 am). In both of these cases, we possess sufficient indications to claim that when the plane left its destination, it was carrying a prisoner to a secret detention centre situated in Kabul.

58.   We can likewise affirm that the plane was not carrying prisoners to further detention when it *left* Timisoara. Its next destination, after all, was Palma de Mallorca, a well-established "staging point", also used for recuperation purposes in the midst of rendition circuits.

59.   There is documentation in this instance that the passengers of the N313P plane, using US Government passports[49] and apparently false identities[50], stayed in a hotel in Palma de Mallorca for two nights before returning to the United States. One can deduce that these passengers, in addition to the crew of the plane, comprised a CIA rendition team, the same team performing all renditions on this circuit.

60.   The N313P plane stayed on the runway at Timisoara on the night of 25 January 2004 for barely one hour. Based on analysis of the flight capacity of N313P, a Boeing 737 jet, in line with typical flight behaviours of CIA planes, it is highly unlikely that the purpose of heading to Romania was to refuel. The plane had the capacity to reach Palma de Mallorca, just over 7 hours away, directly from Kabul that night – twice previously on the same circuit, it had already flown longer distances of 7 hours 53 minutes (Rabat to Kabul) and 7 hours 45 minutes (Kabul to Algiers).

---

[47] See *Flight logs related to the successive rendition operations of Binyam Mohamed and Khaled El-Masri in January 2004*, reproduced in this report in the Appendix to the present document. The landings in question are at Algiers (Algeria) and Timisoara (Romania).
[48] See *Information from the records of the Romanian Civil Aeronautic Authority and the Romanian Ministry of National Defence*, contained as Appenices to the letters sent to me by György Frunda, Chairman of the Romanian delegation to PACE, dated 24 February 2006 and 7 April 2006. I wish to thank my colleague Mr Frunda for his outstanding efforts in gathering information from various Romanian authorities on my behalf.
[49] See Andrew Manreas, *La investigación halla en los vuelos de la CIA decenas de ocupantes con estatus diplomatico*, in El Pais, Palma de Mallorca, 15 November 2005.
[50] See Matias Valles, journalist with Diario de Mallorca, *Testimony before theTDIP Temporary Committee of the European Parliament*, 20 April 2006. Valles researched a total of 42 names he had uncovered from the records of a hotel in Mallorca where the passengers of the N313P plane stayed. Many proved to be "false identities", apparently created using the names of characters from Hollywood movies such as *Bladerunner* and *Alien*. Valles confirmed that at least some of the persons who arrived back in Palma de Mallora from Romania after the rendition circuit were the same persons who had stayed in the hotel at a previous point on the circuit – thus indicating that the "rendition team" remained on the plane throughout its trip.

19

61.   It should be recalled that the rendition team stayed about 30 hours in Kabul after having "rendered" Khaled El-Masri. Then, it flew to Romania on the same plane. Having eliminated other explanations – including that of a simple logistics flight, as the trip is a part of a well-established renditions circuit – the most likely hypothesis is that the purpose of this flight was to transport one or several detainees from Kabul to Romania.

62.   We consider that while all these factual elements do not provide definitive evidence of secret detention centres, they do justify on their own a positive obligation to carry out a serious investigation, which the Romanian authorities do not seem to have done to date.

2.6.2. The case of Poland

63.   Poland was likewise singled out as a country which had harboured secret detention centres.

64.   On the basis of information obtained from different sources we were able to determine that persons suspected of being high level terrorists were transferred out of a secret CIA detention facility in Kabul, Afghanistan in late September and October 2003[51]. During this period, my official database shows that the only arrival of CIA-linked aircraft from Kabul in Europe was at the Polish airport of Szymany. The flights in question, carried out by the well-known "rendition plane" N313P, bear all the hallmarks of a rendition circuit.

65.   The plane arrived in Kabul, on 21 September 2003, from Tashkent, Uzbekistan. The axis between Tashkent and Kabul was well known for detainee transfers[52]. Still, according to information received, the most significant detainee movements at this time probably involved transfers *out of* Kabul. The explanation attributed by NGO sources and journalists who have investigated this period[53] is that the CIA required a more isolated, secure, controlled environment in which to hold its high-level detainees, due to the proliferation of both prison facilities and prisoners in Afghanistan arising from the escalating "war on terrorism".

66.   Thus, the circuit in question continued on 22 September 2003, when the plane flew from Kabul to Szymany airport in Poland. On the same grounds given above for the case of Romania, one may deduce that this flight was a CIA rendition, culminating in a "detainee drop-off" in Poland.

67.   Szymany is described by the Chairman of the Polish delegation to PACE as a "former Defence Ministry airfield", located near the rural town of Szczytno in the North of the country. It is close to a large facility used by the Polish intelligence services, known as the Stare Kiejkuty base. Both the airport and the nearby base were depicted on satellite images I obtained in January 2006[54].

68.   It is noteworthy that the Polish authorities have been unable, despite repeated requests, to provide me with information from their own national aviation records to confirm any CIA-connected flights into Poland. In his letter of 9 May 2006, my colleague Karol Karski, the Chairman of the Polish delegation to PACE, explained:

> "I addressed the Polish authorities competent in gathering the air traffic data, related to these aircraft numbers... I was informed that several numbers from your list were still not found in our flight logs'

---

[51] My team has worked closely with Human Rights Watch to corroborate the available evidence of detainee movements out of Afghanistan. For an indication of the earlier analysis of this information, see *Human Rights Watch Statement on US Secret Detention Facilities in Europe*, 7 November 2005, available at:
http://hrw.org/english/docs/2005/11/07/usint11995.htm.

[52] See Craig Murray, former United Kingdom Ambassador to Uzbekistan, *Exchange of views with the Committee on Legal Affairs and Human Rights (AS/Jur)*, Strasbourg, 24 January 2006. The minutes reflect that Mr Murray spoke of "evidence of the CIA chartering flights to Uzbekistan, between Kabul and Tashkent, and of the use of torture by Uzbek agents, as well as evidence that the American and British authorities were willing to receive and use information obtained under torture by foreign agencies, the relevant decision having been taken at a high level". See also Don van Natta Jr, *Growing Evidence US Sending Prisoners to Torture Capital: Despite Bad Record on Human Rights, Uzbekistan is Ally*, New York Times, 1 May 2005, available at:
www.nytimes.com/2005/05/01/international/01renditions.html?ex=1272600000&en=932280de7e0c1048&ei=5088&partner=rssnyt&emc=rss.

[53] For an excellent account of the motivations for moving detainees to secret locations, see James Risen, *State of War: The Secret History of the CIA and the Bush Administration*, Free Press, New York, 2006, at pages 29 to 31: "The CIA wanted secret locations where it could have complete control over the interrogations and debriefings, free from the prying eyes of the international media, free from monitoring by human rights groups, and, most important, far from the jurisdiction of the American legal system."

[54] See European Union Satellite Centre, information provided to the Rapporteur on 23 January 2006. For further information see the section below at heading 4.1.

records. Being not aware about the source of your information connecting these flight numbers with Polish airspace, I am not able, [nor are] the Polish air traffic control authorities, to comment on the fact of missing them in our records.[55]

69.   Mr. Karski also made the following statement, which reflects the position of the Polish Government on the question of CIA renditions:

"According to the information I have been provided with, none of the questioned flights was recorded in the traffic controlled by our competent authorities – in connection with Szymany or any other Polish airport."

70.   The absence of flight records from a country such as Poland is unusual. A host of neighbouring countries, including Romania, Bulgaria and the Czech Republic have had no such problems in retrieving official data for the period since 2001. Indeed, the submissions of these countries, along with my data from Eurocontrol, confirm numerous flights into and out of Polish airports by the CIA-linked planes that are the subject of this report.

71.   In this light, Poland cannot be considered to be outside the rendition circuits simply because it has failed to furnish information corroborating our data from other sources. I have thus presented in my graphic the suspected rendition circuit involving Szymany airport, in which the landing at Szymany is placed in the category of "detainee drop-off" points.

72.   According to records in our possession, the N313P plane remained at Szymany airport on 22 September 2003 for just 64 minutes. I can also confirm that the plane then flew from Szymany to Romania, where it landed, after a change of course, at Bucharest Baneasa airport. Here, as in the case of Timisoara above, the aircraft landing in Romania fits the profile of a "detainee drop-off".

73.   It is possible that several detainees may have been transported together on the flight out of Kabul, with some being left in Poland and some being left in Romania. This pattern would conform with information from other sources, which indicated the simultaneous existence of secret prisons in these two Council of Europe member States[56].

74.   This suspected rendition circuit continued after Romania by landing in Rabat, Morocco, which several elements point to as a location that harbours a detention facility[57]. It is conceivable that this landing may even have constituted a third "detainee drop-off" in succession before the plane returned to the United States, via Guantanamo Bay.

75.   As for Romania, I find that there is now a preponderance of indications, not to prove the existence of detention centres, but in any case to open a real in-depth and transparent inquiry. One can add that the sources at the origin of the publications by Human Rights Watch, The Washington Post and ABC News, referring to the existence of such centres in Romania and Poland, are multiple, concordant and particularly well informed, as they belong to the very services that have directed these operations.

[...]

3.5. Bisher Al-Rawi and Jamil El-Banna

163.   This case, which concerns two British permanent residents arrested in Gambia in November 2002 and transferred first to Afghanistan and from there to Guantanamo (where they still are), is an example of (ill-conceived) cooperation between the services of a European country (the British MI5) and the CIA in abducting persons against whom there is no evidence justifying their continued detention in prison and whose principal crime is to be on social terms with a leading Islamist, namely Abu Qatada.

164.   The information made public to date[148] shows that the abduction of Messrs Al-Rawi and El-Banna was indeed motivated by information – partly erroneous – supplied by MI5.

[...]

175.   The families of Messrs Al-Rawi and El-Banna and their lawyers at the London firm Birnberg, Peirce & Partners brought an action to oblige the British government to make representations to the United States through diplomatic channels in order to secure the release and repatriation of the two men as soon as possible. According to the latest information, the British government has acted along those lines with regard to Mr Al-Rawi, but not with regard to Mr El-Banna. The judgment at first instance, given in May 2006, dismissed the families' complaints.

176.   In view of these highly disturbing facts, I find that the British authorities must shed light on this case in full. I welcome the fact that our colleague, Andrew Tyrie, has devoted much energy to this matter in order for truth to be established in this disturbing case. Meanwhile, the United Kingdom, even if it has no recognised legal obligation, must make good the consequences of the apparently very imprecise communication between the MI5 and the American services. There is indeed little doubt that the arrest of the two men was largely triggered or at least influenced by the messages of November 2002, only part of which (the afore-mentioned telegrams) is public knowledge.

[...]

198.   Binyam's case is an example for the very numerous detainees – most of whose names and whereabouts we do not know – who have become trapped in the United States' spider's web during the course of the "war on terror". Binyam has been subjected to two CIA renditions, a US military transfer to Guantanamo Bay and several other clandestine transfers by plane and helicopter. He has been held in at least two secret detention facilities, in addition to military prisons. During his illegal interrogations, he has been confronted with allegations that could only have arisen from intelligence provided by the United Kingdom.

[...]

288.   In this sense, it must be stated that to date, the following member States could be held responsible, to varying degrees, which are not always settled definitively, for violations of the rights of specific persons identified below (respecting the chronological order as far as possible):

-   Sweden, in the cases of Ahmed Agiza and Mohamed Alzery ;
-   Bosnia-Herzegovina, in the cases of Lakhdar Boumediene, Mohamed Nechle, Hadj Boudella, Belkacem Bensayah, Mustafa Ait Idir and Saber Lahmar (the "Algerian six") ;
-   The United Kingdom in the cases of Bisher Al-Rawi, Jamil El-Banna and Binyam Mohamed ;
-   Italy, in the cases of Abu Omar and Maher Arar ;
-   "The former Yugoslav Republic of Macedonia", in the case of Khaled El-Masri ;
-   Germany, in the cases of Abu Omar, of the "Algerian six", and Khaled El-Masri ;
-   Turkey, in the case of the "Algerian six".

289.   Some of these above mentioned states, and others, could be held responsible for collusion – active or passive (in the sense of having tolerated or having been negligent in fulfilling the duty to supervise) - involving secret detention and unlawful inter-state transfers of a non specified number of persons whose identity so far remains unknown:

-   Poland and Romania, concerning the running of secret detention centres;
-   Germany, Turkey, Spain and Cyprus for being "staging points" for flights involving the unlawful transfer of detainees;
-   Ireland, the United Kingdom, Portugal, Greece and Italy for being "stopovers" for flights involving the unlawful transfer of detainees.

[...]

(12)　European Parliament Resolution adopting Report by Temporary Committee, 14 February 2007 (extracts)

The European Parliament,

[...]

68.　Welcomes the meeting in London with the UK Minister for Europe and the fact that the UK Government supplied documents and explanations; notes that the UK authorities could not answer all the questions raised by the Temporary Committee delegation to London;

69.　Takes note of the declarations made by UK Secretary of State for Foreign and Commonwealth Affairs, Margaret Beckett, in a written response to a parliamentary question whereby she admitted that the UK Government had been aware of a secret CIA prison network before US President George W. Bush acknowledged its existence in September 2006; asks the UK Government to state whether it has raised the issue with the US authorities and whether, and, if so, when, it informed or discussed the issue with other European governments;

70.　Thanks the UK's All-Party Parliamentary Group on Extraordinary Renditions (APPG), comprising members of the House of Commons and the House of Lords, for its work and for providing the Temporary Committee delegation to London with a number of highly valuable documents;

71.　Condemns the extraordinary rendition of Bisher Al-Rawi, an Iraqi citizen and resident in the United Kingdom, and Jamil El-Banna, a Jordanian citizen and resident in the United Kingdom, who were arrested by Gambian authorities in Gambia in November 2002, turned over to US agents, and flown to Afghanistan and then to Guantánamo, where they remain detained in the absence of a trial or any form of judicial assistance;

72. Points out that the telegrams from the UK security service MI5 to an unspecified foreign government, which were released to the Chairman of the APPG, Andrew Tyrie, suggest that the abduction of Bisher Al-Rawi and Jamil El-Banna was facilitated by partly erroneous information supplied by MI5;

73. Criticises the unwillingness of the UK Government to provide consular assistance to Bisher Al-Rawi and Jamil El-Banna on the grounds that they are not UK citizens;

74. Condemns the extraordinary rendition, on two occasions, of Binyam Mohammed, Ethiopian citizen and resident in the United Kingdom; points out that Binyam Mohammed has been held in at least two secret detention facilities, in addition to military prisons;

75. Is deeply disturbed by the testimony of Binyam Mohammed's lawyer, who gave an account of the most horrific torture endured by his client to the official delegation of the Temporary Committee to the United Kingdom;

76. Emphasises that the former UK Secretary of State for Foreign and Commonwealth Affairs, Jack Straw, conceded in December 2005 that UK intelligence officials met Binyam Mohammed when he was arrested in Pakistan; points out in this respect that some of the questions put by the Moroccan officials to Binyam Mohammed appear to have been inspired by information supplied by the United Kingdom;

77. Condemns the extraordinary rendition of UK citizen Martin Mubanga, who met the official delegation of the Temporary Committee to the United Kingdom, and who was arrested in Zambia in March 2002 and subsequently flown to Guantánamo; regrets the fact that Martin Mubanga was interrogated by UK officials at Guantánamo, where he was detained and tortured for four years without trial or any form of judicial assistance and then released without charge;

78. Takes note of the testimony to the Temporary Committee by Craig Murray, former UK Ambassador to Uzbekistan, on the exchange of intelligence obtained under torture and the legal opinion of Michael Wood, former legal advisor to the UK Foreign and Commonwealth Office;

79. Expresses its concern about Michael Wood's legal opinion, according to which receiving or possessing information extracted under torture, insofar as there is no direct participation in the torture, is not per se prohibited by the UN Convention against Torture and other Cruel, Inhumane or Degrading Treatment or Punishment; expresses its condemnation of any attempt to obtain information by means of torture, regardless of who is involved;

80. Notes the 170 stopovers made by CIA-operated aircraft at UK airports, and expresses serious concern about the purpose of those flights which came from or were bound for countries linked with extraordinary rendition circuits and the transfer of detainees; deplores the stopovers at UK airports of aircraft that have been shown to have been used by the CIA, on other occasions, for the extraordinary rendition of Bisher Al-Rawi, Jamil El-Banna, Abou Elkassim Britel, Khaled El-Masri, Binyam Mohammed, Abu Omar and Maher Arar and for the expulsion of Ahmed Agiza and Mohammed El Zari;

British government documents and statements

13. Foreign Office Memo to 10 Downing Street, 7 December 2005—p.231

This Memorandum, written two days after Condoleezza Rice's statement on rendition (Document 5), offers an assessment of how rendition was affected by the UK's international obligations and the state of knowledge at the time about the use of UK airspace for rendition flights. It also offered 'advice on handling'. The Memo was leaked some weeks later, adding to speculation over the issue.

14. Written Answer by the Foreign Secretary, Rt Hon Jack Straw MP, 12 December 2005—p.235

The first Parliamentary Question on "Extraordinary Rendition" was asked by Chris Mullin MP on 17 October 2005. As interest in the issue grew, the then Foreign Secretary disclosed that two rendition flights had gone through UK airspace in 1998. The details of one or two other possible cases remained unclear

15. Written Statement by the Foreign Secretary, Rt Hon Jack Straw MP, 20 January 2006—p.237

The Foreign Secretary followed up his Written Answer (Document 14) with a Written Statement on 10 January 2006 that added some further detail concerning US requests for use of UK territory or airspace for rendition flights in 1998. However, the leaking of the Memorandum to 10 Downing Street (Document 13) led to a further restatement of the government's position on 20 January. Subsequent disclosures, notably in relation to Diego Garcia, would contradict elements of the Statement.

16. Letter from the Foreign Secretary, Rt Hon Jack Straw MP, to the Shadow Foreign Secretary, Rt Hon William Hague MP, 6 February 2006—p.239

Further to the Foreign Secretary's statements (Documents 14 and 15), his opposition counterpart, William Hague, raised a number of questions in an open letter. Some of the Foreign Secretary's answers, notably on transfers through British Overseas Territories and transfers of those detained by UK armed forces, would later have to be corrected (Documents 17 and 19).

17. Statement by the Foreign Secretary, Rt Hon David Miliband MP, 21 February 2008—p.242

230

The British government consistently denied that any suspects were rendered through Diego Garcia. On 18 July 2007, the Foreign Office Minister of State, Lord Malloch Brown, told the House of Lords that 'The US authorities have repeatedly given us assurances that no terrorist suspects have been, or are being, held at Diego Garcia, or at any time have passed in transit through Diego Garcia or its territorial waters or airspace.'—[Official Report, House of Lords, 18 July 2007; Vol. 694, c. WA25.] On 11 October, the Foreign Office Minister Meg Munn gave a similar answer to a Parliamentary Question in the Commons. All this was invalidated by the Foreign Secretary's Statement, which followed the provision of new information from the US administration. As the then Chairman of the Foreign Affairs Select Committee, Mike Gapes MP, pointed out, it also discredited the government's previous insistence that 'We are clear that the US would not render anyone through UK airspace (including the Overseas Territories) without our permission.'

18. Written Statement by the Foreign Secretary, Rt Hon David Miliband MP, 3 July 2008, and list of flights—p.245

Following the admission that rendition flights had landed at Diego Garcia, the Foreign Secretary sent a list of flights to the US for specific assurances that they had not been used in rendition. The assurances received in response did not address rendition 'circuit flights', nor flights through UK airspace that did not land at a UK airport.

19. Statement by the Defence Secretary, Rt Hon John Hutton MP, 26 February 2009—p.260

A year after David Miliband had corrected previous government statements on rendition through Diego Garcia, another Cabinet Minister had to make a further disclosure to the House of Commons. Following a review of detainee records in Iraq and Afghanistan, Defence Secretary John Hutton confirmed that – contrary to previous statements – two individuals detained in Iraq in 2004 and handed over to the custody of the United States had been transferred to Afghanistan. The government insisted that this was an isolated case; however, claims to the contrary by groups such as Reprieve and the government's inability to disclose details about the individuals transferred were causes for continuing unease.

20. Statement by the Prime Minister, Rt Hon David Cameron MP, 6 July 2010—p.265

Shortly after the formation of the new coalition government, the Prime Minister announced the establishment of an inquiry into allegations of British involvement in the mistreatment of detainees overseas. He confirmed that it would examine rendition and related issues.

(13)   Foreign Office Memo to 10 Downing Street, 7 December 2005

Dear Grace,

Detainees

Summary

1.   An explanation of what is normally meant by "Rendition" and
"Extraordinary Rendition", though these are neither legal nor precise
terms. Discussion also of their legality: Rendition could be legal in certain
limited circumstances; Extraordinary Rendition is almost certainly illegal.
Further advice, too, on what we and the US mean when we talk of
"torture" and "cruel, inhuman and degrading treatment" (CID). And to
what extent knowledge of, or partial assistance in, these operations (eg
permission to refuel) constitutes complicity?

2.   Advice too on handling. We should try to avoid getting drawn on
detail, at least until we have been able to complete the substantial research
required to establish what has happened even since 1997; and to try to
move the debate on, in as front foot a way as we can, underlining all the
time the strong counter-terrorist rationale for close co-operation with the
US, within our legal obligations. Armed with Rice's statement and the
Foreign Secretary's response, we should try to situate the debate not on
whether the US practices torture (and whether the UK is complicit in it):
they have made clear they do not – but onto the strong US statements in
Rice's text on their commitment to domestic and international
instruments. A debate on whether the US test for torture/CID derives from
their commitments under the US Constitution rather than international
law is better ground than the principle of whether they practice torture.

Detail

3.   You asked for further advice on substance and handling, following my
letter of 5 December, including with a view to PMQs on 7 December.
Specifics:

What do we mean by "Rendition"?

4.   This is not a legally defined term. But it is normally understood to mean
the transfer of a person from one jurisdiction to another, outside the normal
legal processes such as extradition, deportation, removal or exclusion. It does
not necessarily carry any connotation of involvement in torture.

"Extraordinary Rendition"?

5.   The use of this term is even more varied. In its recent letters to Chief
Constables and Ministers, Liberty has defined it as transfer from one third
country to another. But it is normally used to connote the transfer of a person
from one third country to another, in circumstances where there is a real risk
(or even intention) that the individual will be subjected to torture or cruel,

inhuman or degrading treatment (CID). Indefinite detention without legal process could be argued to constitute CID.

Is Rendition **lawful**?

6.   We need to look at the facts of each case. In certain circumstances, it could be legal, if the process complied with the domestic law of both countries involved, and their international obligations. Normally, these international obligations, eg under the International Covenant on Civil and Political Rights (ICCPR), would prevent an individual from being arbitrarily detained or expelled outside the normal legal process. Council of Europe countries would also be bound by the ECHR, which has similar obligations in this sense. Against this background, even a Rendition that does not involve the possibility of torture/CID would be difficult, and likely to be confined to those countries not signed up to eg the ICCPR.

7.   Rendition could therefore be legal in certain tightly defined circumstances. Rice's Statement claimed two such examples (the World Trade Centre bomber, Ramzi Yousef, and Carlos the Jackal). But such cases will be rare.

Could Rendition ever be legal in the UK?

8.   This depends how we are using the term "rendition". In most circumstances and in most uses of the term, it will not be legal, including if it contravenes the law of the state from which the individual is transferred. In some limited circumstances, eg where there is no extant extradition procedure between the UK and a third country, transfer without formal extradition might be legal.

Is Extraordinary Rendition legal?

9.   In the most common use of the term (ie involving real risk of torture), it could never be legal, because this is clearly prohibited under the UN Convention Against Torture (CAT). But the CAT prohibition on transfer applies to torture only, not to CID. (This may explain the emphasis on torture in Rice's statement.)

10.   The US government does not use the term "Extraordinary Rendition" at all. They say that, if they are transferring an individual to a country where they believe he is likely to be tortured, they get the necessary assurances from the host government (cf Rice's Statement: "The US has not transported anyone, and will not transport anyone, to a country when we believe he will be tortured. Where appropriate, the US seeks assurances that transferred persons will not be tortured"). (Comment: We would not want to cast doubt on the principle of such government-to-government assurances, not least given our own attempts to secure these from countries to which we wish to deport their nationals suspected of involvement in terrorism: Algeria etc).

What about the US reservation and "understandings" with respect to the CAT?

11.   The US reservation to the CAT states that the US considers itself bound (Article 16) to prevent CID only insofar as this means the CID prohibited by the US Constitution, but not as defined in international instruments such as the ICCPR. So, for example, the US would not (logically enough) consider themselves bound by the ECHR findings in relation to UK practice in Northern Ireland in the 1970s which ruled that five types of treatment did constitute CID (eg sleep deprivation, constant exposure to loud noise).

12.   An "understanding" stated by the US spells out what it understands by mental pain or suffering in the definition of torture. It is not clear whether in practice this gives the US scope to use techniques which would otherwise constitute torture.

Would cooperating with a US Rendition operation be illegal?

13.   If the US were to act contrary to its international obligations, then co-operation with such an act would also be illegal if we knew of the circumstances. This would be the case, for example, in any cooperation over an Extraordinary Rendition without human rights assurances. Conversely, cooperation with a "legal" Rendition, that met the domestic law of both of the main countries involved, and was consistent with their international obligations, would be legal. Where we have no knowledge of illegality but allegations are brought to our attention, we ought to make reasonable enquiries.

How do we know whether those our Armed Forces have helped to capture in Iraq or Afghanistan have subsequently been sent to interrogation centres?

14.   Cabinet Office is researching this with MOD. But we understand the basic answer is that we have no mechanism for establishing this, though we would not ourselves question such detainees while they were in such facilities.

What happened in 1998?

15.   The Security Service have so far identified two cases:

   i)   An individual, Mohammed Rashed Daoud AL-OWHALI, was suspected of involvement in bombing the US Embassy in Nairobi. The US asked on 24 August 1998 for assistance with his return from Kenya to the USA for trial. This was originally via Prestwick, but later changed to Stansted because of the flight range of the aircraft. The request was originally for Al-Owhali and one other, who in the event did not travel. The request was agreed by the Home Secretary, Jack Straw.

   ii)   A similar request the same year was turned down, because the individual concerned was to be transported to Egypt (not yet clear what, if anything, the US said about assurances).

16.   From the information we have at the moment, we are not sure in either case whether the individual's transfer from the country in which he was detained was extra-legal.

17.   The papers we have unearthed so far suggest there could be more such cases. The Home Office, who lead, are urgently examining their files, as are we. But we now cannot say that we have received no such requests for the use of UK territory or air space for "Extraordinary Rendition". It does remain true that "we are not aware of the use of UK territory or air space for the purposes of "Extraordinary Rendition"". But we think we should now try to move the debate on from the specifics of rendition, extraordinary or otherwise, and focus people instead on the Rice's clear assurance that all US activities are consistent with their domestic and international obligations and never include the use of torture.

Handling

18.   As far as possible, we should stick to the terms of the Foreign Secretary's Statement in response to Rice's, and his letter to EU Foreign Ministers covering her reply. We should also try to bring out the other side of the balance, in terms of the huge challenge which the threat of terrorism poses to all countries, and the need to balance the rights of the suspected terrorist against those of his potential victims.

19.   More broadly, we should try to move the debate on from concentrating on whether the US practice torture, which they have clearly said they do not, and try to focus on the US's constructive reassurance that, in all respects, they have acted in a way consistent with their domestic and international legal obligations, and with the sovereignty of those countries with which they have been working.

20.   I am copying this letter to Nigel Sheinwald and Margaret Aldred (Cabinet Office), Ian Forber (MOD), Emma Churchill (Home Office), (Thames House), (Vauxhall Cross), and Sir David Manning (Washington).

(Irfan Siddiq)
Private Secretary

Ms Grace Cassy
10 Downing Street

(14) Written Answer by the Foreign Secretary, Rt Hon Jack Straw MP, 12 December 2005

Terrorist Suspects (Renditions)

Sir Menzies Campbell: To ask the Secretary of State for Foreign and Commonwealth Affairs when he was first informed that the United States was conducting international renditions of terrorist suspects; and what representations he has made to the US administration on such renditions. [36414]

Mr. Straw: The term rendition" is currently being used to describe informal transfers of individuals in a wide range of circumstances. Whether any particular rendition" is lawful depends on the facts of each individual case. Where we are requested to assist another State and our assistance would be lawful, we will decide whether or not to assist taking into account all the circumstances. We would not assist in any case if to do so would put us in breach of UK law or our international obligations. In particular, we would not facilitate the transfer of an individual from or through the UK to another State where there were grounds to believe that the person would face a real risk of torture.

Careful research by officials has been unable to identify any occasion since 11 September 2001, or earlier in the Bush administration, when we received a request for permission by the United States (US) for a rendition through UK territory or airspace, nor are we otherwise aware of such a case.

Additional research covering the remainder of the period of office of this Government (i.e. back to May 1997) has been undertaken. This shows there were some renditions via the UK during that period. Specifically, we have identified two definite occasions in 1998 when requests were made by the US. These occasions, for which records have been identified, were for transfer to the US for the person concerned to stand trial there. As the then Home Secretary I agreed these requests.

Although confirmatory records have yet to be identified, we believe that there may have been one or two other possible cases, also in 1998, which concerned requests by the US but for transfer to a third country. We have information on one such case which is incomplete and does not tell us whether the request was refused. We also have information on a case based on the recollection of officials involved in such matters, without any confirmatory records. The officials' recollection is that the case was refused. It is likely, but not certain, that the two cases are in fact one and the same. I have some recollection of such a case, but, given the passage of time, I cannot be certain. The search for records continues.

(15) Written Statement by the Foreign Secretary, Rt Hon Jack Straw MP, 20 January 2006

FOREIGN AND COMMONWEALTH AFFAIRS

Rendition Allegations (Inquiries)

The Secretary of State for Foreign and Commonwealth Affairs (Mr. Jack Straw): Some media reports over the last 48 hours, based on a leaked Government document, have suggested that the Government may be aware that there have been cases of "extraordinary rendition" through UK territory or airspace about which it has not informed Parliament.

This is not the case. I have given Parliament clear answers, updated as information has become available to me. The following chronology makes this clear:

> 7 December: the leaked document was sent by my office to the Prime Minister's Office, setting out our understanding at that time.

> 12 December: after continuing searches of official records over the following few days, my written answer to the right hon. Member for North East Fife, (Sir Menzies Campbell), Official Report, Column 1652W,set out the facts as they had then been established: there had been three instances in 1998 where the US authorities had requested permission to render a detainee through UK territory or airspace; and in two of these cases, where the detainee was to be transferred to the US for trial, the US request had been granted. In the other case, it had been refused. I added that officials continued to search the records.

> 13 December: I discussed these issues at length in my public evidence session with the Foreign Affairs Committee.

> 10 January: I issued a written ministerial statement saying that Foreign and Commonwealth Office officials had now completed a search of their records back to May 1997. This search had turned up one further case, also in 1998: the Government had declined a US request to refuel a flight carrying two detainees en route to the US.

To summarise the position:

> We have found no evidence of detainees being rendered through the UK or Overseas Territories since 11 September 2001.

We have found no evidence of detainees being rendered through the UK or Overseas Territories since 1997 where there were substantial grounds to believe there was a real arisk of torture.

There were four cases in 1998 where the US requested permission to render one or more detainees through the UK or Overseas Territories. In two of these cases, records show the Government granted the US request, and refused two others.

Since before September 2001 we have worked closely with the US to achieve our shared goal of fighting terrorism. As part of that close co-operation, we have made clear to the US authorities, including in recent months:

that we expect them to seek permission to render detainees via UK territory and airspace (including Overseas Territories);

that we will grant permission only if we are satisfied that the rendition would accord with UK law and our international obligations, and

how we understand our obligations under the UN Convention Against Torture.

We are also clear that the US would not render a detainee through UK territory or airspace (including Overseas Territories) without our permission. As noted above, the US has sought such permission in the past.

The Government are committed to fulfilling their obligations under United Kingdom and international law. I have sought throughout to keep the House informed of developments. And shall do so again if new information comes to light.

239

(16)   Letter from the Foreign Secretary, Rt Hon Jack Straw MP, to the Shadow Foreign Secretary, Rt Hon William Hague MP, 6 February 2006

6 February 2006

DEP 06/356
HOUSE OF COMMONS LIBRARY

Foreign & Commonwealth Office

The Rt Hon William Hague MP
House of Commons
London
SW1A 0AA

London SW1A 2AH

From the Foreign Secretary

Dear William...

Thank you for your letter of 19 January about rendition. I note you planned to make your letter public. I plan to place a copy of this reply in the library of the House.

You will have seen my Written Ministerial Statement of 20 January (copy attached), which summarised what we have ascertained about US requests to render detainees through UK territory or airspace since May 1997. My written Answer to Sir Menzies Campbell on 12 December 2005 (copy attached) is also relevant to your questions.

You ask about approaches by the US authorities since September 2001 to discuss the use of UK territory or airspace for the purpose of rendition flights. For the sake of completeness, I should point out that in 2004 US intelligence officials made a preliminary enquiry of their UK counterparts in respect of a wish they had to transfer a detainee via one of the Overseas Territories. But the US authorities decided subsequently not to pursue this idea, and made no formal request for such a transfer. We reported this to the Intelligence and Security Committee shortly afterwards, in June 2004.

As I said in the Written Ministerial statement, since before September 2001 we have worked closely with the US to achieve our shared goal of fighting terrorism. As part of that close co-operation, we have made clear to the US authorities, including in recent months:

i). that we expect them to seek permission to render detainees via UK territory and airspace (including Overseas Territories);

ii) that we will grant permission only if we are satisfied that the rendition would accord with UK law and our international obligations, and

iii) how we understand our obligations under the UN Convention Against Torture.

We are clear that the US would not render a detainee through UK territory or airspace (including Overseas Territories) without our permission. As for Her Majesty's Government, we would not facilitate the transfer of an individual from or through the UK to another State where there were substantial grounds to believe that the person would face a real risk of torture.

In her statement on 5 September, Condoleezza Rice not only said "*the United States ... will not transport anyone to a country when we believe he will be tortured*", but also said "*where appropriate, the United States seeks assurances that transferred persons will not be tortured*"

As Kim Howells made clear in a written Answer on 20 December to Andrew Tyrie (Official Column 2840W), we are unaware of any cases of individuals detained by the UK Armed Forces and subsequently transferred by the USA to any country. We gave details of detentions in Afghanistan to the Intelligence and Security Committee, which published them in March last year, and Defence Ministers have given several detailed answers about detentions in Iraq, most recently in the last two weeks.

In line with Government practice on disclosure of requests for legal advice generally, I neither confirm nor deny whether or when legal advice was sought or given on this issue, as to do so would not be in the public interest.

Yours ever,

JACK STRAW

(17)   Statement by the Foreign Secretary, Rt Hon David Miliband MP, 21 February 2008

Terrorist Suspects (Renditions)

1.6 pm

The Secretary of State for Foreign and Commonwealth Affairs (David Miliband): With your permission, Mr Deputy Speaker, I would like to make a statement on US rendition operations. On 12 December 2005, in response to a parliamentary question from the right hon. and learned Member for North-East Fife (Sir Menzies Campbell), my right hon. Friend the Member for Blackburn (Mr. Straw), then Foreign Secretary, updated the House on the subject of terrorist suspects and rendition, stating:

> "Careful research by officials has been unable to identify
> any occasion since 11 September 2001, or earlier in the Bush
> administration, when we received a request for permission by the
> United States...for a rendition through UK territory or airspace,
> nor are we otherwise aware of such a case."—[*Official Report*, 12
> December 2005; Vol. 440, c. 1652W.]

That was supplemented by two further statements in January 2006 and a letter of 6 February 2006 to the right hon. Member for Richmond, Yorks (Mr. Hague).

In March 2007, the then Prime Minister, Tony Blair, gave an assurance to the Intelligence and Security Committee that he was satisfied that the US had at no time since 9/11 rendered an individual through the UK or through our overseas territories. In its report on rendition of 28 June 2007, the ISC said:

> "We are satisfied that there is no evidence that US rendition flights
> have used UK airspace (except the two cases in 1998 referred to
> earlier in this Report) and that there is no evidence of them having
> landed at UK military airfields."

The Government welcomed those conclusions in their response to the report in July 2007. Parliamentary answers, interviews and letters followed that evidence. I am very sorry indeed to have to report to the House the need to correct those and other statements on the subject, on the basis of new information passed to officials on 15 February 2008 by the US Government.

Contrary to earlier explicit assurances that Diego Garcia had not been used for rendition flights, recent US investigations have now revealed two occasions, both in 2002, when that had in fact occurred. An error in the earlier US records search meant that those cases did not come to light. In both cases, a US plane with a single detainee on board refuelled at the US facility in Diego Garcia. The detainees did not leave the plane, and the US Government have assured us that no US detainees have ever been held on Diego Garcia. US investigations show no record of any other rendition through Diego Garcia or any other overseas territory, or through the UK itself, since then.

Yesterday, US and UK legal teams discussed the issue, and I spoke with Secretary Rice. We both agree that the mistakes made in those two cases are not acceptable, and she shares my deep regret that the information has only just come to light. She emphasised to me that the US Government came to us with the information quickly after they discovered it.

The House and the Government will share deep disappointment at the news, and about its late emergence. That disappointment is shared by our US allies. They recognise the absolute imperative for the British Government to provide accurate information to Parliament. I reaffirm the Government's commitment to that imperative today. We fully accept that the United States gave its earlier assurances in good faith. We accepted those assurances, and indeed referred to them publicly, also in good faith.

For the avoidance of doubt, I have asked my officials to compile a list of all the flights where we have been alerted to concerns regarding rendition through the UK or our overseas territories. Once it is ready we will be sending the list to the US and seeking their specific assurance that none of those flights was used for rendition purposes.

Our counter-terrorism relationship with the United States is vital to UK security. I am absolutely clear that there must and will continue to be the strongest possible intelligence and counter-terrorism relationship with the US, consistent with UK law and our international obligations. As part of our close co-operation, there has long been a regular exchange with the US authorities, in which we have set out, first, that we expect them to seek permission to render detainees via UK territory and airspace, including overseas territories; secondly, that we will grant that permission only if we are satisfied that rendition would accord with UK law and our international obligations; and thirdly, how we understand our obligations under the UN convention against torture. Secretary Rice has underlined to me the firm US understanding that there will be no rendition through the UK, UK airspace or overseas territories without express British Government permission.

The House will want to know what has become of the two individuals in question. There is a limit to what I can say, but I can tell the House the following. The US Government have told us that neither of the men was a British national or a British resident. One is currently in Guantanamo Bay. The other has been released. The House will know that the British Government's long-standing position is that the detention facility at Guantanamo should be closed.

My officials and their US counterparts continue to work through all the details and implications of this information. We will keep procedures under review to ensure that they meet the standards that we have set, and I will, of course, keep the House updated.

(18)   Written Statement by the Foreign Secretary, Rt Hon David Miliband MP, 3 July 2008, and list of flights

Terrorist Suspects (Rendition)

The Secretary of State for Foreign and Commonwealth Affairs (David Miliband): On 21 February I made a statement to the House regarding new information we had been passed by the United States Government regarding rendition. Contrary to earlier assurances that Diego Garcia had not been used for rendition flights, United States investigations had revealed two occasions, both in 2002, when this had in fact occurred. Since February, I have corresponded with Secretary Rice on this issue and our officials have continued to work through the details and implications of the new information.

I promised the House that, as part of this process, my officials would compile a list of flights where we had been alerted to concern about rendition through the UK or our overseas territories. The list which they have compiled, containing 391 flights, reflects concerns put to us by hon. Members, members of the public, multilateral organisations and non-governmental organisations. Inclusion on this list does not represent an official endorsement of any allegations about a particular flight. On the contrary, US Government flights—as with other Government flights—occur regularly for a variety of purposes. Our intention was to collate in one place those concerns that had been put to us directly. The list was passed to the US on 15 May. I undertook in February to publish the list and have today placed a copy in the Library of the House and published it on the FCO website at www.fco.co.uk

The US Government received the list of flights from the UK Government. The US Government confirmed that, with the exception of two cases related to Diego Garcia in 2002, there have been no other instances in which US intelligence flights landed in the United Kingdom, our overseas territories, or the Crown dependencies, with a detainee on board since 11 September 2001.

Our US allies are agreed on the need to seek our permission for any future renditions through UK territory. Secretary Rice has underlined to me the firm US understanding that there will be no rendition through the UK, our overseas territories and Crown dependencies or airspace without first receiving our express permission. We have made clear that we would only grant such permission if we were satisfied that the rendition would accord with UK law and our international obligations. The circumstances of any such request would be carefully examined on a case-by-case basis.

Our intelligence and counter-terrorism relationship with the US is vital to the national security of the United Kingdom. There must and will continue to be the strongest possible intelligence and counter-terrorism relationship between our two countries, consistent with UK law and our international obligations.

A list of flights where the UK Government has been alerted to concerns regarding rendition through the UK, its Overseas Territories or the Crown Dependencies

No	SOURCE OF ALLEGATION	Serial No	Departure Date	Departure Time	Departure Location	Country	Arrival Location	Country	Arrival Time	Departure Date	Departure Time	Arrival Location	Country	Arrival Time	Departure Date	Departure Time	Arrival Location	Country	Arrival Time
1	REPRIEVE REPORT "ENFORCED DISAPPEARANCE, ILLEGAL INTERSTATE TRANSFER, AND OTHER HUMAN RIGHTS ABUSES INVOLVING THE UK OVERSEAS TERRITORIES"	N8DBMG	17/03/2001	15:04	ORLANDO INTL	USA	PROVIDENCIALES	TURKS & CAICOS	16:34	17/03/2001	17:46	EXECUTIVE AIRPORT	USA	19:14					
2	ANDREW TYRIE MP, APPG ON EXTRAORDINARY RENDITION	N368CE	06/06/2001		BOSTON/LOGAN INTL, MASSACHUSETTS	USA	STANSTED	UK											
3	ANDREW TYRIE MP, APPG ON EXTRAORDINARY RENDITION	N368CE	07/06/2001		STANSTED	UK	ATHENS/ELEFTHERIOS VENIZELOS	GREECE											
4	ANDREW TYRIE MP, APPG ON EXTRAORDINARY RENDITION	N85VM	24/06/2001		TETERBORO NJ	USA	BELFAST ALDERGROVE	UK											
5	ANDREW TYRIE MP, APPG ON EXTRAORDINARY RENDITION	N85VM	29/06/2001		BELFAST ALDERGROVE	UK	TETERBORO, NJ	USA											
6	SNP REPORT "ALLEGED CIA AIRCRAFT FLYING INTO SCOTLAND"	N1HC	03/07/2001		UNSPECIFIED		PRESTWICK	UK											
7	ANDREW TYRIE MP, APPG ON EXTRAORDINARY RENDITION	N368CE	05/08/2001		LUTON	UK	BANGOR INTL, MAINE	USA											
8	ANDREW TYRIE MP, APPG ON EXTRAORDINARY RENDITION	N368CE	05/08/2001		NEWARK, NEW YORK	USA	LUTON	UK											
9	SNP REPORT "ALLEGED CIA AIRCRAFT FLYING INTO SCOTLAND"	N33NJ	26/06/2001		UNSPECIFIED		PRESTWICK	UK											
10	ANDREW TYRIE MP, APPG ON EXTRAORDINARY RENDITION	N85VM	04/09/2001		CONNAUGHT	IRELAND	LONDON/DERRY/EGLINGTON	UK											
11	ANDREW TYRIE MP, APPG ON EXTRAORDINARY RENDITION	N85VM	05/09/2001		LONDON/DERRY/EGLINGTON	UK	BEDFORD/LAURENCE G HANSCOM MASSACHUSETTS	USA											
12	ANDREW TYRIE MP, APPG ON EXTRAORDINARY RENDITION	N85VM	16/09/2001		LUTON	UK	GENEVE COINTRIN	SWITZERLAND											
13	ANDREW TYRIE MP, APPG ON EXTRAORDINARY RENDITION	N368CE	04/10/2001		BANGOR INTL, MAINE	USA	INVERNESS	UK											
14	ANDREW TYRIE MP, APPG ON EXTRAORDINARY RENDITION	N368CE	09/10/2001		INVERNESS	UK	BANGOR INTL, MAINE	USA											
15	ANDREW TYRIE MP, APPG ON EXTRAORDINARY RENDITION	N85VM	14/10/2001		TETERBORO NJ	USA	RAF LEUCHARS	UK											
16	REPRIEVE REPORT "SCOTTISH INVOLVEMENT IN EXTRAORDINARY RENDITION"	N37GP	15/10/2001	23:53	WASHINGTON	USA	PRESTWICK	UK	5:48	16/10/2001	6:40	FRANKFURT	GERMANY	8:09					
17	ANDREW TYRIE MP, APPG ON EXTRAORDINARY RENDITION	N85VM	15/10/2001		EDINBURGH	UK	RAF LEUCHARS	UK											
18	ANDREW TYRIE MP, APPG ON EXTRAORDINARY RENDITION	N85VM	21/10/2001		RAF LEUCHARS	UK	FARMINGDALE	USA											
19	REPRIEVE REPORT "SCOTTISH INVOLVEMENT IN EXTRAORDINARY RENDITION"	N37GP	24/10/2001	4:52	FRANKFURT	GERMANY	PRESTWICK	UK	6:18	24/10/2001	7:30	WASHINGTON	USA	13:41					
20	INTELLIGENCE & SECURITY COMMITTEE REPORT INTO RENDITION	N37GP	24/10/2001		JORDAN	JORDAN	PRESTWICK	UK											
21	REPRIEVE REPORT "SCOTTISH INVOLVEMENT IN EXTRAORDINARY RENDITION"	N37GP	28/10/2001	22:07	WASHINGTON	USA	PRESTWICK	UK	3:51	29/10/2001	10:27	KARSHI	UZBEKISTAN	17:43					
22	REPRIEVE REPORT "SCOTTISH INVOLVEMENT IN EXTRAORDINARY RENDITION"	N37GP	05/11/2001	13:50	FRANKFURT	GERMANY	PRESTWICK	UK	15:19	05/11/2001	16:36	WASHINGTON	USA	23:09					
23	REPRIEVE REPORT "SCOTTISH INVOLVEMENT IN EXTRAORDINARY RENDITION"	N37GP	07/11/2001	22:25	WASHINGTON	USA	PRESTWICK	UK	4:22	08/11/2001	5:44	CAIRO	EGYPT	10:32					
24	REPRIEVE REPORT "SCOTTISH INVOLVEMENT IN EXTRAORDINARY RENDITION"	N37GP	10/11/2001	8:57	FRANKFURT	GERMANY	PRESTWICK	UK	10:24	10/11/2001	11:28	WASHINGTON	USA	17:35					
25	REPRIEVE REPORT "SCOTTISH INVOLVEMENT IN EXTRAORDINARY RENDITION"	N37GP	14/11/2001	1:16	WASHINGTON	USA	PRESTWICK	UK	7:27	14/11/2001	20:18	TASHKENT	UZBEKISTAN	2:34					
26	REPRIEVE REPORT "SCOTTISH INVOLVEMENT IN EXTRAORDINARY RENDITION"	N37GP	15/11/2001	7:05	DUSHANBE	TAJIKISTAN	PRESTWICK	UK	14:24	17/11/2001	11:46	WASHINGTON	USA	17:57					
27	CONTRIBUTION OF THE RAPPORTEUR "RESEARCH ON THE PLANES USED BY THE CIA (EUROPEAN PARLIAMENT)"	N37GP	08/12/2001		WASHINGTON	USA	PRESTWICK	UK											
28	CONTRIBUTION OF THE RAPPORTEUR "RESEARCH ON THE PLANES USED BY THE CIA (EUROPEAN PARLIAMENT)"	N37GP	08/12/2001		PRESTWICK	UK	CAIRO	EGYPT											
29	CONTRIBUTION OF THE RAPPORTEUR "RESEARCH ON THE PLANES USED BY THE CIA (EUROPEAN PARLIAMENT)"	N37GP	09/12/2001		CAIRO	EGYPT	PRESTWICK	UK											
30	CONTRIBUTION OF THE RAPPORTEUR "RESEARCH ON THE PLANES USED BY THE CIA (EUROPEAN PARLIAMENT)"	N37GP	10/12/2001		PRESTWICK	UK	WASHINGTON	USA											
31	REPRIEVE REPORT "SCOTTISH INVOLVEMENT IN EXTRAORDINARY RENDITION"	N37GP	13/12/2001	1:15	WASHINGTON	USA	PRESTWICK	UK	7:40	13/12/2001	8:58	TASHKENT	UZBEKISTAN	15:24	14/12/2001	8:03	PRESTWICK	UK	14:52
32	REPRIEVE REPORT "SCOTTISH INVOLVEMENT IN EXTRAORDINARY RENDITION"	N37GP	14/12/2001	15:40	PRESTWICK	UK	WASHINGTON	USA	22:39										

A list of flights where the UK Government has been alerted to concerns regarding rendition through the UK, its Overseas Territories or the Crown Dependencies

#	SOURCE OF ALLEGATION	Serial No	Departure Date	Departure Time	Departure Location	Country	Arrival Location	Country	Arrival Time	Departure Date	Departure Time	Arrival Location	Country	Arrival Time	Departure Date	Departure Time	Arrival Location	Country	Arrival Time
33	REPRIEVE REPORT 'SCOTTISH INVOLVEMENT IN EXTRAORDINARY RENDITION'	N379P	20/12/2001	6:56	CAIRO	EGYPT	PRESTWICK	UK	12:03	20/12/2001	13:07	WASHINGTON	USA	19:18					
34	SNP REPORT 'ALLEGED CIA AIRCRAFT FLYING INTO SCOTLAND'	N315CR	22/12/2001		UNSPECIFIED		PRESTWICK	UK											
35	ANDREW TYRIE MP, APPG ON EXTRAORDINARY RENDITION	N85VM	26/12/2001		BEDFORD/LAURENCE G HANSCOM FIELD MASSACHUSETTS	USA	LUTON	UK											
36	ANDREW TYRIE MP, APPG ON EXTRAORDINARY RENDITION	N85VM	28/12/2001		LUTON	UK	BEDFORD/LAURENCE G HANSCOM FIELD MASSACHUSETTS	USA											
37	ANDREW TYRIE MP, APPG ON EXTRAORDINARY RENDITION	N85VM	12/01/2002		LARNACA	CYPRUS	LONDON/STANSTED	UK											
38	ANDREW TYRIE MP, APPG ON EXTRAORDINARY RENDITION	N85VM	12/01/2002		LONDON/STANSTED	UK	SCHENECTADY NY	USA											
39	REPRIEVE REPORT 'SCOTTISH INVOLVEMENT IN EXTRAORDINARY RENDITION'	N379P	15/01/2002	8:37	CAIRO	EGYPT	PRESTWICK	UK	13:31	15/01/2002	14:40	WASHINGTON	USA	21:48					
40	SNP REPORT 'ALLEGED CIA AIRCRAFT FLYING INTO SCOTLAND'	N212AZ	28/01/2002		UNSPECIFIED		PRESTWICK	UK											
41	REPRIEVE REPORT 'SCOTTISH INVOLVEMENT IN EXTRAORDINARY RENDITION'	N379P	06/02/2002	13:34	WASHINGTON	USA	PRESTWICK	UK	19:19	06/02/2002	21:19	DUBAI	DUBAI	4:53					
42	REPRIEVE REPORT 'SCOTTISH INVOLVEMENT IN EXTRAORDINARY RENDITION'	N379P	11/02/2002	23:40	AMMAN	JORDAN	PRESTWICK	UK	6:00	13/02/2002	11:43		BAHRAIN	18:58					
43	HIGHLIGHTED BY THE REPORT (WORKING DOC. No.8 DT08415335EN doc) PRODUCED BY IT DP AT THE EUROPEAN PARLIAMENT	N379P	12/02/2002		AMMAN	JORDAN	PRESTWICK	UK											
44	CONTRIBUTION OF THE RAPPORTEUR: RESEARCH ON THE PLANES USED BY THE CIA (EUROPEAN PARLIAMENT)	N8161Q	22/02/2002		FRANKFURT	GERMANY	GLASGOW	UK											
45	CONTRIBUTION OF THE RAPPORTEUR: RESEARCH ON THE PLANES USED BY THE CIA (EUROPEAN PARLIAMENT)	N8161Q	23/02/2002		GLASGOW	UK	REYKJAVIK	ICELAND											
46	CONTRIBUTION OF THE RAPPORTEUR: RESEARCH ON THE PLANES USED BY THE CIA (EUROPEAN PARLIAMENT)	N1HC	25/02/2002		MINNEAPOLIS	USA	BIGGIN HILL	UK											
47	CONTRIBUTION OF THE RAPPORTEUR: RESEARCH ON THE PLANES USED BY THE CIA (EUROPEAN PARLIAMENT)	N1HC	27/02/2002		BIGGIN HILL	UK	WARSAW	POLAND											
48	CONTRIBUTION OF THE RAPPORTEUR: RESEARCH ON THE PLANES USED BY THE CIA (EUROPEAN PARLIAMENT)	N1HC	01/03/2002		MILAN	ITALY	BIGGIN HILL	UK											
49	CONTRIBUTION OF THE RAPPORTEUR: RESEARCH ON THE PLANES USED BY THE CIA (EUROPEAN PARLIAMENT)	N1HC	01/03/2002		BIGGIN HILL	UK	MILWAUKEE	USA											
50	CONTRIBUTION OF THE RAPPORTEUR: RESEARCH ON THE PLANES USED BY THE CIA (EUROPEAN PARLIAMENT)	N379P	10/03/2002		PRESTWICK	UK	WASHINGTON	USA											
51	CONTRIBUTION OF THE RAPPORTEUR: RESEARCH ON THE PLANES USED BY THE CIA (EUROPEAN PARLIAMENT)	N379P	10/03/2002		WASHINGTON	USA	PRESTWICK	UK											
52	CONTRIBUTION OF THE RAPPORTEUR: RESEARCH ON THE PLANES USED BY THE CIA (EUROPEAN PARLIAMENT)	N379P	19/03/2002		PRESTWICK	UK	WASHINGTON	USA											
53	CONTRIBUTION OF THE RAPPORTEUR: RESEARCH ON THE PLANES USED BY THE CIA (EUROPEAN PARLIAMENT)	N379P	19/03/2002		WASHINGTON	USA	PRESTWICK	UK											
54	CONTRIBUTION OF THE RAPPORTEUR: RESEARCH ON THE PLANES USED BY THE CIA (EUROPEAN PARLIAMENT)	N168D	23/03/2002		SEVILLE	SPAIN	REYKJAVIK	ICELAND											
55	CONTRIBUTION OF THE RAPPORTEUR: RESEARCH ON THE PLANES USED BY THE CIA (EUROPEAN PARLIAMENT)	N168D	24/03/2002		PRESTWICK	UK	REYKJAVIK	ICELAND											
56	CONTRIBUTION OF THE RAPPORTEUR: RESEARCH ON THE PLANES USED BY THE CIA (EUROPEAN PARLIAMENT)	N379P	26/03/2002		WASHINGTON	USA	PRESTWICK	UK											
57	CONTRIBUTION OF THE RAPPORTEUR: RESEARCH ON THE PLANES USED BY THE CIA (EUROPEAN PARLIAMENT)	N379P	27/03/2002		PRESTWICK	UK	DUBAI	DUBAI											
58	CONTRIBUTION OF THE RAPPORTEUR: RESEARCH ON THE PLANES USED BY THE CIA (EUROPEAN PARLIAMENT)	N8E13G	24/04/2002		REYKJAVIK	ICELAND	FAIRFORD	UK											
59	CONTRIBUTION OF THE RAPPORTEUR: RESEARCH ON THE PLANES USED BY THE CIA (EUROPEAN PARLIAMENT)	N8E13G	28/04/2002		FAIRFORD	UK	PONTA DELGADA	PORTUGAL											
60	SNP REPORT 'ALLEGED CIA AIRCRAFT FLYING INTO SCOTLAND'	N212AZ	13/05/2002		UNSPECIFIED		PRESTWICK	UK											
61	CONTRIBUTION OF THE RAPPORTEUR: RESEARCH ON THE PLANES USED BY THE CIA (EUROPEAN PARLIAMENT)	N8E13G	17/05/2002		BERGEN	NORWAY	FAIRFORD	UK											
62	CONTRIBUTION OF THE RAPPORTEUR: RESEARCH ON THE PLANES USED BY THE CIA (EUROPEAN PARLIAMENT)	N8E13G	17/05/2002		FAIRFORD	UK	STEPHENVILLE	CANADA											
63	CONTRIBUTION OF THE RAPPORTEUR: RESEARCH ON THE PLANES USED BY THE CIA (EUROPEAN PARLIAMENT)	N2215G	20/05/2002		BUDAPEST	HUNGARY	GLASGOW	UK											
64	CONTRIBUTION OF THE RAPPORTEUR: RESEARCH ON THE PLANES USED BY THE CIA (EUROPEAN PARLIAMENT)	N2215G	20/05/2002		GLASGOW	UK	KEFLAVIK	ICELAND											

	SOURCE OF ALLEGATION	Serial No	Departure Date	Departure Location	Departure Time	Country	Arrival Location	Country	Arrival Time	Departure Date	Departure Time	Arrival Location	Country	Arrival Time	Departure Date	Departure Time	Arrival Location	Country	Arrival Time
65	CONTRIBUTION OF THE RAPPORTEUR: RESEARCH ON THE PLANES USED BY THE CIA (EUROPEAN PARLIAMENT)	N1IHC	05/06/2002	MILAN		ITALY	BIGGIN HILL	UK											
66	REPRIEVE REPORT 'SCOTTISH INVOLVEMENT IN EXTRAORDINARY RENDITION'	N379P	16/06/2002	WASHINGTON	17:14	USA	PRESTWICK	UK	23:01	17/06/2002	17:11	KARACHI	PAKISTAN	2:17					
67	REPRIEVE REPORT 'SCOTTISH INVOLVEMENT IN EXTRAORDINARY RENDITION'	N379P	19/06/2002	TASHKENT	5:00	UZBEKISTAN	PRESTWICK	UK	11:55	20/06/2002	6:59	WASHINGTON	USA	13:48					
68	SNP REPORT 'ALLEGED CIA AIRCRAFT FLYING INTO SCOTLAND'	N47DJF	28/06/2002	UNSPECIFIED			PRESTWICK	UK											
69	REPRIEVE REPORT 'ENFORCED DISAPPEARANCE, ILLEGAL INTERSTATE TRANSFER, AND OTHER HUMAN RIGHTS ABUSES INVOLVING THE UK OVERSEAS TERRITORIES'	N829MG	07/07/2002	CITY OF FORT LAUDERDALE EXECUTIVE AIRPORT	23:11	USA	PROVIDENCIALES	TURKS & CAICOS	0:33	08/07/2002	01:00	FORT LAUDERDALE-HOLLYWOOD INTL. AIRPORT	USA	02:23					
70	SNP REPORT 'ALLEGED CIA AIRCRAFT FLYING INTO SCOTLAND'	N315CR	07/07/2002	UNSPECIFIED			PRESTWICK	UK											
71	CONTRIBUTION OF THE RAPPORTEUR: RESEARCH ON THE PLANES USED BY THE CIA (EUROPEAN PARLIAMENT)	N829MG	17/07/2002	ANTWERP		BELGIUM	EAST MIDLANDS	UK											
72	CONTRIBUTION OF THE RAPPORTEUR: RESEARCH ON THE PLANES USED BY THE CIA (EUROPEAN PARLIAMENT)	N829MG	19/07/2002	EAST MIDLANDS		UK	NUREMBERG	GERMANY											
73	SNP REPORT 'ALLEGED CIA AIRCRAFT FLYING INTO SCOTLAND'	N212AZ	08/08/2002	UNSPECIFIED			PRESTWICK	UK											
74	ANDREW TYRIE MP, APPG ON EXTRAORDINARY RENDITION	N368CE	03/09/2002	GOOSE BAY		CANADA	BIRMINGHAM	UK											
75	ANDREW TYRIE MP, APPG ON EXTRAORDINARY RENDITION	N368CE	03/09/2002	NICE/COTE d'AZUR		FRANCE	FARNBOROUGH	UK											
76	CONTRIBUTION OF THE RAPPORTEUR: RESEARCH ON THE PLANES USED BY THE CIA (EUROPEAN PARLIAMENT)	N368CE	03/09/2002	FARNBOROUGH		UK	NICE	FRANCE											
77	ANDREW TYRIE MP, APPG ON EXTRAORDINARY RENDITION	N368CE	03/09/2002	FARNBOROUGH		UK	NICE/COTE d'AZUR	FRANCE											
78	ANDREW TYRIE MP, APPG ON EXTRAORDINARY RENDITION	N368CE	04/09/2002	NICE/COTE d'AZUR		FRANCE	FARNBOROUGH	UK											
79	CONTRIBUTION OF THE RAPPORTEUR: RESEARCH ON THE PLANES USED BY THE CIA (EUROPEAN PARLIAMENT)	N368CE	04/09/2002	NICE		FRANCE	FARNBOROUGH	UK											
80	CONTRIBUTION OF THE RAPPORTEUR: RESEARCH ON THE PLANES USED BY THE CIA (EUROPEAN PARLIAMENT)	N368CE	04/09/2002	FARNBOROUGH		UK	NICE	FRANCE											
81	ANDREW TYRIE MP, APPG ON EXTRAORDINARY RENDITION	N368CE	04/09/2002	FARNBOROUGH		UK	NICE/COTE d'AZUR	FRANCE											
82	REPRIEVE REPORT 'ENFORCED DISAPPEARANCE, ILLEGAL INTERSTATE TRANSFER, AND OTHER HUMAN RIGHTS ABUSES INVOLVING THE UK OVERSEAS TERRITORIES'	N379P	13/09/2002	ATHENS	8:12	GREECE	DIEGO GARCIA	DIEGO GARCIA	17:14										
83	CONTRIBUTION OF THE RAPPORTEUR: RESEARCH ON THE PLANES USED BY THE CIA (EUROPEAN PARLIAMENT)	N1IHC	25/09/2002	BRAUNSCHWEIG		GERMANY	BLACKPOOL	UK											
84	CONTRIBUTION OF THE RAPPORTEUR: RESEARCH ON THE PLANES USED BY THE CIA (EUROPEAN PARLIAMENT)	N1IHC	26/09/2002	BLACKPOOL		UK	LONDON (UNSPECIFIED)	UK											
85	ANDREW TYRIE MP, APPG ON EXTRAORDINARY RENDITION	N85VM	26/09/2002	FARMINGDALE		USA	RAF LEUCHARS	UK											
86	ANDREW TYRIE MP, APPG ON EXTRAORDINARY RENDITION	N85VM	28/09/2002	RAF LEUCHARS		UK	SCHENECTADY NY	USA											
87	CONTRIBUTION OF THE RAPPORTEUR: RESEARCH ON THE PLANES USED BY THE CIA (EUROPEAN PARLIAMENT)	N368CE	30/09/2002	GOOSE BAY		CANADA	BIRMINGHAM	UK											
88	ANDREW TYRIE MP, APPG ON EXTRAORDINARY RENDITION	N368CE	30/09/2002	BIRMINGHAM		UK	GOOSE BAY	CANADA											
89	ANDREW TYRIE MP, APPG ON EXTRAORDINARY RENDITION	N85VM	05/10/2002	SCHENECTADY NY		USA	RAF LEUCHARS	UK											
90	ANDREW TYRIE MP, APPG ON EXTRAORDINARY RENDITION	N85VM	05/10/2002	RAF LEUCHARS		UK	FARMINGDALE	USA											
91	JOURNALIST, ITN	N379P	18/10/2002	ISLAMABAD		PAKISTAN	RAF NORTHOLT	UK	15:50	20/10/2002	8:43	WASHINGTON DULLES	USA						
92	CONTRIBUTION OF THE RAPPORTEUR: RESEARCH ON THE PLANES USED BY THE CIA (EUROPEAN PARLIAMENT)	N829MG	27/10/2002	STEPHENVILLE		CANADA	BIGGIN HILL	UK											
93	CONTRIBUTION OF THE RAPPORTEUR: RESEARCH ON THE PLANES USED BY THE CIA (EUROPEAN PARLIAMENT)	N829MG	30/10/2002	BIGGIN HILL		UK	BARCELONA	SPAIN											
94	CONTRIBUTION OF THE RAPPORTEUR: RESEARCH ON THE PLANES USED BY THE CIA (EUROPEAN PARLIAMENT)	N1IHC	08/11/2002	PALM BEACH		USA	LONDON (UNSPECIFIED)	UK											
95	SNP REPORT 'ALLEGED CIA AIRCRAFT FLYING INTO SCOTLAND'	N212AZ	10/11/2002	UNSPECIFIED			PRESTWICK	UK											
96	CONTRIBUTION OF THE RAPPORTEUR: RESEARCH ON THE PLANES USED BY THE CIA (EUROPEAN PARLIAMENT)	N1IHC	12/11/2002	PARIS		FRANCE	LONDON (UNSPECIFIED)	UK											

A list of flights where the UK Government has been alerted to concerns regarding rendition through the UK, its Overseas Territories or the Crown Dependencies

	SOURCE OF ALLEGATION	Serial No	Departure Date	Departure Time	Departure Location	Country	Arrival Location	Country	Arrival Time	Departure Date	Departure Time	Arrival Location	Country	Arrival Time	Departure Date	Departure Time	Arrival Location	Country	Arrival Time
97	ANDREW TYRIE MP, APPG ON EXTRAORDINARY RENDITION	N85VM	12/11/2002		DUBAI INTL	DUBAI	LUTON	UK											
98	ANDREW TYRIE MP, APPG ON EXTRAORDINARY RENDITION	N86VM	12/11/2002		LUTON	UK	WASHINGTON	USA											
99	CONTRIBUTION OF THE RAPPORTEUR: RESEARCH ON THE PLANES USED BY THE CIA (EUROPEAN PARLIAMENT)	N1HC	16/11/2002		LONDON (UNSPECIFIED)	UK	PALM BEACH	USA											
100	REPRIEVE REPORT 'ENFORCED DISAPPEARANCE, ILLEGAL INTERSTATE TRANSFER, AND OTHER HUMAN RIGHTS ABUSES INVOLVING THE UK OVERSEAS TERRITORIES'	N85VM	20/11/2002	19:08	GUANTANAMO	US NAVAL BASE, CUBA	PROVIDENCIALES	TURKS & CAICOS	19:39	20/11/2002	23:26	WASHINGTON DULLES	USA	2:14					
101	REPRIEVE REPORT 'ENFORCED DISAPPEARANCE, ILLEGAL INTERSTATE TRANSFER, AND OTHER HUMAN RIGHTS ABUSES INVOLVING THE UK OVERSEAS TERRITORIES'	N85VM	25/11/2002	11:04	KABUL	AFGHANISTAN	EDINBURGH	UK	19:44	25/11/2002	20:40	WASHINGTON DULLES	USA	4:00					
102	ANDREW TYRIE MP, APPG ON EXTRAORDINARY RENDITION	N85VM	25/11/2002		KABUL	AFGHANISTAN	EDINBURGH	UK											
103	ANDREW TYRIE MP, APPG ON EXTRAORDINARY RENDITION	N85VM	25/11/2002		EDINBURGH	UK	WASHINGTON	USA											
104	CONTRIBUTION OF THE RAPPORTEUR: RESEARCH ON THE PLANES USED BY THE CIA (EUROPEAN PARLIAMENT)	N313P	04/12/2002		FRANKFURT	GERMANY	RAF MILDENHALL	UK											
105	CONTRIBUTION OF THE RAPPORTEUR: RESEARCH ON THE PLANES USED BY THE CIA (EUROPEAN PARLIAMENT)	N313P	04/12/2002		RAF MILDENHALL	UK	CAMP SPRING	USA											
106	SNP REPORT 'ALLEGED CIA AIRCRAFT FLYING INTO SCOTLAND'	N822US	08/12/2002		UNSPECIFIED	UK	GLASGOW	UK											
107	CONTRIBUTION OF THE RAPPORTEUR: RESEARCH ON THE PLANES USED BY THE CIA (EUROPEAN PARLIAMENT)	N8213G	13/12/2002		PORTSMOUTH	UK	PONTA DELGADA	PORTUGAL											
108	REPRIEVE REPORT 'SCOTTISH INVOLVEMENT IN EXTRAORDINARY RENDITION'	N1016M	15/12/2002	11:41	REYKJAVIK	ICELAND	GLASGOW	UK	16:09	16/12/2002	11:59	FRANKFURT	GERMANY	18:10					
109	SNP REPORT 'ALLEGED CIA AIRCRAFT FLYING INTO SCOTLAND'	N213AZ	21/12/2002		UNSPECIFIED	UK	PRESTWICK	UK											
110	JOURNALIST, ITN	N379P	16/01/2003		AMMAN/QUEEN ALIA	JORDAN	RAF NORTHOLT	UK	12:50	18/01/2003	10:00	SHANNON	IRELAND						
111	SNP REPORT 'ALLEGED CIA AIRCRAFT FLYING INTO SCOTLAND'	N213AZ	17/01/2003		UNSPECIFIED	UK	PRESTWICK	UK											
112	CONTRIBUTION OF THE RAPPORTEUR: RESEARCH ON THE PLANES USED BY THE CIA (EUROPEAN PARLIAMENT)	N4009L	18/01/2003		PRESTWICK	UK	FRANKFURT	GERMANY											
113	CONTRIBUTION OF THE RAPPORTEUR: RESEARCH ON THE PLANES USED BY THE CIA (EUROPEAN PARLIAMENT)	N4009L	18/01/2003		REYKJAVIK	ICELAND	PRESTWICK	UK											
114	SNP REPORT 'ALLEGED CIA AIRCRAFT FLYING INTO SCOTLAND'	N470JF	23/01/2003		UNSPECIFIED	UK	PRESTWICK	UK											
115	REPRIEVE REPORT 'ENFORCED DISAPPEARANCE, ILLEGAL INTERSTATE TRANSFER, AND OTHER HUMAN RIGHTS ABUSES INVOLVING THE UK OVERSEAS TERRITORIES'	N85VM	31/01/2003	17:18	GUANTANAMO	US NAVAL BASE, CUBA	PROVIDENCIALES	TURKS & CAICOS	18:37	02/02/2003	12:49								
116	CONTRIBUTION OF THE RAPPORTEUR: RESEARCH ON THE PLANES USED BY THE CIA (EUROPEAN PARLIAMENT)	N168BF	04/02/2003		HAMBURG	GERMANY	LONDON (UNSPECIFIED)	UK											
117	CONTRIBUTION OF THE RAPPORTEUR: RESEARCH ON THE PLANES USED BY THE CIA (EUROPEAN PARLIAMENT)	N168BF	07/02/2003		LONDON (UNSPECIFIED)	UK	EDINBURGH	UK											
118	CONTRIBUTION OF THE RAPPORTEUR: RESEARCH ON THE PLANES USED BY THE CIA (EUROPEAN PARLIAMENT)	N168BF	07/02/2003		EDINBURGH	UK	LONDON (UNSPECIFIED)	UK											
119	CONTRIBUTION OF THE RAPPORTEUR: RESEARCH ON THE PLANES USED BY THE CIA (EUROPEAN PARLIAMENT)	N168BF	08/02/2003		LONDON (UNSPECIFIED)	UK	LARNACA	CYPRUS											
120	HIGHLIGHTED BY THE REPORT (WORKING DOC. No.8 DT/634558.doc) PRODUCED BY TDIP AT THE EUROPEAN PARLIAMENT	N379P	11/02/2003		TASHKENT	UZBEKISTAN	GLASGOW	UK											
121	CONTRIBUTION OF THE RAPPORTEUR: RESEARCH ON THE PLANES USED BY THE CIA (EUROPEAN PARLIAMENT)	N379P	12/02/2003		GLASGOW	UK	WASHINGTON	USA											
122	CONTRIBUTION OF THE RAPPORTEUR: RESEARCH ON THE PLANES USED BY THE CIA (EUROPEAN PARLIAMENT)	N379P	24/02/2003		WICK	UK	FRANKFURT	GERMANY											
123	JOURNALIST, ITN	N379P	24/02/2003		WASHINGTON DULLES	USA	RAF NORTHOLT	UK	20:05	26/02/2003	9:00	DOHA	QATAR						
124	CONTRIBUTION OF THE RAPPORTEUR: RESEARCH ON THE PLANES USED BY THE CIA (EUROPEAN PARLIAMENT)	N816IG	24/02/2003		REYKJAVIK	ICELAND	WICK	UK											
125	JOURNALIST, ITN	N379P	28/02/2003		DOHA	QATAR	RAF NORTHOLT	UK											
126	CONTRIBUTION OF THE RAPPORTEUR: RESEARCH ON THE PLANES USED BY THE CIA (EUROPEAN PARLIAMENT)	N379P	01/03/2003		GLASGOW	UK	WASHINGTON	USA	12:49	01/03/2003	9:00	GLASGOW	UK						
127	ANDREW TYRIE MP, APPG ON EXTRAORDINARY RENDITION	N85VM	03/03/2003		DUBAI INTL	DUBAI	GLASGOW	UK											
128	CONTRIBUTION OF THE RAPPORTEUR: RESEARCH ON THE PLANES USED BY THE CIA (EUROPEAN PARLIAMENT)	N168BF	03/03/2003		HAWARDEN	UK	LONDON (UNSPECIFIED)	UK											

A list of flights where the UK Government has been alerted to concerns regarding rendition through the UK, its Overseas Territories or the Crown Dependencies

	SOURCE OF ALLEGATION	Serial Nr	Departure Date	Departure Time	Departure Location	Country	Arrival Location	Country	Arrival Time	Departure Date	Departure Time	Arrival Location	Country	Arrival Time	Departure Location	Departure Time	Arrival Location	Country	Arrival Time
129	ANDREW TYRIE MP, APPG ON EXTRAORDINARY RENDITION	N85VM	03/03/2003		GLASGOW	UK	WASHINGTON	USA											
130	CONTRIBUTION OF THE RAPPORTEUR: RESEARCH ON THE PLANES USED BY THE CIA (EUROPEAN PARLIAMENT)	N168BF	04/03/2003		LONDON (UNSPECIFIED)	UK	HAMBURG	GERMANY											
131	CONTRIBUTION OF THE RAPPORTEUR: RESEARCH ON THE PLANES USED BY THE CIA (EUROPEAN PARLIAMENT)	N168BF	05/03/2003		HAMBURG	GERMANY	LONDON (UNSPECIFIED)	UK											
132	REPRIEVE REPORT 'SCOTTISH INVOLVEMENT IN EXTRAORDINARY RENDITION'	N379P	07/03/2003	20:44	PRAHA RUZYNE	CZECH REPUBLIC	GLASGOW	UK	22:42	08/03/2003	9:56	WASHINGTON	USA	16:16					
133	CONTRIBUTION OF THE RAPPORTEUR: RESEARCH ON THE PLANES USED BY THE CIA (EUROPEAN PARLIAMENT)	N168BF	07/03/2003		LONDON (UNSPECIFIED)	UK	ATHENS	GREECE											
134	CONTRIBUTION OF THE RAPPORTEUR: RESEARCH ON THE PLANES USED BY THE CIA (EUROPEAN PARLIAMENT)	N313P	11/03/2003		WASHINGTON	USA	LUTON	UK											
135	CONTRIBUTION OF THE RAPPORTEUR: RESEARCH ON THE PLANES USED BY THE CIA (EUROPEAN PARLIAMENT)	N313P	11/03/2003		LUTON	UK	KUWAIT	KUWAIT											
136	ANDREW TYRIE MP, APPG ON EXTRAORDINARY RENDITION	N219BM	23/03/2003		STEPHENVILLE	CANADA	PRESTWICK	UK											
137	ANDREW TYRIE MP, APPG ON EXTRAORDINARY RENDITION	N219BM	24/03/2003		PRESTWICK	UK	FRANKFURT MAIN	GERMANY											
138	CONTRIBUTION OF THE RAPPORTEUR: RESEARCH ON THE PLANES USED BY THE CIA (EUROPEAN PARLIAMENT)	N313P	28/03/2003		WASHINGTON	USA	LONDON (UNSPECIFIED)	UK											
139	CONTRIBUTION OF THE RAPPORTEUR: RESEARCH ON THE PLANES USED BY THE CIA (EUROPEAN PARLIAMENT)	N313P	28/03/2003		LONDON (UNSPECIFIED)	UK	PRESTWICK	BAHRAIN											
140	SNP REPORT 'ALLEGED CIA AIRCRAFT FLYING INTO SCOTLAND'	N47LUF	28/03/2003		UNSPECIFIED	UK	LUTON	UK											
141	CONTRIBUTION OF THE RAPPORTEUR: RESEARCH ON THE PLANES USED BY THE CIA (EUROPEAN PARLIAMENT)	N313P	30/03/2003		LUTON	DUBAI	WASHINGTON	USA											
142	CONTRIBUTION OF THE RAPPORTEUR: RESEARCH ON THE PLANES USED BY THE CIA (EUROPEAN PARLIAMENT)	N313P	30/03/2003		LUTON	UK	LUTON	UK											
143	REPRIEVE REPORT 'ENFORCED DISAPPEARANCE, ILLEGAL INTERSTATE TRANSFER, AND OTHER HUMAN RIGHTS ABUSES INVOLVING THE UK OVERSEAS TERRITORIES'	N85VM	02/04/2003	16:25	GUANTANAMO	US NAVAL BASE, CUBA	PROVIDENCIALES	TURKS & CAICOS	17:51	03/04/2003	19:08	GUANTANAMO	US NAVAL BASE, CUBA	19:52					
144	CONTRIBUTION OF THE RAPPORTEUR: RESEARCH ON THE PLANES USED BY THE CIA (EUROPEAN PARLIAMENT)	N313P	15/04/2003		LUTON	KUWAIT	LUTON	UK											
145	CONTRIBUTION OF THE RAPPORTEUR: RESEARCH ON THE PLANES USED BY THE CIA (EUROPEAN PARLIAMENT)	N313P	18/04/2003		LUTON	UK	WASHINGTON	USA											
146	REPRIEVE REPORT 'SCOTTISH INVOLVEMENT IN EXTRAORDINARY RENDITION'	N1016M	18/04/2003	5:37	NUREMBERG	GERMANY	PRESTWICK	UK	10:06	19/04/2003	09:02	KEFLAVIK	ICELAND	13:54					
147	CONTRIBUTION OF THE RAPPORTEUR: RESEARCH ON THE PLANES USED BY THE CIA (EUROPEAN PARLIAMENT)	N168BF	27/04/2003		ISTANBUL	TURKEY	EDINBURGH	UK											
148	CONTRIBUTION OF THE RAPPORTEUR: RESEARCH ON THE PLANES USED BY THE CIA (EUROPEAN PARLIAMENT)	N168BF	28/04/2003		EDINBURGH	UK	HAMBURG	GERMANY											
149	CONTRIBUTION OF THE RAPPORTEUR: RESEARCH ON THE PLANES USED BY THE CIA (EUROPEAN PARLIAMENT)	N168BF	28/04/2003		HAMBURG	GERMANY	LONDON (UNSPECIFIED)	UK											
150	CONTRIBUTION OF THE RAPPORTEUR: RESEARCH ON THE PLANES USED BY THE CIA (EUROPEAN PARLIAMENT)	N168BF	30/04/2003		LONDON (UNSPECIFIED)	UK	PARIS	FRANCE											
151	CONTRIBUTION OF THE RAPPORTEUR: RESEARCH ON THE PLANES USED BY THE CIA (EUROPEAN PARLIAMENT)	N168BF	02/05/2003		GENEVA	SWITZERLAND	EDINBURGH	UK											
152	CONTRIBUTION OF THE RAPPORTEUR: RESEARCH ON THE PLANES USED BY THE CIA (EUROPEAN PARLIAMENT)	N168BF	02/05/2003		EDINBURGH	UK	GENEVE	SWITZERLAND											
153	SNP REPORT 'ALLEGED CIA AIRCRAFT FLYING INTO SCOTLAND'	N212AZ	02/05/2003		UNSPECIFIED	SWITZERLAND	PRESTWICK	UK											
154	CONTRIBUTION OF THE RAPPORTEUR: RESEARCH ON THE PLANES USED BY THE CIA (EUROPEAN PARLIAMENT)	N168BF	04/05/2003		GENEVA	SWITZERLAND	EDINBURGH	UK											
155	CONTRIBUTION OF THE RAPPORTEUR: RESEARCH ON THE PLANES USED BY THE CIA (EUROPEAN PARLIAMENT)	N168BF	04/05/2003		EDINBURGH	UK	LONDON (UNSPECIFIED)	UK											
156	REPRIEVE REPORT 'ENFORCED DISAPPEARANCE, ILLEGAL INTERSTATE TRANSFER, AND OTHER HUMAN RIGHTS ABUSES INVOLVING THE UK OVERSEAS TERRITORIES'	N85VM	05/05/2003	16:32	GUANTANAMO	US NAVAL BASE, CUBA	PROVIDENCIALES	TURKS & CAICOS	17:20	10/05/2003	14:00	GUANTANAMO	US NAVAL BASE, CUBA	14:39					
157	HIGHLIGHTED BY THE REPORT (WORKING DOC. No.8 DT964133/EN.doc) PRODUCED BY TDIP AT THE EUROPEAN PARLIAMENT	N168BF	05/05/2003		LONDON (UNSPECIFIED)	UK	CAIRO	EGYPT											
158	SNP REPORT 'ALLEGED CIA AIRCRAFT FLYING INTO SCOTLAND'	N47LUF	10/05/2003		UNSPECIFIED	UK	PRESTWICK	UK											
159	CONTRIBUTION OF THE RAPPORTEUR: RESEARCH ON THE PLANES USED BY THE CIA (EUROPEAN PARLIAMENT)	N379P	29/05/2003		LARNACA	CYPRUS	GLASGOW	UK											
160	CONTRIBUTION OF THE RAPPORTEUR: RESEARCH ON THE PLANES USED BY THE CIA (EUROPEAN PARLIAMENT)	N379P	29/05/2003		GLASGOW	UK	WASHINGTON	USA											

#	SOURCE OF ALLEGATION	Serial No	Departure Date	Departure Time	Departure Location	Country	Arrival Location	Country	Arrival Time	Departure Date	Departure Time	Arrival Location	Country	Arrival Time	Departure Date	Departure Time	Arrival Location	Country	Arrival Time
161	ANDREW TYRIE MP, APPG ON EXTRAORDINARY RENDITION	N819JJ	31/05/2003		FRANKFURT MAIN	GERMANY	PRESTWICK	UK											
162	ANDREW TYRIE MP, APPG ON EXTRAORDINARY RENDITION	N819JJ	01/06/2003		PRESTWICK	UK	GANDER INTL	CANADA											
163	SNP REPORT "ALLEGED CIA AIRCRAFT FLYING INTO SCOTLAND"	N470JF	07/06/2003		UNSPECIFIED		PRESTWICK	UK											
164	ANDREW TYRIE MP, APPG ON EXTRAORDINARY RENDITION	N368CE	11/06/2003		NEWARK, NEW YORK	USA	INVERNESS	UK											
165	SNP REPORT "ALLEGED CIA AIRCRAFT FLYING INTO SCOTLAND"	N212AZ	13/06/2003		UNSPECIFIED		PRESTWICK	UK											
166	ANDREW TYRIE MP, APPG ON EXTRAORDINARY RENDITION	N368CE	14/06/2003		INVERNESS	UK	GANDER INTL	CANADA											
167	ANDREW TYRIE MP, APPG ON EXTRAORDINARY RENDITION	N368CE	17/06/2003		GANDER INTL	CANADA	LUTON	UK											
168	CONTRIBUTION OF THE RAPPORTEUR: RESEARCH ON THE PLANES USED BY THE CIA (EUROPEAN PARLIAMENT)	N368CE	18/06/2003		GANDER	CANADA	LUTON	UK											
169	ANDREW TYRIE MP, APPG ON EXTRAORDINARY RENDITION	N368CE	18/06/2003		LUTON	UK	RIYADH/KING KHALID INTL.	SAUDI ARABIA											
170	CONTRIBUTION OF THE RAPPORTEUR: RESEARCH ON THE PLANES USED BY THE CIA (EUROPEAN PARLIAMENT)	N379P	29/06/2003		WARSAW	POLAND	GLASGOW	UK											
171	CONTRIBUTION OF THE RAPPORTEUR: RESEARCH ON THE PLANES USED BY THE CIA (EUROPEAN PARLIAMENT)	N379P	28/06/2003		GLASGOW	UK	WASHINGTON	USA											
172	ANDREW TYRIE MP, APPG ON EXTRAORDINARY RENDITION	N129GS	30/06/2003		PARIS	FRANCE	LUTON	UK											
173	REPRIEVE REPORT "ENFORCED DISAPPEARANCE, ILLEGAL INTERSTATE TRANSFER, AND OTHER HUMAN RIGHTS ABUSES INVOLVING THE UK OVERSEAS TERRITORIES"	N850VM	02/07/2003	15:54	GUANTANAMO	US NAVAL BASE, CUBA	PROVIDENCIALES	TURKS & CAICOS	16:18	03/07/2003	16:49	GUANTANAMO	US NAVAL BASE, CUBA	17:32					
174	REPRIEVE REPORT "SCOTTISH INVOLVEMENT IN EXRAORDINARY RENDITION"	N379P	09/07/2003	6:24	BAKU	AZERBAIJAN	GLASGOW	UK	11:51										
175	REPRIEVE REPORT "SCOTTISH INVOLVEMENT IN EXRAORDINARY RENDITION"	N379P	10/07/2003	5:15	BAKU	AZERBAIJAN	GLASGOW	UK	10:25	10/07/2003	8:49	WASHINGTON	USA	16:05					
176	CONTRIBUTION OF THE RAPPORTEUR: RESEARCH ON THE PLANES USED BY THE CIA (EUROPEAN PARLIAMENT)	N313P	10/07/2003		LARNACA	CYPRUS	GLASGOW	UK											
177	CONTRIBUTION OF THE RAPPORTEUR: RESEARCH ON THE PLANES USED BY THE CIA (EUROPEAN PARLIAMENT)	N313P	10/07/2003		GLASGOW	UK	WASHINGTON	USA											
178	SNP REPORT "ALLEGED CIA AIRCRAFT FLYING INTO SCOTLAND"	N313CR	14/07/2003		UNSPECIFIED		PRESTWICK	UK											
179	SNP REPORT "ALLEGED CIA AIRCRAFT FLYING INTO SCOTLAND"	N470JF	26/07/2003		UNSPECIFIED		PRESTWICK	UK											
180	REPRIEVE REPORT "SCOTTISH INVOLVEMENT IN EXRAORDINARY RENDITION"	N4468A	22/07/2003	13:10	PRESTWICK	UK	MUNICH	GERMANY	11:50										
181	REPRIEVE REPORT "SCOTTISH INVOLVEMENT IN EXRAORDINARY RENDITION"	N379P	23/07/2003	23:06	CAIRO	EGYPT	GLASGOW	UK	4:07	25/07/2003	8:03	WASHINGTON	USA	14:30					
182	HIGHLIGHTED BY THE REPORT (WORKING DOC. No 8 DT/64133SEN.doc) PRODUCED BY TDIP AT THE EUROPEAN PARLIAMENT	N379P	24/07/2003		CAIRO	EGYPT	GLASGOW	UK											
183	SNP REPORT "ALLEGED CIA AIRCRAFT FLYING INTO SCOTLAND"	N379P	24/07/2003		CAIRO	EGYPT	GLASGOW	UK											
184	INTELLIGENCE & SECURITY COMMITTEE REPORT INTO RENDITION	N379P	24/07/2003			AFGHANISTAN	PRESTWICK	UK											
185	REPRIEVE REPORT "SCOTTISH INVOLVEMENT IN EXRAORDINARY RENDITION"	N379P	31/07/2003	10:10	TASHKENT	UZBEKISTAN	GLASGOW	UK	16:41										
186	CONTRIBUTION OF THE RAPPORTEUR: RESEARCH ON THE PLANES USED BY THE CIA (EUROPEAN PARLIAMENT)	N379P	01/08/2003		GLASGOW	UK	WASHINGTON	USA											
187	CONTRIBUTION OF THE RAPPORTEUR: RESEARCH ON THE PLANES USED BY THE CIA (EUROPEAN PARLIAMENT)	N313P	18/08/2003		AMMAN	JORDAN	GLASGOW	UK											
188	CONTRIBUTION OF THE RAPPORTEUR: RESEARCH ON THE PLANES USED BY THE CIA (EUROPEAN PARLIAMENT)	N313P	18/08/2003		GLASGOW	UK	WASHINGTON	USA											
189	HIGHLIGHTED BY THE REPORT (WORKING DOC. No 8 DT/64133SEN.doc) PRODUCED BY TDIP AT THE EUROPEAN PARLIAMENT	N379P	17/09/2003		TASHKENT	UZBEKISTAN	PRESTWICK	UK											
190	CONTRIBUTION OF THE RAPPORTEUR: RESEARCH ON THE PLANES USED BY THE CIA (EUROPEAN PARLIAMENT)	N379P	18/09/2003		PRESTWICK	UK	WASHINGTON	USA											
191	SNP REPORT "ALLEGED CIA AIRCRAFT FLYING INTO SCOTLAND"	N470JF	25/09/2003		UNSPECIFIED		PRESTWICK	UK											
192	CONTRIBUTION OF THE RAPPORTEUR: RESEARCH ON THE PLANES USED BY THE CIA (EUROPEAN PARLIAMENT)	N5155A	23/09/2003		REYKJAVIK	ICELAND	WICK	UK											

A list of flights where the UK Government has been alerted to concerns regarding rendition through the UK, its Overseas Territories or the Crown Dependencies

	SOURCE OF ALLEGATION	Serial No	Departure Date	Departure Time	Departure Location	Country	Arrival Location	Country	Arrival Time	Departure Date	Departure Time	Arrival Location	Country	Arrival Time
193	SNP REPORT "ALLEGED CIA AIRCRAFT FLYING INTO SCOTLAND"	N315CR	23/08/2009		UNSPECIFIED		PRIESTWICK	UK						
194	SNP REPORT "ALLEGED CIA AIRCRAFT FLYING INTO SCOTLAND"	N822US	26/08/2003		UNSPECIFIED		PRIESTWICK	UK						
195	CONTRIBUTION OF THE RAPPORTEUR; RESEARCH ON THE PLANES USED BY THE CIA (EUROPEAN PARLIAMENT)	N4009L	27/08/2003		FRANKFURT	GERMANY	GLASGOW	UK						
196	CONTRIBUTION OF THE RAPPORTEUR; RESEARCH ON THE PLANES USED BY THE CIA (EUROPEAN PARLIAMENT)	N4009L	27/09/2003		GLASGOW	UK	REYKJAVIK	ICELAND						
197	ANDREW TYRIE MP, APPG ON EXTRAORDINARY RENDITION	N8183J	31/08/2003		GANDER INTL.	CANADA	PRIESTWICK	UK						
198	ANDREW TYRIE MP, APPG ON EXTRAORDINARY RENDITION	N8183J	01/09/2003		PRIESTWICK	UK	FRANKFURT MAIN	GERMANY						
199	ANDREW TYRIE MP, APPG ON EXTRAORDINARY RENDITION	N9705J	04/09/2003		CARACAS	VENEZUELA	LUTON	UK						
200	CONTRIBUTION OF THE RAPPORTEUR; RESEARCH ON THE PLANES USED BY THE CIA (EUROPEAN PARLIAMENT)	N313P	06/09/2003		LARNACA	CYPRUS	GLASGOW	UK						
201	CONTRIBUTION OF THE RAPPORTEUR; RESEARCH ON THE PLANES USED BY THE CIA (EUROPEAN PARLIAMENT)	N313P	07/09/2003		GLASGOW	UK	WASHINGTON	USA						
202	CONTRIBUTION OF THE RAPPORTEUR; RESEARCH ON THE PLANES USED BY THE CIA (EUROPEAN PARLIAMENT)	N5139A	10/09/2003		WICK	UK	AUGSBURG	GERMANY						
203	TONY LLOYD MP, UK DELEGATION TO THE PARLIAMENTARY ASSEMBLY OF THE COUNCIL OF EUROPE	N510MG	10/09/2003		MUNICH	GERMANY	LONDON GATWICK	UK						
204	CONTRIBUTION OF THE RAPPORTEUR; RESEARCH ON THE PLANES USED BY THE CIA (EUROPEAN PARLIAMENT)	N5139A	10/09/2003		REYKJAVIK	ICELAND	WICK	UK						
205	CONTRIBUTION OF THE RAPPORTEUR; RESEARCH ON THE PLANES USED BY THE CIA (EUROPEAN PARLIAMENT)	N50BH	11/09/2003		GREENSBORO	USA	LONDONDERRY	UK						
206	REPRIEVE REPORT 'SCOTTISH INVOLVEMENT IN EXPADRAINARY RENDITION"	N375P	12/09/2003	8:27	AQABA	JORDAN	PRIESTWICK	UK	14.09	12/09/2003	15.53	WASHINGTON	USA	23.00
207	CONTRIBUTION OF THE RAPPORTEUR; RESEARCH ON THE PLANES USED BY THE CIA (EUROPEAN PARLIAMENT)	N375P	12/09/2003		PRIESTWICK	UK	WASHINGTON	USA						
208	CONTRIBUTION OF THE RAPPORTEUR; RESEARCH ON THE PLANES USED BY THE CIA (EUROPEAN PARLIAMENT)	N50BH	15/09/2003		LONDONDERRY	UK	BIRMINGHAM	UK						
209	CONTRIBUTION OF THE RAPPORTEUR; RESEARCH ON THE PLANES USED BY THE CIA (EUROPEAN PARLIAMENT)	N50BH	15/09/2003		BIRMINGHAM	UK	MANCHESTER	UK						
210	SNP REPORT "ALLEGED CIA AIRCRAFT FLYING INTO SCOTLAND"	N315CR	15/09/2003		UNSPECIFIED		PRIESTWICK	UK						
211	CONTRIBUTION OF THE RAPPORTEUR; RESEARCH ON THE PLANES USED BY THE CIA (EUROPEAN PARLIAMENT)	N50BH	16/09/2003		MANCHESTER	UK	LONDONDERRY	UK						
212	CONTRIBUTION OF THE RAPPORTEUR; RESEARCH ON THE PLANES USED BY THE CIA (EUROPEAN PARLIAMENT)	N50BH	16/09/2003		LONDONDERRY	UK	GANDER	CANADA						
213	SNP REPORT "ALLEGED CIA AIRCRAFT FLYING INTO SCOTLAND"	N47CLIF	18/09/2003		UNSPECIFIED		PRIESTWICK	UK						
214	ANDREW TYRIE MP, APPG ON EXTRAORDINARY RENDITION	N2189MA	20/09/2003		GENOVA/SESTRI	ITALY	PRIESTWICK	UK						
215	ANDREW TYRIE MP, APPG ON EXTRAORDINARY RENDITION	N85VM	20/09/2003		FARMINGDALE	USA	RAF LEUCHARS	UK						
216	ANDREW TYRIE MP, APPG ON EXTRAORDINARY RENDITION	N2189MA	21/09/2003		PRIESTWICK	UK	GANDER INTL.	CANADA						
217	REPRIEVE REPORT 'ENFORCED DISAPPEARANCE, ILLEGAL INTERSTATE TRANSFER, AND OTHER HUMAN RIGHTS ABUSES INVOLVING THE UK OVERSEAS TERRITORIES'	N313P	24/09/2003	7:46	GUANTANAMO	US NAVAL BASE, CUBA	PROVIDENCIALES	TURKS & CAICOS	8:39	25/09/2003	13.00	WASHINGTON DULLES	USA	15:47
218	HIGHLIGHTED BY THE REPORT (WORKING DOC. No.8 DT964333SEM.doc) PRODUCED BY TDIP AT THE EUROPEAN PARLIAMENT	N279P	24/09/2003		TASHKENT	UZBEKISTAN	PRIESTWICK	UK						
219	CONTRIBUTION OF THE RAPPORTEUR; RESEARCH ON THE PLANES USED BY THE CIA (EUROPEAN PARLIAMENT)	N379P	25/09/2003		PRIESTWICK	UK	WASHINGTON	USA						
220	ANDREW TYRIE MP, APPG ON EXTRAORDINARY RENDITION	N85VM	27/09/2003		RAF LEUCHARS	UK	FARMINGDALE	USA						
221	CONTRIBUTION OF THE RAPPORTEUR; RESEARCH ON THE PLANES USED BY THE CIA (EUROPEAN PARLIAMENT)	N379P	30/09/2003		WASHINGTON	USA	LUTON	UK						
222	CONTRIBUTION OF THE RAPPORTEUR; RESEARCH ON THE PLANES USED BY THE CIA (EUROPEAN PARLIAMENT)	N379P	30/09/2003		LUTON	UK	RIYADH	SAUDI ARABIA						
223	CONTRIBUTION OF THE RAPPORTEUR; RESEARCH ON THE PLANES USED BY THE CIA (EUROPEAN PARLIAMENT)	N379P	09/10/2003		DELHI	INDIA	LUTON	UK						
224	CONTRIBUTION OF THE RAPPORTEUR; RESEARCH ON THE PLANES USED BY THE CIA (EUROPEAN PARLIAMENT)	N379P	09/10/2003		LUTON	UK	WASHINGTON	USA						

A list of flights where the UK Government has been alerted to concerns regarding rendition through the UK, its Overseas Territories or the Crown Dependencies

#	SOURCE OF ALLEGATION	Serial No	Departure Date	Departure Time	Departure Location	Country	Arrival Time	Arrival Location	Country	Departure Date	Departure Time	Arrival Location	Country	Arrival Time
225	CONTRIBUTION OF THE RAPPORTEUR: RESEARCH ON THE PLANES USED BY THE CIA (EUROPEAN PARLIAMENT)	N313P	17/10/2003		WASHINGTON	USA	17:30	RAF BRIZE NORTON	UK					
226	JOURNALIST, ITN	N313P	17/10/2003		LONDON GATWICK	UK	16:35	RAF BRIZE NORTON	UK	19/10/2003	12:45	TRIPOLI	UNSPECIFIED	10:13
227	SNP REPORT 'ALLEGED CIA AIRCRAFT FLYING INTO SCOTLAND'	N212AZ	18/10/2003		UNSPECIFIED	UNSPECIFIED		PRESTWICK	UK					
228	JOURNALIST, ITN	N313P	22/10/2003		TRIPOLI	LIBYA	15:35	RAF NORTHOLT	UK					
229	HIGHLIGHTED BY THE REPORT (WORKING DOC: No 8 DT/641333EN.doc) PRODUCED BY TDIP AT THE EUROPEAN PARLIAMENT	N313P	22/10/2003		MISURATA	LIBYA		RAF NORTHOLT	UK					
230	HIGHLIGHTED BY THE REPORT (WORKING DOC: No 8 DT/641333EN.doc) PRODUCED BY TDIP AT THE EUROPEAN PARLIAMENT	N313P	28/10/2003		RAF NORTHOLT	UK		MISURATA	LIBYA					
231	JOURNALIST, ITN	N313P	29/10/2003		TRIPOLI	UNSPECIFIED	17:10	RAF NORTHOLT	UK	29/10/2003	17:45	SHANNON	IRELAND	
232	HIGHLIGHTED BY THE REPORT (WORKING DOC: No 8 DT/641333EN.doc) PRODUCED BY TDIP AT THE EUROPEAN PARLIAMENT	N313P	29/10/2003		MISURATA	LIBYA		RAF NORTHOLT	UK					
233	SNP REPORT 'ALLEGED CIA AIRCRAFT FLYING INTO SCOTLAND'	N212AZ	09/11/2003		UNSPECIFIED	LIBYA		PRESTWICK	UK					
234	JOURNALIST, ITN	N379P	29/11/2003		WASHINGTON	USA	7:37	RAF BRIZE NORTON	UK					
235	CONTRIBUTION OF THE RAPPORTEUR: RESEARCH ON THE PLANES USED BY THE CIA (EUROPEAN PARLIAMENT)	N379P	29/11/2003		RAF BRIZE NORTON	UK		WASHINGTON	USA					
236	REPRIEVE REPORT 'ENFORCED DISAPPEARANCE, ILLEGAL INTERSTATE TRANSFER, AND OTHER HUMAN RIGHTS ABUSES INVOLVING THE UK OVERSEAS TERRITORIES'	N313P	22/11/2003		GUANTANAMO	US NAVAL BASE, CUBA	19:23	PROVIDENCIALES	TURKS & CAICOS					
237	REPRIEVE REPORT 'ENFORCED DISAPPEARANCE, ILLEGAL INTERSTATE TRANSFER, AND OTHER HUMAN RIGHTS ABUSES INVOLVING THE UK OVERSEAS TERRITORIES'	N85VM	28/11/2003	14:29	FARMINGDALE REPUBLIC AIRPORT	USA	17:32	PROVIDENCIALES	TURKS & CAICOS					
238	REPRIEVE REPORT 'ENFORCED DISAPPEARANCE, ILLEGAL INTERSTATE TRANSFER, AND OTHER HUMAN RIGHTS ABUSES INVOLVING THE UK OVERSEAS TERRITORIES'	N85VM	28/11/2003	22:23	PROVIDENCIALES	TURKS & CAICOS	1:14	FARMINGDALE REPUBLIC AIRPORT	USA					
239	JOURNALIST, ITN	N313P	01/12/2003		WASHINGTON	USA		RAF NORTHOLT	UK					
240	HIGHLIGHTED BY THE REPORT (WORKING DOC: No 8 DT/641333EN.doc) PRODUCED BY TDIP AT THE EUROPEAN PARLIAMENT	N313P	01/12/2003	18:49	RAF NORTHOLT	UK	8:50	MISURATA	LIBYA					
241	REPRIEVE REPORT 'ENFORCED DISAPPEARANCE, ILLEGAL INTERSTATE TRANSFER, AND OTHER HUMAN RIGHTS ABUSES INVOLVING THE UK OVERSEAS TERRITORIES'	N85VM	03/12/2003		GUANTANAMO	US NAVAL BASE, CUBA	19:23	PROVIDENCIALES	TURKS & CAICOS					
242	ANDREW TYRIE MP APPG ON EXTRAORDINARY RENDITION	N2189M	03/12/2003		GOOSE BAY	CANADA		PRESTWICK	UK					
243	JOURNALIST, ITN	N313P	03/12/2003		TRIPOLI	UNSPECIFIED	13:00	RAF NORTHOLT	UK	03/12/2003	12:00	LUCA	MALTA	
244	HIGHLIGHTED BY THE REPORT (WORKING DOC: No 8 DT/641333EN.doc) PRODUCED BY TDIP AT THE EUROPEAN PARLIAMENT	N313P	03/12/2003		MISURATA	LIBYA		RAF NORTHOLT	UK					
245	ANDREW TYRIE MP APPG ON EXTRAORDINARY RENDITION	N2189M	04/12/2003		PRESTWICK	UK		FRANKFURT MAIN	GERMANY					
246	SNP REPORT 'ALLEGED CIA AIRCRAFT FLYING INTO SCOTLAND'	N47UF	06/12/2003		UNSPECIFIED	UK		PRESTWICK	UK					
247	JOURNALIST, ITN	N313P	12/12/2003		WASHINGTON	USA	9:00	RAF BRIZE NORTON	UK	12/12/2003		TRIPOLI	UNSPECIFIED	
248	HIGHLIGHTED BY THE REPORT (WORKING DOC: No 8 DT/641333EN.doc) PRODUCED BY TDIP AT THE EUROPEAN PARLIAMENT	N313P	12/12/2003		MISURATA	LYBIA		RAF BRIZE NORTON	UK					
249	HIGHLIGHTED BY THE REPORT (WORKING DOC: No 8 DT/641333EN.doc) PRODUCED BY TDIP AT THE EUROPEAN PARLIAMENT	N313P	12/12/2003		RAF NORTHOLT	UNSPECIFIED		TRIPOLI	LYBIA					
250	REPRIEVE REPORT 'ENFORCED DISAPPEARANCE, ILLEGAL INTERSTATE TRANSFER, AND OTHER HUMAN RIGHTS ABUSES INVOLVING THE UK OVERSEAS TERRITORIES'	N829MG	15/12/2003	13:36	CITY OF FORT LAUDERDALE EXECUTIVE AIRPORT	USA	14:49	PROVIDENCIALES	TURKS & CAICOS					
251	CONTRIBUTION OF THE RAPPORTEUR: RESEARCH ON THE PLANES USED BY THE CIA (EUROPEAN PARLIAMENT)	N313P	16/12/2003		TETERBORO	USA		LUTON	UK					
252	CONTRIBUTION OF THE RAPPORTEUR: RESEARCH ON THE PLANES USED BY THE CIA (EUROPEAN PARLIAMENT)	N1HC	16/12/2003		TETERBORO	USA		RAF NORTHOLT	UK					
253	CONTRIBUTION OF THE RAPPORTEUR: RESEARCH ON THE PLANES USED BY THE CIA (EUROPEAN PARLIAMENT)	N1HC	17/12/2003		LONDON (UNSPECIFIED)	UK		TETERBORO	USA					
254	CONTRIBUTION OF THE RAPPORTEUR: RESEARCH ON THE PLANES USED BY THE CIA (EUROPEAN PARLIAMENT)	N313P	17/12/2003		LUTON	UK		WASHINGTON	USA					
255	HIGHLIGHTED BY THE REPORT (WORKING DOC: No 8 DT/641333EN.doc) PRODUCED BY TDIP AT THE EUROPEAN PARLIAMENT	N379P	18/12/2003		KARJUKH/KADJA RAWASH	AFGHANISTAN		GLASGOW	UK					
256	CONTRIBUTION OF THE RAPPORTEUR: RESEARCH ON THE PLANES USED BY THE CIA (EUROPEAN PARLIAMENT)	N379P	18/12/2003		GLASGOW	UK		WASHINGTON	USA					

#	SOURCE OF ALLEGATION	Serial No	Departure Date	Departure Time	Departure Location	Country	Arrival Location	Country	Arrival Time	Departure Date	Departure Time	Arrival Location	Country	Arrival Time
257	REPRIEVE REPORT 'ENFORCED DISAPPEARANCE, ILLEGAL INTERSTATE TRANSFER, AND OTHER HUMAN RIGHTS ABUSES INVOLVING THE UK OVERSEAS TERRITORIES'	N826MG	26/12/2005	16:34	WESTCHESTER COUNTY	USA	PROVIDENCIALES	TURKS & CAICOS	19:32	26/12/2005	20:07	EXECUTIVE AIRPORT	USA	21:42
258	REPRIEVE REPORT 'ENFORCED DISAPPEARANCE, ILLEGAL INTERSTATE TRANSFER, AND OTHER HUMAN RIGHTS ABUSES INVOLVING THE UK OVERSEAS TERRITORIES'	N313P	26/12/2003	18:19	WASHINGTON DULLES	USA	PROVIDENCIALES	TURKS & CAICOS	20:56	27/12/2003	22:31	GUANTANAMO	US NAVAL BASE, CUBA	23:15
259	ANDREW TYRIE MP APPG ON EXTRAORDINARY RENDITION	N818JJ	01/01/2004		FRANKFURT MAIN	GERMANY	PRESTWICK	UK						
260	ANDREW TYRIE MP APPG ON EXTRAORDINARY RENDITION	N818JJ	02/01/2004		PRESTWICK	UK	GANDER INTL.	CANADA						
261	REPRIEVE REPORT 'ENFORCED DISAPPEARANCE, AND OTHER HUMAN RIGHTS ABUSES INVOLVING THE UK OVERSEAS TERRITORIES'	N85VM	05/01/2004		GUANTANAMO	US NAVAL BASE, CUBA	PROVIDENCIALES	TURKS & CAICOS	17:42	09/01/2004	15:26	GUANTANAMO	US NAVAL BASE, CUBA	16:10
262	CONTRIBUTION OF THE RAPPORTEUR RESEARCH ON THE PLANES USED BY THE CIA (EUROPEAN PARLIAMENT)	N19RD	10/01/2004	17:03	SEVILLE	SPAIN	EDINBURGH	UK						
263	REPRIEVE REPORT 'ENFORCED DISAPPEARANCE, ILLEGAL INTERSTATE TRANSFER, AND OTHER HUMAN RIGHTS ABUSES INVOLVING THE UK OVERSEAS TERRITORIES'	N85VM	15/01/2004	16:21	PROVIDENCIALES	TURKS & CAICOS	GUANTANAMO	CUBA	17:02					
264	CONTRIBUTION OF THE RAPPORTEUR RESEARCH ON THE PLANES USED BY THE CIA (EUROPEAN PARLIAMENT)	N19RD	16/01/2004		EDINBURGH	UK	REYKJAVIK	ICELAND						
265	ANDREW TYRIE MP APPG ON EXTRAORDINARY RENDITION	N2189M	18/01/2004		GANDER INTL.	CANADA	PRESTWICK	UK						
266	ANDREW TYRIE MP APPG ON EXTRAORDINARY RENDITION	N2189M	19/01/2004		PRESTWICK	UK	AMMAN / MARKA	JORDAN						
267	CONTRIBUTION OF THE RAPPORTEUR RESEARCH ON THE PLANES USED BY THE CIA (EUROPEAN PARLIAMENT)	N818JJ	21/01/2004		FRANKFURT	GERMANY	PRESTWICK	UK						
268	CONTRIBUTION OF THE RAPPORTEUR RESEARCH ON THE PLANES USED BY THE CIA (EUROPEAN PARLIAMENT)	N818JJ	22/01/2004		PRESTWICK	UK	GANDER	CANADA						
269	ANDREW TYRIE MP APPG ON EXTRAORDINARY RENDITION	N970SJ	06/02/2004		MADRID	SPAIN	LUTON	UK						
270	REPRIEVE REPORT 'ENFORCED DISAPPEARANCE, AND OTHER HUMAN RIGHTS ABUSES INVOLVING THE UK OVERSEAS TERRITORIES'	N85VM	09/02/2004	16:40	GUANTANAMO	US NAVAL BASE, CUBA	PROVIDENCIALES	TURKS & CAICOS	17:19	13/02/2004	15:29	GUANTANAMO	US NAVAL BASE, CUBA	18:13
271	JOURNALIST, ITN	400065	03/03/2004		RAF LAKENHEATH	UK	RAF NORTHOLT	UK	14:20					
272	JOURNALIST, ITN	400065	04/03/2004	12:05	RAF NORTHOLT	UK	SHANNON	IRELAND						
273	REPRIEVE REPORT 'ENFORCED DISAPPEARANCE, AND OTHER HUMAN RIGHTS ABUSES INVOLVING THE UK OVERSEAS TERRITORIES'	N85VM	11/03/2004	20:01	GUANTANAMO	US NAVAL BASE, CUBA	PROVIDENCIALES	TURKS & CAICOS	20:42	12/03/2004	12:34	GUANTANAMO	US NAVAL BASE, CUBA	13:17
274	REPRIEVE REPORT 'ENFORCED DISAPPEARANCE, ILLEGAL INTERSTATE TRANSFER, AND OTHER HUMAN RIGHTS ABUSES INVOLVING THE UK OVERSEAS TERRITORIES'	N8068V	12/03/2004	7:44	GUANTANAMO	US NAVAL BASE, CUBA	PROVIDENCIALES	TURKS & CAICOS	8:17	13/03/2004	14:54	WASHINGTON DULLES	USA	17:33
275	REPRIEVE REPORT 'SCOTTISH INVOLVEMENT IN EXTRAORDINARY RENDITION'	N4465A	18/03/2004	10:20	REYKJAVIK	ICELAND	PRESTWICK	UK	5:03					
276	CONTRIBUTION OF THE RAPPORTEUR RESEARCH ON THE PLANES USED BY THE CIA (EUROPEAN PARLIAMENT)	N157A	01/04/2004		MUNICH	GERMANY	PRESTWICK	UK						
277	CONTRIBUTION OF THE RAPPORTEUR RESEARCH ON THE PLANES USED BY THE CIA (EUROPEAN PARLIAMENT)	N157A	01/04/2004		PRESTWICK	UK	REYKJAVIK	ICELAND						
278	SNP REPORT 'ALLEGED CIA AIRCRAFT FLYING INTO SCOTLAND'	N315CR	04/04/2004		UNSPECIFIED		PRESTWICK	UK						
279	CONTRIBUTION OF THE RAPPORTEUR RESEARCH ON THE PLANES USED BY THE CIA (EUROPEAN PARLIAMENT)	N818J	08/04/2005		GANDER INTL.	CANADA	PRESTWICK	UK						
280	ANDREW TYRIE MP APPG ON EXTRAORDINARY RENDITION	N818J	07/04/2004		PRESTWICK	UK	IRAKLION NIKOS KAZANZAKIS	GREECE, CRETE						
281	HIGHLIGHTED BY THE REPORT (WORKING DOC. No 8 DT\634133SEN.doc) PRODUCED BY TDIP AT THE EUROPEAN PARLIAMENT	N188BF	08/04/2004		CASABLANCA/MOHAMMED	MOROCCO	FARNBOROUGH CIV	UK						
282	HIGHLIGHTED BY THE REPORT (WORKING DOC. No 8 DT\634133SEN.doc) PRODUCED BY TDIP AT THE EUROPEAN PARLIAMENT	N188BF	08/04/2004		CASABLANCA/MOHAMMED	MOROCCO	FARNBOROUGH CIV	UK						
283	REPRIEVE REPORT 'ENFORCED DISAPPEARANCE, ILLEGAL INTERSTATE TRANSFER, AND OTHER HUMAN RIGHTS ABUSES INVOLVING THE UK OVERSEAS TERRITORIES'	N8068V	08/04/2004	14:32	GUANTANAMO	US NAVAL BASE, CUBA	PROVIDENCIALES	TURKS & CAICOS	15:22	09/04/2004	19:25	GUANTANAMO	US NAVAL BASE, CUBA	19:11
284	REPRIEVE REPORT 'ENFORCED DISAPPEARANCE, ILLEGAL INTERSTATE TRANSFER, AND OTHER HUMAN RIGHTS ABUSES INVOLVING THE UK OVERSEAS TERRITORIES'	N8068V	09/04/2004	21:27	PROVIDENCIALES	TURKS & CAICOS	JACKSONVILLE INTL.	USA	23:42	09/04/2004				
285	TONY LLOYD MP, UK DELEGATION TO THE PARLIAMENTARY ASSEMBLY OF THE COUNCIL OF EUROPE	N5103MG	25/04/2004		CLEVELAND, OHIO	USA	LONDON LUTON	UK						
286	ANDREW TYRIE MP APPG ON EXTRAORDINARY RENDITION	N818JJ	03/05/2004		GANDER INTL.	CANADA	PRESTWICK	UK						
287	ANDREW TYRIE MP APPG ON EXTRAORDINARY RENDITION	N818JJ	04/05/2004		PRESTWICK	UK	IRAKLION NIKOS KAZANZAKIS	GREECE, CRETE						
288	ANDREW TYRIE MP APPG ON EXTRAORDINARY RENDITION	N360CE	08/05/2004		NEWARK, NEW YORK	USA	STANSTED	UK						

A list of flights where the UK Government has been alerted to concerns regarding rendition through the UK, its Overseas Territories or the Crown Dependencies

	SOURCE OF ALLEGATION	Serial No	Departure Date	Departure Time	Departure Location	Country	Arrival Location	Country	Arrival Time	Departure Date	Departure Time	Arrival Location	Country	Arrival Time	Departure Date	Departure Time	Arrival Location	Country	Arrival Time
289	ANDREW TYRIE MP APPG ON EXTRAORDINARY RENDITION	N368CE	09/05/2004		STANSTED	UK	BANGOR INTL. MAINE	USA	12:55										
290	JOURNALIST, ITN	400085	12/05/2004		RAMSTEIN	GERMANY	RAF NORTHOLT	UK											
291	JOURNALIST, ITN	400085	13/05/2004	6:00	RAF NORTHOLT	UK	ALGIERS	ALGERIA											
292	CONTRIBUTION OF THE RAPPORTEUR: RESEARCH ON THE PLANES USED BY THE CIA (EUROPEAN PARLIAMENT)	N16RD	13/05/2004		REYKJAVIK	ICELAND	EDINBURGH	UK											
293	CONTRIBUTION OF THE RAPPORTEUR: RESEARCH ON THE PLANES USED BY THE CIA (EUROPEAN PARLIAMENT)	N16RD	13/05/2004		EDINBURGH	UK	FRANKFURT	GERMANY											
294	JOURNALIST, ITN	N806BV	16/05/2004		MARRAKECH	MOROCCO	RAF NORTHOLT	UK	12:10	15/05/2004	13:00	LUTON	UK						
295	JOURNALIST, ITN	N806BV	17/05/2004		LUTON	UK	RAF NORTHOLT	UK	11:05	18/05/2004	8:00	SHANNON	IRELAND						
296	CONTRIBUTION OF THE RAPPORTEUR: RESEARCH ON THE PLANES USED BY THE CIA (EUROPEAN PARLIAMENT)	N81ISJ	23/05/2004		GANDER	CANADA	PRESTWICK	UK											
297	CONTRIBUTION OF THE RAPPORTEUR: RESEARCH ON THE PLANES USED BY THE CIA (EUROPEAN PARLIAMENT)	N81ISJ	24/05/2004		PRESTWICK	UK	IRAKLION	GREECE											
298	ANDREW TYRIE MP APPG ON EXTRAORDINARY RENDITION	N219BM	25/05/2004		PRAHA/RUZYNE	CZECH REPUBLIC	PRESTWICK	UK											
299	ANDREW TYRIE MP APPG ON EXTRAORDINARY RENDITION	N219RM	26/05/2004		PRESTWICK	UK	GANDER INTL	CANADA											
300	CONTRIBUTION OF THE RAPPORTEUR: RESEARCH ON THE PLANES USED BY THE CIA (EUROPEAN PARLIAMENT)	N173S	28/05/2004		MUNICH	GERMANY	PRESTWICK	UK											
301	CONTRIBUTION OF THE RAPPORTEUR: RESEARCH ON THE PLANES USED BY THE CIA (EUROPEAN PARLIAMENT)	N173S	29/05/2004		PRESTWICK	UK	REYKJAVIK	ICELAND											
302	CONTRIBUTION OF THE RAPPORTEUR: RESEARCH ON THE PLANES USED BY THE CIA (EUROPEAN PARLIAMENT)	N1HC	12/09/2004		KILIMANJARO	TANZANIA	FARNBOROUGH	UK											
303	CONTRIBUTION OF THE RAPPORTEUR: RESEARCH ON THE PLANES USED BY THE CIA (EUROPEAN PARLIAMENT)	N1HC	12/09/2004		FARNBOROUGH	UK	WHITE PLAINS	USA											
304	CONTRIBUTION OF THE RAPPORTEUR: RESEARCH ON THE PLANES USED BY THE CIA (EUROPEAN PARLIAMENT)	N1HC	17/09/2004		WESTHAMPTON BEACH	USA	LONDON (UNSPECIFIED)	UK											
305	CONTRIBUTION OF THE RAPPORTEUR: RESEARCH ON THE PLANES USED BY THE CIA (EUROPEAN PARLIAMENT)	N1HC	18/09/2004		LONDON (UNSPECIFIED)	UK	MILWAUKEE	USA											
306	CONTRIBUTION OF THE RAPPORTEUR: RESEARCH ON THE PLANES USED BY THE CIA (EUROPEAN PARLIAMENT)	N187D	20/09/2004		SEVILLE	SPAIN	EDINBURGH	UK											
307	CONTRIBUTION OF THE RAPPORTEUR: RESEARCH ON THE PLANES USED BY THE CIA (EUROPEAN PARLIAMENT)	N187D	21/09/2004		EDINBURGH	UK	REYKJAVIK	ICELAND											
308	HIGHLIGHTED BY THE REPORT (WORKING DOC. No.8 DT1841332IEN.doc) PRODUCED BY TDIP AT THE EUROPEAN PARLIAMENT	N37IP	25/09/2004		AMMAN	JORDAN	PRESTWICK	UK											
309	CONTRIBUTION OF THE RAPPORTEUR: RESEARCH ON THE PLANES USED BY THE CIA (EUROPEAN PARLIAMENT)	N806BV	25/09/2004		PRESTWICK	UK	WASHINGTON	USA											
310	CONTRIBUTION OF THE RAPPORTEUR: RESEARCH ON THE PLANES USED BY THE CIA (EUROPEAN PARLIAMENT)	N168BF	09/07/2004		ZURICH	SWITZERLAND	LONDON (UNSPECIFIED)	UK											
311	CONTRIBUTION OF THE RAPPORTEUR: RESEARCH ON THE PLANES USED BY THE CIA (EUROPEAN PARLIAMENT)	N168BF	09/07/2004		LONDON (UNSPECIFIED)	UK	ZURICH	SWITZERLAND											
312	CONTRIBUTION OF THE RAPPORTEUR: RESEARCH ON THE PLANES USED BY THE CIA (EUROPEAN PARLIAMENT)	N1611Q	24/07/2004		MARSEILLE	FRANCE	BOURNEMOUTH	UK											
313	ANDREW TYRIE MP APPG ON EXTRAORDINARY RENDITION	N368CE	24/07/2004		LIVERPOOL	UK	NEWARK	USA											
314	CONTRIBUTION OF THE RAPPORTEUR: RESEARCH ON THE PLANES USED BY THE CIA (EUROPEAN PARLIAMENT)	N1611Q	07/08/2004		BOURNEMOUTH	UK	KERKIRA	GREECE											
315	CONTRIBUTION OF THE RAPPORTEUR: RESEARCH ON THE PLANES USED BY THE CIA (EUROPEAN PARLIAMENT)	N445BA	24/08/2004		GLASGOW	UK	PRAHA	CZECH REPUBLIC											
316	CONTRIBUTION OF THE RAPPORTEUR: RESEARCH ON THE PLANES USED BY THE CIA (EUROPEAN PARLIAMENT)	N16RD	01/09/2004		FRANKFURT	GERMANY	WICK	UK											
317	CONTRIBUTION OF THE RAPPORTEUR: RESEARCH ON THE PLANES USED BY THE CIA (EUROPEAN PARLIAMENT)	N16RD	03/09/2004		WICK	UK	REYKJAVIK	ICELAND											
318	SNP REPORT "ALLEGED CIA AIRCRAFT FLYING INTO SCOTLAND"	N315CR	06/09/2004		UNSPECIFIED		PRESTWICK	UK											
319	CONTRIBUTION OF THE RAPPORTEUR: RESEARCH ON THE PLANES USED BY THE CIA (EUROPEAN PARLIAMENT)	N227SV	04/10/2004		FARMINGDALE	USA	RAF LEUCHARS	UK											
320	CONTRIBUTION OF THE RAPPORTEUR: RESEARCH ON THE PLANES USED BY THE CIA (EUROPEAN PARLIAMENT)	N227SV	09/10/2004		RAF LEUCHARS	UK	FARMINGDALE	USA											

A list of flights where the UK Government has been alerted to concerns regarding rendition through the UK, its Overseas Territories or the Crown Dependencies

SOURCE OF ALLEGATION	Serial No	Departure Date	Departure Location	Departure Time	Country	Arrival Location	Country	Arrival Time	Departure Date	Departure Time	Arrival Location	Country	Arrival Time	Country	Arrival Location	Country	Arrival Time
321 REPRIEVE REPORT 'ENFORCED DISAPPEARANCE, ILLEGAL INTERSTATE TRANSFER, AND OTHER HUMAN RIGHTS ABUSES INVOLVING THE UK OVERSEAS TERRITORIES'	N313P	26/10/2004	GUANTANAMO	20:24	US NAVAL BASE, CUBA	PROVIDENCIALES	TURKS & CAICOS	20:51	28/10/2004	14:57							
322 ANDREW TYRIE MP, APPG ON EXTRAORDINARY RENDITION	N816SJ	02/11/2004	FRANKFURT MAIN		GERMANY	PRESTWICK	UK										
323 ANDREW TYRIE MP, APPG ON EXTRAORDINARY RENDITION	N816SJ	03/11/2004	PRESTWICK		UK	GANDER INTL	CANADA										
324 CONTRIBUTION OF THE RAPPORTEUR: RESEARCH ON THE PLANES USED BY THE CIA (EUROPEAN PARLIAMENT)	N816SJ	12/11/2004	FRANKFURT		GERMANY	PRESTWICK	UK										
325 CONTRIBUTION OF THE RAPPORTEUR: RESEARCH ON THE PLANES USED BY THE CIA (EUROPEAN PARLIAMENT)	N816SJ	13/11/2004	PRESTWICK		UK	GANDER	CANADA										
326 SNP REPORT 'ALLEGED CIA AIRCRAFT FLYING INTO SCOTLAND'	N216BM	13/11/2004	UNSPECIFIED			PRESTWICK	UK										
327 CONTRIBUTION OF THE RAPPORTEUR: RESEARCH ON THE PLANES USED BY THE CIA (EUROPEAN PARLIAMENT)	N465?C	29/11/2004	GANDER		CANADA	PRESTWICK	UK										
329 CONTRIBUTION OF THE RAPPORTEUR: RESEARCH ON THE PLANES USED BY THE CIA (EUROPEAN PARLIAMENT)	N467?C	30/11/2004	PRESTWICK		UK	IRAKLION	GREECE										
329 CONTRIBUTION OF THE RAPPORTEUR: RESEARCH ON THE PLANES USED BY THE CIA (EUROPEAN PARLIAMENT)	N227SV	14/12/2004	WASHINGTON		USA	LUTON	UK										
330 HIGHLIGHTED BY THE REPORT (WORKING DOC. No 8 DT\664\1333EN.doc) PRODUCED BY TDIP AT THE EUROPEAN PARLIAMENT	N227SV	15/12/2004	LUTON		UK	PAPHOS	CYPRUS										
331 HIGHLIGHTED BY THE REPORT (WORKING DOC. No 8 DT\664\1333EN.doc) PRODUCED BY TDIP AT THE EUROPEAN PARLIAMENT	N168BF	16/12/2004	CASABLANCA		MOROCCO	LONDON (UNSPECIFIED)	UK										
332 CONTRIBUTION OF THE RAPPORTEUR: RESEARCH ON THE PLANES USED BY THE CIA (EUROPEAN PARLIAMENT)	N168BF	18/12/2004	NEWCASTLE		UK	LONDON (UNSPECIFIED)	UK										
333 CONTRIBUTION OF THE RAPPORTEUR: RESEARCH ON THE PLANES USED BY THE CIA (EUROPEAN PARLIAMENT)	N168BF	18/12/2004	LONDON (UNSPECIFIED)		UK	NEWCASTLE	UK										
334 CONTRIBUTION OF THE RAPPORTEUR: RESEARCH ON THE PLANES USED BY THE CIA (EUROPEAN PARLIAMENT)	N168BF	20/12/2004	LONDON (UNSPECIFIED)		UK	GENEVA	SWITZERLAND										
335 CONTRIBUTION OF THE RAPPORTEUR: RESEARCH ON THE PLANES USED BY THE CIA (EUROPEAN PARLIAMENT)	N168BF	15/01/2005	LARNACA		CYPRUS	LONDON (UNSPECIFIED)	UK										
336 HIGHLIGHTED BY THE REPORT (WORKING DOC. No 8 DT\664\1333EN.doc) PRODUCED BY TDIP AT THE EUROPEAN PARLIAMENT	N168BF	16/01/2005	LUTON		UK	CASABLANCA/MOHAMMED	MOROCCO										
337 HIGHLIGHTED BY THE REPORT (WORKING DOC. No 8 DT\664\1333EN.doc) PRODUCED BY TDIP AT THE EUROPEAN PARLIAMENT	N313P	18/01/2005	MISURATA		LIBYA	GLASGOW	UK										
338 CONTRIBUTION OF THE RAPPORTEUR: RESEARCH ON THE PLANES USED BY THE CIA (EUROPEAN PARLIAMENT)	N447RS	19/01/2005	MISURATA		LYBIA	GLASGOW	UK										
339 CONTRIBUTION OF THE RAPPORTEUR: RESEARCH ON THE PLANES USED BY THE CIA (EUROPEAN PARLIAMENT)	N447RS	19/01/2005	GLASGOW		UK	WASHINGTON	USA										
340 HIGHLIGHTED BY THE REPORT (WORKING DOC. No 8 DT\664\1333EN.doc) PRODUCED BY TDIP AT THE EUROPEAN PARLIAMENT	N168BF	05/02/2005	CASABLANCA/MOHAMMED		MOROCCO	FARNBOROUGH CIV	UK										
341 HIGHLIGHTED BY THE REPORT (WORKING DOC. No 8 DT\664\1333EN.doc) PRODUCED BY TDIP AT THE EUROPEAN PARLIAMENT	N168BF	05/02/2005	CASABLANCA/MOHAMMED		MOROCCO	FARNBOROUGH CIV	UK										
342 CONTRIBUTION OF THE RAPPORTEUR: RESEARCH ON THE PLANES USED BY THE CIA (EUROPEAN PARLIAMENT)	N447RS	07/02/2005	WASHINGTON		USA	GLASGOW	UK										
343 CONTRIBUTION OF THE RAPPORTEUR: RESEARCH ON THE PLANES USED BY THE CIA (EUROPEAN PARLIAMENT)	N447RS	07/02/2005	GLASGOW		UK	BAGHDAD	IRAQ										
344 CONTRIBUTION OF THE RAPPORTEUR: RESEARCH ON THE PLANES USED BY THE CIA (EUROPEAN PARLIAMENT)	N1HC	11/03/2005	DALLAS		USA	FARNBOROUGH	UK										
345 HIGHLIGHTED BY THE REPORT (WORKING DOC. No 8 DT\664\1333EN.doc) PRODUCED BY TDIP AT THE EUROPEAN PARLIAMENT	N1HC	13/03/2005	FARNBOROUGH		UK	BANGALORE	INDIA										
346 HIGHLIGHTED BY THE REPORT (WORKING DOC. No 8 DT\664\1333EN.doc) PRODUCED BY TDIP AT THE EUROPEAN PARLIAMENT	N168BF	14/03/2005	FARNBOROUGH CIV		UK	CAIRO	EGYPT										
347 CONTRIBUTION OF THE RAPPORTEUR: RESEARCH ON THE PLANES USED BY THE CIA (EUROPEAN PARLIAMENT)	N50BH	02/04/2005	TETERBORO		USA	COVENTRY	UK										
348 HIGHLIGHTED BY THE REPORT (WORKING DOC. No 8 DT\664\1333EN.doc) PRODUCED BY TDIP AT THE EUROPEAN PARLIAMENT	N168BF	02/04/2005	TANGER/BOUKHALF		MOROCCO	LUTON	UK										
349 HIGHLIGHTED BY THE REPORT (WORKING DOC. No 8 DT\664\1333EN.doc) PRODUCED BY TDIP AT THE EUROPEAN PARLIAMENT	N50BH	03/04/2005	COVENTRY		UK	BANGOR	USA										
350 HIGHLIGHTED BY THE REPORT (WORKING DOC. No 8 DT\664\1333EN.doc) PRODUCED BY TDIP AT THE EUROPEAN PARLIAMENT	N168BF	08/04/2005	FARNBOROUGH CIV		UK	CASABLANCA ANFA	MOROCCO										
351 ANDREW TYRIE MP, APPG ON EXTRAORDINARY RENDITION	N816SJ	08/04/2005	GANDER INTL		CANADA	PRESTWICK	UK										
352 CONTRIBUTION OF THE RAPPORTEUR: RESEARCH ON THE PLANES USED BY THE CIA (EUROPEAN PARLIAMENT)	N816SJ	07/04/2005	PRESTWICK		UK	IRAKLION	GREECE										

A list of flights where the UK Government has been alerted to concerns regarding rendition through the UK, its Overseas Territories or the Crown Dependencies

No	SOURCE OF ALLEGATION	Serial No	Departure Date	Departure Time	Departure Location	Country	Arrival Location	Country	Arrival Time	Departure Date	Departure Time	Arrival Location	Country	Arrival Time
353	HIGHLIGHTED BY THE REPORT (WORKING DOC. No 8 DT9641333EN.doc) PRODUCED BY EDIP AT THE EUROPEAN PARLIAMENT	N1968BF	24/04/2005		FARNBOROUGH CIV	UK	CASABLANCA ANFA	MOROCCO						
354	CONTRIBUTION OF THE RAPPORTEUR: RESEARCH ON THE PLANES USED BY THE CIA (EUROPEAN PARLIAMENT)	N447BG	25/04/2005		DUBROVNIK	CROATIA	MANCHESTER	UK						
355	CONTRIBUTION OF THE RAPPORTEUR: RESEARCH ON THE PLANES USED BY THE CIA (EUROPEAN PARLIAMENT)	N1968BF	02/05/2005		CASABLANCA	MOROCCO	FARNBOROUGH	UK						
356	REPRIEVE REPORT 'SCOTTISH INVOLVEMENT IN EXORDINARY RENDITION'	N968BW	14/05/2005	11:20	WICK	ICELAND	REYKJAVIK	ICELAND	15:47					
357	CONTRIBUTION OF THE RAPPORTEUR: RESEARCH ON THE PLANES USED BY THE CIA (EUROPEAN PARLIAMENT)	N2560SK	14/05/2005		LONDONDERRY	UK	MALAGA	SPAIN						
358	JOURNALIST, SUNDAY TIMES	N129GS	18/05/2005		WASHINGTON	USA	RAF BRIZE NORTON	UK	9:00					
359	REPRIEVE REPORT 'SCOTTISH INVOLVEMENT IN EXTRAORDINARY RENDITION'	N400XL	20/05/2005	8:54	REYKJAVIK	ICELAND	WICK	UK	11:59					
360	REPRIEVE REPORT 'SCOTTISH INVOLVEMENT IN EXTRAORDINARY RENDITION'	N400XL	20/05/2005	11:04	REYKJAVIK	ICELAND	ABERDEEN	UK	-	20/05/2005	14:12	MUNICH	GERMANY	17:18
361	JOURNALIST, SUNDAY TIMES	N123GS	24/05/2005	14:00	RAF BRIZE NORTON	UK	STOCKHOLM	SWEDEN						
362	JOURNALIST, SUNDAY TIMES	N129GS	27/05/2005	12:00	RAF BRIZE NORTON	UK	STANSTEAD	UK						
363	JOURNALIST, SUNDAY TIMES	N123GS	27/05/2005		STOCKHOLM	SWEDEN	RAF BRIZE NORTON	UK	10.30					
364	ANDREW TYRIE MP. APPG ON EXTRAORDINARY RENDITION	N129GS	28/05/2005		STANSTED	UK	WASHINGTON	USA						
365	JOURNALIST, ITN	40085	09/06/2005		RAMSTEIN	UK	RAF NORTHOLT	UK	12:47					
366	EMILY WILSON, ITN	40085	07/06/2005	7:55	RAF NORTHOLT	UK	SARAJEVO	BOSNIA						
367	HIGHLIGHTED BY THE REPORT (WORKING DOC. No 8 DT9641333EN.doc) PRODUCED BY EDIP AT THE EUROPEAN PARLIAMENT	N1968BF	15/06/2005		FARNBOROUGH CIV	UK	CASABLANCA/MOHAMMED	MOROCCO						
368	HIGHLIGHTED BY THE REPORT (WORKING DOC. No 8 DT9641333EN.doc) PRODUCED BY EDIP AT THE EUROPEAN PARLIAMENT	N1968BF	18/06/2005		TANGER/BOUKHALF	MOROCCO	FARNBOROUGH CIV	UK						
369	SNP REPORT 'ALLEGED CIA AIRCRAFT FLYING INTO SCOTLAND'	N187D	20/06/2005		UNSPECIFIED	UK	EDINBURGH	UK						
370	ANDREW TYRIE MP. APPG ON EXTRAORDINARY RENDITION	N129GS	27/06/2005		LUTON	UK	TEL AVIV	ISRAEL						
371	CONTRIBUTION OF THE RAPPORTEUR: RESEARCH ON THE PLANES USED BY THE CIA (EUROPEAN PARLIAMENT)	N1968BF	24/08/2005		LJUBLJANA	SLOVENIA	EDINBURGH	UK						
372	CONTRIBUTION OF THE RAPPORTEUR: RESEARCH ON THE PLANES USED BY THE CIA (EUROPEAN PARLIAMENT)	N1968BF	25/08/2005		EDINBURGH	UK	GENEIVE	SWITZERLAND						
373	CONTRIBUTION OF THE RAPPORTEUR: RESEARCH ON THE PLANES USED BY THE CIA (EUROPEAN PARLIAMENT)	N1968BF	09/08/2005		MALMOE	SWEDEN	FARNBOROUGH	UK						
374	CONTRIBUTION OF THE RAPPORTEUR: RESEARCH ON THE PLANES USED BY THE CIA (EUROPEAN PARLIAMENT)	N1968BF	24/08/2005		FARNBOROUGH	UK	EAST MIDLANDS	UK						
375	CONTRIBUTION OF THE RAPPORTEUR: RESEARCH ON THE PLANES USED BY THE CIA (EUROPEAN PARLIAMENT)	N1968BF	24/08/2005		EAST MIDLANDS	UK	EDINBURGH	UK						
376	CONTRIBUTION OF THE RAPPORTEUR: RESEARCH ON THE PLANES USED BY THE CIA (EUROPEAN PARLIAMENT)	N1968BF	25/08/2005		EDINBURGH	UK	EAST MIDLANDS	UK						
377	CONTRIBUTION OF THE RAPPORTEUR: RESEARCH ON THE PLANES USED BY THE CIA (EUROPEAN PARLIAMENT)	N1968BF	26/08/2005		EAST MIDLANDS	UK	GENEIVE	SWITZERLAND						
378	CONTRIBUTION OF THE RAPPORTEUR: RESEARCH ON THE PLANES USED BY THE CIA (EUROPEAN PARLIAMENT)	N227BV	26/09/2005		FARMINGDALE	USA	RAF LEUCHARS	UK						
379	CONTRIBUTION OF THE RAPPORTEUR: RESEARCH ON THE PLANES USED BY THE CIA (EUROPEAN PARLIAMENT)	N1968BF	27/09/2005		LJUBLJANA	SLOVENIA	EDINBURGH	UK						
380	CONTRIBUTION OF THE RAPPORTEUR: RESEARCH ON THE PLANES USED BY THE CIA (EUROPEAN PARLIAMENT)	N1968BF	27/09/2005		EDINBURGH	UK	LONDON (UNSPECIFIED)	UK						
381	CONTRIBUTION OF THE RAPPORTEUR: RESEARCH ON THE PLANES USED BY THE CIA (EUROPEAN PARLIAMENT)	N1968BF	28/09/2005		LONDON (UNSPECIFIED)	UK	EDINBURGH	UK						
382	CONTRIBUTION OF THE RAPPORTEUR: RESEARCH ON THE PLANES USED BY THE CIA (EUROPEAN PARLIAMENT)	N1968BF	28/09/2005		EDINBURGH	UK	LONDON (UNSPECIFIED)	UK						
383	CONTRIBUTION OF THE RAPPORTEUR: RESEARCH ON THE PLANES USED BY THE CIA (EUROPEAN PARLIAMENT)	N1968BF	30/09/2005		LONDON (UNSPECIFIED)	UK	FARNBOROUGH	UK						
384	CONTRIBUTION OF THE RAPPORTEUR: RESEARCH ON THE PLANES USED BY THE CIA (EUROPEAN PARLIAMENT)	N227BV	03/10/2005		RAF LEUCHARS	UK	BEDFORD	USA						

A list of flights where the UK Government has been alerted to concerns regarding rendition through the UK, its Overseas Territories or the Crown Dependencies

	SOURCE OF ALLEGATION	Serial No	Departure Date	Departure Time	Departure Location	Country	Arrival Location	Country	Arrival Time	Departure Date	Departure Time	Arrival Location	Country	Arrival Time	Departure Date	Departure Time	Arrival Location	Country	Arrival Time
385	JOURNALIST: SUNDAY TIMES	N129QS	16/10/2005		CONNECTICUT	USA	LONDON (UNSPECIFIED)	UK	15:00										
386	JOURNALIST: SUNDAY TIMES	N129QS	17/10/2005	10:00	RAF BRIZE NORTON	UK	JEDDAH	SAUDI ARABIA											
387	CONTRIBUTION OF THE RAPPORTEUR: RESEARCH ON THE PLANES USED BY THE CIA (EUROPEAN PARLIAMENT)	N1HC	13/12/2005		WHITE PLAINS	USA	LONDON (UNSPECIFIED)	UK											
388	CONTRIBUTION OF THE RAPPORTEUR: RESEARCH ON THE PLANES USED BY THE CIA (EUROPEAN PARLIAMENT)	N1HC	13/12/2005		LONDON (UNSPECIFIED)	UK	FRANKFURT	GERMANY											
389	ANDREW TYRIE MP: APPG ON EXTRAORDINARY RENDITION	N129QS	15/12/2005		HEATHROW	UK	BARBADOS	BARBADOS											
390	CONTRIBUTION OF THE RAPPORTEUR: RESEARCH ON THE PLANES USED BY THE CIA (EUROPEAN PARLIAMENT)	N219BM	21/09/2003		PRESTWICK	UK	GANDER	CANADA											
391	CONTRIBUTION OF THE RAPPORTEUR: RESEARCH ON THE PLANES USED BY THE CIA (EUROPEAN PARLIAMENT)	N44982A	24/05/2004		REYKJAVIK	ICELAND	GLASGOW	UK											

(19)   Statement by the Defence Secretary, Rt Hon John Hutton MP, 26 February 2009

Records of Detention (Review Conclusions)

1.9 pm

The Secretary of State for Defence (Mr. John Hutton): Before I begin my statement, I should like to pay tribute to the three soldiers from 1st Battalion The Rifles who died on operations in Afghanistan yesterday, and to the Royal Marine from 45 Commando who died yesterday from wounds received earlier this month. Today is a sad day for our armed forces and a reminder of the exceptional challenge that our personnel meet with such extraordinary resolve every day. We owe our security to these brave servicemen and women, and I am sure that the whole House will join me in sending condolences to the families and friends of those whom we lost yesterday.

I wish to make a statement on the results of a recent Ministry of Defence review of records of detention resulting from security operations carried out by UK armed forces in Iraq and Afghanistan. It is, I believe, essential that our armed forces are able to detain people who pose a real threat to our troops, our allies or the local population whom we are seeking to protect. These operations are conducted by our forces with courage, integrity and professionalism. In undertaking them, we take fully into account our obligations under international law.

In February last year, allegations were made that persons captured by UK forces in Iraq were transferred to US detention facilities and were mistreated and removed unlawfully from Iraq. My predecessor, my right hon. Friend the Member for Kilmarnock and Loudoun (Des Browne), rightly launched a review, and much of the work was led personally by a very senior British Army general. My right hon. Friend was right to satisfy himself that appropriate procedures were in place to ensure that persons captured by UK forces and transferred to US detention in Iraq were treated in accordance with UK policy and legal requirements. Separately, he also set in hand work to examine all available documentary material relating to detention operations in Iraq and Afghanistan, and to review the parliamentary record.

The Ministry of Defence has now completed a detailed review of records of detention in Iraq and Afghanistan since the start of each campaign. I am today placing in the Library details of all detentions in southern Iraq in each year since 2003.

In Iraq, we have reviewed the record of detainee numbers listing all individuals held in UK detention facilities, first at the Shaibah logistics base and subsequently at the contingency operating base at Basra. In December 2003, when the facility at Shaibah was first opened, records show that 105 internees captured by UK forces were transferred into it from US custody at Camp Bucca. A further 19 were released at that stage. After December 2003, an additional 546 individuals were interned in these facilities. The majority, 491, were released once it was judged that they no longer represented an imperative threat to security, while 141 were transferred to the Iraqi authorities. A further 12 escaped, six were transferred to US detention facilities and, as hon. Members will know, one sadly died in custody.

In conducting this review, it became apparent that, in three parliamentary answers since February 2007, Ministers had overstated by approximately 1,000 the numbers of detainees held by UK forces in the period since January 2004. Nine further answers contained minor inaccuracies. I have written separately today to hon. Members setting the record straight, and I have also placed copies of the letters in the Library of the House. I want to apologise unreservedly for these inaccuracies.

We have also reviewed our records of detentions in the period from March to December 2003, when large numbers of individuals were captured by UK forces during the initial, high-intensity combat phase of the operation. Many of them were held for very short periods or were transferred to the US facility at Umm Qasr and then released. This facility was run by the UK from late March to mid-April 2003, at which point it was transferred to US control.

Given the circumstances in which the database was compiled, we cannot be confident that the data that we hold today are entirely complete. On a small number of occasions, answers or statements provided by my Department have included figures relating to the position in 2003 that indicated that we initially held up to 5,000 Iraqi prisoners during that period. However, a significant number of these were held on behalf of other coalition forces. We now believe that UK forces transferred around 3,000 individuals to the detention facility at Umm Qasr between March and December 2003, but I would ask the House to treat this figure as a best estimate.

In areas outside multinational division south east, UK forces have undertaken operations to capture individuals who were subsequently detained by the United States. These individuals do not feature in the data that I have set out today, but I want to reassure the House that the review has concluded that UK forces have exercised appropriately their responsibilities towards all captured personnel handed to US custody, whether in Multi-national Division (South-East) or elsewhere, and that it has uncovered no evidence of mistreatment.

During the final stages of the review of records of detentions, we found information about one case relating to a security operation conducted in February 2004. I am sure that hon. Members will recall that that period saw an increased level of insurgent activity as the transfer to Iraqi sovereignty drew closer. During the operation, two individuals were captured by UK forces in and around Baghdad. They were transferred to US detention, in accordance with normal practice, and subsequently moved to a US detention facility in Afghanistan.

This information was brought to my attention on 1 December 2008, and I instructed officials to investigate the case thoroughly and quickly so that I could bring a full account to Parliament. Following consultations with US authorities, we confirmed that they transferred the two individuals from Iraq to Afghanistan in 2004 and they remain in custody there today.

I regret that it is now clear that inaccurate information on this particular issue has been given to the House by my Department. However, I want to stress that that was based upon the information available to Ministers and those who were briefing them at that time. My predecessors as Secretaries of State for Defence have confirmed to me that they had no knowledge of these events. I have written to the hon. Members concerned correcting the record, and am placing a copy of these letters also in the Library of the House. Again, I want to apologise to the House for these errors.

The individuals transferred to Afghanistan are members of Lashkar-e-Taiba, a proscribed organisation with links to al-Qaeda. The US Government have explained to us that those individuals were moved to Afghanistan because of a lack of relevant linguists to interrogate them effectively in Iraq. The US has categorised them as unlawful enemy combatants and continues to review their status on a regular basis. We have been assured that the detainees are held in a humane, safe and secure environment that meets international standards that are consistent with cultural and religious norms. The International Committee of the Red Cross has had regular access to the detainees.

A due diligence search by US officials of the list of all those individuals captured by UK forces and transferred to US detention facilities in Iraq has confirmed that this was the only case in which individuals were subsequently transferred outside Iraq. This review has established that officials were aware of the transfer in early 2004. It has also shown that brief references to this case were included in lengthy papers that went to the then Foreign Secretary and the Home Secretary in April 2006. It is clear that the context provided did not highlight its significance at that point to my right hon. Friends.

In retrospect, it is clear to me that the transfer to Afghanistan of these two individuals should have been questioned at the time. We have discussed the issues surrounding this case with the US Government. They have reassured us about their treatment but confirmed that, as the individuals continue to represent significant security concerns, it is neither possible nor desirable to transfer them to either their country of detention or their country of origin. The UK no longer has power to detain suspects in Iraq, and only limited powers of detention in Afghanistan.

For Afghanistan, robust checks have confirmed that we have detailed and precise numbers of all those detained by UK forces since we deployed Task Force Helmand in July 2006. As of 31 December 2008, our database holds the capture details of 479 individuals, including 254 who were subsequently transferred to the authority of the Government of Afghanistan, 217 who were released, and eight who died as a result of injuries sustained on the battlefield.

We hold capture details relating to a total of a further seven individuals detained by UK forces between 2001 and April 2006, and I believe that this represents a complete record. I am also placing the complete details of the detainee numbers for Afghanistan in the Library of the House.

Our detention operations in Iraq and Afghanistan are underpinned by arrangements with our international partners. We have a memorandum of understanding in place with the Government of Afghanistan, signed on 23 April 2006, covering the treatment of individuals detained by UK forces and transferred to Afghan custody. We also have a memorandum of understanding with Iraq, agreed on 8 November 2004, on the treatment of detainees transferred to Iraqi custody. Iraqi Interior, Justice and Defence Ministers have confirmed to us that Iraqi detention procedures remain consistent with the principles set out in that memorandum of understanding.

For the initial stages of the campaign in Iraq, we also had in place a memorandum of understanding with the US and Australian Governments covering arrangements for the treatment and transfer of detainees. We worked on the mutual understanding that the key provisions of the memorandum of understanding continued to apply until it was replaced last year by a further memorandum of understanding with the US. We have also confirmed with the US that the provisions on arrangements for the treatment and transfer of captured prisoners remain under the new legal framework in Iraq and that no person captured with assistance from UK forces will be removed from the territory of Iraq without prior consultation with the UK.

Let me make a final observation. We ask our armed forces to operate in highly dangerous environments, where there is often a limit to the capacity of local agencies to enforce security and the rule of law. In those circumstances, it is essential that we provide our forces with the authority and capabilities to deal effectively with individuals who represent a serious threat to our troops or those they are there to protect; the two detainees to whom I referred earlier fall into that category. We recognise the sensitivity of detention operations. We have put in place rigorous safeguards to ensure that detainees are treated properly. We will continue to carry out detention operations in accordance with our legal and policy obligations, in concert with the US and other allies. This is, and will remain, absolutely central to the way our armed forces conduct these vital operations.

(20) Statement by the Prime Minister, Rt Hon David Cameron MP, 6 July 2010

Treatment of Detainees

3.32 pm

The Prime Minister (Mr David Cameron): I am sure that the whole House will wish to join me in paying tribute to the Royal Marine who died on Thursday, the soldier from the Royal Dragoon Guards who died yesterday, and the soldier from 1st Battalion the Mercian Regiment who died from wounds sustained in Afghanistan in Birmingham yesterday. We should constantly remember the service and the sacrifices made on our behalf by our armed forces and their families, keep them in our thoughts and prayers and thank them for what they do on our behalf.

With permission, Mr Speaker, I would like to make a statement on our intelligence services and allegations made about the treatment of detainees. For the past few years, the reputation of our security services has been overshadowed by allegations about their involvement in the treatment of detainees held by other countries. Some of those detainees allege that they were mistreated by those countries. Other allegations have also been made about the UK's involvement in the rendition of detainees in the aftermath of 9/11. Those allegations are not proven, but today we face a totally unacceptable situation. Our services are paralysed by paperwork as they try to defend themselves in lengthy court cases with uncertain rules. Our reputation as a country that believes in human rights, justice, fairness and the rule of law-indeed, much of what the services exist to protect-risks being tarnished. Public confidence is being eroded, with people doubting the ability of our services to protect us and questioning the rules under which they operate. And terrorists and extremists are able to exploit those allegations for their own propaganda.

I myself, the Deputy Prime Minister and the coalition Government all believe that it is time to clear up this matter once and for all, so today I want to set out how we will deal with the problems of the past, how we will sort out the future and, crucially, how we can make sure that the security services are able to get on and do their job to keep us safe. But first, let us be clear about the work that they do. I believe that we have the finest intelligence services in the world. In the past, it was the intelligence services that cracked the secrets of Enigma and helped deliver victory in world war two. They recruited Russian spies such as

Gordievsky and Mitrokhin, and kept Britain safe in the cold war. They helped disrupt the Provisional IRA in the 1980s and 1990s.

Today, these tremendous acts of bravery continue. Every day, intelligence officers track terrorist threats and disrupt plots. They prevent the world's most dangerous weapons from falling into the hands of the world's most dangerous states. And they give our forces in Afghanistan the information that they need to take key decisions. They do this without any public-or, often, even private-recognition, and despite the massive personal risks to their safety.

We should never forget that some officers have died for this country. Their names are not known; their loved ones must mourn in secret. The service that they have given to our country is not publicly recognised. We owe them, and every intelligence officer in our country, an enormous debt of gratitude. As Minister for the intelligence services, I am determined to do everything possible to help them get on with the job that they trained to do and that we desperately need them to do.

However, to do that, we need to resolve the issues of the past. While there is no evidence that any British officer was directly engaged in torture in the aftermath of 9/11, there are questions over the degree to which British officers were working with foreign security services who were treating detainees in ways they should not have done. About a dozen cases have been brought in court about the actions of UK personnel-including, for example, that since 9/11 they may have witnessed mistreatment such as the use of hoods and shackles. This has led to accusations that Britain may have been complicit in the mistreatment of detainees. The longer these questions remain unanswered, the bigger will grow the stain on our reputation as a country that believes in freedom, fairness and human rights.

That is why I am determined to get to the bottom of what happened. The intelligence services are also keen publicly to establish their principles and integrity. So we will have a single, authoritative examination of all these issues. We cannot start that inquiry while criminal investigations are ongoing, and it is not feasible to start it while so many civil law suits remain unresolved. So we want to do everything that we can to help that process along. That is why we are committed to mediation with those who have brought civil claims about their detention in Guantanamo. And wherever appropriate, we will offer compensation.

As soon as we have made enough progress, an independent inquiry, led by a judge, will be held. It will look at whether Britain was implicated in the improper treatment of detainees, held by other countries, that may have occurred in the aftermath of 9/11. The inquiry will need to look at the relevant Government Departments and intelligence services. Should we have realised sooner that what foreign agencies were doing may have been unacceptable and that we should not have been associated with it? Did we allow our own high standards to slip, either systemically or individually? Did we give clear enough guidance to officers in the field? Was information flowing quickly enough from officers on the ground to the intelligence services and then on to Ministers, so that we knew what was going on and what our response should have been?

We should not be for one moment naive or starry-eyed about the circumstances under which our security services were working in the immediate aftermath of 9/11. There was a real danger that terrorists could get their hands on a dirty bomb, chemical or biological weapons, or even worse. Threat levels had been transformed. The urgency with which we needed to protect our citizens was pressing. But let me state clearly that we need to know the answers, if things went wrong, why, and what we must do to uphold the standards that people expect. I have asked the right hon. Sir Peter Gibson, former senior Court of Appeal judge and currently the statutory commissioner for the intelligence services, to lead the inquiry. The three-member inquiry team will also include Dame Janet Paraskeva, head of the Civil Service Commissioners, and Peter Riddell, former journalist and senior fellow at the Institute for Government.

I have today made public a letter to the inquiry chair setting out what the inquiry will cover, so Sir Peter Gibson can finalise the details with us before it starts. We hope that it will start before the end of this year and report within a year. This inquiry cannot and will not be costly or open-ended; that would serve neither the interests of justice nor national security. Neither can it be a full public inquiry. Of course, some of its hearings will be in public. However, we must be realistic; inquiries into our intelligence services are not like other inquiries. Some information must be kept secret-information about sources, capabilities and partnerships. Let us be frank: it is not possible to have a full public inquiry into something that is meant to be secret. So any intelligence material provided to the inquiry panel will not be made public, and nor will intelligence officers be asked to give evidence in public.

But that does not mean we cannot get to the bottom of what happened. The inquiry will be able to look at all the information relevant to its work, including secret information; it will have access to all relevant Government papers, including those held by the intelligence services; and it will be able to take evidence-in public-including from those who have brought accusations against the Government, and their representatives and interest groups. Importantly, the head of the civil service and the intelligence services will ensure that the inquiry gets the full co-operation it needs from Departments and agencies. So I am confident the inquiry will reach an authoritative view on the actions of the state and our services, and make proper recommendations for the future.

Just as we are determined to resolve the problems of the past, so we are determined to have greater clarity about what is and what is not acceptable in the future. That is why today we are also publishing the guidance issued to intelligence and military personnel on how to deal with detainees held by other countries. The previous Government had promised to do this, but did not, and we are doing it today. It makes clear the following: first, our services must never take any action where they know or believe that torture will occur; secondly, if they become aware of abuses by other countries, they should report it to the UK Government so we can try to stop it; and thirdly, in cases where our services believe that there may be information crucial to saving lives but where there may also be a serious risk of mistreatment, it is for Ministers, rightly, to determine the action, if any, that our services should take. My right hon. Friends the Foreign Secretary, Home Secretary and Defence Secretary have also today laid in the House further information about their roles in those difficult cases.

There is something else we have to address, and that is how court cases deal with intelligence information. Today, there are serious problems. The services cannot disclose anything that is secret in order to defend themselves in court with confidence that that information will be protected. There are also doubts about our ability to protect the secrets of our allies and stop them ending up in the public domain. This has strained some of our oldest and most important security partnerships in the world-in particular, that with America. Hon. Members should not underestimate the vast two-way benefit this US-UK relationship has brought in disrupting terrorist plots and saving lives.

So we need to deal with these problems. We hope that the Supreme Court will provide further clarity on the underlying law within the next few months. And next year, we will publish a Green Paper which will set out our proposals for how intelligence is treated in the full range of judicial proceedings, including addressing the concerns of our allies. In this process, the Government will seek the views of the cross-party Intelligence and Security Committee. I can announce today that I have appointed my right hon. and learned Friend the Member for Kensington (Sir Malcolm Rifkind) as the Chair of that Committee for the duration of this Parliament.

As we meet in the relative safety of this House today, let us not forget this: as we speak, al-Qaeda operatives in Yemen are meeting in secret to plot attacks against us; terrorists are preparing to attack our forces in Afghanistan; the Real IRA is planning its next strike against security forces in Northern Ireland; and rogue regimes are still trying to acquire nuclear weapons. At the same time, men and women, young and old, all of them loyal and dedicated, are getting ready to work again around the world. They will be meeting sources, translating documents, listening in on conversations, replaying CCTV footage, installing cameras, following terrorists-all to keep us safe from these threats. We cannot have their work impeded by these allegations, and we need to restore Britain's moral leadership in the world. That is why we are determined to clear things up, and why I commend this statement to the House.

Parliamentary reports

21. Intelligence and Security Committee, 'Report on the Handling of Detainees by UK Intelligence Personnel in Afghanistan, Guantánamo Bay and Iraq', March 2005 (extracts)—p.272

This report by the ISC relates to the incident in January 2002 which triggered guidance (see Document 30) being sent to British intelligence officers which the Committee viewed as inadequate. It also argues that the maltreatment of suspects tended to be viewed as a series of isolated incidents. The report further records the intelligence services' awareness of prisoners being held in unknown locations, and their belief that valuable intelligence was being gained from them.

22. Foreign Affairs Select Committee, 'Foreign Policy Aspects of the War Against Terrorism', April 2005 (extracts)—p.276

With interest in the rendition issue starting to stir, and in advance of the revelations at the end of the year concerning the CIA's secret prisons, the Foreign Affairs Committee was sharply critical of the government's stance of 'obfuscation'.

23. Joint Committee on Human Rights, Nineteenth Report of 2005-06, 'The UN Convention Against Torture', May 2006 (extracts)—p.277

The Committee addressed the question of the UK's international obligations, notably under the Convention Against Torture, and the role of the Chicago Convention with respect to flights landing within the UK and also those transiting through UK airspace.

24. Intelligence and Security Committee, 'Report on Rendition', July 2007 (extracts)—p.283

These paragraphs summarise the conclusions of the ISC's report on rendition. The report painted a picture of poor record-keeping, concerns over the handling of individual cases and British authorities generally slow to grasp the change to a more aggressive US policy. However, subsequent disclosures – notably concerning Diego Garcia (Document 17) and the Binyam Mohamed case (Documents 37 and 38) – made clear that the Committee's account was inaccurate and severely incomplete.

(21) Intelligence and Security Committee, 'Report on the Handling of Detainees by UK Intelligence Personnel in Afghanistan, Guantánamo Bay and Iraq', March 2005 (extracts)

[...]

46. On 10 January 2002, the first day that the SIS had access to US-held detainees, an SIS officer conducted an interview of a detainee. Whilst he was satisfied that there was nothing during the interview which could have been a breach of the Geneva Conventions, he reported back to London his:

> "... *observations on the circumstances of the handling of* [the] *detainee by the US military before the beginning of the interview.* ***
> ***
> ***.
> ***
> ***
> ***."[11]

47. These comments raised concerns about the US treatment of detainees and the following day – 11 January 2002 – instructions were sent to the SIS officer and copied to all SIS and Security Service officers in Afghanistan, as follows:

> "With regard to the status of the prisoners, under the various Geneva Conventions and protocols, all prisoners, however they are described, are entitled to the same levels of protection. You have commented on their treatment. It appears from your description that they may not be being treated in accordance with the appropriate standards. Given that they are not within our custody or control, the law does not require you to intervene to prevent this. That said, HMG's stated commitment to human rights makes it important that the Americans understand that we cannot be party to such ill treatment nor can we be seen to condone it. In no case should they be coerced during or in conjunction with an SIS interview of them. If circumstances allow, you should consider drawing this to the attention of a suitably senior US official locally.

---

[11] *Letter from the SIS to the Intelligence and Security Committee, 24 September 2004*

It is important that you do not engage in any activity yourself that involves inhumane or degrading treatment of prisoners. As a representative of a UK public authority, you are obliged to act in accordance with the Human Rights Act 2000 which prohibits torture, or inhumane or degrading treatment. Also as a Crown Servant, you are bound by Section 31 of the Criminal Justice Act 1948, which makes acts carried out overseas in the course of your official duties subject to UK criminal law. In other words, your actions incur criminal liability in the same way as if you were carrying out those acts in the UK."

48. Following receipt of these instructions, the SIS officer in Afghanistan took no further action and the SIS informed us that while he remained in Afghanistan for a further three weeks, he did not witness any further instances of this kind. The SIS told us that they regarded this as an isolated incident. Ministers were not informed about this incident until July 2004.

49. However, from January 2002 the Security Service ensured that all officers involved in interviews of detainees were briefed individually by a senior manager prior to their deployments.

50. There are many lessons to be learnt from this episode. The SIS officer correctly reported his observations and SIS headquarters responded promptly with instructions. But these instructions did not go far enough: they should have required the SIS officer to report his concerns to the senior US official. They should also have required all officers to report any similar matters in the future to both the US authorities and to their respective headquarters in the UK. Furthermore, the Foreign Secretary should have been informed immediately that an officer had reported that a serious potential abuse by the US military had occurred and that instructions had, as a consequence, been issued to all deployed staff from the SIS and Security Service.

51. As we have previously noted, the UK regarded all the detainees as subject to the provisions of the Geneva Conventions. However, on 7 February 2002 the US President stated as US policy that the Geneva Conventions did not apply to the conflict with Al Qaeda. He continued that, although the Conventions did apply to the conflict with Afghanistan, the Taliban were unlawful combatants and therefore did not qualify for prisoner of war status. The President, however, ordered that detainees were to be treated *"humanely and, to the extent appropriate and consistent with military necessity, in a manner consistent with the principles of Geneva".*

52. We have been told that in March 2002 an SIS officer in Afghanistan was told *** *** .
The SIS officer returned the matter back to London but no action was taken either locally or by the SIS in London. Again we were told that this was because it was regarded as an isolated incident. Ministers were not informed of this matter until August 2004.

274

53. In April 2002 *"an SIS officer was present at an interview conducted by the US military of a detainee in Afghanistan who complained of time in isolation and who had previously had a nervous breakdown. The detainee was aware that he was in isolation for his own protection ****
***. The SIS officer asked the US officer in charge of the interview for better treatment"[12] but we were told that he was unable to follow up the situation. Ministers were not told about this event until August 2004.

54. In June 2002, the Security Service discussed with FCO officials a US report that referred to the hooding, withholding of blankets and sleep deprivation of a detainee in Afghanistan. The matter was raised promptly with the US authorities, although there is no record that any further action was taken or that the matter was pursued by either the Security Service or the FCO. The Security Service has stated that the general terms of this report were raised with Ministers in late 2002 (although no Minister has confirmed this) and the specifics of the case were not drawn to Ministers' attention until June 2004.

55. In July 2002, a Security Service officer reported to senior management that whilst in Afghanistan a US official had referred to *"getting a detainee ready"*, which appeared to involve sleep deprivation, hooding and the use of stress positions. The officer reported that they had commented to the US official that this was inappropriate but that the Security Service's senior management took no further action. We were told that this was primarily because the report was based on second-hand information and the Security Service had raised the general point the previous month. The detainee, when re-interviewed later that month, provided a list of grievances, which included the use of constant bright lights. The Security Service officer raised the complaints with the US officer in charge of the facility at the time but no further follow-up action was taken. Ministers were not informed about this case until June 2004.

[...]

"Ghost Prisoners"

77. Concern has been raised by the media and human rights organisations about the treatment and welfare of the so-called "*ghost prisoners*". These are individuals that the US authorities are holding at undisclosed locations under unknown conditions and to whom the International Committee of the Red Cross does not have access. The US authorities authorised the 9/11 Commission to identify 10 of these individuals,[19] as the product of their interrogations was key to the Commission's report. We asked the UK Agencies if they had any knowledge of these individuals and whether they had interviewed them or received intelligence from them.

78. The Security Service made the following comments, which are shared by the SIS:

"*Clearly the US is holding some Al Qaida members in detention, other than at Guantanamo, but we do not know the locations or terms of their detention and do not have access to them. The US authorities are under no obligation to disclose to us details of all their detainees and there would be no reason for them to do so unless there is a clear link to the UK. We have however received intelligence of the highest value from detainees, to whom we have not had access and whose location is unknown to us, some of which has led to the frustration of terrorist attacks in the UK or against UK interests.*"

[...]

---

[19] *Khalid Sheikh Mohammed, Abu Zubaydah, Riduuan Isamuddin (also known as Hambali), Abd al Rahim al Nashiri, Tawfiq bin Attash (also known as Khallad), Ramzi Binalshibh, Mohamed al Kahtani, Ahmad Khalil Ibrahim Samir al Ani, Ali Abd al Rahman al Faqasi al Ghamdi (also known as Abu Bakr al Azdi) and Hassan Ghul*

(22) Foreign Affairs Select Committee, 'Foreign Policy Aspects of the War Against Terrorism', April 2005 (extracts)

[...]

Rendition of terrorist suspects

96. On 25 February, we wrote to the FCO about extraordinary rendition. We asked the Government:

- whether the United Kingdom has used extraordinary rendition or any other practice of sending suspects to third countries for interrogation;

- whether the United Kingdom has allowed any other country to use its territory or its airspace for such purposes or received information which has been gained using these methods; and

- whether the Government regards the use of such methods as (a) legally and (b) morally acceptable?

97. In its response to this letter, the Government told us:

> The British Government's policy is not to deport or extradite any person to another state where there are substantial grounds to believe that the person will be subject to torture or where there is a real risk that the death penalty will be applied. Whether rendition is contrary to international law depends on the particular circumstances of each case. We encourage all members of the international community to respect international law and human rights standards... The British Government is not aware of the use of its territory or airspace for the purposes of "extraordinary rendition". The British Government has not received any requests, nor granted any permissions, for the use of UK territory or airspace for such purposes... As you will be aware, this issue was the subject of a comprehensive inquiry by the Intelligence and Security Committee, whose report (CM6469) has just been published. Ministers have also answered a number of Parliamentary questions on this.

This response does not provide a satisfactory answer to our questions. Similarly, parliamentary questions put by a Member of this Committee have met with obfuscation.

98. **We conclude that the Government has failed to deal with questions about extraordinary rendition with the transparency and accountability required on so serious an issue. If the Government believes that extraordinary rendition is a valid tool in the war against terrorism, it should say so openly and transparently, so that it may be held accountable. We recommend that the Government end its policy of obfuscation and that it give straight answers to the Committee's questions of 25 February.**

[...]

(23)   Joint Committee on Human Rights, Nineteenth Report of 2005-06, 'The UN Convention Against Torture', May 2006 (extracts)

[...]

8   Extraordinary Renditions

[...]

Human rights compliance

156. In regard to extraordinary renditions, as elsewhere, compliance with the Convention against Torture and other human rights standards requires more than passive non-

cooperation in torture; it requires active investigative and law enforcement action to prevent torture or inhuman and degrading treatment. Credible allegations that UK airports or airspace is being used to render suspects to face torture engage the UK's positive obligations to prevent and investigate acts of torture under UNCAT, as well as under Article 3 of the European Convention on Human Rights, given force in domestic law by the Human Rights Act,[217] and under the customary international law prohibition on torture.

157. Under Article 3 of UNCAT, there is an obligation not to return anyone to a country where there are substantial grounds to consider that they will face a real risk of torture; this is reflected by similar obligations under Article 3 ECHR[218] and Article 7 ICCPR.[219] This obligation is also likely to apply where an individual is "rendered" through the UK by foreign intelligence agents, to face such a risk of torture outside the UK.[220]

158. Liberty and JUSTICE further suggest that extraordinary renditions may in themselves amount to torture, since "detaining someone where the detainee is aware that the purpose of the detention is to bring him to a place where he will be subjected to physical torture might in itself amount to torture as it will undoubtedly inflict severe mental suffering on the detainee".[221] This argument relies on an analogy with the case of *Soering v UK*, where it was held that the prolonged wait for the death penalty known as the "death row phenomenon", amounted to inhuman and degrading treatment in breach of Article 3 ECHR.

159. The Convention places a number of specific duties on states to investigate allegations of torture, both within the jurisdiction, and elsewhere. Under Article 12, there is a duty to investigate wherever there are reasonable grounds to suspect that an act of torture has been committed in the jurisdiction. Under Article 6, where persons alleged to have committed offences of torture or complicity in torture are present in the territory of the State, there is an obligation to take the suspect into custody or otherwise secure his presence in the territory, and make a preliminary inquiry into the facts, with a view to either prosecution or extradition in accordance with Article 7.[222] Therefore, the effect of UNCAT is that where there are credible allegations that an aircraft present at a UK airport is involved in the transport of a suspect to torture, or that persons present on the aircraft are involved in the transfer of suspects to torture, there is an obligation to conduct a preliminary investigation into its involvement in any possible offences of torture. Where this preliminary investigation unearths sufficient information to justify arrests, there is an obligation to prevent the aircraft from leaving UK territory, and to arrest any suspects present on the

---

217 *Soering v UK* (1989) 11 EHRR 439; *Chahal v UK* (1997) 23 EHRR 413;

218 *Chahal v UK, op. cit.*

219 Liberty, JUSTICE and REDRESS argue in their evidence that this obligation will be breached where the UK permits a transfer to torture by foreign agents through the UK.

220 See the comments of the Venice Commission (The Council of Europe Commission on Democracy through Law, Opinion on the International Legal Obligations of Council of Europe Member States in Respect of Secret Detention Facilities and Inter-State Transport of Prisoners, 17 March 2006, CDL-AD (2006) 009

221 Ev 159–169

222 Article 5.2 UNCAT provides for universal jurisdiction over crimes of torture, stipulating that states must establish jurisdiction over offences of torture, including complicity and participation in torture, and attempted torture, where the alleged offender is present within the jurisdiction, irrespective of where the offence has occurred.

aircraft. Where there is sufficient evidence, the suspects must be either prosecuted, or extradited.

The Chicago Convention

160. The principal international treaty which regulates civil aviation is the Chicago Convention on International Civil Aviation 1944 (The Chicago Convention). Under the Convention, if extraordinary rendition aircraft are identified as state aircraft, then in order to fly through UK airspace, or land at UK airports, they require prior authorisation, and must abide by the terms of such authorisation (Article 3(d)). If extraordinary rendition aircraft are identified as civil aircraft, then under Article 5 of the Chicago Convention, they must be permitted to fly through UK airspace and to stop for refuelling or other similar ("non-traffic") purposes at UK airports, without obtaining prior permission. However, the Chicago Convention expressly permits State authorities to search the aircraft on landing or departure, and to inspect relevant certificates and other documents relating to the aircraft (Article 16). Under Article 23, these include the journey log book of the aircraft, a list of passengers, their names and places of embarkation and destination, and a detailed description of any cargo. There is therefore nothing in the Convention which would prevent a police search of a civil aircraft stopped for refuelling at a UK airport, or the arrest of persons aboard the aircraft who were suspected of crimes of torture.

161. Furthermore, Article 4 of the Chicago Convention stipulates that states must not use civil aviation for any purpose inconsistent with the overall aims of the Convention.[223] Civil flights established to be transporting suspects to torture would be likely to be considered inconsistent with the aims of the Convention, and therefore outside its protection, in particular given the need to interpret and apply the Convention in light of the UK's obligations under UNCAT and under customary international law. Given the status of the prohibition on torture as a norm of higher international law or *jus cogens*, an interpretation of the Chicago Convention which permitted free passage to aircraft known to be involved in renditions to torture would be likely to render the relevant provisions of the Chicago Convention inapplicable, since under the Vienna Convention on the Law of Treaties, a treaty which conflicts with a norm of *jus cogens* is void.[224]

Status of Aircraft

162. The status of aircraft alleged to be used in extraordinary renditions, as either State or civil aircraft, is unclear. The question is significant, since a State aircraft, though it will require permission to land in the UK, will not be subject to search by UK authorities, except by agreement. Whether an aircraft is classified as State or civil may depend on the nature of the aircraft. Where it is a military aircraft or lands at a military base for example, its status as a civil aircraft may be open to question. The Venice Commission on Democracy through Law, in its recent legal opinion on renditions, considered that where an aircraft, chartered by agents of a foreign State, represents itself as a civil aircraft, then it forfeits the right to claim State aircraft status under the Chicago Convention as well as the

---

223 The Preamble to the Convention notes that development of international civil aviation can "create and preserve friendship and understanding among the nations and peoples of the world" whilst its abuse can "become a threat to the general security" and states the Convention's aim to develop international civil aviation in a "safe and orderly manner."

224 Vienna Convention on the Law of Treaties, Article 53 and Article 64

right to state immunity.[225] It nevertheless considered that aircraft presenting themselves as State aircraft would enjoy immunity and could not be searched.[226] The Secretary General of the Council of Europe, in a recent Report on these matters, recommended clarification of the law on human rights exceptions to State immunity, and co-operation between the Governments of Council of Europe states to achieve this.[227]

The Government view

163. Although there has been some confusion as to the effect of international civil aviation law on the Government and police powers to investigate allegations of extraordinary rendition, it now appears to be accepted that the current law creates no barrier to investigation. Initial Government suggestions that the Chicago Convention prevented investigation of the matter[228] were later withdrawn. At report stage debates on the Civil Aviation Bill in the House of Lords, in response to amendments tabled by Baroness D'Souza which would have provided for express powers to require aircraft to land, and to board and search aircraft where they were suspected of involvement in extraordinary rendition, Lord Davies of Oldham argued that the amendments were unnecessary since such powers already existed under international civil aviation law. He stated:

> The Chicago Convention is clear on this. We certainly have the right to investigate an aircraft, but, of course, we have to have good grounds for doing so. If credible intelligence of serious illegal activity comes to light regarding an aircraft in flight, the Government can certainly require the aircraft to land. Article 3 of the Chicago Convention allows states to require aircraft to land if there are reasonable grounds to conclude that the aircraft is being used for any purpose that is inconsistent with the aims of the Convention.
>
> If the aircraft is on the ground the control authorities—police, Customs and immigration—have a variety of powers to enter, take evidence and make arrests.[229]

164. In evidence to us, Ms Harman accepted there was an obligation to investigate allegations of flights transporting individuals to torture. She further accepted that the Chicago Convention should not "be a shield behind which acts preparatory to torture should take place".[230] She considered that the primary duty of investigation lay with the police, rather than with central government.[231] **We welcome the Government's acceptance that international civil aviation law permits thorough investigation of civil flights alleged to be involved in extraordinary rendition.**

---

225 Venice Commission legal opinion, *op. cit.*, para 103 and para 148

226 *Ibid.*, para 149

227 Secretary General's report under Article 52 ECHR on the question of secret detention and transport of detainees suspected of terrorist acts, 28 February 2006, SG/Inf (2006) 5, para 71

228 HL Deb., 12 October 2005, col 376

229 HL Deb, 8 March 2006, col 844

230 Q 165

231 Q 168

165. The Government's position has been that whilst in principle it would be willing to investigate where there is evidence of extraordinary renditions passing through the UK, at present there is no such evidence.[232] It does not consider information that aircraft landing in the UK can be demonstrated to have been previously involved in extraordinary renditions, to be sufficient in itself to warrant further investigation. Mr Ingram stated, in respect of the aircraft disclosed to have landed at RAF bases: "there is no evidence to show that any of those aircraft were carrying any passengers of the type [alleged to be transported in renditions]".[233] Baroness Ashton of Upholland confirmed the Government's view that there was "no basis for further action".[234]

Conclusions

166. One obstacle to obtaining clear evidence that a particular flight is transporting a detainee as part of a rendition is the current lack of a requirement for chartered civil aircraft passing through the UK to provide lists of passengers on board. Ms Harman confirmed that such information was not required or recorded.[235] We note, however, that there is nothing in the Chicago Convention which would prevent the UK from requiring transiting civil aircraft to provide such information. Given the potential for abuse of free passage for civil aircraft under the Chicago Convention, by aircraft involved in extraordinary renditions, **we recommend that the Government should take steps to require staff and passenger lists to be provided to the UK authorities when chartered civil aircraft land at UK airports, or transit UK airspace. In the long term, if effective unilateral Government action is not taken, there would be a case for amendment of the Chicago Convention, to require the provision of passenger lists.**

167. In relation to the question of whether there have been extraordinary renditions in the past few years using UK airspace or airports, and the extent to which the Government should initiate an investigation, we note that the Government has recently rejected the view of the House of Commons Foreign Affairs Committee that it is under a duty to enquire into the allegations of extraordinary rendition and black sites under the Convention against Torture. In its response to the Foreign Affairs Committee's Annual Report on Human Rights for 2005, the Government states that a "search of all relevant records" has not found any evidence of detainees being rendered through UK airspace since 11 September 2001, and that in the absence of such evidence it does not consider that there is a requirement under Article 12 UNCAT for it to carry out a further investigation.[236] This accords with the Government's view expressed in evidence to us, as described above.

168. We consider that there is now a reasonable suspicion that certain aircraft passing through the UK may have been carrying suspects to countries where they may have faced torture, or to have been returning from rendering suspects to such countries. This reasonable suspicion is in our view sufficient to trigger the duty to investigate, and to look

---

232 Lord Davies of Oldham, report stage debate on Civil Aviation Bill, *op. cit*; Rt Hon Adam Ingram MP, Qq 236–270; DCA Qq 137–180

233 Q 251

234 Ev 85–88

235 Q 180

236 Response of the Secretary of State for Foreign and Commonwealth Affairs to the First Report from the Foreign Affairs Committee, Session 2005–06, *Annual Report on Human Rights 2005*, Cm 6774, paras 27 and 28

behind the assurances received from foreign Governments. It follows that we do not accept the Government's view that, by the means described in its response to the Foreign Affairs Committee, it has adequately demonstrated that it has satisfied the obligation under domestic and international human rights law to investigate credible allegations of renditions of suspects through the UK to face torture abroad. In order to satisfy the obligation to investigate in relation to possible renditions to face torture which may already have taken place, we believe the Government should now take active steps to ascertain more details about the flights which it is now known used UK airports, including, in relation to each flight, who was on them, and their precise itinerary and the purpose of their journey. If evidence of extraordinary renditions come to light from such investigations, the Government should report such evidence promptly to Parliament.

169. We recognise that there are growing calls for an independent public inquiry into alleged use of UK airports in extraordinary renditions, and that the piecemeal way in which information has so far reached the public domain does not inspire confidence in the Government's willingness to investigate, but nevertheless we consider that such an inquiry would be premature. Whether a public inquiry is necessary should be determined in light of the extent to which inquiries by the Government leads to the publication of the detailed information required.

170. For the future, in addition to the steps which the Government has taken to make its position on extraordinary renditions clear to the United States authorities,[237] we believe the Government should establish a clear policy as to the action to be taken in cases where aircraft alleged to have been previously involved in renditions transit the UK. Where there are credible allegations arising from previous records that a particular civil aircraft transiting UK airspace has been involved in renditions, and where the aircraft is travelling to or from a country known to practise torture or inhuman or degrading treatment, it should be required to land. Where such an aircraft lands at a UK airport for refuelling or similar purposes, it should be required to provide a full list of all those on board, both staff and passengers. On landing, it should be boarded and searched by the police, and the identity of all those on board verified. Wherever appropriate, a criminal investigation should be initiated. Where an aircraft suspected of involvement in extraordinary renditions identifies itself as a state aircraft, it should not be permitted to transit UK airspace, in the absence of permission for UK authorities to search the aircraft. We consider that these steps are not only permitted by the current law, but required to ensure full compliance with the Convention Against Torture.

---

237 *Ibid.*, para 29

[...]

(24) Intelligence and Security Committee, 'Report on Rendition', July 2007 (extracts)

[...]

SUMMARY OF CONCLUSIONS AND RECOMMENDATIONS

A.   Our intelligence-sharing relationships, particularly with the United States, are critical to providing the breadth and depth of intelligence coverage required to counter the threat to the UK posed by global terrorism. These relationships have saved lives and must continue.

B.   We are concerned that Government departments have had such difficulty in establishing the facts from their own records in relation to requests to conduct renditions through UK airspace. These are matters of fundamental liberties and the Government should ensure that proper searchable records are kept.

C.   Prior to 9/11, assistance to the U.S. "Rendition to Justice" programme – whether through the provision of intelligence or approval to use UK airspace – was agreed on the basis that the Americans gave assurances regarding humane treatment and that detainees would be afforded a fair trial. These actions were appropriate and appear to us to have complied with our domestic law and the UK's international obligations.

D.   Those operations detailed above, involving UK Agencies' knowledge or involvement, are "Renditions to Justice", "Military Renditions" and "Renditions to Detention". They are not "Extraordinary Renditions", which we define as *"the extra-judicial transfer of persons from one jurisdiction or State to another, for the purposes of detention and interrogation outside the normal legal system, where there is a real risk of torture or cruel, inhuman or degrading treatment"*. We note that in some of the cases we refer to, there are allegations of mistreatment, including whilst individuals were detained at Guantánamo Bay, although we have not found evidence that such mistreatment was foreseen by the Agencies. The Committee has therefore found no evidence that the UK Agencies were complicit in any "Extraordinary Rendition" operations.

E.   In the immediate aftermath of the 9/11 attacks, the UK Agencies were authorised to assist U.S. "Rendition to Justice" operations in Afghanistan. This involved assistance to the CIA to capture "unlawful combatants" in Afghanistan. These operations were approved on the basis that detainees would be treated humanely and be afforded a fair trial. In the event, the intelligence necessary to put these authorisations into effect could not be obtained and the operations did not proceed. The Committee has concluded that the Agencies acted properly.

F.   SIS was subsequently briefed on new powers which would enable U.S. authorities to arrest and detain suspected terrorists worldwide. In November 2001, these powers were confirmed by the Presidential Military Order. We understand that

SIS was sceptical about the supposed new powers, since at the time there was a great deal of "tough talk" being used at many levels of the U.S. Administration, and it was difficult to reach a definitive conclusion regarding the direction of U.S. policy in this area. Nonetheless, the Committee concludes that SIS should have appreciated the significance of these events and reported them to Ministers.

G. The Security Service and SIS were also slow to detect the emerging pattern of "Renditions to Detention" that occurred during 2002. The UK Agencies, when sharing intelligence with the U.S. which might have resulted in the detention of an individual subject to the Presidential Military Order, should always have sought assurances on detainee treatment.

H. The cases of Bisher al-Rawi and Jamil el-Banna and others during 2002 demonstrated that the U.S. was willing to conduct "Rendition to Detention" operations anywhere in the world, including against those unconnected with the conflict in Afghanistan. We note that the Agencies used greater caution in working with the U.S., including withdrawing from some planned operations, following these cases.

I. By mid-2003, following the case of Khaled Sheikh Mohammed and suspicions that the U.S. authorities were operating "black sites", the Agencies had appreciated the potential risk of renditions and possible mistreatment of detainees. From this point, the Agencies correctly sought Ministerial approval and assurances from foreign liaison services whenever there were real risks of rendition operations resulting from their actions.

J. After April 2004 – following the revelations of mistreatment at the U.S. military-operated prison at Abu Ghraib – the UK intelligence and security Agencies and the Government were fully aware of the risk of mistreatment associated with any operations that may result in U.S. custody of detainees. Assurances on humane treatment were properly and routinely sought in operations that involved any risk of rendition and/or U.S. custody.

K. The Committee has strong concerns, however, about a potential operation in early 2005 which, had it gone ahead, might have resulted in the ***. The operation was conditionally approved by Ministers, subject to assurances on humane treatment and a time limit on detention. These were not obtained and so the operation was dropped. ***
***
***.

L. We are satisfied that the UK intelligence and security Agencies had no involvement in the capture or subsequent "Rendition to Detention" of Martin Mubanga and that they acted properly.

M.   There is a reasonable probability that intelligence passed to the Americans was used in al-Habashi's subsequent interrogation. We cannot confirm any part of al-Habashi's account of his detention or mistreatment after his transfer from Pakistan.

N.   We agree with the Director General of the Security Service that, with hindsight, it is regrettable that assurances regarding proper treatment of detainees were not sought from the Americans in this case.

O.   Whilst this was not a rendition but a deportation, and the Security Service and SIS were not in a strong position to impose conditions on it, we accept their view that they should nevertheless have sought greater assurances that the individual would be treated humanely.

P.   Given el-Banna's and al-Rawi's backgrounds and associations, it was reasonable to undertake a properly authorised covert search of the men's luggage. The decision to arrest the men was taken by the police on the basis of the suspicious items they found and was not instigated by the Security Service.

Q.   The sharing of intelligence with foreign liaison services on suspected extremists is routine. There was nothing exceptional in the Security Service notifying the U.S. of the men's arrest and setting out its assessment of them. The telegram was correctly covered by a caveat prohibiting the U.S. authorities from taking action on the basis of the information it contained.

R.   In adding the caveat prohibiting action, the Security Service explicitly required that no action (such as arrests) should be taken on the basis of the intelligence contained in the telegrams. We have been told that the Security Service would fully expect such a caveat to be honoured by the U.S. agencies – this is fundamental to their intelligence-sharing relationship. We accept that the Security Service did not intend the men to be arrested.

S.   The Security Service and Foreign Office acted properly in seeking access to the detained British nationals, asking questions as to their treatment and, when they learnt of a possible rendition operation, protesting strongly.

T.   We note that eventually the British nationals were released, but are concerned that, contrary to the Vienna Convention on Consular Relations, access to the men was initially denied.

U.   This is the first case in which the U.S. agencies conducted a "Rendition to Detention" of individuals entirely unrelated to the conflict in Afghanistan. Given that there had been a gradual expansion of the rendition programme during 2002, it could reasonably have been expected that the net would widen still further and that greater care could have been taken. We do, however, note that Agency priorities at the time were – rightly – focused on disrupting attacks rather than scrutinising American policy. We also accept that the Agencies could not have foreseen that the U.S. authorities would disregard the caveats placed on the intelligence, given that they had honoured the caveat system for the past 20 years.

V. This case shows a lack of regard, on the part of the U.S., for UK concerns. Despite the Security Service prohibiting any action being taken as a result of its intelligence, the U.S. nonetheless planned to render the men to Guantánamo Bay. They then ignored the subsequent protests of both the Security Service and the Government. This has serious implications for the working of the relationship between the U.S. and UK intelligence and security agencies.

W. Whilst we note that Bisher al-Rawi has now been released from Guantánamo Bay and that el-Banna has been cleared for release, we nevertheless recommend that the UK Government ensures that the details of suspicious items found during the Gatwick luggage search (including the police's final assessment of these items) are clarified with the U.S. authorities.

X. We recognise the contribution of the Foreign and Commonwealth Office in securing Bisher al-Rawi's release. However, having seen the full facts of the case – and leaving aside the exact nature of al-Rawi's relationship with the Security Service – we consider that the Security Service should have informed Ministers about the case at the time, and are concerned that it took *** years, and a court case, to bring it to their attention.

Y. What the rendition programme has shown is that in what it refers to as "the war on terror" the U.S. will take whatever action it deems necessary, within U.S. law, to protect its national security from those it considers to pose a serious threat. Although the U.S. may take note of UK protests and concerns, this does not appear materially to affect its strategy on rendition.

Z. It is to the credit of our Agencies that they have now managed to adapt their procedures to work round these problems and maintain the exchange of intelligence that is so critical to UK security.

AA. The Committee notes that the UK Agencies now have a policy in place to minimise the risk of their actions inadvertently leading to renditions, torture or cruel, inhuman or degrading treatment (CIDT). Where it is known that the consequences of dealing with a foreign liaison service will include torture or CIDT, the operation will not be authorised.

BB. In the cases we have reviewed, the Agencies have taken action consistent with the policy of minimising the risks of torture or CIDT (and therefore "Extraordinary

Rendition") based upon their knowledge and awareness of the CIA rendition programme at that time.

CC. Where, despite the use of caveats and assurances, there remains a real possibility that the actions of the Agencies will result in torture or mistreatment, we note that the current procedure requires that approval is sought from senior management or Ministers. We recommend that Ministerial approval should be sought in all such cases.

DD. The Committee considers that "secret detention", without legal or other representation, is of itself mistreatment. Where there is a real possibility of "Rendition to Detention" to a secret facility, even if it would be for a limited time, then approval must never be given.

EE. GCHQ has played no role in any U.S. renditions, whether "ordinary" or "extraordinary". Theoretically, given the close working relationship between GCHQ and the National Security Agency (NSA), GCHQ intelligence could have been passed from the NSA to the CIA and could have been used in a U.S. rendition operation. However, GCHQ's legal safeguards and the requirement for explicit permission to take action based on their intelligence provide a high level of confidence that their material has not been used for such operations.

FF. The use of UK airspace and airports by CIA-operated aircraft is not in doubt. There have been many allegations related to these flights but there have been no allegations, and we have seen no evidence, that suggest that any of these CIA flights have transferred detainees through UK airspace (other than two "Rendition to Justice" cases in 1998 which were approved by the UK Government following U.S. requests).

GG. It is alleged that, on up to four occasions since 9/11, aircraft that had previously conducted a rendition operation overseas transited UK airspace during their return journeys (without detainees on board). The Committee has not seen any evidence that might contradict the police assessment that there is no evidential basis on which a criminal inquiry into these flights could be launched.

HH. We consider that it would be unreasonable and impractical to check whether every aircraft transiting UK airspace might have been, at some point in the past, and without UK knowledge, involved in a possibly unlawful operation. We are satisfied that, where there is sufficient evidence of unlawful activity on board an aircraft in UK airspace, be it a rendition operation or otherwise, this would be investigated by the UK authorities.

II.   The system of flight plans and General Aviation Reports is outside the remit of this inquiry, although we are concerned that it appears to be systemically flawed. The Home Secretary has assured the Committee that the e-Borders and Border Management Programme (being introduced from 2008) will address our concerns relating to general aviation documentation and security risks. This would, however, be a matter for the Transport and Home Affairs Select Committees to review in greater depth, if they felt it merited it.

JJ.   The alleged use of military airfields in the UK by rendition flights has been investigated in response to our questions to the Prime Minister. We are satisfied that there is no evidence that U.S. rendition flights have used UK airspace (except the two cases in 1998 referred to earlier in this Report) and that there is no evidence of them having landed at UK military airfields.

[...]

(25) Foreign Affairs Select Committee, 'Overseas Territories', July 2008 (extracts)

[...]

Extraordinary rendition

52. As the FCO told us, the terms of the US-UK agreement on BIOT require the US to seek prior approval from the UK for "any extraordinary use of the US base or facilities, such as combat operations or any other politically sensitive activity".[98] For a number of years before we announced our inquiry claims had been made that Diego Garcia had been used in the United States' rendition programme. On 20 January 2006, the then Foreign Secretary, Rt Hon Jack Straw MP, responded to allegations about use of the UK's territory or airspace for rendition operations, summarising the results of a search of files stretching back to 1997. The search found just four cases of rendition requests by the US, all in 1998. Two were accepted; two were rejected. He told the House that the Government had found "no evidence of detainees being rendered through the UK or its Overseas Territories" since 1998.[99]

53. However, allegations continued and in a Report in 2007 we recommended:

> that the Government ask the United States administration to confirm whether aircraft used in rendition operations have called at airfields in the United Kingdom or in the Overseas Territories en route to or from a rendition and that it make a clear statement of its policy on this practice.[100]

In response, the Government reiterated the statement made by the then Foreign Secretary Jack Straw and argued that, given US assurances, further clarification from the US administration of its policy was unnecessary.[101] In its response to our Report the Government also stated:

> We are clear that the US would not render anyone through UK airspace (including the Overseas Territories) without our permission.[102]

54. In October 2007 we received evidence from the All Party Parliamentary Group on Extraordinary Rendition and from Reprieve for this inquiry, which claimed that Diego Garcia had been used to land a plane linked to "rendition circuits" and that ships in or near its territorial waters had also been used to hold detainees or otherwise facilitate the United

---

[96] Public Accounts Committee, Seventeenth Report of Session 2007-08, *Foreign and Commonwealth Office: Managing Risk in the Overseas Territories*, HC 176, Q 20

[97] Ev 105

[98] Ev 345

[99] HC Deb, 20 January 2006, col 38WS

[100] Foreign Affairs Committee, Third Report of Session 2006-07, *Human Rights Annual Report 2006*, HC 269, para 80

[101] Foreign and Commonwealth Office, *Response of the Secretary of State for Foreign and Commonwealth Affairs to the Third Report from the Foreign Affairs Committee Session 2006-07*, Cm 7127, June 2007, paras 43 - 46

[102] *Ibid.*, para 44

States' renditions programme.[103] Both organisations urged further investigation of these allegations and argued that the UK was wrong to rely on US assurances to the contrary.[104]

55. On 21 February 2008, the current Foreign Secretary, Rt Hon David Miliband MP, reported to the House that the US had now informed him, contrary to its previous assurances, that on two occasions in 2002 Diego Garcia had been used for renditions flights. In both cases a US plane "with a single detainee refuelled at the US facility" on the island. Neither detainee was a British national or British resident. One was currently in Guantánamo Bay and the other had been released. The Foreign Secretary added:

> [...] the detainees did not leave the plane, and the US Government have assured us that no US detainees have ever been held on Diego Garcia. US investigations show no record of any other rendition through Diego Garcia or any other overseas territory, or through the UK itself, since then.

He explained that he had asked FCO officials to compile a list of all the flights where the Government had been alerted to concerns regarding rendition through the UK or the Overseas Territories and said he would be sending this list to the US to seek specific assurances about each flight.[105]

56. Following the Foreign Secretary's statement, we wrote to ask him a number of questions. One of these was whether the list of allegations being sent to the US would include claims relating to ships serviced from Diego Garcia.[106] In response the Foreign Secretary told us that the Government had "previously received assurances from the US in 2005, 2006 and 2007 that no detainees had been transferred through the territorial waters of Diego Garcia". However, he did not address the allegation of detainees being held on ships serviced from Diego Garcia.[107] In oral evidence Meg Munn was also unclear as to whether the list being sent to the US would include this particular allegation.[108]

57. We also asked the Foreign Secretary whether the list being sent to the US would include allegations about flights through UK airspace of planes alleged to have been on their way to or from carrying out a rendition, as well as allegations about flights carrying detainees at the time of transit through UK airspace.[109] He told us that his purpose in preparing the list being sent to the US was "to identify whether rendition through UK territory or airspace in fact occurred" and that the Government did "not consider that an empty flight transiting through our territory falls into this category."[110] As part of our Human Rights inquiry we questioned Lord Malloch-Brown about this position. He replied:

> I do not think that it is more or less okay, but there is a limit to what we can do effectively to monitor empty planes, whose purposes it is not really reasonable for us

[103] Reprieve also made claims about stopovers of rendition planes in the Turks and Caicos Islands.

[104] Ev 182 and 203

[105] HC Deb, 21 February 2008, col 547-8

[106] Ev 310

[107] Ev 343

[108] Qq 304-306

[109] Ev 310

[110] Ev 345

to investigate. If an American military flight requests refuelling or access and is empty of any passengers, I am not sure that it is possible for us to demand what it might be doing on its return flight.[111]

58. Regarding the announcement that Diego Garcia had been used for rendition flights, Lord Malloch-Brown told us:

Obviously, from the Foreign Secretary downwards, and the Prime Minister as well, we were all pretty shocked that those assurances, given in good faith to the Committee and to the House, had proven inaccurate. That is why, in the Foreign Secretary's conversations with Condi Rice, we secured a commitment that we would submit a list of all flights about which there were suspicions-that is, any flights whose details were given to us by Amnesty, Human Rights Watch and others-to the US and would ask them to give us an assurance that there was not any such activity around any of those flights. I think we should wait for the outcome of that. We have made it clear that we would publish both the list of flights we submitted and the responses that we got. We should wait until that is over to see what, if any, steps are necessary after that.[112]

During the evidence session, held on 30 April, the Minister also said the list was "shortly" and "about to be" sent to the US.[113] The FCO later confirmed that it had sent the list to its US counterparts. The FCO also told us that it would lay the list and the US response in both Houses as soon as it had received the response.

59. We also asked the FCO about the extent of UK supervision of activities on Diego Garcia. It replied:

A wide range of activities are conducted by US personnel on Diego Garcia which are routine in nature and are covered by entries in the Exchange of Notes. These activities are not normally supervised by UK personnel, nor at 42 personnel is there capacity to do so.[114]

60. We asked the FCO what discussions it had had with the US on extension of the "lease" beyond 2016. In writing the FCO told us that the UK and US "would of course continue to consult closely on their mutual defence needs and expectations well in advance of that time."[115] However, Meg Munn informed us that the UK had not yet had any discussions with the US about the possibility of terminating the lease in 2016. She also told us that she had not discussed changing the terms of the agreement to increase UK oversight if it did continue beyond 2016.[116]

---

[111] Oral evidence taken before the Foreign Affairs Committee on 7 May 2008, HC (2007-08) 533-ii, Q 59

[112] *Ibid.*, Q 60

[113] *Ibid.*, Q 61

[114] Ev 345

[...]

70. On Diego Garcia itself, we conclude that it is deplorable that previous US assurances about rendition flights have turned out to be false. The failure of the United States Administration to tell the truth resulted in the UK Government inadvertently misleading our Select Committee and the House of Commons. We intend to examine further the extent of UK supervision of US activities on Diego Garcia, including all flights and ships serviced from Diego Garcia.

[...]

(26) Foreign Affairs Select Committee, 'Human Rights Annual Report 2007', July 2008 (extracts)

[...]

Rendition

42. The FCO report notes that the terms 'rendition' and 'extraordinary rendition' have yet to "attain a universally accepted meaning, other than a transfer of an individual between jurisdictions outside normal legal processes". It adds that many commentators understand the term 'extraordinary rendition' to refer to the extra-judicial transfer of persons from one jurisdiction to another "specifically for the purposes of detention and interrogation", giving rise to an increased risk of torture. The Government sets out its policy on extraordinary rendition, stating: "We have not approved and will not approve a policy of facilitating the transfer of individuals through the UK to places where there are substantial grounds to believe they would face a real risk of torture."[63]

43. We have followed the issue of US Government policy and the use of extraordinary rendition closely in recent years, as part of our annual human rights reports, our discontinued series into the *Foreign Policy Aspects of the War against Terrorism* and as part of our recent report into *Overseas Territories*. This latter report sets out the Government's repeated acceptance in recent years of US assurances that UK territory had not been used for the purposes of rendition since 1998. We then noted:

> On 21 February 2008, the current Foreign Secretary, Rt Hon David Miliband MP, reported to the House that the US had now informed him, contrary to its previous assurances, that on two occasions in 2002 Diego Garcia had been used for renditions flights. In both cases a US plane "with a single detainee refuelled at the US facility" on the island. Neither detainee was a British national or British resident. One was currently in Guantánamo Bay and the other had been released.[64]

In the human rights report, the FCO expresses "concern and disappointment" that UK territory was used for the purposes of rendition without the permission of the Government.[65] In our report, we deplored the fact that US assurances "have turned out to be false".[66]

44. There has been a question in recent years over the Government's obligations with regard to flights that use UK airspace or land on UK territory on the way to, or back from, a rendition operation but without a detainee on board. Amnesty International has claimed that it has evidence to prove that flights on the "rendition circuit" have used UK airports. We asked Kate Allen for her assessment of the Government's legal obligation with regard to allowing such flights to use UK facilities. She replied:

---

[63] Foreign and Commonwealth Office, *Human Rights Annual Report 2007*, Cm 7340, March 2008, p 15

[64] Foreign Affairs Committee, Seventh Report of Session 2007–08, *Overseas Territories*, HC 147-I, para 55

[65] Foreign and Commonwealth Office, *Human Rights Annual Report 2007*, Cm 7340, March 2008, p 16

[66] Foreign Affairs Committee, Seventh Report of Session 2007–08, *Overseas Territories*, HC 147-I, para 70

Very clear: if the British Government know what the flights are used for, they have legal responsibility to challenge [...]We have never said that we have known that people were on those flights, but we have said that we know that those flights either picked somebody up and delivered them and have been returning, or have been involved in that rendition circuit. It is very clear that the UK Government have legal responsibility, because they know what those planes have been involved in.[67]

45. Lord Malloch-Brown told us that the Government was to:

submit a list of all flights about which there were suspicions - that is, any flights whose details were given to us by Amnesty, Human Rights Watch and others – to the US and [...] ask them to give us an assurance that there was not any such activity around any of those flights.[68]

As part of our *Overseas Territories* inquiry, we asked the Foreign Secretary if this list included flights that may have been on the way to or from a rendition, but without a detainee on board. He told us that the Government's purpose was "to identify whether rendition through UK territory or airspace in fact occurred" and that the Government did "not consider that an empty flight transiting through our territory falls into this category."[69] We asked Lord Malloch-Brown whether it was "more or less okay" for the US to use UK territory if a flight was empty. His reply appeared to differ from the Foreign Secretary, focusing more on practical issues rather than any question of principle:

I do not think that it is more or less okay, but there is a limit to what we can do effectively to monitor empty planes, whose purposes it is not really reasonable for us to investigate. If an American military flight requests refuelling or access and is empty of any passengers, I am not sure that it is possible for us to demand what it might be doing on its return flight.[70]

We asked the FCO whether it had taken any legal advice with regard to its obligations in these cases. It replied that "legal advice given to the Government is confidential and we are therefore unable to disclose the contents of any such advice".[71] On 3 July 2008, the Foreign Secretary told the House in a written statement that the US had received the list and replied to the FCO, stating that there have been no other US intelligence flights "with a detainee on board" landing in the UK, Overseas Territories or Crown Dependencies since 9/11. We note that this assurance does not address the issue of flights without detainees on board.[72]

---

[67] Q 17

[68] Q 60

[69] Foreign Affairs Committee, Seventh Report of Session 2007–08, *Overseas Territories*, HC 147-II, Ev 346

[70] Q 59

46. In its submission, REDRESS argues that the UK is under a "positive duty" to ensure that it has an effective framework in place to prevent extraordinary renditions. It argues that "an overhaul of the current laws and policies on aviation is urgently required". It notes that the former Foreign Secretary, Rt Hon Margaret Beckett MP, has already acknowledged the deficiencies in record keeping which she conceded are "not all that marvellous, frankly", and argues that this may have contributed to failures to detect renditions in the past.[73] Human Rights Watch adds that "the key question [...] is not just does the UK approve of renditions to torture. It is whether the UK does anything meaningful to stop such renditions from taking place."[74] REDRESS, Amnesty International, and Human Rights Watch all call in their submissions for the Government to hold a full public inquiry into the use of renditions in UK territory.[75]

47. **We conclude that the Government has a moral and legal obligation to ensure that flights that enter UK airspace or land at UK airports are not part of the "rendition circuit", even if they do not have a detainee on board during the time they are in UK territory. We recommend that the Government should immediately raise questions about such flights with the US authorities in order to ascertain the full scale of the rendition problem, and inform the Committee of the replies it receives in its response to this Report.**

The US and Torture

48. This is the last of our human rights reports to be published during the course of the George W Bush Presidency in the United States. We and our predecessor Committees have considered various aspects of the Bush Presidency over the past eight years, in particular through the series of reports on *Foreign Policy Aspects of the War against Terrorism* and our report on *Guantánamo Bay*. One of the most important issues that we have addressed is that of alleged mistreatment of detainees by the US Government.

49. In 2005, President Bush said that "we do not torture".[76] The FCO report welcomes "US government statements that have made clear its opposition to torture, and the cruel, inhuman and degrading treatment of terrorist suspects".[77] This welcome is one example of the Government's apparent trust in the US on this issue, and its willingness to take these remarks at face value. The FCO has previously relied on US statements to deflect questions from this Committee and others. In its response to our human rights report last year (in which we sought clarification over rendition policy), the Government provided a further very clear example of how it uses the statements of US officials in this way when it said:

---

[73] Ev 99–102

[74] Ev 23

In her statement of 5 September 2006, the US Secretary of State, Condoleezza Rice said, referring to allegations of rendition flights:

"The United States has respected – and will continue to respect – the sovereignty of other countries. The United States does not transport, and has not transported, detainees from one country to another for the purpose of interrogation using torture. The United States does not use the airspace or the airports of any country for the purpose of transporting a detainee to a country where he or she will be tortured. The United States has not transported anyone, and will not transport anyone, to a country when we believe he will be tortured. Where appropriate, the United States seeks assurances that transferred persons will not be tortured."

In these circumstances, the Government does not consider that seeking a further clarification from the US administration of its policy is necessary.[78]

50. There is one exception to this general approach, which is the attitude of the British Government to the practice known as "water-boarding", during which a prisoner is bound to a board with feet raised, and cellophane is wrapped round his head. Water is then poured onto his face, which is said to produce a fear of drowning. This leads to a "rapid demand for the suffering to end".[79] The Central Intelligence Agency (CIA) of the US Government has admitted using water-boarding against detainees in recent years. In February 2008, the US Director of National Intelligence Michael McConnell told a Senate intelligence committee that:

The question is, is waterboarding a legal technique? And everything I know, based on the appropriate authority to make that judgment, it is a legal technique used in a specific set of circumstances. You have to know the circumstances to be able to make the judgment.[80]

As Andrew Tyrie MP pointed out in a letter to us, on 8 March 2008, "President Bush vetoed a bill that would have outlawed the use of 'waterboarding' and other 'enhanced' interrogation techniques."[81]

51. David Miliband, the Foreign Secretary, has said: "I consider that water-boarding amounts to torture".[82] Lord Malloch-Brown told us that there is "no ambiguity" about the Government's view.[83] We asked him if he was aware of any other practices carried out by the US Government that the UK would consider torture. An official replied that the

---

[78] Foreign and Commonwealth Office, *Annual Report on Human Rights 2006: Response of the Secretary of State for Foreign and Commonwealth Affairs*, Cm 7127, June 2007, p 9

[79] "Defining torture in a new world war", *BBC News Online*, 8 December 2005, news.bbc.co.uk

[80] "Hearing of the Senate Select Committee on Intelligence", 5 February 2008, www.dni.gov

[81] Ev 111

Government was aware "of the variety of techniques that have been discussed in the US", but Lord Malloch-Brown said he was not aware of any other methods that would be viewed as torture. He added that Congress is currently considering the matter.[84] Writing to us at a later date, he said: "We have not conducted an exhaustive analysis of current US interrogation techniques but we expect all countries to comply with their international obligations".[85] We note that this expectation does not specifically answer our question.

52. There appears to be a striking inconsistency in the Government's approach to this matter. As noted above, it has relied on assurances by the US Government that it does not use torture. However, it is evident that, in the case of water-boarding and perhaps other techniques, what the UK considers to be torture is viewed as a legal interrogation technique by the US Administration. With the divergence in definitions, it is difficult to see how the UK can rely on US assurances that it does not torture. As Amnesty International argues, "what the USA considers torture does not match international law".[86] Human Rights Watch adds that "President Bush's statements on torture need to be considered in the light of the memoranda from his legal advisers that re-defined torture so narrowly as to make the prohibition virtually meaningless."[87]

53. **We conclude that the Foreign Secretary's view that water-boarding is an instrument of torture is to be welcomed. However, given the recent practice of water-boarding by the US, there are serious implications arising from the Foreign Secretary's stated position. We conclude that, given the clear differences in definition, the UK can no longer rely on US assurances that it does not use torture, and we recommend that the Government does not rely on such assurances in the future. We also recommend that the Government should immediately carry out an exhaustive analysis of current US interrogation techniques on the basis of such information as is publicly available or which can be supplied by the US. We further recommend that, once its analysis is completed, the Government should inform this Committee and Parliament as to its view on whether there are any other interrogation techniques that may be approved for use by the US Administration which it considers to constitute torture.**

[...]

(27)   Foreign Affairs Select Committee, 'Human Rights Annual Report 2008', August 2009 (extracts)

[...]

2 Rendition

[...]

Details of the 2002 renditions through Diego Garcia

26. The Government has claimed to have only limited information about the flights that landed on Diego Garcia in 2002 and the individuals in question. When we questioned the Foreign Secretary about why details of the cases had not been published by the Government he answered that "we have no confirmation of their names, and that is why we have not put them into the public domain".[40] In answer to a Parliamentary Question by Andrew Tyrie MP, the FCO Minister of State, Bill Rammell MP, stated that "We have very limited specific information about these flights and, despite enquiry, have not been able to establish further details that would be essential for purposes of further investigation."[41] Mr Tyrie told us that "the implication is that the US is withholding information about these flights" and that this information would be essential for investigation of whether criminal offences were committed.[42]

27. From the information provided, Reprieve believe that have identified one of the men rendered through Diego Garcia in 2002 as Mohammed Saad Iqbal Madni. They urge that the Government should clarify further what it knew of his apprehension, transfer and treatment, whether British personnel had contact with him and provide details of assurances sought by the UK regarding his treatment.[43] Clive Stafford Smith told us that evidence for this assertion was "pretty much indisputable" but that the Government had

---

36   HC Deb 21 February 2008 Col 547

37   http://www.fco.gov.uk/resources/en/pdf/3052790/fs-wms-rendition-030708

38   HC Deb 3 July 2008, col 58 WS

39   Ev 64

40   Q 95

41   HC Deb 26 February 2009 Col 948W

42   Ev 64

43   http://www.reprieve.org.uk/static/downloads/Microsoft_Word_-_2009_05_20_FAC_Submission_DG.pdfand Q11

failed to respond to the claim. He believes the second prisoner was Shaikh Ibn Al-Libi but told us that "we are by no means certain."[44]

28. **We conclude that it is unacceptable that the Government has not taken steps to obtain the full details of the two individuals who were rendered through Diego Garcia. We recommend that the Government presses the new US Administration to provide these details, and that it should then either publish them, or explain the reasons why it considers it would not be in the public interest to publish them.**

The agreement between the US and UK on the use of Diego Garcia

In our 2008 Report on Overseas Territories we noted that the US lease on Diego Garcia is due to expire in 2016. The FCO told us that the 1966 Exchange of Notes which established the agreement would "continue in force for a further twenty years beyond 2016", unless it was ended by "either government giving notice of termination, in accordance with its terms".[45] However, at that time, Ministers had not discussed the possibility of terminating the lease or altering the terms of the agreement to increase UK oversight of activities on the Island.[46] Referring to the acknowledge rendition through Diego Garcia, Andrew Tyrie MP has argued that "if the agreements in place were not breached, then they appear inadequate for the purpose of preventing British involvement in extraordinary renditions."[47]   Clive Stafford Smith also told us that

> there is no doubt that it violated that agreement, but it violated a lot of other things. British law applies in Diego Garcia, notwithstanding what some other people have said. It has very interesting aspects. In fact, the law provides for a Diego Garcia supreme court that is meant to apply British law, of which there is no such thing. [...] The whole process has been one to skirt the law[48]

29. We questioned the Foreign Secretary about whether the use of Diego Garcia for rendition flights would breach the terms of the agreement between the UK and the US on the use of the island. He told us:

> In our view there should be consultation. I think there was consultation about a previous case—there were a couple of cases in the 1990s. That is certainly the procedure that now exists [...] the US Administration have said that they will consult us if they ever want to use it. So they obviously share that view.[49]

He did not believe that there were grounds to examine the terms of the agreement that govern the use of the island, adding:

> If the American Administration were now saying that they did not need to consult us, that would be a *prima facie* case for reviewing the arrangements. I am sure in

---

44   Q 11

45   Foreign Affairs Committee, Seventh Report of Session 2007–08, *Overseas Territories*, HC 147, para 49

46   *Ibid.*, para 60

47   Ev 64

48   Q 9

2016 we will want to look at whether they are adequate for the times; there is no limitation on that. In respect of the use of Diego Garcia for rendition there is an absolutely clear position from the British Government and the American Government about the appropriate way to act. In that respect, there is no lack of clarity.[50]

30. **We conclude that the use of Diego Garcia for US rendition flights without the knowledge or consent of the British Government raises disquieting questions about the effectiveness of the Government's exercise of its responsibilities in relation to this territory. We recommend that in its response to this Report, the Government indicates whether it considers that UK law has effect in British Indian Ocean Territory, and whether it considers that either UK law or the agreements between the US and UK over the use of BIOT were broken by the admitted US rendition flights in 2002.**

Flight records

31. The Intelligence and Security Committee's July 2007 report on rendition commented that:

> We are concerned that Government departments have had such difficulty in establishing the facts from their own records in relation to requests to conduct renditions through UK airspace. These are matters of fundamental liberties and the Government should ensure that proper searchable records are kept.[51]

The Government has admitted that flight records from Diego Garcia covering the period during which renditions are known to have occurred through the island have been destroyed.[52] In its submission, Reprieve questioned why accurate records were not kept and argued that the Government should make available details of how, why and by whom records were destroyed.[53] When we asked the Foreign Secretary whether the Government would be willing to do this, he replied: ""I have never been asked that before and there is no proposal to do it."[54] He stated that on Diego Garcia since 2008 "all flight records are now held by the British representative"[55] and outlined his intention to make improvements in record keeping:

> The record-keeping systems that have to be improved are partly a matter of what happens on the base and partly a matter of what happens back in London. In respect of all detainee issues, there is now a central point in the Foreign Office for arranging that, and I think that is the right way forward.[56]

---

50   Q 101

51   Intelligence and Security Committee, *Rendition*, Cm 7171, July 2007, page 17

52   HC Deb 6 November 2008, c688W

53   http://www.reprieve.org.uk/static/downloads/Microsoft_Word_-_2009_05_20_FAC_Submission_DG.pdf

54   Q 109

55   Q 110

32. Non-commercial, non-state flights do not require permission to land in the UK.[57] Redress has previously suggested that the law covering the use of civil aircraft for rendition and the procedures for authorising the entry of 'state aircraft' into UK territory should be assessed.[58] They comment in particular that although many rendition flights are designated as 'civil' flights, they might more accurately be described as 'state' flights and therefore should require more explicit authorisation.[59] Benjamin Ward was

> supportive of the initiative by the all-party parliamentary group on rendition to create a permission system for rendition flights, including for overflights, similar to that which exists already in extradition cases under the European Convention on Extradition. That proposal was put forward to the Government in 2006 and, as far as I am aware, nothing ever came of it. Obviously that would not entirely eliminate the risk of transfers, but effectively requiring a transferring state to certify, in advance, what opportunity the prisoner had had to challenge any risk of human rights abuse that they might be subject to would make it much more difficult and much less attractive to use UK territory and UK airspace for such transfers. It would be a very important and symbolic change and it is not clear to me why that was not taken up.

33. **We conclude that, in the light of the controversy over the use of British Indian Ocean Territory for purposes of rendition by the US, it is important that full records of flights through the territory are kept, and retained for an indefinite period. We conclude that it is to be welcomed that the British representative on Diego Garcia now keeps flight records. We recommend that the Government discloses how, why and by whom the records relating to flights through Diego Garcia since the start of 2002 were destroyed. We further recommend that the Government provides, in its response to this Report, full details of its record-keeping and record-disposal policy in relation to flights through British territory, particularly BIOT, and state for how long it now retains such records. We recommend that, in its response, the Government addresses the question of whether it considers that current aviation law and aircraft identification procedures are sufficient to identify flights which may be carrying out rendition both through Diego Garcia or elsewhere through UK airspace.**

Further allegations in relation to Diego Garcia

34. The lack of historical flight data makes it very difficult to test allegations that the two flights in 2002 do not represent the full extent of Diego Garcia's involvement in the rendition circuit. It is claimed that the island was used by the CIA as a 'black site'. During our inquiry into Overseas Territories it was further alleged that ships in or near the island's territorial waters had been used to hold detainees and facilitate rendition.[60] Such allegations include the following:

- US Army General Barry McCaffrey, former head of Southcom, has stated twice in public that Diego Garcia has been used by the US to hold prisoners, stating in a

---

57 Intelligence and Security Committee, *Rendition*, Cm 7171, July 2007, para 188

58 Redress, The United Kingdom, *Torture and Anti-Terrorism: Where the Problems Lie*, December 2008, page 28

59 Redress, The United Kingdom, *Torture and Anti-Terrorism: Where the Problems Lie*, December 2008, page 30

radio interview in May 2004 "We're probably holding around 3,000 people, you know, Bagram Air Field, Diego Garcia, Guantánamo, 16 camps throughout Iraq."[61]

- In October 2003 Time magazine reported that the Al-Qaeda operative known as Hambali had been interrogated on the island.[62]

- A former senior American official told Time magazine in July 2008 that "a CIA counterterrorism official twice said that a high-value prisoner or prisoners were being held and interrogated on the island. The identity of the captive or captives was not made clear."[63]

- In August 2008, the Observer reported that former American intelligence officers "unofficially told senior Spanish judge Baltasar Garzón that Mustafa Setmarian, a Spanish-based Syrian accused of running terrorist training camps in Afghanistan, was taken to Diego Garcia in late 2005 and held there for months."[64]

- Reprieve allege that Abu Zubaydah and Khaled Skeikh Mohammed, currently held at Guantánamo, were also held on the island.[65]

- The Observer has reported that Manfred Novak, the United Nations special investigator on torture, told the paper that "he had talked to detainees who had been held on the archipelago in 2002, but declined to name them."[66]

35. In its 2008 Annual Report on Human Rights the FCO stated that:

The US government denies having interrogated any terrorist suspect or terrorism-related detainee on Diego Garcia since 11 September 2001. They have also informed us that no detainees have been held on ships within Diego Garcia's territorial waters over that period, and that they do not operate detention facilities for terrorist suspects on board ships.[67]

36. We asked the Foreign Secretary whether this assurance extended to the use of Diego Garcia as a victualling point for ships outside its territorial water which may have been used for renditions. He stated that "we have no information, either of vessels inside territorial waters being used for rendition or of supplies from Diego Garcia going to ships outside the territorial waters.[68] The FCO state that such re-victualling would be "highly unlikely to occur" because:

---

61 http://www.msnbc.msn.com/id/4924989 ; http://www.reprieve.org.uk/static/downloads/Microsoft_Word_-_2009_05_20_FAC_Submission_DG.pdf

62 The Terrorist Talks, TIME magazine, 5 October 2003 http://www.time.com/time/magazine/article/0,9171,1101031013–493256,00.html

63 US Used UK Isle for Interrogations, TIME magazine, 31 July 2008 http://www.time.com/time/world/article/0,8599,1828469,00.html

64 US 'held suspects on British territory in 2006', The Observer, 3 August 2008

65 http://www.reprieve.org.uk/static/downloads/Microsoft_Word_-_2009_05_20_FAC_Submission_DG.pdf

66 US 'held suspects on British territory in 2006', The Observer, 3 August 2008

67 Foreign and Commonwealth Office, Annual Report on Human Rights 2008, Cm 7557, page 17

68 Q 104

The territorial waters of Diego Garcia extend to 3 nautical miles. Replenishment at Sea [...] requires a stable transfer system between the two vessels concerned. This would usually be provided by an auxiliary vessel. No such vessels are currently berthed in Diego Garcia and consequently all vessels have to come into port to be replenished.[69]

The Foreign Secretary undertook to supply us with an assessment of whether, under the US/UK agreements on the use of BIOT, the British Government's prior consent would be required for the use of the territory as a re-victualling point for vessels outside territorial waters. He later told us that:

Under the UK/US Exchange of Notes which govern the use of the British Indian Ocean Territory for Defence purposes, the US undertakes to inform the UK of intended movements of its ships in BIOT territorial waters in "normal circumstances".[70]

37. **We conclude that it is a matter of concern that many allegations continue to be made that the two acknowledged instances of rendition through British Indian Ocean Territory in 2002 do not represent the limit of the territory's use for this purpose. We further conclude that it is extremely difficult for the British Government to assess the veracity of these allegations without active and candid co-operation from the US Administration. We recommend that the Government requests the Obama Administration to carry out a further, comprehensive check on its records relating to the use of BIOT with a view to testing the truth of the specific allegations (including those set out in paragraph 34 above) relating to rendition through the territory. We conclude that it is unsatisfactory that the Government is not able to give us a categorical assurance that re-victualling of ships anchored outside BIOT's territorial waters by any vessel from BIOT, for purpose of assisting rendition, has not occurred. We further conclude that it is unsatisfactory that the US has only undertaken to inform the UK of the movement of ships in Diego Garcia's territorial waters in normal circumstances but not in all cases. We recommend that the Government requests the US Administration to supply details of any movement of ships in Diego Garcia's waters since January 2002 that were not notified at the time to the UK authorities, and seek assurances that at no point were these or other vessels used for re-victualling of vessels outside Diego Garcia's territorial waters which were being used for purposes of rendition.**

Acceptance of US assurances

38. The Government has repeatedly demonstrated a willingness to accept US assurances in relation to the use of BIOT for rendition flights. A report from the Council of Europe in 2007 criticised the Government for having accepted these assurances "without ever independently or transparently inquiring into the allegations itself, or accounting to the public in a sufficiently thorough manner".[71] The 2007 ISC report on rendition exonerated

---

the Government from this charge, but did so before the revelation in February 2008 about the use of BIOT for rendition purposes.[72] In our own Report on the Overseas Territories, published in July 2008, we concluded that "it is deplorable that previous US assurances about rendition flights have turned out to be false."

39. The Foreign Secretary continues to argue that US assurances, such as those given by former Secretary of State Condoleeza Rice, can be relied upon:

> I have had assurances, as I say, at the highest level that there are no cases beyond those two, and also that if there was any desire on the part of the United States to use Diego Garcia for so-called extraordinary rendition, or for any kind of rendition, the British Government would be consulted.

> We can be confident that our closest intelligence and foreign policy ally seeks to honour its trust with us in all respects. The degree of intelligence co-operation that exists between the US and the UK is of a unique standard and standing. It is based on mutual trust. It is not only one-way traffic. The US Government understand the importance of transparency and full openness with us. When the Secretary of State of the United States gives you her word, you take it very seriously. [73]

40. Mr Miliband argued that:

> It was certainly proactive on the part of the US to notify us in the first place of this new evidence that arose in February 2008. That did not emerge because I had been in touch with them about a particular case—they came to us. They were clearly proactive in that instance. I think that they have subsequently looked hard at their own systems, but they have been clear with me, in a way that I have then reported in full to Parliament, about the limits of their use of Diego Garcia. [74]

The Foreign Secretary assured us that in future the US would seek agreement for use of Diego Garcia for rendition flights:

> Just to be clear, the information came out because the Americans found it; they found it and they told us. We said, very clearly, that our understanding of the agreement in respect of Diego Garcia was that there had to be agreement. They subsequently said, "We give you absolute assurance that, in all future cases, there will be; we will see that agreement." So there is no mystery about that.[75]

41. We reiterate our previous conclusion that it is deplorable that previous US assurances about rendition flights through Diego Garcia have turned out to be false. We further conclude that the basis of trust in subsequent US assurances about the use of BIOT has been undermined. We recommend that the Government outline what practical action it is taking to ensure that it has full sources of information about US rendition activity on BIOT.

---

72   Intelligence and Security Committee, *Rendition*, Cm 7171, July 2007, para 210

73   Qq 96, 98

74   Q 97

Empty flights and the use of UK airports

42. In our last human rights Report we commented on the use of UK territory by aircraft on their way to conduct rendition operations or returning empty from such operations.[76] In its response to that Report, the Government stated that it:

> does not consider that a flight transiting UK territory or airspace on its way to or from a rendition operation constitutes rendition. Nor do we consider that permitting transit or refuelling of an aircraft without detainees on board without knowledge of what activities that aircraft had been or would be involved in, or indeed whether or not those activities were unlawful, to be unlawful in itself. There are more than two million flights through UK airspace annually. It would be unreasonable and impractical to check every aircraft transiting UK airspace on the basis that it may have been, at some point in the past, and without UK knowledge, involved in a possible unlawful operation. Instead an intelligence-led approach is and must be employed.[77]

In his submission, Andrew Tyrie MP pointed out that the list of flights which was sent to the US in May 2008 "did not include flights through UK airspace that did not land at UK airports". He added that "the Foreign Secretary failed to ask the US to confirm whether any of the flights on the list were 'rendition circuit' flights. He appeared not to know whether the US had cross-checked the list of flights with their own records before providing renewed assurances on this issue."[78]

43. **We reiterate our earlier conclusion that the Government has a moral and legal obligation to ensure that flights that enter UK airspace or land at UK airports are not part of the rendition circuit. We acknowledge the practical difficulties in the way of monitoring all empty flights transiting UK territory or airspace. We recommend that the Government, in its response to this Report, sets out options for more effectively establishing whether flights, including those by civilian aircraft, are on their way to or from a rendition operation.**

---

76 Foreign Affairs Committee, Ninth Report of Session 2007–08, *Human Rights Annual Report 2007*, HC 533, para 47

77 Government response to Foreign Affairs Committee, Ninth Report of Session 2007–08, *Human Rights Annual Report*, Cm 7463, para 23

78 Ev 64

[...]

4 Transfers of detainees

86. At a joint evidence session held with the Defence Committee in October 2008, we questioned the Foreign Secretary and the then Defence Secretary on issues relating to transfers of prisoners from UK custody in Iraq and Afghanistan, and the possibility that transferred prisoners may have subsequently suffered ill treatment.[166] In our current inquiry we have returned to some of the issues raised at that hearing.

The Government's review of records of detention

87. The then Secretary of State for Defence, Rt Hon John Hutton MP, made a Statement to the House on 26 February 2009 giving the results of a Ministry of Defence review of records of detention resulting from security operations carried out by UK armed forces in Iraq and Afghanistan.[167] The review had been prompted by the allegations made by Ben Griffin, a former member of UK special forces. The website of the 'Stop the War Coalition' reports Mr Griffin as stating that:

Individuals detained by British soldiers [...] have ended up in Guantánamo Bay Detention Camp, Bagram Theatre Internment Facility, Balad Special Forces Base, Camp Nama BIAP and Abu Ghraib Prison. [...] I have no doubt in my mind that non-combatants I personally detained were handed over to the Americans and subsequently tortured.[168]

In February 2009 Mr Griffin was served with a High Court order preventing him from repeating these allegations or making any fresh allegations of a similar nature arising from his experience of UK special forces' operations.[169]

88. The Defence Secretary's statement on 26 February detailed that of 479 individuals detained by the UK between July 2006 and December 2008, 254 were subsequently transferred to Afghan authorities, 217 were released and 8 had died. The statement asserts that there were "a further seven individuals detained by UK forces between 2001 and April 2006", but it does not state what became of them.[170] The Foreign Secretary gave us an updated set of figures when he gave oral evidence to us in June 2009, but later revised these in writing to clarify that there had been 549 detentions in the period between July 2006 and 16 June 2009. Of these "257 have been released, 283 transferred to the Afghans, 8 died, and 1 is receiving medical treatment".[171]

89. In his February 2009 statement, the Defence Secretary noted that previous estimates of the number of prisoners held by the UK in Iraq had been considerably overstated, and he

166 Oral evidence taken before the Defence and Foreign Affairs Committees on 28 October 2008, HC (2007-08) 1145-i

167 HC Deb, 26 February 2009, cols 394-97

168 Statement of Ben Griffin, 25 February 2008, http://stopwar.org.uk/content/view/533/27/

169 The Guardian, "Court gags ex-SAS man who made torture claims", 29 February 2009

170 HC Deb, 26 February 2009, col 394

apologised for this and other inaccuracies in information given to the House. In addition, he admitted that one category of detainee was not included in the review figure:

> In areas outside multi-national division South East, UK forces have undertaken operations to capture individuals who were subsequently detained by the US. These individuals do not feature in the data I set out above, and I do not intend to provide further details on these detentions today.[172]

We remain unclear as to what has been the fate of detainees captured in this way. Reprieve highlighted this issue in a press release in February 2009, stating that it was "deeply concerned about the inadequate scope of the MOD review [...] specifically that it does not include the participation of UK personnel in joint operations under the overall command of the US".[173] In his evidence to us Clive Stafford Smith questioned

> whether their review has been enough. The letter that the Minister wrote is very carefully written, and it is very carefully written to exclude, for example, Task Force 36, where the British were working with the Americans on the big-name people—Al-Zarqawi and people like that. The people who have been reviewed and admitted publicly are by definition the less significant people, [...] It is important to follow up on that, because we are responsible for those people. [174]

90. **We conclude that it is a matter of concern that the Government has not provided details of the fate of individuals detained by US forces in Iraq as a result of operations by UK forces, or those captured by UK forces and detained by US forces. We recommend that, in its response to this Report, the Government informs us of the number of such detainees, relevant details of the circumstances of their capture and the degree of involvement of UK forces, and any assurances it has received from the US authorities about their treatment and whereabouts, on an individual basis. We further recommend that the Government, in its response, provides us with a full statement of its record-keeping practice in respect of persons captured by UK forces in Iraq and Afghanistan, whether or not UK forces make the eventual detention.**

---

172 HC Deb, 26 February 2009, col 394

173 Reprieve press release, 26 February 2009,

174 Q 49

[...]

Transfers to US forces in Iraq

96. In his February 2009 statement (see paragraph 87 above), the Defence Secretary reported that two detainees originally captured by UK forces were, in February 2004, transferred to the US authorities and subsequently moved to Afghanistan, where they remain. In their written submission, the FCO state that the position of the US is that "it is neither possible nor desirable to transfer them to either their country of detention or their country of origin".[186] A due-diligence search by US officials has found that this was the only occasion on which UK-detained personnel transferred to US forces in Iraq were subsequently transferred out of the country. Mr Hutton admitted that brief references to the case were included in "lengthy" papers which went to the then Foreign and Home Secretaries (Rt Hon Jack Straw MP and Rt Hon Charles Clarke MP respectively) in April 2006, but that "the context provided did not highlight its significance at that point".[187] A subsequent Parliamentary Question revealed that an MoD official was copied a document noting the transfer on 7 October 2004. According to the Government, the document has not been found in MoD records and the official does not recollect receiving it. The then

184 Ev 75

185 Q 52

186 Ev 46

187 HC Deb, 26 February 2009, col 394

Defence Secretary stated that he was satisfied that his officials "were unaware of the case and that they acted in good faith at all times".[188] The two individuals were Pakistani members of the Lashkar-e-Taiba organisation in Iraq,[189] and the US claims the transfer occurred " because of a lack of relevant linguists to interrogate them effectively in Iraq"[190]

97. Amnesty International expressed concern about the transfer, stating that:

> On the basis of the limited public information about these two cases, it appears that the detainees would have been "protected persons" under the Fourth Geneva Convention and that the USA would have violated this provision when it transferred them to Afghanistan. Unlawful deportation or transfer or unlawful confinement, as well as torture and other inhuman treatment, in violation of the Geneva Conventions, are war crimes.[191]

They recommended that the Government should give further details of the cases of the two men transferred to Afghanistan from Iraq, including

> whether the two men [...] were held in secret detention by the USA at any time; whether they were subjected to interrogation techniques or detention conditions that violated the prohibition of torture or other ill-treatment; and, if so, whether anyone has been held accountable.[192]

Reprieve recommended that the prisoners should be identified and given legal representation, and that a review take place to investigate possible UK involvement in such activities elsewhere.[193] Clive Stafford Smith argued that

> the British Government have admitted that we were involved in something that is illegal under British law [...] It is inconceivable to me, quite frankly, that the British Government can say publicly, "We admit that we committed two criminal acts, but we are not going to tell you who the victims of those acts are." [194]

98. The Foreign Secretary told us that the transfer did not indicate shortcomings in record keeping, adding that:

> When the former Defence Secretary made his statement to the House of Commons, he made it clear that the transfer to Afghanistan should have been questioned at the time [...] the future course of those two people should have been questioned at the time. There was no question of British personnel collaborating or colluding in rendition to Afghanistan.[195]

---

188 HC Deb, 3 March 2009, col 1439W

189 Q 145, 147; Ev 146

190 Ev 46

191 Ev 76

He promised to provide us with the FCO's assessment of the legality of the transfer, adding that the answer would be:

> part governed by the fact that Iraq was under a chapter 7 mandate at the time and the law of armed conflict was in issue at the time in Iraq. I think that there would be a large number of unique legal issues at stake. That is what makes a difference. Iraq and Afghanistan have been and are governed by international legal commitments that are different from some of the other cases mentioned.[196]

The FCO later informed us that

> The US believes they had legal authority to make this transfer [...] however, the United States is currently reviewing its policy in this area. We welcome this review and look forward to its outcome. In the particular case in question, we have sought and received assurances about the welfare of the individuals concerned and have put into place safeguards and guarantees to prevent repetition.[197]

99. We asked the Foreign Secretary whether he would provide details about these men's identities and give assurances about their treatment since the transfer. He replied that "the former Defence Secretary gave all the information that we had at the time of the statement to Parliament; I am not aware of any further information having come to light since then."[198] Correcting the transcript of the session, the Foreign Secretary subsequently noted that it would have been more correct to state that "We are unable to provide further information on this matter other than that given by my Rt. Hon. Friend the former Secretary of State for Defence in his statement of 26 February 2009."[199]

100. Clive Stafford Smith asserted that that this was not an isolated case:

> we have identified at least one other person. The facts are a bit different. He was not originally in British custody; he was turned over to the British, the British carried him around for a while and then turned him back over to the Americans, and the guy was then rendered—and that is certainly not included in the British report.[200]

He also suggested that the allegations made by Ben Griffin related to additional cases:

> Taking it a step further, you will be familiar with the gag order that was applied to Mr. Griffin when he started talking about these materials [see paragraph 87 above]. You will know that he was in Iraq only from 2005 onward—after the 2004 renditions that are discussed in the Minister's letter. To the extent that Mr. Griffin was talking about renditions that Britain was involved in that he knows about, those happened after the two that were dealt with in the Minister's letter[201]

---

196 Q 148

197 Ev 52

101. We conclude that the onward transfer to Afghanistan of two Pakistani men transferred from UK to US custody in Iraq in 2004 is of great concern. We do not regard the stated reason for this transfer, that US forces did not have sufficient linguists available in Iraq, as being convincing. We further conclude that it is not acceptable that the Government is unable to identify these detainees, or to provide assurances about their subsequent treatment. We recommend that the Government, in its response to this Report, identifies these men, and inform us of what steps it has taken to discover whether they have been treated in an acceptable way since being transferred to US forces. We conclude that the allegation by Reprieve that these two cases were not, as the Government asserts, isolated ones, gives cause for concern. We recommend that the Government investigates in detail any specific allegations put before it by Reprieve and reports to us the outcome of those investigations.

[...]

Legal responsibility for detainees after transfer

107. During our joint evidence session with the Defence Committee on Iraq and Afghanistan in October 2008, we explored the issue of the responsibility that the UK retains for detainees following their transfer. During that session the then Defence Secretary, Mr Hutton, appeared to suggest that such a responsibility existed,[211] but in a subsequent memorandum he corrected his position:

> I [...] want to take this opportunity to confirm our legal position with regard to detainees. The UK does not have legal obligations towards the treatment of individuals we have detained once they have been transferred to the custody of another state, whether in Iraq or Afghanistan or through the normal judicial extradition process.[212]

In a subsequent letter the Foreign Secretary confirmed that the FCO concurred with this position, adding:

> HMG takes meticulous care that any transfer takes place in accordance with the strategic framework of memoranda of understanding and other assurances, so that we can be abundantly certain that it is consistent with any applicable international human rights obligations of the United Kingdom.[213]

108. Andrew Tyrie MP provided us with a legal opinion published on 29 September 2008, prepared by Michael Fordham QC and Tom Hickman, barristers at Blackstone Chambers who specialise in human rights law. Mr Tyrie told us that:

> The Opinion makes clear that assurances provided by another state, that an individual handed over by UK forces would not be mistreated, would not absolve the UK government of the obligation to examine whether the assurances provide a sufficient guarantee that the individual will be protected against the risk of ill-treatment. Importantly, the Legal Opinion highlights "specific concerns about the legality of the UK having accepted such assurances" from the US.[214]

109. Mr Tyrie subsequently wrote to the Chairman of the Defence Committee, Rt Hon James Arbuthnot MP, setting out his grounds for challenging the validity of Mr Hutton's statement:

> if an individual has been transferred in circumstances where the transfer arguably breached the European Convention on Human Rights, and the Human Rights Act,

---

210 Q161

211 Evidence taken before the Defence and Foreign Affairs Committees on 28 October 2009, Iraq and Afghanistan, HC (2007–08) 1145–I, Q24-25

212 Evidence taken before the Defence and Foreign Affairs Committees on 28 October 2009, Iraq and Afghanistan, HC (2007–08) 1145–I, Ev 20

213 Foreign Affairs Committee, Eighth Report of Session 2008–09, HC 302, Ev 161

then there may be a continuing obligation on the UK to investigate the circumstances of that transfer. This appears to have been contradicted by the Secretary of State's letter;

although there are obligations up to the point of transfer to ensure that a detainee is treated in accordance with the rights set out in the ECHR, this is not mentioned by the Secretary of State in his letter;

agreements between the UK and the Afghan authorities and between the UK, Australia and the US, give the UK powers that appear inconsistent with the Secretary of State's assertion that the UK no longer has any legal obligations towards transferred detainees;

there may also be continuing obligations under criminal law or tort law once a detainee has been transferred. This also appears to have been contradicted by the Secretary of State's letter.[215]

110. Kate Allen of Amnesty International was clear that "the legal obligation still rests with the UK", [216] and Benjamin Ward indicated that the UK has

to make a risk assessment before the transfer. If there is a real risk, they are responsible for any treatment that the person is subject to after the transfer. They would then be obliged to take steps to remedy that, such as providing compensation and carrying out an investigation. Obviously, if a person has been tortured, you cannot untorture them.[217]

111. A further issue is the extent to which the Government follows up in individual cases the welfare of detainees that have been transferred. Clive Stafford Smith told us that

You cannot assess whether you have got it right if you do not find out what happened to the guys. I cannot answer this quite frankly, but I doubt very much that our Government know what happened to all the people who were turned over.[218]

112. The Foreign Secretary told us that the Government does follow up what has happened to the detainees that are transferred:

If you mean by systematic an ongoing, detailed, in person investigation, then that has been going on. To put that in perspective, it is useful to have some numbers. As of last week, 544 people had been detained, 295 had been transferred to the Afghan authorities and 259 had been released. That gives you some idea of the scale that we are talking about. That is why, when I talk about British embassy officials from Kabul, or the Royal Military Police investigating it, given the scale of that detention, it is reasonable to talk about an ongoing, in person, careful review of the situation.[219]

---

215 http://www.extraordinaryrendition.org/index.php/appg-letters-on-extraordinary-rendition/uk-committees?start=5

216 Q 55

217 Q 55

218 Q 55

219 Q 163

113. We conclude that although there may be scope for argument about the extent of the legal obligation on the UK to monitor the welfare of individual detainees after it has transferred them to another country, there is no doubt in our view that the UK is under a moral obligation to do so. Such monitoring is desirable not only to enable the Government to intervene if it receives information that an individual is being ill-treated, but also because any evidence thus revealed of systematic ill-treatment will call into question whether future transfers to that country should take place. We recommend that the Government takes the necessary action to ensure that it has mechanisms in place to allow it effectively to monitor the welfare of individuals transferred, and in its response to this Report sets out what specific steps it is taking.

[...]

(28) Joint Committee on Human Rights, Sixteenth Report of 2009-10, 'Counter-Terrorism Policy and Human Rights: Bringing Human Rights Back In', March 2010 (extracts)

[...]

3 Complicity in torture

[...]

39. It seems to us that the Minister (in his evidence to us), the Director General of MI5, and both the Home and Foreign Secretaries, in their recent public statements, come very close to saying that, at least in the wake of 9/11, the lesser of two evils was the receipt and use of intelligence which was known, or should have been known, to carry a risk that it might have been obtained under torture, in order to protect the UK public from possible terrorist attack. This is no defence to the charge of complicity in torture.

40. We cannot find any legal basis for the Government's narrow formulation of the meaning of complicity in its Response to our Report on Complicity in Torture. The

Government's formulation of its position changes the relevant question from "does or should the official receiving the information know that it has or is likely to have been obtained by torture?" to "does the official receiving the information know or believe that receipt of the information would encourage the intelligence services of other states to commit torture?" As we made clear in our earlier report, 'complicity', in the sense used in the relevant international standards, does not require active encouragement. The systematic receipt of information obtained by torture is a form of aquiescence, or tacit consent, and the relevant state of mind is whether the official receiving the information knew or should have known that it was or was likely to have been obtained by torture.

41. The Government's formulation appears to us to be carefully designed to enable it to say that, although it knew or should have known that some intelligence it received was or might have been obtained through torture, this did not amount to complicity in torture because it did not know or believe that such receipt would encourage the use of torture by other States.

Guidance on interrogation overseas

42. In March 2009 the Government agreed to provide the ISC with its guidance to the intelligence services on the detention and interrogation of suspects overseas. In September, the ISC expressed its disappointment at the delay in providing it with the guidance, despite repeated requests, which meant it could not begin its inquiry. Following the ISC's public criticism, the Government finally provided the ISC with the guidance on 18 November, a delay of 8 months. The ISC states on its website:

> We have been told that this delay was due to the complex legal nature of these issues, and the need to consolidate previously separate guidance into one version. The Committee will consider the material, take further evidence and seek independent legal advice, before reporting our findings to the Prime Minister.

43. We asked the Minister and his official, Ms Byrne, a number of questions about exactly what guidance has been provided to the ISC and in particular whether it has been provided with unedited versions of all the guidance that existed at the time of the various allegations of complicity. However, we remained unclear about whether all of the earlier versions have been provided. Ms Byrne said, for example (Q32), that "they have all the sets of material that we were able to give."

44. We therefore wrote to the Minister after our evidence session asking him to confirm that the ISC has been provided with all versions of the guidance that were current at the time of the various allegations of the UK's complicity in torture, and that nothing had been deleted from those versions of the guidance. The Minister's response was that "all *current* versions of relevant guidance were provided to the ISC in May. These were then consolidated into a single version which was provided to the ISC on 18 November 2009".[30] If all relevant versions were indeed provided to the ISC in May 2009, why would the ISC complain publicly in September that they had not received the guidance and why was it necessary to provide a consolidated version in November 2009?

---

30   Letter from David Hanson, 13 January 2010, above n. 10 (emphasis added).

45. We regret to say that, despite the clear intent of our questions, the Government's answers leave us no clearer about whether the ISC has been provided with all versions of the guidance which was current at the time of the various allegations of complicity, which date back to 2002. We look to the ISC to provide clarification on this point.

46. It is, however, clear that the Government does not intend to make public the guidance which was current at the relevant time to which the various allegations relate. The Prime Minister, in his evidence to the Liaison Committee, confirmed that the Government is refusing to publish the earlier guidance.[31] Asked whether he will make public the guidance which was in place at the time the complicity in torture was alleged to have taken place, he said "I would not want to go back in time and publish previous recommendations. I would want to publish the recommendations that are going to be in force from now on." He gave no reason for that refusal, other than to refer generally to the fact that there are cases about the allegations of complicity being dealt with at the moment through the courts.

47. We welcome the Prime Minister's commitment to publish the new guidelines which will be drawn up by the Intelligence and Security Committee. However, the Prime Minister's statements on this issue, from his first written statement on 18 March 2009 on, are in the present tense. He draws a clear line between the new guidance, which will come out of the process that he has set in motion, and the old guidance, which the Government has decided not to publish. No convincing justification has been offered for the decision not to publish the previous guidance. As we have pointed out before, in the United States, the Obama administration has put into the public domain significant Justice Department memos, including legal advice, about matters as sensitive as interrogation techniques. In our view, there can be no justification for not publishing the guidelines that were in place at the time the alleged complicity in torture took place. In order to learn lessons for the future, as well as to ensure proper accountability for past wrongs where appropriate, it is essential that the earlier guidance be published. We also repeat our earlier recommendation that the relevant legal advice also be made public. The Government has not convincingly explained what makes the UK different from the United States, where the legal advice has been published.

The urgent need for an independent inquiry

48. In our report on Complicity in Torture, we concluded that, in view of the large number of unanswered questions, there was now no other way to restore public confidence in the intelligence services than by setting up an independent inquiry into the numerous allegations about the UK's complicity in torture.[32] Since the publication of our report, there has been a number of significant developments which have led to many further calls for a public inquiry into these allegations about complicity in torture, both from within and outside Parliament.

49. On 24 November 2009 Human Rights Watch ("HRW") published its Report, *Cruel Britannia: British Complicity in the Torture and Ill-Treatment of Terror Suspects in Pakistan*. The HRW Report contains accounts from victims and their families about the cases of five UK citizens of Pakistani origin who were tortured in Pakistan by Pakistani

---

31 Oral evidence taken before the Liaison Committee on 2 February 2010, HC (2009–10) 346-i, Qs 81-83

32 Report on Complicity in Torture, above n. 24, at para. 99

security agencies between 2004 and 2007. It claims that, while there is no evidence of UK officials directly participating in torture, UK complicity is clear. It argues that the UK government was fully aware of the systematic use of torture in Pakistan, and that UK officials knew that torture was taking place in these five cases. Some of the individuals are said to have met UK officials while detained in Pakistan, in some cases shortly after the individuals had been tortured. UK officials are said to have supplied questions and lines of enquiry to Pakistan intelligence sources in cases where detainees were tortured, and to have put pressure on Pakistani authorities for results, passing questions and offering other co-operation without ensuring that the detainees were treated appropriately. The Report claims that members of Pakistan's intelligence agencies have corroborated the information from the detainees themselves that UK officials were aware of specific cases of mistreatment.

50. On 10 February 2010 the Court of Appeal rejected the Foreign Secretary's attempt to prevent the publication of seven redacted sub-paragraphs in the judgment of the High Court in Binyam Mohamed's case.[33] The paragraphs were immediately published. In our view they represent strong evidence to suggest that the Security Service was complicit in the torture of Binyam Mohamed by the US authorities. Sub-paragraph (ix) states:

> We regret to have to conclude that the reports provided to the SyS [Security Service] made clear to anyone reading them that BM was being subjected to the treatment that we have described and the effect upon him of that intentional treatment.

51. The publication of the previously withheld paragraphs led to a renewed flurry of calls for an independent inquiry into the extent of the UK's complicity in torture. These calls were fortified by the suggestion in the Court of Appeal's judgments that the apparent complicity in Binyam Mohamed's case called into question the reliability of the Security Services's denials of allegations that there was a wider problem of the Security Services' complicity in torture. In particular, the Master of the Rolls, Lord Neuberger, said in para. 168 of his judgment:

> "168. Fourthly, it is also germane that the Security Services had made it clear in March 2005, through a report from the Intelligence and Security Committee, that 'they operated a culture that respected human rights and that coercive interrogation techniques were alien to the Services' general ethics, methodology and training' (paragraph 9 of the first judgment), indeed they 'denied that [they] knew of any ill–treatment of detainees interviewed by them whilst detained by or on behalf of the [US] Government' (paragraph 44(ii) of the fourth judgment). Yet, in this case, that does not seem to have been true: as the evidence showed, some Security Services officials appear to have a dubious record relating to actual involvement, and frankness about any such involvement, with the mistreatment of Mr Mohamed when he was held at the behest of US officials. I have in mind in particular witness B, but the evidence in this case suggests that it is likely that there were others. The good faith of the Foreign Secretary is not in question, but he prepared the certificates partly, possibly largely, on the basis of information and advice provided by Security Services personnel. Regrettably, but inevitably, this must raise the question whether

any statement in the certificates on an issue concerning the mistreatment of Mr Mohamed can be relied on, especially when the issue is whether contemporaneous communications to the Security Services about such mistreatment should be revealed publicly. Not only is there some reason for distrusting such a statement, given that it is based on Security Services' advice and information, because of previous, albeit general, assurances in 2005, but also the Security Services have an interest in the suppression of such information."

52. Paradoxically, the case for a wide-ranging inquiry was forcibly made by the barrister representing the Foreign Office in the Binyam Mohamed case, Jonathan Sumption QC, in his letter to the Court of Appeal asking for the first draft of this paragraph in the draft judgment to be removed. The essence of his objection was that there is a limit to the extent to which the litigation of an individual case can lead to credible findings on systemic issues. Objecting to a part of the paragraph which suggested that there was an obvious reason for distrusting any UK Government assurance based on Security Service advice and information, because of previous 'form',[34] which Mr. Sumption said constituted an exceptionally damaging criticism of the good faith of the Security Service as a whole, he identified a number of questions which would need answering before the Court was able to make findings as to how systemic the problem was, for which a much wider inquiry would be needed:

> To categorise a problem as systemic is rarely a straightforward matter. In this case at the very least it would be necessary to examine the methods and procedures of the Security Service in relation to the interviewing of detainees as well as the giving of information and advice to ministers; the basis on which the statement to the Intelligence and Security Committee was made, and what further information was provided to them, in particular about the treatment of detainees; what (if any) other instances there are of the Services' knowledge of ill-treatment of the detainees interviewed by them, how information of this kind is stored, on what occasions it is retrieved, how widely it is disseminated within the Service and what the Service's response was. The Court has not been in a position to do any of this. It simply does not have the material.

53. **To the extent that the analysis in the letter of Jonathan Sumption QC draws attention to the inherent limitations of litigation as a means of inquiring into a wider systemic problem, we agree. It powerfully makes the case for an independent inquiry into these grave matters, which would not be constrained from looking at the wider issues in the way that the court adjudicating on Binyam Mohamed's claims inevitably is. In our view, the case for setting up an independent inquiry into the allegations of complicity in torture is now irresistible.**

---

34   The first draft of the relevant paragraph of Lord Neuberger's draft judgment (para 168) is set out in full at para 18 of the Court of Appeal's judgment in *R (on the application of Binyam Mohamed) v Secretary of State for Foreign and Commonwealth Affairs* (26 February 2010).

[...]

The British role: policy

29. Foreign Office memorandum on detainees in Afghanistan, 10 January 2002—p.323

In early January 2002, the Foreign Office faced increasing questions over the fate of British nationals detained in Afghanistan. One memorandum had noted that 'Public opinion has on the whole shown little concern about the welfare of the British detainees, or the legal terms of their detention. But the issue is clearly of sensitivity to Muslim opinion in the UK and abroad.' This paper sought to establish a position, seeing transfer to Guantánamo as a desirable resolution of the problem, while seeking to ensure that British officials would have consular access and that British nationals would not face the death penalty. Like others in this section, this document was released as a result of litigation brought by former Guantánamo detainees against the British authorities.

30. Guidance to SIS officer on treatment of a detainee, 11 January 2002—p.326

In an incident later highlighted by the ISC, in January 2002 an SIS officer became concerned at the treatment he observed of a detainee in US custody, and asked his superiors for guidance. The response, set out below and sent to all intelligence officers serving in Afghanistan, was considered by the ISC and others to be inadequate in failing to make clear that the officer was required to raise concerns with the US authorities. The full scope of guidance available at that time remains unclear.

31. Note on 'Warriors', 14 January 2002—p.328

This note, apparently written by a British intelligence officer, is cryptic but indicates both awareness of harsh interrogation conditions ('cold beaten up') and a weighing up of the options for dealing with the detainees, including 'collusive deportation [deleted] extradition'.

32. Telegram from the Foreign Secretary to Washington and other Embassies, 17 January 2002—p.330

In this telegram, the then Foreign Secretary, Jack Straw, set out the thinking about British nationals held in Afghanistan already indicated in the internal Foreign Office memorandum a week earlier (Document 29). While the Foreign Secretary hoped that the detainees would stay in Afghanistan long enough to be interviewed by the intelligence services, their subsequent removal to Guantánamo was seen as 'the best way to meet our counter-terrorism objective'. However, as the next document shows, in other parts of Whitehall concern was already growing at the conditions in Guantánamo.

33. Foreign Office memo and Prime Minister's comments, 18 January 2002—p.332

This Foreign Office memorandum to the then Prime Minister, Tony Blair, is most striking for the accompanying handwritten comments, believed to have been written by the Prime Minister, which read 'The key is to find out how they are being treated. Though I was initially sceptical about claims of torture we must make it clear to the US that any such action wd be totally unacceptable & v quickly establish that it isn't happening.' These concerns, however, did not translate into a changed British approach to the transfer of nationals to Guantánamo.

34. Memorandum from Stuart Horlock concerning detainees, 26 February 2002—p.334

This memorandum, from a senior Home Office official, is revealing of one of the strongest factors in official thinking about transfers to Guantánamo: that they represented a lesser evil than the possibility of the detainees returning to the UK and having to be released. This approach would later manifest itself in the handling of individual cases, such as that of Martin Mubanga (see Document 39).

35. Memorandum from Stuart Horlock, 12 April 2002—p.335

This memorandum suggests that official concern about handling of the issue was diminishing, and indicates interesting differences in approach between the Foreign Office and Number 10.

(29) Foreign Office memorandum on detainees in Afghanistan, 10 January 2002

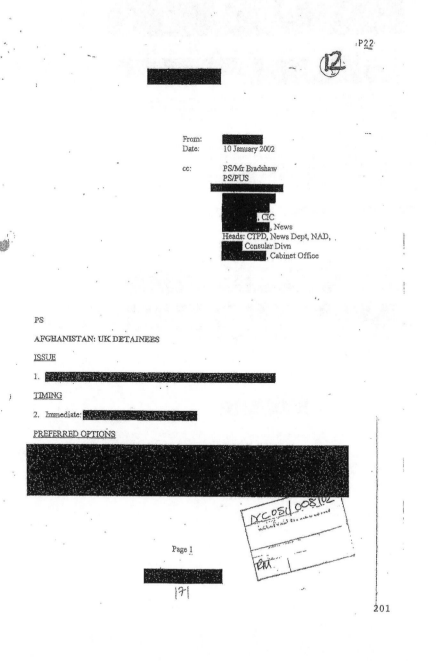

P22

From:
Date: 10 January 2002

cc: PS/Mr Bradshaw
PS/PUS

, CIC
, News
Heads: CTPD, News Dept, NAD, .
Consular Divn
, Cabinet Office

PS

AFGHANISTAN: UK DETAINEES

ISSUE

1.

TIMING

2. Immediate:

PREFERRED OPTIONS

Page 1

|7|

ARGUMENT

3. Transfer of UK nationals held by US forces in Afghanistan to the US base in Guantanamo is the best way to meet our counter-terrorism objective by ensuring that they are securely held. The only alternative is for the UK to take custody of them, either by UK forces in Afghanistan (who do not have the capacity to hold prisoners) or repatriation.

4. The security services are currently in Afghanistan interviewing detainees with a UK connection.

5. If British nationals are to remain in US custody we will need to continue to meet our consular obligations. In agreeing to this plan, we would need a number of reassurances from the Americans, notably:

- full information on who is being detained and who will be transferred;
- a guarantee of consular access in accordance with international obligations;
- information in due course of US intentions for handling these cases;
- if they plan to prosecute, full information on the procedure to be used (ie whether they will use military tribunals and details of how they would operate) including reassurances that any trial will conform with international standards and that no UK national will be sentenced to death.

BACKGROUND

6. We are aware of up to 12 possible British nationals held in Afghanistan, 5 by the US in Kandahar and 3 in Bagram. Washington telno 30 reports that the US now plan to start transferring detainees to the base in Guantanamo Bay in Cuba. The first batch, who might leave today, could include some who claim UK nationality.

7. There will inevitably be questions from MPs and the press about whether they will be tried by military tribunals and possibly executed. We should seek reassurances from the Americans on these points.

172

RESOURCE IMPLICATIONS

8. None.

PRESS LINES

9. News Department have had a lot of inquiries about UK detainees. Transfer of UK nationals to Guantanamo will quickly raise in the mind of the press the issue which we have so far been able to avoid publicly: are these British nationals to be tried in US military tribunals and be subject, possibly, to the death penalty. Our line – that we are seeking information and reassurances and that the US is aware of our opposition to the death penalty – is not strong, but a stronger line is difficult until policy is clearer. As the detainees will still be abroad, the FCO will remain the lead Whitehall department in press terms.

10. If asked about transfer to Guantanamo, we can say:

- We are aware of US plans to transfer detainees, including some UK nationals, to Guantanamo.
- The issue of how these prisoners should be handled is a matter for the US authorities. They have told us that they would be treated humanely.
- We have asked the Americans for full information on who will be transferred and what will happen to them. We are asking for consular access and reassurances that any trial will conform to international norms.

CTPD
Tel:

(30) Guidance to SIS officer on treatment of a detainee, 11 January 2002

67

DATE: 11/01/02

AL QAIDA DETAINEES

1. Thank you for making such a good and determined start on interviewing Al Qaida detainees; we can see all sorts of likely ⬛⬛⬛⬛⬛ benefits.

2. There are one or two legal points worth repeating and/or clarifying, some with particular reference to ⬛⬛⬛ some more general. ⬛⬛⬛ has asked that you share these with ⬛⬛⬛⬛

3. ⬛⬛⬛⬛⬛⬛⬛⬛⬛⬛⬛⬛⬛⬛⬛⬛⬛⬛⬛⬛⬛⬛⬛⬛⬛⬛⬛⬛⬛⬛⬛⬛⬛⬛⬛

4. With regard to the status of the prisoners, under the various Geneva conventions and protocols, all prisoners, however they are described, are entitled to the same level of protection. You have commented on their treatment. It appears from your description that they may not be being treated in accordance with the appropriate standards. Given that they are not within our custody or control, the law does not require you to intervene to prevent this. That said, HMG's stated commitment to human rights makes it important that

the Americans understand that we cannot be party to such ill treatment nor can we be seen to condone it. In no case should they be coerced during or in conjunction with an SIS interview of them. If circumstances allow, you should consider drawing this to the attention of a suitably senior US official locally.

5. It is important that you do not engage in any activity yourself that involves inhumane or degrading treatment of prisoners. As a representative of a UK public authority, you are obliged to act in accordance with the Human Rights Act 2000 which prohibits torture, or inhumane or degrading treatment. Also, as a Crown Servant, you are bound by Section 31 of the Criminal Justice Act 1948, which makes acts carried out overseas in the course of your official duties subject to UK criminal law. In other words, your actions incur criminal liability in the same way as if you were carrying out those acts in the UK.

6. If you require further guidance ▮▮▮▮▮ on this or related issues, please contact either ▮▮▮▮▮▮▮▮▮

(31) Note on 'Warriors', 14 January 2002

HQ Instructions Item 005

Warriors 14/1

1. interview conditions cold beaten up

2. mil. police: but flawed

(i) circs of arrest

(ii) ill-treatment

(iii) SS interviews: intelligence battlefield
planned attacks

(iv) take them back: (iv) access to sol[icitors]

collusive deportation extradition

vol[untary] return

options to stay

Army Legal Service: status

5

Waris 14/1 (2.4) Ⓢ

1. intonic writing   add   beaten up

2. nil. police. but flames

    (i) crs f— aud

    (ii) ill— treatment

    (iii) SS intonic. — intellgnce Justtifica)
                    — plan) attnds:

    (iv) take the bane:

                      (iv) accus to sa'
                                   extra

Any legal Service; status
                                  Communic deportdurs.
                                    nof. retn
                                    opti bsty.

(32) Telegram from the Foreign Secretary to Washington and other Embassies, 17 January 2002

ZCZC FCA500
OO CRN NDO LOG
.C 01 FSXAD
FM FCO 021
BT
FSX254

LNSXAN 9254 MAMIAN 2491
Internal Addressees
Action:▮▮▮▮▮▮▮▮▮▮▮▮▮▮▮▮▮▮▮▮▮▮▮▮▮▮▮

Info:▮▮▮▮

Date:101748Z JAN 02

Originator:FCO

Telegram Number:21

ADDRESSEES:
TO DESKBY 101800Z WASHINGTON
INFO IMMEDIATE UKMIS NEW YORK, UKMIS GENEVA, KABUL , HAVANA
INFO IMMEDIATE ISLAMABAD, TASHKENT, ANKARA, MODUK, PJHQUK
INFO IMMEDIATE CABINET OFFICE,▮▮▮▮▮▮▮▮▮▮▮▮ HOME OFFICE,▮▮▮▮▮▮▮
INFO IMMEDIATE RIYADH, SANAA, CANBERRA
INFO PRIORITY EU POSTS, NATO POSTS

PROTECTIVE MARKING:
▮▮▮▮▮▮▮▮▮▮▮▮▮

Subject:AFGHANISTAN: DETAINEES

SIC 19S
WASHINGTON TELNO 30
PJHQ PLEASE FORWARD TO NCC CENTCOM
CABINET OFFICE FOR ▮▮▮▮▮▮▮ NC 10
HEADS OF MISSION SECTION PLEASE PASS TO SIR C MEYER

SUMMARY

1. No objection to American plans to transfer UK detainees from
Afghanistan to Guantanamo Bay. We hope that UK nationals will not be
included in the first group of transfers. We should also insist on
consular access and full information on future handling.

DETAIL

2. The UK approach on the repatriation and prosecution of UK
nationals is still being considered. Nevertheless, we accept that
the transfer of UK nationals held by US forces in Afghanistan to the
US base in Guantanamo is the best way to meet our counter-terrorism
objective by ensuring that they are securely held. However, a
specialist team is currently in Afghanistan seeking to interview any
detainees with a UK connection to obtain information on their
terrorist activities and connections. We therefore hope that all
those detainees they wish to interview will remain in Afghanistan and
will not be among the first groups to be transferred to Guantanamo.
A week's delay should suffice. UK nationals should be transferred as
soon as possible thereafter.

▮▮

17/1/02

4.   We note that NSC were surprised by a reference to the Vienna
Convention. We are taking a consular access approach because we
believe that these rights and responsibilities apply under the
bilateral UK/US Consular Convention irrespective of whether or not
the detainee is being held as a POW under the Geneva Convention.

5. In response to any press enquiries about transfer to
Guantanamo, we can say:

- We are aware of US plans to transfer detainees, including some
UK nationals, to Guantanamo.
- It is for the US authorities to determine the details of how these
prisoners should be handled. They have told us that they would be
treated humanely.
- We have asked the Americans for full information on who will be
transferred and what will happen to them. We are asking for consular
access and reassurances that any trial and treatment will conform to
international norms.

6.   Please draw on these points in responding to State and NSC.
Advice on wider policy issues will follow.

STRAW

MAMIAN 2491

NNNN

(33) Foreign Office memo and Prime Minister's comments, 18 January 2002

12a

18 January 2002

Prime Minister
During the weekend we
may get feedback from
ICRC and from our team.

**Foreign &
Commonwealth
Office**

London SW1A 2AH

file

UK Nationals Held in Afghanistan and Guantanamo

You asked for a round up of the latest position.

I attach a chart listing the detainees who might be British. We still need to verify their identities and confirm their nationality. There might be other British detainees that have not yet been drawn to our attention.

The team from the Security Service and the Embassy in Washington is now in Guantanamo. They will be interviewing the detainees in accordance with the agreement reached with the Americans. Their dual aim is to obtain information on any terrorist activities affecting the UK and to establish the identity of any British nationals. We have asked for an initial report on Monday morning. The team will report back to Ministers after their visit; they will not speak to the press.

The ICRC are due to arrive in Guantanamo today. There will be intense press interest in any conclusions they reach on humanitarian issues. However it is highly unlikely that they will make public any judgements on conditions in the camp or make statements on individual cases.

This will continue to be a difficult issue to handle, both in procedural and legal terms with the US and in handling Parliament and the media here.

10 Downing Street

The key is to find out how they are being treated. Though I was initially sceptical about claims of torture we must make it clear to the U.S. that any such action wd be totally unacceptable & v. quickly establish that it isn't happening.

(34)   Memorandum from Stuart Horlock concerning detainees, 26 February 2002

13

From   Stuart Horlock
        Terrorism & Protection Unit
        6ᵗʰ Floor West Wing
        ▉ ▉▉▉▉▉▉▉

cc   John Gieve
        John Warne
        Bob Whalley

26 February 2002

<u>Emily Miles</u>

UK NATIONALS HELD IN GUANTANAMO BAY

Bob Whalley mentioned to you that this issue was raised at TIDO(O) yesterday and said I would provide a short note in advance of the minutes.

- FCO said that despite Rumsfield's comments and subsequent press coverage the American position remained unchanged and that no decisions had been taken in respect of the detainees. It was not expected that the Americans would decide to deport the British detainees quickly and certainly not without advance warning.

- Indeed, the Americans currently take the view that "the ball in the UK court" and wish to know from us how we would handle any returnees. TIDO(O) commissioned an outline of the process that could be passed to the Americans and I am to circulate a draft today. ▉▉▉▉▉▉▉▉▉▉▉▉▉▉▉▉▉▉▉▉▉▉▉▉▉▉▉▉▉▉▉▉▉▉▉

- The meeting agreed that UK should not be in any hurry to take back the detainees though FCO was quiet on the point.

- If the difficulties we face steers the Americans to make more use of military tribunals FCO will have some obvious problems of public presentation (which are already beginning to emerge) but these are likely to be preferable to those associated with the detainees being released in the UK.

- ▉▉▉▉▉▉▉▉▉▉▉▉▉▉▉▉▉▉▉▉▉▉▉▉▉▉▉▉▉▉

STUART HORLOCK

(35)   Memorandum from Stuart Horlock, 12 April 2002

From   Stuart Horlock
       Terrorism & Protection Unit
       6th Floor West Wing

cc   John Warne
       Bob Whalley

12 April 2001

Paul Oldfield

JOHN GIEVE'S MEETING WITH SIR ANTHONY JAY -
DETAINEES AT GUATANAMO BAY

You asked for briefing on this issue.

There have been no significant developments in these cases since a flurry of activity
in mid March. We know of no issues of particular concern to FCO requiring
immediate attention.

In mid-March a number of tricky issues were being considered.

Level of protection (by HMG) to be afforded to British citizens held

- British Embassy officials told Americans informally that it was possible
  that we would revert with formal (and public) requests for legal access.
  FCO had wanted to do this (and wanted to be seen to be doing it) but had
  been overruled by No.10.

Legal proceedings here

- An application for judicial review of HMG's role in assisting the
  Americans in detaining and interrogating one of the British detainees
  (ABASSI) was refused.

Military tribunals

- Regulation for the Military Commissions were published by the
  Americans. The presumption of innocence until proven guilty, standards
  of proof 'beyond reasonable doubt' and safeguards akin to those
  available to military court martials took some of the steam out of press
  and public criticism.

- Statements from President Bush referring to the detainees as "killers" on
  the same day that the regulations were published did not draw criticism
  here that minds had already been made up.

Intelligence gathering

- British detainees have been interviewed by Security Service on two separate occasions. The detainees were co-operative and provided good information.

- SIS and the Security Service are now ▮▮▮▮▮▮▮▮▮▮ interviewing other nationals ▮▮▮▮▮▮▮▮▮▮

Return of detainees to UK

▮▮

Prosecutions here

- ▮▮▮▮▮▮▮▮▮▮▮▮▮▮▮▮▮▮▮▮▮▮▮▮▮▮▮▮▮▮▮▮▮▮▮▮▮▮ The Home Secretary felt there would also be questions about public interest in prosecuting young and ill-informed individuals who may have been manipulated by others.

- The Americans are prepared to assist the police here in compiling admissible evidence.

Handling

- No press coverage here during the last four weeks.

STUART HORLOCK

The British role: individual cases

36. Bisher al-Rawi and Jamil el-Banna—p.339

The role of the security services in the arrest of Bisher al-Rawi and Jamil el-Banna in The Gambia in November 2002, and their subsequent rendition to Afghanistan and finally to Guantánamo, remains unclear. The first of this group of documents indicates an apparent attempt by the security services to elicit cooperation from el-Banna (referred to in the report as Abu Anas) shortly before his journey to The Gambia. The later documents are telegrams sent by SyS to their American counterparts, detailing the arrest of the men at Heathrow because of suspicious items in al-Rawi's luggage, and notifying the Americans of their later flight to The Gambia. A final telegram, which was sent to SIS and the Foreign Office, describes their arrest on arrival in Banjul. The security services were later criticised for failing to clarify in telegrams to the Americans that the devices in al-Rawi's luggage were found to be innocent, and for not telling Ministers until 2006 of information relevant to al-Rawi's case, possibly relating to his alleged relationship with the security services (see Document 24).

37. Binyam Mohamed judgment (extracts)—p.350

Binyam Mohamed, an Ethiopian national resident in Britain since 1994, was arrested in Pakistan in April 2002 on suspicion of terrorist activities. He arrived in Guantánamo in September 2004, having allegedly been rendered via Morocco (in which he reportedly suffered severe torture) and Afghanistan. Released in 2009, he was the central figure in a court case in which the British authorities were found to have 'facilitated' his interrogation at times when he was known to be held incommunicado and when at least some within the security services were aware that he was subject to maltreatment. These extracts from the High Court judgment of 21 August 2008 describe the main features of his case. Deletions and text in bold indicate amendments to the judgment made on 31 July 2009.

38. Binyam Mohamed: the US threat and the redacted paragraphs—p.363

This judgment of 4 February 2009, on whether a short summary of Binyam Mohamed's treatment could be published by the court, considered the US's opposition to publication and the role of the ISC. Regarding the former, in spite of the Court's clear reservations about suppression, it concluded that the then Foreign Secretary was acting in good faith and on the basis of a real threat from the US to reconsider its intelligence sharing relationship with the UK if the paragraphs were published.

The High Court overturned this ruling on 16 October 2009 and on 10 February 2010 the Court of Appeal upheld the decision to publish the redacted paragraphs. At the end of the extract are the seven paragraphs in question; they had been redacted from the original judgment (Document 37) but were published as an appendix to the Court of Appeal's 10 February judgment.

39. Martin Mubanga—p.368

Martin Mubanga, a dual British-Zambian national, was arrested in Zambia in March 2002. As indicated by these documents, released in connection with the litigation brought by former Guantánamo detainees, the British authorities had no desire to take consular responsibility for him; the telegram from the Deputy Head of Mission in Lusaka, written some months later, indicates that clear instructions to this effect came from No. 10. The memorandum from the head of SyS, Eliza Manningham-Buller, to the Permanent Secretary at the Home Office indicates the dilemma: the security services did not believe that there was enough evidence to charge Mubanga, but their interviews with him led them to believe that he was dangerous. There was also fear that his release would trigger a 'hostile American reaction'. In these circumstances, some officials at least appear to have viewed his transfer to Guantánamo as a desirable outcome, although the circumstances in which this eventually took place (in April) remain unclear.

40. Omar Deghayes—p.382

Omar Deghayes, a Libyan refugee from the Gaddafi regime and long-term British resident, was arrested in Pakistan in early 2002. Intelligence officers who inter-viewed him thought him uncooperative. In a section of interview notes released in the detainee court case – undated, but clearly before March 2002 – one of his interviewers recommended that 'If he sticks to his story and gives us just a few more details, we propose disengaging and allowing events here to take their course.' Notes of subsequent interviews in Islamabad and Bagram are heavily redacted and in some cases fragmentary, but suggest that officers used threats of long-term detention by the Americans, or (by implication) his return to Libya. Deghayes was transferred to Guantánamo in the autumn of 2002 and alleges serious maltreatment during his detention there. He was released in December 2007.

(36)   Bisher al-Rawi and Jamil el-Banna

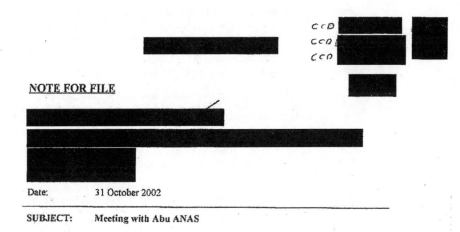

CCD
CCD
CCD

NOTE FOR FILE

Date: 31 October 2002

SUBJECT: Meeting with Abu ANAS

Summary
Unannounced visit to ANAS at home by ▓▓▓▓ and MPSB D/Sgt ▓▓▓▓ ANAS welcoming and apparently friendly; denies any involvement in extremist activity; concerned about being arrested or turned back when leaving for Gambia, or being excluded once outside the country; asks about progress of application for British nationality and possibility of a return of personal items seized during police raid last year; shows no interest in resettlement package in return for co-operation.

Detail

2.   On 31 October at 0845hrs, I and ▓▓▓▓ of MPSB called at ANAS's home at 15 Tintern Ave, NW9. This is a reasonably well maintained 1930's semi, probably worth around £300,000 if the local estate agents window is anything to go by. Parked on the drive at the front was a small silver coloured car, VRN ?M439 ELB displaying a green L plate.

3.   ANAS opened the door himself; in Arabic, I introduced us as Michael from the British Government and Andy from Scotland Yard and asked if we could have a brief chat with him. He immediately invited us in and took us into the living room at the back of the house; his wife, dressed in traditional full length hijab but with the face uncovered, and three young children were already in there so we waited in the corridor in case either ANAS or his wife were sensitive about us being in the same room as her, but they beckoned us in and then said that they were in the middle of checking ANAS's blood sugar level - for the last five days he had been suffering health problems and had just been diagnosed by the doctor as having diabetes. Eventually the wife shooed the children out but hovered around the door to listen to the conversation. The meeting was conducted in Arabic throughout.

4.   ANAS asked me to repeat who we were and I said that I was from the Security Service - Scotland Yard ? he queried; so I explained that Andy was from Scotland Yard and that I was from 'the mukhaberaat', although it was important for him to understand that we were not like the mukhaberaat in most Arab countries. He immediately agreed with this comment and said that he had previously been interviewed by Alan Macdonald ▓▓▓▓▓▓▓▓

5.   I then said that, with the arrest of Abu QATADA, we would be able to focus more

5

340

attention on other members and groups in the extremist community. ANAS immediately said that he was not a member of such a group, although he conceded in response to my naming their names that he was a friend of Abu QATADA and Abu RASMEE. He explained that as a youth he had led a dissolute life but had then rediscovered Islam and had been to Afghanistan. It was there that he had met QATADA whom he considered to be a friend; there was no way that he would allow QATADA's family to go without food or assistance during QATADA's detention.

5. I told him that in addition to increased focus on UK based extremists, we were investigating reports of terrorists based abroad who were keen to mount attacks in the UK, possibly using biological or chemical weapons. He agreed that such people were correctly labelled terrorist. I told him that the use of such techniques would pose a threat to all residents of the UK, as biological weapons would not differentiate between Muslims and Christians, and that as the father of young children he should be concerned by such a possibility. Both ANAS and his wife who was standing by the door agreed with this. She then left to look after the children.

6. I continued saying that in the event of a successful attack in the UK, it was not possible to predict the government's reaction. It was quite possible that he could find himself swept up in a further round of detentions. He did however have a choice - he could continue with his current life or ...; at this point he interrupted to ask what I meant by his current life. I told him that I meant his association with members of the extremist community and also his involvement in criminal activity, like his recent arrest and caution for petty shoplifting in an Asda supermarket. He laughed and shook my hand saying that I knew everything. He went on to say that he was not involved in any extremist activity; he did not believe that people like RASMEE could be considered a threat to the UK and, indeed, there was a fatwa saying that Muslims should respect UK laws. I pointed out that there was also a fatwa which declared that Muslims in the UK could consider themselves to be in a state of jihad and could therefore take 'ghaneema' (spoils of war) from non Muslims. He again laughed but did not deny this.

7. He then went on to say that he was not a well man; in addition to diabetes he had trouble with his back due to beatings at the hands of the Jordanian authorities. He was only interested in providing for his children the opportunities that he himself had not had as a child. He assumed we knew about his business venture in Gambia with WAHAAB, which he hoped would prove profitable. He said he would be travelling the next day and asked whether he would be arrested or turned back at the airport. I said that if he had a valid travel document he should be able to travel without a problem. He then asked whether he would be able to get back into the country. I repeated the travel document point.

8. I returned to the choice which he could make; he could either continue as at present, with the risks that entailed, or he could start a new life with a new identity, new nationality, money to set himself up in business and to provide for his family, and an opportunity to move to a Muslim country where his children could be brought up away from the bad influences in Western society. He asked if I wanted him to leave the UK. I told him that that would be for him to decide but that I could help him if that was what he wanted. He said that his children were being brought up as British nationals, going to normal English schools; his life was now in UK. He then asked about progress on his application for UK nationality as he had completed the required years of residency. I told him that this was a decision for the Home Secretary; he queried whether the Home Secretary decided all cases or only his; I told him that the Home Secretary decided all

6

cases. I added that I was in a position to make recommendations to the Home Secretary but that the final decision rested with the Home Secretary. ANAS asked if the Home Secretary intended to grant his application; I said I did not know but that, if we were asked for a view, we would be obliged to report ANAS' previous involvement in Afghanistan and his association with persons currently detained for extremist activities.

9. I again returned to the choice he had; if he chose to help us by providing details of all his activities and contacts, we would assist him to create a new life for himself and his family. I told him that I did not expect him to give me an immediate answer; it was an important decision and he needed to think carefully about it.

10. ANAS then asked when he could expect the return of the items seized during a police raid on his house some time ago; he explained that his computer, videos, address books had all been taken and not returned. He was particularly keen to get family photographs back. I told him that I would try to find out what was happening and would let him know.

11. ANAS' wife had come back in by this time and asked whether we wanted some tea; we declined saying that we were ready to leave. Abu ANAS saw us to the door and waved us off cheerfully.

Comment

12. ANAS appeared cheerful and relaxed throughout, although always ready to learn what we knew about him. He maintained that he was not involved in any extremist activity and was focused on his family's's welfare. He did not give any hint of willingness to co-operate with us. His desire for British nationality and the security that this would provide may be worth exploring further with him, should he return to the UK ▮▮▮▮▮▮▮▮ will make enquiries of SO 13 to establish the status of ANAS' possessions. It may be possible to arrange for the return of some of these items, even in ANAS's absence, to generate some goodwill.

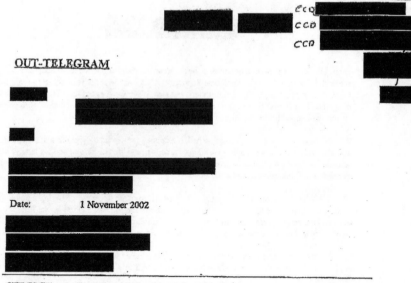

OUT-TELEGRAM

Date: 1 November 2002

SUBJECT: Detention of Islamists at Gatwick Airport

THIS INFORMATION HAS BEEN COMMUNICATED IN CONFIDENCE TO THE RECIPIENT GOVERNMENT AND SHOULD NOT BE RELEASED WITHOUT THE AGREEMENT OF THE BRITISH GOVERNMENT. IT IS FOR RESEARCH AND ANALYSIS PURPOSES ONLY AND MAY NOT BE USED AS THE BASIS FOR OVERT, COVERT OR EXECUTIVE ACTION.

1.   Three individuals associated with the prominent spiritual cleric Omar OTHMAN@ Abu QATADA were detained by members of the Anti-Terrorist branch at Gatwick airport on the 1 November 2002 under the Terrorism Act 2000. A search of their baggage revealed some form of home-made electronic device. Preliminary inquiries including X-ray suggest that it may be a timing device or could possibly be used as some part of a car-based IED. All three individuals were due to fly to Banjul, Gambia. At this time, this is for your information only. We intend to do further analysis of the recovered items and will revert in due course.

2.   The three individuals were Bishr AL RAWI (23/12/67) , an Iraqi Islamic extremist who is a member of Abu QATADA's close circle of associates, Abu ANAS@ Jamil Abdulatif Iylayan EL-BANNA@ Mohammed AL-QURAYSHI (28/5/62), formerly assessed to be Abu QATADA's financier and Abdallah ELJANOUDI (18/9/62). ▮▮▮▮▮▮▮▮▮▮ ELJANOUDI ▮▮▮ has been based in the UK for twelve years and was travelling on a UK passport. Secret and reliable intelligence indicated that these individuals were travelling to Gambia to invest in a peanut oil factory.

3.   Kind regards.

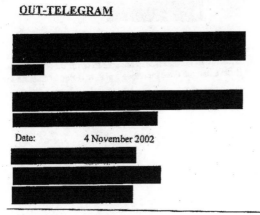

OUT-TELEGRAM

Date: 4 November 2002

SUBJECT: Travellers to Gambia

THIS INFORMATION HAS BEEN COMMUNICATED IN CONFIDENCE TO THE
RECIPIENT GOVERNMENT AND SHOULD NOT BE RELEASED WITHOUT THE
AGREEMENT OF THE BRITISH GOVERNMENT. IT IS FOR RESEARCH AND
ANALYSIS PURPOSES ONLY AND MAY NOT BE USED AS THE BASIS FOR OVERT,
COVERT OR EXECUTIVE ACTION.

1.   The following form of words can be passed to Gambian liaison:

BEGINS

1.   Three individuals associated with the prominent spiritual cleric Omar OTHMAN@ Abu
QATADA are due to travel to Gambia in the near future with the intention of opening a peanut
oil factory. The three individuals are Bishr AL RAWI (23/12/67) , an Iraqi Islamic extremist who
is a member of Abu QATADA's close circle of associates, Abu ANAS@ Jamil Abdulatif Iylayan
EL-BANNA@ Mohammed AL-QURAYSHI (28/5/62), formerly assessed to be Abu QATADA's
financier and Abdallah ELJANOUDI (18/9/62). Little is known about ELJANOUDI but he has
been based in the UK for twelve years and is travelling on a UK passport.

2.   Abu QATADA is one of the leading Islamist spiritual advisors in Europe with extensive
links to a wide range of terrorist groups, including Usama Bin LADEN's Al Qaida network. In
1995 he issued a fatwa justifying the killing of women and children who were relatives of the
security forces in Algeria. Abu QATADA lends spiritual advice to and raises funds for terrorist
groups. AL RAWI and Abu ANAS are part of Abu QATADA's inner circle of associates.

ENDS

11

344

3. We would be grateful for feedback on the reaction of the Gambians to this intelligence. In particular, we would be interested to learn if they are able to cover these individuals whilst they are in Gambia. We believe that the three individuals plan to reside in Gambia for around three months.

4. Kind regards.

LOOSE MINUTE

Date: 6 November 2002

SUBJECT: ███████████ Baggage Search of Abu ANAS; 1 November 2002

We have spoken at length about this operation but, for the record, I thought you might wish to have a detailed list of what was found in each of the six bags ██████████ As you are aware, the bags belonged to Abu ANAS and his two travelling companions; only one of them (bag 4) was labelled with the target's name.

2.   The contents of the bags were as follows:

BAG 1 - a holdall containing c.20 copies of the Quran, sealed in shrink wrap plastic. ██████ copied one of these. ██████ offered to X-Ray the books and they were passed to HMCE officers. We discovered later that HMCE had found nothing untoward.

BAG 2 - a holdall containing c.300 copies of a card-bound pamphlet entitled "Three Letters on 1) The Description of the Prophet's Gusl, 2) The Description of the Prophet's Wudu, 3) The Description of the Prophet's Prayer". One of these was copied by ██████

Also in this bag were 2 copies of the Quran, one of which had a very small amount of Arabic writing in the back (copied by ██████ and 5 copies of Tafsir Ibn Kathir (abridged), another hardback book.

BAG 3 - a very large suitcase containing only clothes.

BAG 4 - a large suitcase with "Jamil" written in felt pen on the outside, containing clothes and a variety of medical products (bandages, plasters, *Panadol*, etc) and toiletries (deodorants, razors, etc).

Bag 5 - a rucksack containing, in no particular order:

a) A bundle of electric wires wrapped around a set of tweezers and a small pair of scissors;
b) A "folding plotter";
c) 3 Manuals for VHM FM Handheld Tranceivers manufactured by ALINCO Inc. Written on these papers were several telephone numbers (already passed to you): 0870 9005505, 0870

346

1541102, 07774 507240, 01753 512600.
d) An air pump manual;
e) A retractable spade;
f) FIELD AND TREK small bag with various equipment;
g) Lo- tech drill bits etc;
h) a gas cylinder;

As well as these (which is not an exhaustive list), there was an item which can best be described as a quantity of masking tape wrapped around an unidentified object. This had a metal sheet stuck to it, and wires leading from it to a battery pack (without batteries). Also connected to this were a series of clips on the ends of several other wires.

Bag 6- a standard size suitcase, containing:

a) 5 pairs of *Salter* weighing scales (all boxed as new);
b) a TECNICA INVERTOR 1000 (voltage invertor);
c) various bits of electronic equipment.

3.   made copies of most of the above, and this should be available to you shortly. In the meantime, please do not hesitate to contact me if you wish to discuss any of the above.

OUT-TELEGRAM

Date: 8 November 2002

SUBJECT: Individuals Travelling to Gambia

THIS INFORMATION HAS BEEN COMMUNICATED TO THE RECIPIENT GOVERNMENT IN CONFIDENCE AND SHALL NOT BE RELEASED WITHOUT THE AGREEMENT OF THE BRITISH GOVERNMENT.

1.   Further to ▓▓▓▓▓ dated 1 November and our telephone conversation today.

2.   We are able to confirm that the three individuals associated with the prominent spiritual cleric Omar OTHMAN@ Abu QATADA who were arrested at Gatwick on 1 November have today boarded Sierra National Airlines Flight LJ054 to Banjul, Gambia. The flight was due to depart from the UK at 1230 but the departure was delayed until 1310.

3.   The three individuals checked-in at the airport using the following variations of their names:

    JAMIL ABDUL LATIF IYLAN (28/5/62)
    BISHR QALID (23/12/67)
    ABDALLAH GHAZI (18/9/62)

4.   Regards.

15

OUT-TELEGRAM

Date: 11 November 2002

SUBJECT: Individuals Detained in Gambia

1. Three individuals associated with the prominent spiritual cleric Omar OTHMAN @ Abu QATADA were detained in Banjul by the Gambian authorities on 8 November. Secret and reliable reporting had indicated that Jamil EL-BANNA @ Abu ANAS, Bishr AL RAWI and Wahab AL RAWI were travelling to Gambia to set up a groundnut oil factory.

2. Abu ANAS (28/5/62) is a Jordanian Palestinian veteran of the Afghan-Soviet war and is assessed to be Abu QATADA's financier. Abu ANAS is in close contact with members of the GSPC and FIT and his home is reported to have been used by these groups as a meeting place.

3. Bishr AL RAWI (23/12/67) is an Iraqi Islamist extremist who is a member of Abu QATADA's close circle of associates. He has previously come to our attention for his financial activities in connection with Abu ANAS. Bishr's enthusiasm for extreme sports has often brought him to the attention of the police. For example, he was seen driving away from the M4 flyover at Brentford in March 2001, which he and two other individuals had been seen climbing. He is also a qualified diver, a keen dinghy sailor and parachutist.

4. Wahab AL RAWI, Bishr's brother, is a close associate of Abu ANAS. Secret and reliable reporting has indicated that Wahab was taking the lead in the plans for setting up the peanut oil factory. Further reporting has revealed that he travelled to Gambia on 28 October, in advance of Bishr and Abu ANAS.

5. Bishr AL RAWI, Abu ANAS and a further individual Abdallah Ghazi EL JANOUDI attempted to travel to Gambia on 1 November. However, they were detained by members of the

Anti-Terrorist Branch at Gatwick Airport under the Terrorism Act 2000. A search of their baggage revealed that they were carrying some form of suspicious home made electronic device. All three individuals were released on 4 November after it was assessed that the device was a commercially available battery charger that had been modified by Bishr AL RAWI in order to make it more powerful.

6. ███████████ EL JANOUDI (18/9/62), ███████████████████ He was born in Beirut and is now a naturalised British Citizen. Secret and reliable reporting has indicated that EL JANOUDI is a close associate of Bishr AL RAWI.

7. Bishr AL RAWI, Abu ANAS and EL JANOUDI returned to Gatwick on 8 November and departed for Gambia. Special Branch enquiries on the day revealed that a forth individual, Ibrahim YOUSIF, had the same booking reference as the other three, indicating that he was travelling with them. YOUSIF removed himself from the aircraft before the gate closed, claiming that he was too ill to travel. Special Branch were notified and he was detained under the Terrorism Act 2000. During a police interview YOUSIF admitted that he was carrying a bag for the other three (a subsequent search of this bag had revealed numerous Qu'rans). YOUSIF was later released ███████████████

8. On arrival in Gambia on the evening of 8 November Bishr AL RAWI, Abu ANAS and EL JANOUDI were detained by the local authorities for questioning. Wahab AL RAWI and an individual called Omar OMARI ████████████████████████████████ were also detained when they came to meet the other three at Banjul airport.

9. We are receiving updates from ███████████ regarding these detainees. We will forward any further relevant information in due course.

10. Regards,

(37)   Binyam Mohamed judgment (extracts)

[...]

7. BM is an Ethiopian national and not a British national. He was born in Ethiopia on 24 July 1978. He came to the United Kingdom on 9 March 1994 after a short period in the United States and sought asylum on the basis of his family's opposition to the then government of Ethiopia. Although the application was rejected, in May 2000 he was given exceptional leave to remain in the United Kingdom for 4 years. During that period he lived in London. He worked and studied. His studies included vocational studies for electrical and electronics engineering. Other members of his family sought asylum in the United States; this was granted and some are now United States citizens and reside in the United States. He was converted to Islam. In 2001 he left the United Kingdom to travel to Pakistan. He went on to Afghanistan in June 2001. His account is that he wanted to try and "kick" a drug habit by moving away from the places he frequented in London and to see the Taliban with his own eyes to see if it was a good Islamic country or not. He then returned to Pakistan.

8. It is alleged in the charges brought against him in May 2008 (see paragraph 47.i) below) that whilst in Afghanistan he trained in Al-Qaida camps and was brought to the front line to participate in combat operations between the Taliban and the Northern Alliance. That he was thereafter chosen by Al-Qaida, because of his refugee status in the United Kingdom, to train for and participate in terrorist actions; he was then trained in the building of remote controlled devices to be used to attack United States forces in Afghanistan. That when he went to Pakistan he worked with others on the construction of an improvised radioactive bomb to be detonated in the United States and other matters to which we refer at paragraph 47.i).

[...]

10. On 10 April 2002 BM was arrested at Karachi Airport by the Pakistani authorities when he was attempting to leave Pakistan to fly to London. This was his second attempt to leave Pakistan using the British passport of a British national.

11. On 22 April 2002 the SyS and the SIS were notified by the United States authorities that an individual, subsequently identified as BM, had been detained in Pakistan using a fake British passport; that this was the second time he had sought to leave Pakistan using that same passport. The passport was in fact genuine, but BM's photograph had been substituted for the real holder, Fouad Zouaoui.

12. On 26 April 2002, the SyS and the SIS were notified by the United States authorities that the person arrested, after initially claiming to have been born in Nigeria, claimed he was BM and that he was an Ethiopian citizen with refugee status in the United Kingdom; that he had been an engineering student and gave a United Kingdom address. The United States authorities asked the SyS to assist in his identification and verify the information. The SIS and SyS were told that BM was being interviewed by the United States authorities in Pakistan and reports of those interviews during April 2002 were passed to the SIS and SyS. It is clear from those reports (which, as is

apparent from the telegrams, included information that BM was planning to construct and detonate a dirty bomb) that BM was a person whose activities would be of importance to the SyS in protecting the vital interests of the national security of the United Kingdom.

13. Preliminary enquiries by the SyS resulted in information being provided to the United States authorities on 29 April 2002 that the person arrested had lived at the address he had claimed in London and that he was who he claimed to be.

14. Given the information provided by the United States authorities, the SyS were concerned that he might fit the profiles of persons who, although they seemed innocuous whilst in the United Kingdom, might have graduated to serious terrorist activity in Afghanistan. In order to protect the vital interests of the national security of the United Kingdom and in accordance with their usual procedures, in a telegram of 1 May 2002 they asked that BM be carefully questioned about his time in the United Kingdom (as appeared in the open evidence), before setting out the detailed questions to be asked in relation to BM's activities and activities in Afghanistan and Pakistan and his plans and intentions on his return to the United Kingdom. The telegram included the following passage:

> "We would also like to explore the possibility of Security Service officers conducting a debrief of *** regarding his time spent in the UK. As has been the case with other UK nationals/residents detained in Pakistan and Afghanistan, we believe that our knowledge of the UK scene may provide contextual background useful during any continuing interview process. This may enable individual officers to identify any inconsistencies during discussions. This will place the detainee under more direct pressure and would seem to be the most effective way of obtaining intelligence on BM's activities/plans concerning the UK. Grateful for your views"

In a further telegram of 8 May 2002 further questions were sent to be asked of BM by the United States authorities; the telegram made clear that answers would assist the SyS greatly. An update on the plans of the United States authorities for BM was also sought.

15. Reports of the interviews of BM by the United States authorities during May 2002 were passed to the SyS. The SyS provided BM's Home Office file to the United States authorities on 15 May 2002. Such exchanges are a normal and vital part of protecting the United Kingdom and its residents.

(d)   The interview of BM by the Security Service

16. On 10 May 2002 the United States authorities indicated that the SyS would be permitted access to BM and arrangements were made for a SyS officer to travel to Pakistan to interview BM as part of a programme of interviewing others.

17. On 17 May 2002 an officer of the SyS, who gave evidence before us as Witness B, travelled to Pakistan and interviewed BM at an interviewing facility in Karachi. Before going he reviewed information about BM. There was a dispute **at the hearing** as to what information he saw in the course of that review. **Since that hearing,**

further documents disclosed to us make clear that a composite document was prepared for sending to Witness B for his attention in Karachi; it contained a detailed briefing package which included questions he should ask of BM and details of the reports provided by the United States authorities. No determination can be made by us as to whether it was sent to or received by Witness B.

18. It is important to emphasise that the purpose of that interview was to obtain intelligence about serious threats to United Kingdom national security, including intelligence about BM's background and contacts in the United Kingdom, his activities and contacts in Afghanistan and Pakistan and about his plans and intentions on his return to the United Kingdom.

19. The officer made notes during the interview which he put into a long report which he sent to his more senior officers by telegram on 17 May 2002. That report records BM telling Witness B about his time in the United Kingdom, how he obtained his United Kingdom passport from a criminal and the mosques he attended in London. He was recruited to travel to Afghanistan. He was trained in Afghanistan on weapons and explosives and thereafter, after the collapse of the Taliban, on remote devices, including landmines to be used against United States forces. Witness B did not cover BM's time in Pakistan because this had been covered in depth in previous interviews, but questioned him about his meeting with Abu Zubeida, a person alleged to be a close associate of Osama Bin Laden. The report records that BM had been asked to return to the United Kingdom to help in the provision of passports. BM said the report of a dirty bomb was "the FBI perception". The real story was that he had seen a file on a computer in Lahore and decided it was a joke – part of the instructions included adding bleach to uranium 238 in a bucket and rotating it around one's head for 45 minutes. He thought another major attack would happen – this was his assessment, but he did not know although the FBI thought he did.

20. Under the heading, closing remarks, the report then stated:

> "I told [BM] that he had an opportunity to help us and help himself. The US authorities will be deciding what to do with him and this would depend to a very large degree on his degree of cooperation. I said that if he could persuade me he was telling the complete truth I would seek to use my influence to help him. He asked how, and said he didn't expect ever to get out of the situation he was in. I said it must be obvious to him that he would get more lenient treatment if he cooperated. I said that I could not and would not negotiate up front, but if he persuaded me he was cooperating fully then (and only then) I would explore what could be done for him with my US colleagues. It was, however, clear that, while he appeared happy to answer any questions, he was holding back a great deal of information on who and what he knew in the UK and in Afghanistan. I said I wanted to come back and see him again. In the meantime, he should reflect on what I had told him and, if he wanted my help, he would need to be completely forthcoming. [BM] did not argue and appeared to accept what I said. We closed the interview on an amicable note."

> "[BM] is intelligent and patient. If he chooses not to cooperate
> he has the personal qualities and I believe strength of will to
> maintain his story indefinitely. He showed no signs of being
> anxious about his position, I suspect that he will only begin to
> provide information of genuine value if he comes to believe
> that it is genuinely in his interests to do so. I don't think he has
> yet reached this point."

22.   In his open evidence to us, Witness B stated that what he meant was that no members
        of the United States authorities would have taken any interest in what he, Witness B,
        had to say unless he could persuade them that BM was being fully cooperative; if BM
        was prepared to be completely forthcoming and honest, then he would do what he
        could to help him, but if he was not, he would be unable to. He denied the suggestion
        put to him by Ms Rose QC, counsel for BM, that he was threatening BM or putting
        any pressure on him.

(e)   The lawfulness of BM's detention in Pakistan

23.   During the period from 10 April 2002 until May 2004, it is common ground that BM
        was held incommunicado and was denied access to a lawyer. During the period in
        which it is known he was in Pakistan (and it is common ground that on all the
        evidence, both closed and open, it is only known he was in Pakistan until 17 May
        2002), his detention was not reviewed by any court or tribunal in Pakistan.

24.   On the evidence of Pakistani law given by Mr Afzal H Mufti of Cornelius, Lane and
        Mufti, an experienced advocate of considerable standing before the Supreme Court of
        Pakistan, it is clear that the detention was unlawful under the laws of Pakistan. The
        suspension of the constitution of Pakistan by General Musharraf and the issuing of a
        Provisional Constitution Order in October 1999, did not affect the position under the
        law of Pakistan that fundamental rights remained in full force. It was therefore
        unlawful in Pakistan to hold BM incommunicado, without access to legal
        representation, and to hand him over to United States agents without due judicial
        process. That was the only evidence of Pakistani law before us and we accept it.

25.   It was the open evidence of Witness B that the question of interviewing detainees had
        been discussed at length by his management, with legal advisers and the Government;
        his task was to interview BM in accordance with what had been approved by his
        management. He accepted that he was aware in some circles that it was believed that
        the Pakistani authorities had demonstrated a poor human rights record.

(f)   BM's allegations as to his treatment when held in Pakistan

26.   In the evidence before us, there is an account given by BM of what he says he did and
        what happened to him after 17 May 2002. During his period of unlawful and
        incommunicado detention in Pakistan which he contends lasted from 10 April 2002 to
        22 July 2002, he alleges:

        i)   After an initial period of custody by the Pakistani police, he was taken to the
                interrogation centre of the Pakistan Security Services where he was

interrogated, not by the Pakistani Security Services but by United States agents whom he believed to be the FBI. They believed he was a top Al-Qaida person and involved in the creation of a dirty bomb and would be sent to the United States to commit terrorist attacks. As we have set out above and as is set out at paragraph 47.i) below, these are amongst the matters with which he was charged on 28 May 2008.

ii)   He told the United States agents that he would not talk until he was given access to a lawyer. He was told by the United States agents that the law had been changed and there were no lawyers. He was hung by a leather strap around his wrists so he could only just stand, he was allowed to go to the toilet only twice a day and was given food only once every second day. He was told by them that he must co-operate with them the hard or the easy way. If he did not do so he would be taken to Jordan. "We can't do what we want here, the Pakistanis can't do exactly what we want them to do. The Arabs will deal with you."

iii)   In consequence of this threat he made admissions as to his identity and his address. That was checked out with the United Kingdom authorities and he was told it was true. He then admitted that he had been to Afghanistan.

iv)   He was then beaten by the Pakistani authorities and threatened with a gun.

v)   When the British agent visited him, the torture stopped. The agent introduced himself as "John". BM provided a description of him. He was interviewed in the presence of a United States agent who had previously been part of the team that interrogated him:

> "They gave me a cup of tea with a lot of sugar in it. I initially only took one. 'No, you need a lot more. Where you are going you need a lot of sugar' I didn't know exactly what he meant by this, but I figured he meant some poor country in Arabia. One of them did tell me I was going to get tortured by the Arabs."

BM asked for a lawyer. The British agent also asked what he could do to help. BM said he did not know. The agent told BM he would see what he could do with the Americans, promising to tell BM what would happen to him, but he did not see him again.

vi)   He thereafter refused to talk until he was given an access to a lawyer.

27.   Witness B had observed in his report that BM looked thinner than in his photograph and that had given him sufficient concern to be noticed. In his open evidence to us, Witness B made clear that he considered that BM was in a fit state to be interviewed and that BM made no complaints about his treatment, though he gave him the opportunity of doing so. Witness B strongly denied that there was any conversation to the effect we have set out in paragraph 26v); as obviously we had no oral evidence from BM, it would not be appropriate for us to express any view on this allegation made by BM.

[...]

29.   After the interview on 17 May 2002, the SyS determined that, as a result of what BM had said in the interviews as well as in the reports of interviews conducted by the United States authorities, BM might have further relevant information to provide and that it was necessary in the interests of the national security of the United Kingdom to seek his responses to further questions, ideally through a further interview conducted by the SyS:

i)   Witness A of the SyS stated in his open witness statement that the United States authorities suggested that BM might be transferred to Afghanistan at that time; that in the circumstances prevalent at the time, the transfer of detainees by the United States authorities to detention facilities in Afghanistan was not unusual or regarded as unlawful or improper. In a further statement witness A said that it was widely known that there were other transfers of detainees from Pakistan to Afghanistan at the time. He was not aware that the United Kingdom Government objected and did not know if anyone had given specific consideration to its lawfulness at the time. The issue of the United Kingdom's position on rendition by the United States was considered by the ISC in its report of 28 June 2007 on the practice of rendition to which we have referred at paragraph 28.

ii)   On 11 June 2002 the SyS sought information as to his whereabouts in Pakistan or Afghanistan and asked to interview BM. The United States authorities noted that efforts were underway to have him moved to Afghanistan and suggested that a further interview be deferred until after the transfer had taken place. Logistically this was more convenient to the SyS and, as the SyS informed the United States authorities, it made more sense to wait until his transfer. The United States authorities indicated that they would keep the SyS informed about his transfer.

iii) In the event this did not happen. On 7 July 2002 the SyS recorded in a telegram that, frustratingly, they had no information of the whereabouts of BM who was described as one of their highest priorities. Urgent clarification of his whereabouts was sought and whether they were likely to see him at Bagram in the near future.

iv) On 15 July 2002 the United States authorities told the SyS in a briefing on an unrelated matter that BM was to be moved to Afghanistan, when a further interview could be facilitated. The SyS sought information on 31 July 2002 as to whether BM was in Pakistan or Afghanistan and for an indication as to when the interview could take place. No response was received. Witness A stated that, although this would not have been regarded as particularly unusual or suspicious, no further information was received as to whether the transfer had taken place.

v) On 12 August 2002 the SyS sought information from the SIS. They asked if on their routine visits to Bagram the SIS could check whether three individuals, including BM were at Bagram; the telegram stated "*** appear to have no information on his current whereabouts exclam".

v)(a) By 19 August 2002, the SyS were aware that BM was being held in a covert location where he was being debriefed. Direct access was not possible but the SyS were able to send questions to the US authorities to be put to him.

v)(b) On 28 August 2002 the SIS told the SyS that there was no record of BM having arrived ~~there~~ **at Bagram**.

vi) On 22 August 2002 the SyS again sought **direct** access to BM; no response was received. On 28 August 2002 the SIS informed the SyS that BM had not arrived at Bagram.

vii) In late September 2002 the SyS received a report from the United States authorities of an interview with BM.

viii) On 30 September 2002 the SyS discussed the case of BM with the United States authorities at a meeting at Thames House, the headquarters of the SyS. The SyS asked for direct access to BM, but were told that SyS access could not be facilitated at that time.

(i) The provision by the SyS of further information and questions to the United States authorities

30. Faced with this prolonged refusal to allow **direct** access, witness A stated that it was regarded as essential in the interests of the national security of the United Kingdom to send further questions to the United States authorities to be put to BM. The SyS had other information which suggested current plans for an attack on the United Kingdom and it was thought that BM might have relevant information

0) An agenda for a video conference on 23 October 2002 included an update by the US authorities on their continued interviewing of BM.

i)   On 25 October 2002, the SyS sent a telegram referring to the meeting at Thames House. It included the following passage:

> "We would like to stress that we regard [BM] as a key focus point for our investigations into the activities of UK passport holders in Afghanistan and elsewhere. ... We feel in the light of [BM]'s recent cooperation further debriefs by these same officers **** may have a positive effect on our intelligence gathering operation into this subject area. However we are grateful for the opportunity to provide material to be used in the current debriefing at this stage."

The telegram then set out further information about BM and the questions to be asked of BM including information relating to Fouad Zouaoui and general questions. The telegram indicated the SyS would provide further information if it discovered further intelligence and asked for updates regarding direct access to BM for the SyS.

ii)   Further questions were raised on 5 November 2002 and a photobook sent. Witness A stated that no reply was ever received by the SyS to these two telegrams despite a chasers on 8 **and 12** November 2002 which made clear that although the SyS appreciated that this might be "a long winded process", the urgent nature of the enquiries was obvious.

iii)   In February 2003, the SyS received **5** reports from the United States authorities of an interview with BM, though they did not relate directly to the questions put by the SyS. We were told by witness A **at the hearing** that **two of** these were the last interview reports received.

iv)   **On 15 April 2003, the SyS requested, in the light of BM's reported co-operation, a further interview by Witness B; a list of over 70 further questions was also sent.**

v)   **Further information from debriefings of BM was supplied to the United Kingdom authorities by the United States authorities on 14 November 2003, 14 January 2004 and 15 March 2004.**

(j)   *The ~~total absence of~~ information as to BM's whereabouts between May 2002 and May 2004*

31.   On the totality of the open and closed evidence before the court, it is clear that the United States authorities have never informed either the SyS or any other part of the United Kingdom Government **of the covert location at which BM was held** ~~about BM's whereabouts~~ in the period between 17 May 2002 and his transfer to Bagram in May 2004.

32.   That remains the position to this day. It was, however, accepted in evidence filed on behalf of the Foreign Secretary that, although the SyS was not aware ~~of his~~ **where the covert** location **was** when they received the information to which we have referred in

sub-paragraphs 29.vii) to 30   it was "apparent that he was in the custody of a third country and not yet in United States custody."

33. The evidence before us made clear that the United States Government has also, so far, refused to provide BM's lawyers with any information as to where he was or indeed what they contend happened to him in the period of 2 years between May 2002 and May 2004.

34. We refer to the procedures for disclosure under the Military Commissions Act of 2006 at paragraph 117.

   (k)   BM's allegations as to his rendition to Morocco and his torture there

35. In the account of the evidence of BM before us, BM alleges that he was taken to Morocco in July 2002 and was held incommunicado and tortured there until January 2004:

   i)   He was taken from Karachi to Islamabad and then subjected to extraordinary rendition by United States personnel to Morocco on 22 July 2002. He was handed over to other people in Morocco. His lawyers have obtained evidence which suggests that a Gulfstream V aircraft operated on behalf of the CIA left Islamabad and landed at Rabat on that day.

   ii)   After arrival in Morocco he was handed over to other persons and held in various facilities. He was told that the United States wanted a story from him and he was to testify against others in relation to matters such as the dirty bomb. He was then tortured by some persons who were masked. A detailed account of that alleged torture has been given to us in a note provided by his lawyers; it is only necessary to mention, for reasons that are made clear at paragraph 103.ii) below, that he contends that apart from being severely beaten and subjected to sleep deprivation, his penis and private parts were cut with a scalpel. One of those who interrogated him stated she was a Canadian; it is alleged by BM's lawyers that she was an agent of the CIA.

   iii) During the course of his interrogation he was questioned about his links with the United Kingdom, told of personal information about himself (such as details of his education, the name of his kick boxing trainer and friendships in London). He was told that they had been working with the British and had seen photographs of people given to them by MI5.

35.A) It is clear from documents subsequently supplied to us that Witness B visited Morocco once in November 2002 and twice in February 2003. As no information about these visits was available at the hearing Witness B was not questioned in the open or closed sessions about these visits or the document referred to at paragraph 30.iv). We have been informed that the SyS maintains that it did not know that BM was in Morocco in the period in question.

(l)   BM's allegations of rendition from Morocco to Afghanistan

36. BM then alleges that on 21 or 22 January 2004, he was transferred back into the custody of the United States at an airport in Morocco. He alleges that he was then

subject to extraordinary rendition to what he describes as "The Prison of Darkness" near Kabul in January 2004 where he remained until May 2004. He alleges that before the flight photographs were taken of his penis. BM's lawyers have provided materials that they contend suggest that there was a flight on 22 January 2004 by a Gulfstream V aircraft operated by the CIA from Rabat to Kabul.

37.   He alleges that he was held in a black hole at the "Prison of Darkness" where he was deprived of sleep, blasted with sound, starved and then beaten and hung up. During this period he alleges that he was interrogated by the CIA and threatened with further torture if he did not provide the story that the United States wanted.

(m)   The statements made by him at Bagram and Guantanamo Bay between May and November 2004 and the use made of them by the United States

38.   BM contends that he was transferred to Bagram in May 2004. There he was subjected to further mistreatment. In the result he signed statements put before him by the United States authorities at Bagram between May and September 2004. These were made as a result of that unlawful detention, torture and cruel inhuman or degrading treatment.   He had confessed during the torture and cruel, inhuman or degrading treatment to anything those inflicting that treatment on him wanted him to say. This was also his state when he signed statements at Bagram.

39.   On 20 September 2004 BM was transferred to Guantanamo Bay and for the same reasons made further confessions prior to November 2004.

[...]

87.   The summary of our findings necessary for this open judgment is as follows:

    (i)   The SyS and the SIS were interested in BM because of his residence in the United Kingdom, his connections with suspected persons in the United Kingdom, the period of time spent in Pakistan and Afghanistan, those whom he was said to have been with and the gravity of the allegations made against him at the time.

    (ii)   We have no doubt that on the basis of that information the SIS and SyS were right to conclude that BM was a person of great potential significance and a serious potential threat to the national security of the United Kingdom. There was therefore every reason to seek to obtain as much intelligence from him as was possible in accordance with the rule of law and to cooperate as fully as possible with the United States authorities to that end.

    (iii)   It was clear from reports that BM was held incommunicado from 10 April 2002 whilst a series of interviews was conducted by the United States authorities in April 2002 during which he had asked for a lawyer and had been refused.

    (iv)   In May 2002, the SyS and the SIS received reports containing information relating to BM's detention and treatment in Pakistan. The details of the reports are set out in the closed judgment.

(v)   **Our finding after the hearing was that** the probability is that Witness B read the reports either before he left for Karachi or before he conducted the interview.   **Since the hearing we have been provided with the documents to which we have referred at paragraph 17 which show a briefing document was prepared for sending to him.**

(vi)   If, contrary to ~~that~~ the finding **we made after the hearing,** Witness B had not read them prior to going to Karachi or after arrival at Karachi and prior to the interview, we have no doubt that other persons within the SyS, including persons more senior to Witness B, must have read the reports and must have appreciated what they said about BM's detention and treatment at Karachi. Those officers should have drawn to the attention of Witness B these matters either before or after the interview. **It is now clear that the reports were studied by other desk officers.**

(vii)   In the light of Witness B's continued involvement with BM and the importance attached to BM by the SyS, it is inconceivable that he did not carefully read the materials after his return.

(viii)   During the interview Witness B saw himself as having a role to play in conjunction with the United States authorities in inducing BM to cooperate by making it clear that the United Kingdom would not help unless BM cooperated. We can well understand why, given the exigencies of the time, Witness B put matters in such stark terms as he did. It is clear that what he said to BM was, in effect, that the United Kingdom would not attempt to assist him unless BM persuaded him that he was cooperating fully with the United States authorities.

(ix)   By 30 September 2002, it was clear to the SyS that BM was being held **at a covert location** (either by the authorities of the United States or under the direct control of the United States) ~~at a facility~~ which was not a United States military facility, such as Bagram. It is clear to us that they ~~must have appreciated~~ **knew** that he was not in a regular United States facility, that the facility in which he was being detained and questioned was that of a foreign government (other than Afghanistan) and that the United States authorities had direct access to information being obtained from him.

(x)   The SyS were supplying information as well as questions which they knew were to be used in interviews of BM from the time of his arrest whilst he was held incommunicado and without access to a lawyer or review by a court or tribunal. They continued to supply information and questions after they knew of the circumstances of BM's detention and treatment as contained in the reports of the series of interviews in May 2002 and after September 2002 when they ~~must have appreciated~~ **knew** the circumstances related to his continued detention which we have described in sub-paragraph (ix).

88.   We have concluded that in the light of those findings that

i)   The conduct of the SyS facilitated interviews by or on behalf of the United States when BM was being detained by the United States incommunicado and without access to a lawyer.

ii)   The SyS continued to facilitate the interviewing of BM by providing information and questions after 17 May 2002 until ~~November 2002~~ **at least April 2003** in the knowledge of what had been reported to them in relation to the conditions of his detention and treatment and his interviews in Karachi in May 2002 to which we have referred.

iii) Witness B worked with the United States authorities to the extent of making it clear to BM that the United Kingdom Government would not help BM unless he cooperated fully with the United States authorities.

iv)   The SyS continued to facilitate interviews by the United States authorities after September 2002 when also they knew BM was still incommunicado and when they **knew** ~~must also have appreciated~~ that he was not in a United States facility and that the **undisclosed** facility in which he was being detained and questioned was that of a foreign government (other than Afghanistan) and that the United States authorities had direct access to information being obtained from him.

v)   If the question of facilitation is considered as one where an important factor is the relationship between the person from whom the information is sought and the alleged wrongdoer (as some of the authorities to which we have referred at paragraph 70a suggest), then by seeking to interview BM in the circumstances described and supplying information and questions for his interviews, the relationship of the United Kingdom Government to the United States authorities in connection with BM was far beyond that of a bystander or witness to the alleged wrongdoing.

vi)   **We are unable to determine the significance (if any) of Witness B's visits to Morocco discussed in paragraph 35A.**

[...]

(38)   Binyam Mohamed: the US threat and the redacted paragraphs

[...]

67. In considering the submission, we have reminded ourselves of our initial view that the redacted paragraphs should form part of our first open judgment as essential to open justice. It was also our view that making clear what in fact was reported by officials of the United States Government would prevent the uninformed speculation to which we have referred and which might be damaging to the SyS.

68. That view was formed in the light of the fact that there was nothing in the redacted paragraphs that would identify any agent or any facility or any secret means of intelligence gathering. Nor could anything in the redacted paragraphs possibly be described as "highly sensitive classified US intelligence." It followed that it was (and remains) our view that the ordinary business of intelligence gathering would not be affected by putting into the public domain the redacted paragraphs as they contain only a short summary of what was reported to the United Kingdom authorities by the officials of the United States Government as to what they say happened to BM during his detention in Pakistan in April and May 2002.

69. Moreover, in the light of the long history of the common law and democracy which we share with the United States, it was, in our view difficult to conceive that a democratically elected and accountable government could possibly have any rational objection to placing into the public domain such a summary of what its own officials reported as to how a detainee was treated by them and which made no disclosure of sensitive intelligence matters. Indeed we did not consider that a democracy governed by the rule of law would expect a court in another democracy to suppress a summary of the evidence contained in reports by its own officials or officials of another State where the evidence was relevant to allegations of torture and cruel, inhuman or degrading treatment, politically embarrassing though it might be.

70. We had no reason at that time to anticipate there would be made a threat of the gravity of the kind made by the United States Government that it would reconsider its intelligence sharing relationship, when all the considerations in relation to open justice pointed to us providing a limited but important summary of the reports.

71. Since our initial view was formed, other matters have lent support to it:

i) It is accepted that the reports summarised in the redacted paragraphs gave rise to an arguable case of cruel, inhuman or degrading treatment and torture.

ii) No argument has been made that any of the ordinary considerations relating to the secrecy of intelligence gathering (such as the identity of agents or the location of facilities) would be affected.

iii) No reason has emerged, particularly in the light of the statement made by Ms Crawford to which we have referred at paragraph 12, why the United States Government has not itself put the matters contained in the redacted passage into the public domain. There has been ample time for the United States Government to do so.

In the circumstances, it is still difficult to understand how objection can properly be made to a court in the United Kingdom doing so in all the circumstances we have set out.

72. It therefore would have remained our view, absent the evidence adduced by the Foreign Secretary as to the position taken by the Government of the United States, that there was every reason to put the paragraphs into the public domain. The suppression of reports of wrongdoing by officials (in circumstances which cannot in any way affect national security) would be inimical to the rule of law and the proper functioning of a democracy. Championing the rule of law, not subordinating it, is the cornerstone of a democracy. Moreover as the Foreign Secretary has made clear in his Certificate of 5 September 2008, the protection of human rights is central to the efforts of the United Kingdom to counter radicalisation.

[...]

(a) The ISC.

85. The ISC was established under s.10 of the Intelligence Services Act 1994 to examine the expenditure, administration and policy of the SyS and the SIS. It is required to make an annual report on the discharge of its functions to the Prime Minister and the Prime Minister is under a duty to lay the report before Parliament, subject to his right to exclude from the report any matter that may be prejudicial to the continued discharge of the functions of the SIS or SyS.

86. As is clear from the narrative set out in paragraph 9 of our first judgment, the ISC has very carefully examined issues relating to the treatment of detainees arrested in Pakistan and Afghanistan or

held in Guantanamo Bay after the US military action commenced in Afghanistan in 2001. It has published two Reports on these matters -1 March 2005 (Cm 6469) and July 2007 (Cm 7171). Highly material to the present issue is the reference at paragraph 54 of the ISC Report of 1 March 2005 to a United States report in June 2002 of treatment accorded to a detainee in Afghanistan, including hooding, withholding of blankets and sleep deprivation. We were told this US report was a public report. Paragraph 55 of the same ISC Report referred to a SyS officer reporting to senior management in July 2002 "that whilst in Afghanistan, a US official had referred to 'getting a detainee ready', which appeared to involve sleep deprivation, hooding and the use of stress positions.

87. The ISC considered the case of BM in its Report of July 2007 at paragraphs 98 to 106 after the allegations of torture and cruel, inhuman and degrading treatment made by BM had been made known to the ISC. The Report records at paragraph 105 that the Director General of the SyS expressed regret that assurances as to BM's treatment had not been sought from the United States; the Report expressed the view that this was understandable given the lack of knowledge at the time of any possible consequences of United States custody of detainees.

88. It is now clear that the 42 documents disclosed as a result of these proceedings were not made available to the ISC. The evidence was that earlier searches made had not discovered them. The ISC Report could not have been made in such terms if the 42 documents had been made available to it. However, as a result of these proceedings, the 42 documents have since been supplied to the ISC along with our closed judgment and the transcript of Witness B's open and closed evidence.

89. Although the express provisions of the Act do not, as the Special Advocates rightly submitted, permit the ISC to investigate particular cases, we understand that with the agreement of the Prime Minister, it has extended its remit to do so, as part of its general Parliamentary scrutiny of the operation of the SyS and the SIS. This is an important constitutional development as the ISC is being made a powerful means of ensuring that the SIS and SyS can be made democratically accountable for their conduct and of ensuring that they act in accordance with the rule of law and do not facilitate action by other States which is contrary to our law and values.

90. We also have little doubt that the ISC, in the light of the information from these proceedings, will conduct a further investigation into the

illegal incommunicado detention of BM, his treatment in April and May 2002 and the role of the SyS in relation to it. When it does so, it will be able to ask searching and difficult questions of witnesses from the SyS and SIS on the very important issues identified. It will also be in a position to know from the 42 documents the kind of documentation that may be held in relation to other detainees and which it should therefore request. There can be no doubt that it is in a position to conduct a most thorough and wide ranging enquiry. As an important all party Parliamentary Committee possessed of the information available to us and in the position to seek much more, the ISC will be in a position, if the results of their investigation so require, to hold those in charge of the SIS and SyS and her Majesty's Government to account in Parliament in relation to all the matters, including those set out in the redacted paragraphs. All of this can be done without exposing the United Kingdom to the real risks identified by the Foreign Secretary. This is a very significant means of democratic accountability.

91. However, s.10 of the Act permits the Prime Minister to delete from the annual report any matter which may be prejudicial to the continued discharge of the functions of the SyS and the SIS; this practice has been followed in relation to the specific reports to which we have referred. Thus, although the ISC will, as a result of what has emerged from these proceedings, be able to hold Her Majesty's Government and others to account for the actions of the SyS or SIS (if it finds on investigation there is reason to do so), it therefore will not be in a position to put the matters covered in the redacted paragraphs into the public domain, given the view that the Foreign Secretary has set out in his certificates to the Court, unless the United States Government changes its position. Thus information necessary for the purposes of debate on the important issues of torture and cruel, inhuman or degrading treatment or compliance by other states with provisions of international law cannot be brought into the public domain through the ISC.

[...]

The redacted paragraphs

(iv) It was reported that a new series of interviews was conducted by the United States authorities prior to 17 May 2002 as part of a new strategy designed by an expert interviewer.

(v) It was reported that at some stage during that further interview process by the United States authorities, BM had been intentionally subjected to continuous sleep deprivation. The effects of the sleep deprivation were carefully observed.

(vi) It was reported that combined with the sleep deprivation, threats and inducements were made to him. His fears of being removed from United States custody and "disappearing" were played upon.

(vii) It was reported that the stress brought about by these deliberate tactics was increased by him being shackled during his interviews.

(viii) It was clear not only from the reports of the content of the interviews but also from the report that he was being kept under self-harm observation, that the interviews were having a marked effect upon him and causing him significant mental stress and suffering.

(ix) We regret to have to conclude that the reports provided to the SyS made clear to anyone reading them that BM was being subjected to the treatment that we have described and the effect upon him of that intentional treatment.

(x) The treatment reported, if had been administered on behalf of the United Kingdom, would clearly have been in breach of the undertakings given by the United Kingdom in 1972. Although it is not necessary for us to categorise the treatment reported, it could easily be contended to be at the very least cruel, inhuman and degrading treatment of BM by the United States authorities.

(39) Martin Mubanga

<u>OUT-TELEGRAM</u>

Action:

Info:

Section/Desk:

From:

Date: 26 March 2002

File Ref:

Copied To:

Our Ref:

SUBJECT: MARTIN MUBANGA

1.

2. We have sought legal and political advice ▓▓▓▓▓▓▓▓▓▓ The option of MUBANGA's transfer to US custody through UK officials will not be accepted by HMG under any circumstances.

3.

4.

5. Meanwhile, we are investigating legal possibilities in the UK with the Metropolitan Police Anti-Terrorist Branch. ▓▓▓▓▓▓▓▓▓ But it is equally important that undue hopes about the potential success of a UK prosecution are not raised.

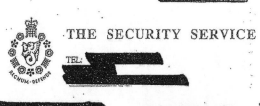

THE SECURITY SERVICE

TEL:

27 March 2002

Dear John

UPDATE ON MARTIN MUBANGA

I wrote to you on 20 and 22 March about Martin MUBANGA, who has been detained in Zambia. I am writing with a further update.

2.   A Security Service officer travelled to Zambia and interviewed MUBANGA on 23 and 24 March███████████████████████████████. The interviews focused on MUBANGA's links to the Islamist community in the UK and his activities in, and departure from, Afghanistan.

3.   MUBANGA admitted during interview that, prior to September 11, he had conducted training in AL Qa'ida associated camps in Afghanistan, having formerly attended mosques in London associated with the Islamist extremists Abu QATADA and Faisal AL-JAMAIKEE. MUBANGA also admitted that, following this training, ███ MUBANGA also said that the list of ████████ Jewish organisations ███████████ had been given to him ██████████ and that the organisations could be targeted for "some action". He denied that he had been given (or agreed to) any specific tasking.

4.   It is the belief of those who interviewed MUBANGA that his account of his escape from Afghanistan after September 11 lacked credibility and that MUBANGA's escape may have been arranged by an Islamist network and that he could well have been given a terrorist remit to pursue. It is our assessment that MUBANGA remains committed to his cause and would pose a serious threat if he were to be released.

5.   ███ We fear, and the Anti-Terrorist branch of the Metropolitan Police (SO13) have since confirmed, that there is insufficient evidence at present to charge MUBANGA if he were to be returned to the UK. ██████████████████████████████████ ███ ███████████████ This would obviously be untenable legally.

John Gieve Esq
Home Office

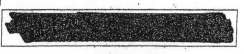

2.

6.   We are therefore faced with the prospect, as anticipated in earlier discussions, of the return of a British citizen to the UK about whom we have serious concerns, whom it may be difficult to prosecute and whose release could trigger hostile US reaction.

7.   Copies of this letter go to Richard Wilson, ▓▓▓▓▓▓▓▓▓▓▓▓▓▓▓▓ and David Veness.

Yours,

Eliza.

E L Manningham-Buller

LOOSE MINUTE

To:
From:
Ext. No:
Date: 2 April 2002
File Ref.:
Copied To:

SUBJECT: Martin MUBANGA: Interviews

Summary

    Martin MUBANGA (MM) was interviewed for four and a half hours on Saturday 23 March and seven hours on Sunday 24 March by ▓▓▓▓▓▓▓▓▓▓▓▓▓▓▓▓▓▓▓▓▓▓▓▓▓

- ▓▓

- Although MM engaged with his interviewers, his account was short of checkable facts, full of names and events that he could not remember and in many cases unbelievable.

- ▓▓ More information was obtained during the interviews and despite lack of detail and obvious lies there are certainly some leads for ▓▓▓

- ▓▓▓

- MM said that the ▓▓▓▓▓▓▓▓▓▓▓▓▓▓▓ the list of the ▓▓▓▓▓▓ Jewish organisations ▓▓▓▓▓▓▓▓▓▓▓▓▓▓▓ MM said that it was obvious that the organisations shown could/should be targeted for "some action" but denied that by accepting it he had been given (or agreed to) any specific tasking.

- ▓▓▓▓▓▓▓▓▓▓▓▓▓▓▓▓▓▓▓▓▓▓▓▓▓ there were significant reasons to doubt MM's account of his departure from Afghanistan. ▓▓▓▓▓▓▓▓▓▓▓▓ this lacked credibility and, coupled with MM's continued belief in Jihad and reluctance to denounce events such as the Embassy bombings in 1998, think that it is possible that MM left Afghanistan with some form of tasking. ▓▓▓▓▓▓▓▓▓▓▓▓▓▓

372

- MM appears to be emotionally unstable and committed to violence. We assess that he has spent his life looking for something to give meaning to his existence. Although boxing briefly provided this, Islam has long been the focus. MM's commitment occasionally lapses (his continuing fixation with women, returns to drug dealing, non-Islamic friends, smoking) but when he returns to his faith, he continues to have extremist beliefs. At the end of the interviews, MM was refusing to condemn the bombings in East Africa ('innocents who die go to heaven'), was defending future jihad and the right of wronged people to take action against those who are responsible. He is prepared to accept at face value the advice of spiritual leaders claiming that until he can understand Arabic, he is not qualified to doubt their word.

2. ▓▓▓▓▓ were convinced that, if released, Martin MUBANGA was likely to continue to try to further the cause in which he believes. As such, he would be a danger to national (and international) security.

Future Action

3. ▓▓▓▓▓▓▓▓▓▓▓▓▓▓▓▓▓▓▓▓▓▓▓▓▓▓▓▓▓▓▓ If this were to take place, MM is likely to be sent to Guantanamo Bay. It will certainly be worth further ▓ interviews of MM if further access can be arranged. In the mean time ▓ would provide clarification and provide further lines of questioning.

Background

4. ▓▓▓

Interview

5. MM was sleeping when we arrived at the guesthouse ▓▓▓▓▓ He was woken and joined us in the meeting room at 0845. Strangely, MM, a well-muscled individual, had refused to wear a shirt (an attempt to intimidate?). He looked fit and well - there was no sign of any bad treatment. ▓▓▓ introduced himself ▓ Tony as MI5 ▓

256

...stressed that he was there to gather information...

MM was slowly taken through his life from the beginning of his conversion to Islam to date. The interview ended at about 1315.

6. Throughout both this and the subsequent day's interview, MM did answer all the questions put to him. However, he seemed to be providing as little information as possible at all times. MM normally paused for a long time before providing an answer and, especially on day two when we were talking specifics, we assessed that he was often denying knowledge that he had or fabricating. MM regularly resorted to monosyllabics. Most of the time, MM was defiant, often fixing his interviewers with hard stares and trying not to be the first to look away.

Pre-Bosnia

7. MM moved to Britain with his mother, brother (Anthony) and sisters (Constance and Kate) in the mid-1970s following the death in a car crash of his father. The family was Roman Catholic and MM was sent to a boarding school in North Wales (St Mary's College). He spent the last three years of his education at St Gregory's High School in London. His mother died in 1988. By the time he left school he was already involved in criminality. He described his life as centring on drugs, sex and a desire to make money. He was an enthusiastic football hooligan (Arsenal) and admitted to deriving significant enjoyment from street battles between opposing groups of fans. He dealt in drugs (he mentioned selling fake Es) although he stressed that he did not deal in hard drugs. He described his conversion to Islam as a gradual change that took three years. He refused to identify his inspiration to make this change although the six months (for attempted vehicle theft) he spent in Feltham prison (young offenders?) seemed to have a big impact. Whilst there he briefly attended a prayer circle but soon fell out with the Iman (he was disruptive). He said that he spend his time reading books on Islam provided by his long term white non-Muslim girlfriend. He said that he did not mix with any Muslim inmates.

8. Following release he did a short course in construction at Hendon College and began to return to his old criminal ways. He also worked part time as a pizza deliverer. Throughout this time, he continued to read and think about Islam. Eventually, in 1993, he saw a Muslim woman wearing hijab, approached her and explained that he wanted help becoming a Muslim. She put him in contact with her brother, an Ethiopian called Daoud. Daoud helped him swear to Islam at Baker St Mosque.

Bosnia

9. MM would not give a clear account of how he ended up attending Mosque - a brother had suggested it. MM said that he would go on most Fridays but that he did not get to know any of the names of his fellow attendees. As he did not speak Arabic, he relied on others to translate Abu QATADA's khutbas or just listened to the intensity of AQ's speaking.

Page 3

374

18

From: ████████ Lusaka -Conf
Sent: 17 May 2002 08:33
To: ████████ (London)
Subject: RE: High profile consular case.

████████

This is getting ridiculous. What disturbs us most here is the determination to blame us for the schizophrenic way in which policy on this whole case was handled in London. I will gladly send you a personal secret telegram - spelling out exactly the constraints under which were placed by edicts from London ████████████ - of which you, or at least CTPD, must surely be aware. These placed us in an impossible position. But it will not be today, as I have several other pressing priorities and will not be in the office much.

██
██
██

████████, I repeat, yet again, that the person concerned at no time requested any consular assistance from us.

█████

-----Original Message-----
From: ████████ (London)
Sent: 16 May 2002 16:48
To: ████████ Lusaka -Conf
Subject: High profile consular case.

Thanks for your message. I'm sorry if we appear to be misinterpreting your messages: we really don't understand what has been going on, ████████████████████████████████████

██
██
████████████████████████ We potentially had a responsibility for his welfare. ████
██

██
██

██. Neither CTPD or Thames House can understand why security considerations would prevent you from explaining this. Content for you to send me a personal secret telegram explaining this if you would prefer. We will then at least be able to formulate a response to any further questions about this. Even better, of course, we all hope that interest in it will die away completely.

16/5/02

1

1L

52

FRIOR LUSAKA / FCO 122 OF 22 MAY 2002
PERSONAL: ZAMBIA/KELVIN MUBANGA

SUMMARY

1. Conflicting instructions and expectations on this case placed us in an impossible situation. We cannot always have our cake and eat it.

DETAIL

2. Our exchange of e-mails refers. The following is a summary of the Mubanga case.

3. Mubanga is a dual national who entered Zambia on his Zambian passport. ▮▮▮▮ ▮▮▮▮ But instructions from London were unequivocal. We should not accept responsibility for, or take custody of him. This was subsequently reinforced by the message from No 10 that under no circumstances should Mubanga be allowed to return to the UK. ▮▮▮▮▮▮▮▮▮▮▮▮▮▮▮▮ ▮▮▮▮▮▮▮▮▮▮▮▮ And it became clear that if we requested consular access ▮▮▮▮▮▮ thereby de facto acknowledging him as a UK national, he would have been handed over to us. This would have gone against all other instructions from London.

4. ▮▮▮▮▮▮▮▮▮▮▮▮▮▮▮▮ We had also decided we should speak to the Permanent Secretary of the MFA (the Head of Consular Department was not an appropriate contact in this case — ▮▮▮▮▮▮▮▮▮▮ But before the PS was available to see me, Mubanga was removed from Zambia. We could not in any case have requested formal consular access. Chapter 1.3 of the Consular handbook refers.

5. ▮▮▮▮▮▮▮▮▮▮▮▮▮▮▮▮▮▮▮▮▮▮

COMMENT

6. On the face of it, I am sure Consular Division might like to interpret this story to mean we did not do enough to seek access to Mubanga. But apart from the fact that Mubanga was a dual national in the country of his second nationality, our hands were tied by policy directed from London. ▮▮▮▮▮▮▮▮▮▮ Different action by us would in all likelihood have resulted in Mubanga being delivered to our doorstep.

7. We fully agree with the basic tenet that any UK national, no matter what they are alleged to have done, has a right to Consular assistance. But the handling of the Mubanga case placed us in an

6

53

impossible no. [redacted] One half of the FCO say we should not take
responsibility for [redacted] and the other half said we should. We need
to realise that [attractive] as it may seem, we must not always play
things all ways. We need co-ordinated thinking to avoid such
dilemmas arising again, other posts having to face the difficulties
we have had to face, and any UK national having to go without the
consular protection to which they are entitled.

8.   You may wish to show this to CTPD.

[redacted]

```
YYYY
MAIN            0
SINGLE COPIES
CONSULAR D//[redacted]        0
CTPD//[redacted]              0
[JC]                          0
```

SVMDAN 0294

From:
Sent: 15 August 2002 10:24
To:
Cc:
Subject: : FW: Martin Mubanga - request for Mutual Legal Assistance

Please see e-mail below from the DHM in Lusaka.

We have been asked to arrange co-operation with the Zambians over prosecuting/investigating Mubanga. We need to think carefully about how we handle it, I would have thought a prosecution in the UK is going to be hampered by technicalities. I wonder if should consider flagging these potential problems up to the appropriate authorities.

- Mubanga is a British passport holder and has British Nationality. His family are in Britain and we are treating him as British at G-Bay.

- As an apparent 'dual national' Mubanga was entitled for us to try and get consular access (as was his sister arrested at the same time and then released) in accordance with our stated policy. We didn't seek consular access in Zambia, which meant we broke our policy despite us knowing there was a significant question mark over the Zambian aspect of his nationality. Zambia is not a signatory to VCCR though and there is no bi-lateral consular convention.

- ▓▓▓▓▓▓▓▓▓▓▓▓▓▓▓▓▓▓▓▓▓▓▓▓▓▓▓▓▓▓▓

- ▓▓▓▓▓▓▓▓▓▓▓▓▓▓▓▓▓▓▓▓▓▓▓▓▓▓▓▓ we are going to be open to charges of a concealed extradition.

- This isn't to appear negative, ▓▓▓▓▓▓▓▓▓▓▓▓▓▓▓▓▓▓▓▓

- Out of interest Mubanga's sister who also holds the same nationality as him, (British with a Zambian nationality which appears doubtful) was deported from Zambia after his transfer. You can't deport your own national so it follows the Zambians are going to say Mubanga is also British and has no Zambian nationality.

regards,

Desk Officer
Special Cases, Consular Division

-----Original Message-----
From:
Sent: 14 August 2002 15:51
To: (London);
Subject: FW: Martin Mubanga - request for Mutual Legal Assistance

I would be grateful for your advice on a response to Lusaka. From a registry search I note that you have both been involved in the Guantanamo Bay case in which case you might be better placed to respond than me.
Thanks for your help.

Desk Officer Angola, Zambia, Sao Tome and Principe
Foreign and Commonwealth Office
Telephone (direc▓▓▓▓▓▓▓▓▓▓▓▓
Fax

1

616

378

----Original Message----
From: Lusaka -Conf
Sent: 13 August 2002 10:47
To:
Subject: Martin Mubanga - request for Mutual Legal Assistance

I first tried to send this to you last week, but looking back at my records, I don't think you received it - we had a temporary e-mail glitch.

Apologies for writing to you on this in the first instance, but to be quite honest I was not quite sure to whom I should send it. I suspect it may fall somewhere between CTPD and Consular Division.

I am not sure how much you know about Martin Mubanga - a dual Zambian/UK national who was detained in Zambia earlier this year and then removed by the Americans to Guantanamo Bay.

Mubanga entered Zambia on his Zambian passport, and we were clearly instructed by London to take no responsibility for him, though Consular Division wanted us to seek Consular access. Had we done so, the Zambians, who do not recognise dual nationality, would have promptly handed him over to us. I did a telegram (our 123) to   in Consular Div outlining the difficulties under which we had been placed by contradictory instructions from FCO. The case also put the Zambians in a difficult position.

I have now received (by DHL) a request from the CPS, via the UK Central Authority in the Home Office, for Mutual Legal Assistance from the Zambians in putting together the case to prosecute Mubanga in the UK for treason.

The High Commissioner is concerned there might be some contradictions in our position. Eg: here we treated Mubanga as a Zambian national, and we are now treating him as a UK national. I suspect the answer is that he has been treated in the same way that any dual national would be treated in these circumstances - as a national of that country in the country of his second nationality, and as a UK national for the purposes of trying him in the UK (though what is he being treated as at Guantanamo Bay?)

also wondered if the UK should ask that he be tried in the US rather than in the UK. I have been at least partly following this issue in the media, and thought there had been some sort of US court ruling which effectively meant that Guantanamo Bay inmates could only be tried by a US military tribunal or in the country of their nationality (I could easily be wrong). But grateful if someone could clarify this.

And one further point concerns us. The MLA request assumes Mubanga was arrested here - he was not, he was only detained (we made this clear throughout).

But despite all the questions/reservations, we are assuming we should do as the CPS ask. I propose to execute the request as we would normally do - via the MFA. But it will cause the Zambians some difficulties, and my be a thorn in our relatoinship - especially if they come in for any criticism eg in the media.

There may be something we can do to encourage co-operation - eg in permitting Anti-terrorist squad officers to be present at interviews here with some of Mubanga's associates (also part of the request). But we need to be aware this will not necessarily be easy.

If you would like me to send you a copy of the MLA request, I will airtech it

62

NOTE FOR FILE

For PA on:
Copied To:
Author:
Ext. No:
Date: 22 August 2002

SUBJECT: MUBANGA: Background to case

1.   The following is background to Martin MUBANGA's detention in Zambia and subsequent transfer to GTMO.

- Also on 19 March, ▮▮▮ informed ▮▮▮ that we were keen to obtain access to MUBANGA and could deploy at short notice. ▮▮▮ also discussed the possibility of MUBANGA's release,

380

 The telegram raises the possibility that MUBANGA might be sent to GTMO, stating that "Whether they do so is a matter solely for the US. However, we would hope that they would have legitimate reasons, and see real advantage in taking this action."

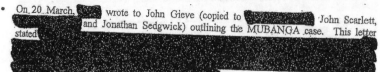

briefed senior FCO officials, but not Consular Division. On the same day,

- On 20 March, wrote to John Gieve (copied to John Scarlett, and Jonathan Sedgwick) outlining the MUBANGA case. This letter stated

- MUBANGA was interviewed by in Lusaka on 23 and 24 March, judged him to be in many cases unbelievable.

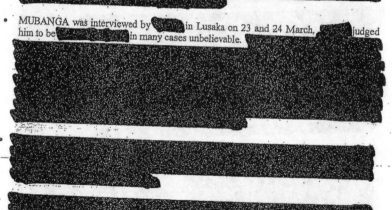

- On 26 March, the MUBANGA case was discussed by , FCO Consular Department and SO13. Consular were supportive of actions to date but wanted to avoid inconsistencies in the way in which detainees were treated: Consular Department has requested access in other cases and therefore planned to send a message to Consul in Lusaka to ask them to seek consular access for MUBANGA on normal channels.

Page 2

259

381

- Also on 26 March, ▮▮▮▮ informed ▮▮▮▮ that HMG would not accept the transfer of MUBANGA to US custody through UK officials ▮▮▮▮

- Subsequent to this, MUBANGA was handed over to the US authorities in Zambia and rendited to GTMO, ▮▮▮▮

Page 3

260

(40)   Omar Deghayes

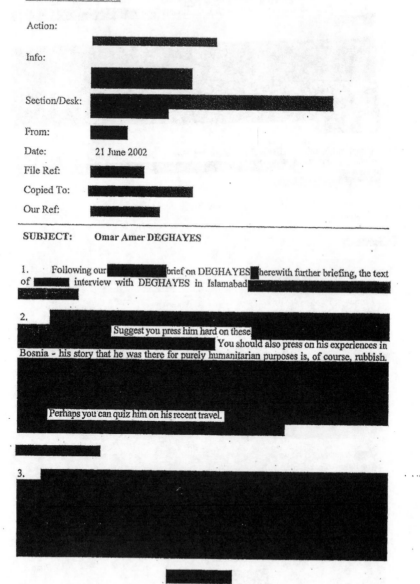

OUT-TELEGRAM

Action:

Info:

Section/Desk:

From:

Date: 21 June 2002

File Ref:

Copied To:

Our Ref:

SUBJECT: Omar Amer DEGHAYES

1.   Following our ▮▮▮▮▮▮ brief on DEGHAYES ▮herewith further briefing, the text
of ▮▮▮▮ interview with DEGHAYES in Islamabad ▮▮▮▮▮▮▮▮▮▮▮▮▮▮▮▮▮▮▮▮
▮▮▮▮▮▮

2. ▮▮▮▮▮▮▮▮▮▮▮▮▮▮▮▮▮▮▮▮▮▮▮▮▮▮▮▮▮▮▮▮▮▮
▮▮▮▮▮▮▮▮▮ Suggest you press him hard on these ▮▮▮▮▮▮
▮▮▮▮▮▮▮▮▮▮▮▮▮▮ You should also press on his experiences in
Bosnia - his story that he was there for purely humanitarian purposes is, of course, rubbish.

▮▮▮▮▮ Perhaps you can quiz him on his recent travel. ▮▮▮▮▮

3.

▮ Interview with DEGHAYES

TEXT BEGINS

Summary

1. DEGHAYES attempts to persuade his ▮▮▮▮ that he is, in fact, his older brother▮▮
▮▮▮▮▮▮▮ Maintains that his work in Bosnia and Afghanistan was purely
charitable, although admits some (limited) contact with the LIFG. Clearly lying about depth of
his involvement, and refuses during this interview to cooperate further. No point in
re-interviewing him during this deployment unless he indicates he is willing to cooperate.

Detail

2. I ▮▮▮▮ Andrew ▮ interviewed Omar Amer DEGHAYES ▮▮▮ from 1430-1630
on 22 May 2002 ▮▮▮
▮▮▮▮ The interview lasted approx. two hours with a
30-minute break. DEGHAYES was unrestrained throughout and drank a glass of water. He
appeared fit and mentally competent, and confirmed that he was willing to be interviewed.

DEGHAYES Claims He Is Abu Bakr DEGHAYES

3. Immediately after introductions, DEGHAYES started on a list of demands (his word): he
wanted news of his wife and child, whom he had not seen for two months; he wanted the British
High Commission to intervene on his behalf; and he wanted my full-name as he intended to
launch a prosecution on his return to the UK. He said he had been held for two months without
charge and this was illegal. He added that he was a British citizen and demanded that the British
authorities secure his release. Comment: DEGHAYES was confrontational and energetic at this
point▮▮▮▮▮▮

4. ▮ asked him if he was a British passport holder. He was: he had a passport in the name of
Abu Bakr Amer DEGHAYES. ▮▮▮▮ DEGHAYES said that
he was, in fact, Abu Bakr (Omar s older brother). ▮▮▮
DEGHAYES said that it QUOTE did not look good UNQUOTE if the British High Commission
got involved in his case. He had expected he would be released in a matter of days but now, after
two months, he decided he needed the protection afforded by his British citizenship and so
revealed his true identity. ▮ remarked that this was scarcely credible but asked him to provide
detail on his background to support his story. ▮ warned him that he would need to tell the
absolute truth. ▮ wanted to help him but ▮ could not do so unless he was honest.
DEGHAYES said he was willing to cooperate and asked for my full-name. I declined to give

384

it and (in response to him pressing me) said I was under no legal obligation to do so.

5. ▮▮▮▮▮▮▮▮▮▮▮▮▮▮▮▮▮▮▮▮▮▮▮▮▮▮▮▮▮▮▮▮▮▮▮▮ He admitted being QUOTE more on the muqatila side UNQUOTE, which he clarified as meaning the LIFG. ▮▮▮

6. ▮▮▮▮▮▮▮▮▮▮▮▮▮▮▮▮▮▮▮▮▮▮▮▮▮▮▮▮▮▮▮▮▮▮

7. ▮▮▮▮▮▮▮▮▮▮▮▮▮▮▮▮▮▮▮▮▮▮▮▮▮▮▮▮▮▮▮▮

8. ▮▮▮▮▮▮▮▮▮▮▮▮▮▮▮▮▮▮▮▮▮▮▮▮▮▮▮▮▮▮▮▮

9. ▮▮▮▮▮▮▮▮▮▮▮▮▮▮▮▮▮▮▮▮▮▮▮▮▮▮▮▮▮▮▮▮

10. ▮▮▮▮▮▮▮▮▮▮▮▮▮▮▮▮▮▮▮▮▮▮▮▮▮▮▮▮▮▮

DEGHAYES Changes His Story

15. ▮ suspended the interview for 30 minutes and, after recommencing, asked DEGHAYES if there was anything he wanted to change about his story. No. ▮ then made it clear that ▮ had been inclined to help him but that ▮ couldn t if he wasn t telling ▮ the truth. ▮ had little

time and so he needed to think very carefully about what he now told ████████ ██ DEGHAYES admitted that he was frightened about being repatriated to Libya. ████ asked him if he was telling ██ he was Abu Bakr

(and a UK passport holder) because of this. He admitted that he was, and he was in reality Omar (and therefore not a UK citizen). But (he said immediately) that was the only thing that was untrue about what he had just told ██. It was Abu Bakr who had travelled to Libya and he had done so in order to see his family (Abu Bakr was still married to his children s mother). ████ expressed incredulity again about this, but DEGHAYES insisted it was true, and that Abu Bakr had been imprisoned. ██████████████████████

16. ██

17. ██

18. ██

19. ██

Bosnia

20. DEGHAYES admitted having been to Bosnia for 2-3 months, specifically Zagreb. He insisted he worked only with the NGO Human Concern. He said did not fight in the Katiba.

Links to the LIFG

21. ▮▮▮ asked DEGHAYES to provide information on his LIFG contacts.

22.

23.

24.

SECRET

25. ██
██

Conclusion

26. ██
██
██

27. ██ closed the interview by telling DEGHAYES he needed to think very carefully about the gravity of the situation he was in. He was a Libyan citizen who had been arrested in Pakistan as an illegal entrant. ██ may well be able to help him but ██ would not and could not if he continued to withhold information or seek to mislead ██ It was obvious from what he had told ██ that this is what he was doing. ██
██

██████ DEGHAYES reacted rather sarcastically to this by thanking ██ for ██ QUOTE concern UNQUOTE, complained that he had cooperated and all he got in return was disbelief, and said he would not cooperate in future. His future, he said, lay not in ██ hands but in God s. And if God wanted him to be sent to Libya, so be it. The interview ended on a decidedly frosty note.

Comments

28. DEGHAYES turned out to be a surprisingly forceful character whose denials of anything beyond a superficial involvement in the LIFG were robust - although not believable. He is obviously lying about the depth and extent of his involvement. He fits the pattern of a mujahid recruited in the UK, although we found it interesting that he spent so long in Afghanistan ██
██
██
████████████████████ His apparent acceptance of the possibility of repatriation to Libya was surprising as he had appeared ████████████████████████ sufficiently worried during this interview to lie outrageously about his own identity.

29. ██
██

Text Ends

██████████████████████████████████
██
██████████████████████

Internal Addressees
Action: ██████ ████████████████████████████

Info: ████████

Date:261516Z JUN 02

Originator: ████████████

Telegram Number: ████

ADDRESSEES:
TO ██████████████
TO
TO ████

PROTECTIVE MARKING:
████████████████████

Subject:DEGHAYES

BEGINS
████ 26 June 2002
Immediate
To ██
████████████████████████████████████

SUMMARY

DEGHAYES continues to lie about his involvement in extremism.
Some progress made though, particularly his admission of being a
Bosnian vet. Having been confronted with accurate information
regarding his past we believe that DEGHAYES probably now realises the
sedriousness of his position. This may provide an opening in future
interviews.

DETAIL

On 24 June, ██████ and ██████ interviewed Omar DEGHAYES in the
Bagram detention centre. The interview commenced at 1345 GMT and
finished at 1600 GMT. DEGHAYES was brought to the interview room
manacled and hooded. When the hood was removed, DEGHAYES looked pale
and shaky. We asked if he was ill and he replied that he was
suffering from Malaria. We immediately asked if he was well enough to
be interviewed and he replied that he was. We offered him some water,
which he accepted. DEGHAYES stated that his condition was being made
worse by the food provided for the detainees and claimed that he had
not eaten for two days. However, his condition appeared to fluctuate
throughout the interview, worsening whenever he was found out to be
lying. After we had ensured he was well enough to continue we
introduced ourselves, and explained the role of MI5.

2. We went on to explain that he was being held in custody solely by
the Americans, and as we understood it he could face a long period of
incarceration. We may be able to help him but the only circumstances
in which we would even consider this is if he were to be completely
honest and tell us everything that we wanted to know. DEGHAYES
assured us he had nothing to hide and would be completely honest with

207

8

us, as he had been ████████████████ We responded that there was
little point continuing with the interview if he maintained that
attitude. We knew he had lied ██████████████ and we expected him
to be more truthful with us today.

3. He acknowledged that he had made some mistakes but pleaded with
us to believe that he was now being honest. We said that we had
evidence of his dishonesty, and hoped he would recognise that he was
making a big mistake. Give me evidence, he said. We asked him if he
had been to Chechnya. He said, never. ████████████████████████
██ He said,
forcefully, that this must be a mistake. He swore to Allah that he
had never been to Chechnya. ████████████
██ What
really mattered was that we believed it to be the case. Until he
convinced us otherwise we would be unable to help him. ████████████
██████████ He said no. We remained silent.

4. The interview stalled at this point. DEGHAYES was clearly
irritated that we disbelieved him and didn t appear to be willing to
debate the issue. After a brief period of silence we told him that
we would listen to his version of events. He should start from his
conversion.

CONVERSION

5. ████████████████████ DEGHAYES explained that before his
conversion he had led a Western lifestyle; drinking, going to bars
and nightclubs and enjoying his wealth. As was the case throughout
the interview, DEGHAYES could not remember precise dates but said
that in the early 90s he had been visited by some Tablighis who had
encouraged him to embrace Islam. He went with them to the Madina
Mosque on one occasion and from then on started praying regularly at
home. After some time he started attending the Madina Mosque. ████████
████████████ He denied ever being a
member of Tablighi Jamaat but said he supported their aims. ██████

6. In 1992 or 1993, he couldn t remember which, he moved to London
to attend University. He lived in Kilburn but couldn t remember the
address. He went to Holborn College, London to read law. The
College offered degrees from the University of London and the
University of Wolverhampton. DEGHAYES graduated after 2 years with a
degree for Wolverhampton. DEGHAYES said he had not been involved
with any Islamic groups at university but had arranged with the
course director for a room to be provided for prayer, which he used
regularly. We took this opportunity to explain to DEGHAYES that we
were, of course, not concerned by the fact that he had embraced Islam
and led a devout life. Our only interest in these events was in the
sense that it informed our understanding of his association with
others who we knew to be extreme. He said he never travelled
overseas during the time he was at university.

7. We asked DEGHAYES if he had become involved with the LIFG when
at university. He said he had never been involved with the Fighting
Group . We said that we knew that not to be the case and we would
like him to tell us about his involvement with the group. He said he
supported the aims of the group because Qadaffi had destroyed his
people, but he had never been a member. We asked why he hadn t
joined if he supported the group. He said that joining any group
entailed a commitment which he was not prepared to give.

8. ██
██
██

DEGHAYES started mumbling unconvincingly at this point, saying that Afghanistan was not such an important issue in those days, there was no reason to talk about it.

14.

Again, DEGHAYES started rambling, saying that he lived in a very distinctive house in Brighton and everyone knew he lived there. Consequently many Libyans came to visit him.

15.

Did you talk about he GIA. No, never, the LIFG wouldn t co-operate with the GIA, they were animals and criminals. Whereas the LIFG was only interested in overthrowing Qaddafi, the GIA was so extreme it would even kill women and childern.

16.

17.

He repeated the rather tame excuse that it was merely because of his family name. He said, emotionally, that, yes he supported the LIFG, if they wanted him to go and fight in Libya he would go. He told us that he had never told anyone else that, so would we now believe him. We told him this was simply not good enough. We repeated that we wanted to help him but as it was he would be staying in prison for a long time because we knew he was lying. We stressed that we knew about most of his activities already and merely wanted him to confirm

392

Internal Addressees
Action:

Info:

Date:050658Z JUL 02

Originator:

Telegram Number:

ADDRESSEES:

PROTECTIVE MARKING:

Subject:Interview with Omar Amer DEGHAYES, 3 July 2002

Summary

Some progress made on specific topics but DEGHAYES clearly lying and
holding back on many issues, including   operations in
Afghanistan.

Detail

1.   and   interviewed DEGHAYES from 1630 to 1930 (local
time) on 3 July 2002 at the Bagram detention centre. We learned
shortly before the interview that a medical examination had
pronounced DEGHAYES clear of both TB and malaria. Comment:
throughout the interview DEGHAYES expectorated rather disgustingly
into a tissue as if he were still tubercular. These moments usually
coincided with those answers where he was most evasive. At other
times he smiled in an embarrassed way when making admissions

2.   When DEGHAYES was brought in to the interview room he appeared
fit
and mentally alert, although noticeably thinner than   previous
interview with him in Islamabad. DEGHAYES recognised   and was
introduced to   as 'Jeff'. We told him that we wanted to
continue where our predecessors left off, and asked him if he was fit
to be interviewed. He said he was, although complained that he had
internal bleeding. We told him that, as we understood, he did not
have malaria or TB. DEGHAYES said he knew this but he was definitely
ill - the doctor just couldn't work out what it was. He said the
medical staff thought he was malingering and challenged us to explain
how anyone could feign internal bleeding.

3.   DEGHAYES then launched into an extended complaint about why he
was
being held. No evidence had been presented yet he was still in
custody. He was also being treated badly, with head-braces and lock-
down positions being the order of the day. He was treated better by
the Pakistanis; what kind of world was it where the Americans were
more barbaric than the Pakistanis? We listened but did not comment.

210

15

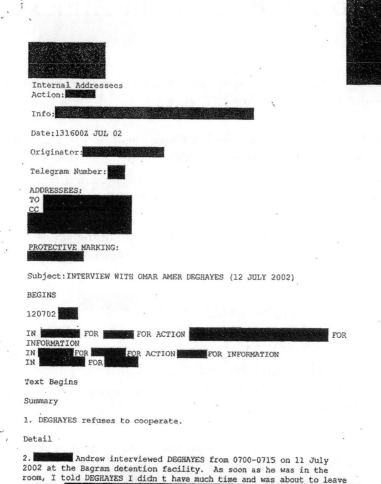

Internal Addressees
Action:

Info:

Date:131600Z JUL 02

Originator:

Telegram Number:

ADDRESSEES:
TO
CC

PROTECTIVE MARKING:

Subject:INTERVIEW WITH OMAR AMER DEGHAYES (12 JULY 2002)

BEGINS

120702

IN _____ FOR _____ FOR ACTION _____ FOR
INFORMATION
IN _____ FOR _____ FOR ACTION _____ FOR INFORMATION
IN _____ FOR _____

Text Begins

Summary

1. DEGHAYES refuses to cooperate.

Detail

2. _____ Andrew interviewed DEGHAYES from 0700-0715 on 11 July
2002 at the Bagram detention facility. As soon as he was in the
room, I told DEGHAYES I didn t have much time and was about to leave
Bagram. _____

_____ For these reasons, and
others which I did not want to go into, we knew DEGHAYES s story was
not true. I told him that before I left Bagram I was required to
provide an assessment to the authorities at the facility on the level
of his cooperation. Would he come clean?

3. DEGHAYES said he had told the truth. If I didn t believe him it
was my fault.

4. I asked _____ a senior officer in the facility, to come into the
room. I told _____ in DEGHAYES s hearing that DEGHAYES was not
cooperating. _____

_____ DEGHAYES mumbled that he had

Note on Sources for the Annex

Documents 1–4 and 7–9 are reproduced from the National Security Archive website, http://www.gwu.edu/~nsarchiv/

Documents 5 is reproduced from the US Department of State's website, http://2001-2009.state.gov/secretary/rm/2005/57602.htm as is the President's speech in Document 6, http://www.america.gov/st/texttrans-english/2006/September/20060906155503eaifas0.8319666.html.

The DNI assessment in Document 6 is reproduced from the US Department of Defense's website, http://www.defense.gov/pdf/thehighvaluede-taineeprogram2.pdf .

Document 10 is extracted from SELECTED DECISIONS OF THE HUMAN RIGHTS COMMITTEE UNDER THE OPTIONAL PROTOCOL: INTERNATIONAL COVENANT ON CIVIL AND POLITICAL RIGHTS, VOLUME 9 (SALES NUMBER E.08.XIV.9, reproduced by kind permission of United Nations Secretariat, Publications Board, New York.

Document 11 is reproduced from the Council of Europe website, http://assembly.coe.int/Documents/WorkingDocs/doc06/edoc10957.pdf

Document 12 is reproduced with kind permission of the European Parliament (© European Union, 2007 – Source: European Parliament)

Documents 13–40 are subject to Crown Copyright and are reproduced under the terms of the Open Government Licence http://www.nationalarchives.gov.uk/doc/open-government-licence/open-government-licence.htm)

Index